FROM FORTRESS TO DEMOCRACY:

THE POLITICAL BIOGRAPHY OF SIR JOSHUA HASSAN

Sir William G F Jackson
and
Francis J Cantos

Gibraltar Books
Grendon – Gibraltar
1995

This book was first published in Great Britain in 1995 by
Gibraltar Books Ltd, Rosehill Farm.
Grendon, Northants NN7 1JW

ISBN 0 948466 35 9

© W G F Jackson
and
F J Cantos

Typeset by Priory Publications, Haywards heath, West Sussex RH16 4DG
Printed in the UK by Antony Rowe Ltd,
Bumper's Farm, Chippenham, Wiltshire SN14 6QA

CONTENTS

ILLUSTRATIONS

(between pages 160 and 161 and 176 and 177)

Plate 1. A recent photograph of Sir Joshua (Salvador) Hassan.

Plate 2. Salvador at the age of three.

Plate 3. Greeting Her Majesty the Queen in 1954; on the left are HRH the Duke of Edinburgh and Mr Chiappe, the City Engineer.

Plate 4. A.W. Serfaty demonstrates a Japanese mini-camera (a novelty in those days) to Her Majesty; the Duke of Edinburgh and Salvador look on.

Plate 5. Greeting Her Majesty the Queen, and the Duke of Edinburgh, in 1954

Plate 6. Salvador with Harold Wilson.

Plate 7. The young Salvador at a dinner of the Association of Labour Mayors in 1954.

Plate 8. Salvador with Sir Winston and Lady Churchill during their visit to Gibraltar in 1961.

Plate 9. Greeting HRH Princess Margaret with Lieutenant-General Sir Harold Redman, in 1957.

Plate 10. Addressing the Committee of 24, with Peter Isola sitting on his left.

Plates 11 & 12. A triumphant election night.

PREFACE

Salvador – Sir Joshua Hassan – has carved his name in the history of the Rock and, indeed, of the world, as the man who fought for and won internal self-government for the Gibraltarians, and successfully resisted Spain's continuing attempts to impose Spanish rule upon them. In 1975, Spain echoed with the cry: Franco is dead; long live the King!

The significance of Franco's death escaped few people in Gibraltar, least of all Salvador, who had already been the Rock's political leader for some 30 years. He was by then at the height of his political career, in his early 60s, and with his reputation already secured by winning constitutional rights for his people, and enhanced by his successful resistance to Franco's attempted takeover. A third and far greater challenge now faced him: could the post-Franco Spain be persuaded to become a good neighbour of Gibraltar to the mutual benefit of the people living on both sides of the frontier?

In his first New Year's message after Franco's death, Salvador, as chief minister of the British Colony of Gibraltar, expressed a glimmer of hope that newly democratized Spain might, if nothing else, adopt a more humane approach towards the people of the Rock, who had been shut off from the outside world by Madrid since 1969.

His optimism had been based on the temporary restoration of telephone links between Gibraltar and Spain during the Christmas season. 'It has brought about,' he said, 'an element of comfort and satisfaction to quite a number of people who have been able to speak to their dear ones.' He noted that as many, if not more, calls came from Spain as from Gibraltar, suggesting that the desire for communication was mutual. For the first time, Salvador saw a real possibility of raising the 15th siege of the Rock. 'One would hope,' he wrote, 'that these small beginnings will be extended to other spheres which will ultimately result in the re-establishment of normal relations with our neighbours.' Henceforth his political leadership would be focussed on bringing this about, knowing full well from the start that he had set himself no easy task, and one which had to be approached with caution. One swallow does not make a summer: the Christmas telephone link-up might not be the harbinger of better cross-border relations. His caution was soon to be vindicated. Almost in the same breath as Arias Navarro, the Franco-appointed prime minister of Spain, announced plans to set up new democratic institutions, he made it clear that the proposed changes would not carry with them an abandonment of Spain's long-standing claim to sovereignty over the Rock. Arias said that he hoped that the first opportunity would be taken to re-establish the territorial integrity of the Spanish realm. In this he was reiterating King Juan Carlos's own words in his accession speech.

Some months later, the Spanish foreign minister, José María Areilza, went to London to enlist support for new Spain's ambition to become 'a respectable member of the Western fold, aiming at eventual membership of the EEC and NATO'. He suggested that, in his view, a democratic Spain could be more flexible in easing the Gibraltar restrictions.

Salvador began to realize that his real task was to convince Spain that lifting the 15th siege would, indeed, be mutually beneficial, although its end would not signify any weakening of Spain's centuries old claim to territorial sovereignty over the Rock. But – and this was a very big 'but' – he had to do so without losing sight of the reason why he was Gibraltar's political leader. Throughout his career, he had fought for complete Gibraltarian internal self-government: he must never jeopardize the wish of the Gibraltarians to stay British.

This biography falls quite naturally into three parts, each covering one of his three great challenges. Part I embraces his successful struggle with Whitehall to achieve internal self-government, which was won with the enactment of the 1969 Constitution. Part II deals with his resistance to Franco's political and economic coercion of the Rock. And Part III covers his struggle to persuade the new Spain to become a good neighbour after Franco's death. The Prologue describes his formative years in Gibraltar and London; and the Epilogue assesses the successes and failures of his 42 years as Gibraltar's popular leader.

WGFJ
FJC
September 1995

CHAPTER 1

A COLONIAL UPBRINGING
Or lesser breeds without the Law
(Kipling's *Recessional*, 1897, Verse 4)

On 21st August 1915, Joshua Abraham Hassan – the first Gibraltarian political leader of international standing – was born at 138 Main Street, Gibraltar. He was the fifth child of Abraham M Hassan, a Jewish cloth merchant, who had inherited property and a business from his father, a leading merchant with family and business connections in Lancashire. The firm imported cotton goods from Manchester for re-export to Spain and Morocco, and had built up a reputation for quality and reliability. Although Joshua's father placed the firm in the hands of a manager, it continued to thrive, and was successful enough for him to be able to give his three sons and two daughters carefree childhoods and good educations within the limits of what was available in Gibraltar during the painful aftermath of the First World War: unemployment had soared and poverty was so widespread amongst the Rock's civilian population that soup kitchens had to be opened by the Colonial government in 1923 to feed the destitute.

The Hassans were Sephardic Jews, who had migrated to Spain during the Jewish Diaspora after the incorporation of Judaea into the Roman Empire during the last century BC. It has been suggested that they had risen in the service of an important Moorish family, and had followed the custom of adopting its name. This is probably a myth: in Moorish times, many Jewish families adopted the name Hassan, which meant 'benefactor' in

Arabic. The custom of Jews taking the name of the family they served did not start until after the Moors had left Spain, and so, if they had adopted such names, they would be Spanish and not Arabic.

The various branches of the Hassan family, one of which was eventually to settle in Gibraltar, fled to Morocco or the eastern Mediterranean after Queen Isabella decreed the expulsion from Spain in 1492 of all Jews who were not prepared to espouse the Christian faith. The future Gibraltar branch of the Hassans chose Morocco where they settled mainly in the Tetuan area just across the Strait, opposite the Rock. The first Hassans recrossed the Straits in about 1735, seeking business in British Gibraltar some 30 years after its capture by Sir George Rooke in 1704.

Abraham Hassan's mother came from the Cansino family. Moses Cansino was one of the first Jews to receive a property grant in Gibraltar in 1723. He was probably a grandson of Jacob Cansino, called '*el sabio*' (the wise), who was adviser to the Count-Duke of Olivares, the chief minister of Philip IV of Spain, in the 17th century. Such was his importance that he had been allowed to live in Madrid for many years despite the Inquisition. An Abraham Hassan, who was no relation of the future Chief Minister, was specifically mentioned by General Sir George Elliott for his excellent work during the Great Siege of 1779-83, and was granted a small property near Southport as a reward. Most of Joshua's paternal and maternal forbears came from Tetuan, but the Cansino family had settled in Minorca for a time.

Salvador, as the young Joshua Hassan was known, naturally played little part in Gibraltar's affairs during the 1920s and 30s, which are sketched here. Nevertheless, these were his formative years when the foundations of his political philosophy and ambitions were laid. Conditions on the Rock in those day kindled within him a burning desire to help to improve the lot of his fellow Gibraltarians within the ambiance of the British fortress and naval base.

The means by which he would achieve this aim developed slowly in his mind over the years: he experienced no sudden call like St

Paul on the road to Damascus. At first, he saw only the need to articulate and represent Gibraltarian views to the colonial government; then he realized the importance of winning local representation within that government; and finally he set his sights on achieving the fullest practicable level of internal self-government compatible with the military needs of the fortress, upon which Gibraltar's economy depended, and without breaching Article X of the Treaty of Utrecht that gave Spain first refusal if Britain ever abrogated her sovereignty over the Rock. During the evolution of his thinking he came to realize that he must avoid either alienating Britain or over-placating Spain. He had to ride these two powerful but unevenly matched horses in such a way that Gibraltar could prosper. Judicious compromise would become the key to his political success.

Living in Main Street, the young Salvador soon experienced – subconsciously at first, no doubt – the gross disparity in the standards of living that had always prevailed in British Gibraltar, and, indeed, in most British colonies. Civilians were treated rather worse in Gibraltar than elsewhere in the Empire because the Rock was a vital fortress in which the civilian population was deemed by its military governors to be a necessary but embarrassing encumbrance.

Military requirements were paramount and generally accepted as such by the inhabitants. In theory, they had no need to live on the Rock if they did not like fortress conditions, but having lived, bred, prospered and often suffered acute hardship there for nearly three centuries – literally 'through storm and tempest, fire and foe', as the traditional English seafarer's hymn puts it – the Rock had become their home, and they had no wish to live anywhere else.

But it was not only the fortress mentality that led to Gibraltarians having so little say in their own government. Despite being Europeans, the British establishment treated most of them as if they were no different from Kipling's 'Lesser breeds without the law', who inhabited the non-white territories of the Colonial Empire. The language barrier – most Gibraltarians spoke only

Andalusian Spanish – did not help; nor did their excitable Latin temperament, which often led to misunderstandings. The unvarnished truth was that Gibraltarians were not trusted to run anything that could remotely impinge on the security of the garrison. As few things did not do so, the scope for running their own affairs was extraordinarily limited.

It was not until Gibraltar had become a Crown Colony in 1830, administered by the Colonial Office instead of the War Office, that some belated recognition was given to the rights of the local people. Nevertheless, the reins of government were still held firmly in the hands of military governors and their staffs, and military requirements remained paramount and scarcely questioned. Little was done officially to develop civilian representation, but unofficially, and almost accidentally, action was taken by leading merchants and professional men. After the Great Siege was raised in 1783, Colonel Drinkwater, its notable historian, set up the Garrison Library, which became the social, as well as the intellectual, hub of the garrison. Such was the deep divide between the military and civilian communities that civilians, however eminent, were barred from membership. In consequence, Gibraltar's men of substance and public conscience came together to establish their own club, calling it the Exchange and Commercial Library. Over the years it developed into the focus for the expression of popular and commercial grievances. Its management committee, although it had no official standing, was elected by all householders in Gibraltar who wished to vote, and it thus became the civilian community's mouthpiece as the only popularly elected representative body on the Rock. Some of its more influential members had friends in high places in Westminster and Whitehall and among the cotton magnates of Manchester, which enabled them to bring indirect but effective pressure to bear upon awkward governors.

The Exchange Committee's most notable victory came in 1855 when they succeeded in engineering the recall of Gibraltar's most unpopular and obtuse governor, General Sir Robert Gardiner (1848-55), through a lobbying campaign in Manchester and

Westminster. Gardiner's principal crime in the eyes of the Gibraltarians was ruining their local trade with Spain. First of all he refused to quarantine British ships coming from England where cholera was raging. The Spaniards took the reasonable precaution of closing the frontier, stopping all trade. And secondly, he tried to stop smuggling, which enraged people on both sides of the frontier who had always prospered from illicit trade of one kind or another. In one of his dispatches Gardiner warned the Colonial Office that the Exchange Committee was beginning to 'affect a representative character, designating the inhabitants of Gibraltar as its constituents, and pursuing with pertinacious demand an attainment of political independence of the Fortress'. He added that it had had the effrontery to be constituted as a chamber of commerce, which, he believed, would 'shake the permanent safety of the Fortress of Gibraltar'. Despite Gardiner's fulminations, the Chamber of Commerce was, indeed, established as a separate institution, but not until 1881. Whilst the Exchange Committee strove to articulate Gibraltarian political opinion, repeated epidemics of malignant fever, cholera, typhus and typhoid compelled the colonial government to do something about the squalor in which most of the civilian population and the lower ranks of the garrison lived. It was the cholera epidemic of 1865 that persuaded the Governor, General Sir Richard Airey, to set up a Board of Sanitary Commissioners – all of whom were appointed by the Governor – to grapple with the unhealthy conditions by providing new water supply, drainage and sewerage systems. When Salvador was born in the middle of the First World War, the Exchange Committee, the Chamber of Commerce and the Sanitary Commissioners were still the only local bodies looking after civilian interests within the Fortress. There was no properly constituted municipal authority or city council.

The Gibraltarian society, into which Salvador was born, had a typically stratified Victorian class structure, made all the more complex by the superimposition of separate colonial service, naval and army hierarchies. On the civilian side, there was a thin crust of financially well-heeled and Anglicized families, who sent their sons to English public schools and universities, and who tended to be 'more English than the English'. The fact that many of their fortunes had been founded upon smuggling in the 18th and 19th centuries was no social disadvantage. They were the people – the Millionaires – from whom governors tended to seek advice and were very much part of the English-speaking colonial establishment. Their social centres were the Royal Calpe Hunt and the Royal Gibraltar Yacht Club with their coveted and select memberships.

Just below the Millionaires came the bilingual professional men: lawyers, bankers, clerics, merchants and entrepreneurs, who formed the middle class, and to which the Hassan family belonged. Although some were members of the Hunt and Yacht clubs, their meeting places were the Casino Calpe, the Gibraltar Club and the Calpe and Mediterranean Rowing Clubs. At the bottom of the pyramid there was the numerous Spanish-speaking working class. They provided most of the labour needed in the colony except for the really hard physical work such as coal-heaving, which was mostly undertaken by so-called Spaniards, who crossed the frontier daily from poverty stricken Andalusia and were only too willing to work for a pittance. Mostly, is an exaggeration: the coal-heavers were about half and half Spaniards and Gibraltarians, but, since many of the Gibraltarian coal-heavers lived in La Linea where the cost of living was significantly lower than in Gibraltar, and because many had Spanish mothers anyway, they were all looked upon as Spaniards.

The inequality in standards of living was grotesque. The upper-class Gibraltarian families, the colonial officials and the officers of the garrison enjoyed the standards of Edwardian England; the middle class lived well too but in more cramped surroundings; the majority of the population slummed it in crowded tenements with whole families living in single rooms and with the most primitive communal sanitary arrangements. Conditions were not as bad as in, say, Calcutta, but the 'lesser breeds' syndrome prevailed nevertheless.

Such disparities still existed at the end of the First World War because Gibraltar was at least 50 years behind Britain in political thinking and practice. The growing influence of socialism, backed by the trade unions, had not, as yet, spread to the Colonial Empire; nor, for that matter, had communism. The wretched conditions which the working class had to endure were accepted as part of the natural order of life, which could be and was relieved by the generous charity of the better off Gibraltarians, but not by government action. The first trade union, the Gibraltar branch of the Transport and General Workers Union, was not set up until 1919. Such industrial unrest as there was in Gibraltar was generated among the coal-heavers, who attempted striking over pay and working conditions in 1890, 1898 and 1919, but with little success: British bayonets, and the use of alternative Moroccan labour, ensured the *status quo* was maintained without much difficulty by the governors.

The disparity in standards of living was also reflected in education. Gibraltar was proud of its rudimentary educational system, which was ahead of most other colonial territories, but this was thanks to the dedicated work of religious orders and private enterprise, and not to the colonial administration. It was not until 1917 that primary education was subsidized by the government and came within the reach of the poorer families. Secondary education remained unsubsidized and had to be paid for by parents. In consequence, many able men of Salvador's generation were lost to the service of the Gibraltarian community during its long struggle for internal self-government because they were largely uneducated.

There was, however, one psychological thread that bound all Gibraltarians together. Whether rich or poor, educated or partially educated, well housed or tenement dwellers, they had an inbred Victorian pride not only in being loyal subjects of the Crown and members of the great British Empire on which the sun never set, but also through being the inhabitants of the Rock – the strategically vital fortified naval base on the Imperial lines of communication to India and Australasia via Suez, and to South Africa. Gibraltar was the first coaling and revictualling stop for outward-bound ships and the last on the way home to England; and it was the only secure port between Portsmouth and Cape Town capable of docking the battleships of the Atlantic and Mediterranean Fleets. Looking over the border into impoverished Andalusia and politically unstable Spain, they were eternally thankful to be British and not Spanish subjects. Salvador was proud of this inheritance: nothing hurt him more than the steady decline of British power during his lifetime.

Salvador's family background and education were to make him the extreme left-wing political activist that he became in his younger days, and ensured that he stayed left of centre throughout his career. His father could and did find the money to give him the best education available in Gibraltar, and later, in London, and introduced him to the political arguments of the day. Not managing his own business, he preferred to spend his time putting the world to rights with his cronies and attending bullfights in Spain. Thus, Salvador grew up in an essentially Gibraltarian environment in which Spanish culture predominated; and in which he imbibed political debate rather than acquiring the business experience and familiarization with management skills that might have been useful to him in government later. It is, however, worth remarking that the whole of the Western Mediterranean had been culturally Spanish since the Moors were driven out of Spain in 1492. Enjoying the Spanish way of life did not make Gibraltarians politically pro-Spanish as Salvador's career was to demonstrate; indeed, after Franco came into power the great majority were rabidly anti-Spanish.

While many of Salvador's contemporaries were sent off to English public schools, his father was content with local schooling for his sons. This gave Salvador an early sense of undeserved social inferiority *vis-à-vis* his English educated contemporaries, and reinforced the radical trends already evident in his character. He certainly became an ardent supporter of the republican cause during the Spanish Civil War whereas those educated in England generally supported Franco's nationalists.

Salvador's primary education was, nevertheless, conservative.

In 1921, at the age of six, he was sent to the coeducational Loretto Convent School then at Gavino's Passage – where he received an excellent grounding in the three Rs from the Catholic nuns despite being a Jew. His religious education was provided within the Jewish community itself. One of the remarkable things about Gibraltar has always been the religious tolerance shown by all Gibraltarians, stemming, according to the Spanish 18th century historian, Lopez de Ayala, from firm military rule. While there may have been some truth in his suggestion, the suffering of the whole closely packed community during sieges, economic depressions and distressingly unpredictable epidemics created mutual understanding and tolerance amongst the people of all walks of life; coupled with religious tolerance, and derived from the same shared experiences, is the Gibraltarians' great generosity in supporting worthy charities of all kinds and their sense of community. At the age of twelve, Salvador was already displaying his own generosity of spirit and social conscience by collecting the weekly subscriptions of 15 centimos for the Jewish Sick Fund *Hozer Dalim*, and he was taking an intuitive interest in people and their individual problems. Unlike most boys, he enjoyed talking to older people and making friends with them because he found that they could teach him more and their company was more congenial to him. The seeds of his political future were already developing at that early age.

His secondary education started in September 1926 at the Christian Brothers College on Line Wall Road, a building on the site where he now has his chambers. He proved himself a very popular, highly intelligent and gifted student. Gregarious by nature like his father, he maintained close touch throughout his life with all those who had been at school with him. He is remembered by his elders as a loquacious and precocious youngster, who quickly absorbed the details of everything going on around him. He was an avid reader and a frequent visitor to the Tabera book shop in La Linea, where he enjoyed discussing Spanish literature and art with Pepe Tabera, its owner. The SPQR tobacconist, at 146 Main Street, was another of his haunts where he learnt much about horse-racing and its punters; and he enjoyed going to bullfights in the nearby Andalusian towns with his father and friends where he imbibed Spanish culture. A keen cyclist, he enjoyed the rough and tumble of playing bicycle-polo with his contemporaries, but he and his family never aspired to joining the prestigious Royal Calpe Hunt or owning horses.

Salvador went through all the classes at the Christian Brothers School and finished with the London University Matriculation, including Latin which he needed to read for the bar. At the age of fifteen, some five years before leaving for London to join the Middle Temple as a law student in February 1935, he took his first conscious step towards a political career by joining the Exchange and Commercial Library as its Assistant Honorary Librarian and so became a lowly member of its Committee. He was thus able to observe at first hand its successive attempts to win locally elected representation within the Gibraltar government and an official Gibraltarian voice in the Rock's internal affairs.

The governors in the 1920s were all generals, who had held high command in the First World War. Sir Horace Smith-Dorien (1918-23) commanded the 2nd Corps in the retreat from Mons and at the battle of Le Cateau, and later the 2nd Army at Ypres. Sir Charles Monro (1923-28) commanded the 3rd Army in France and organised the withdrawal from Gallipoli before returning to France to command the 1st Army and then becoming the C-in-C India. And Sir Alexander Godley (1928-33) commanded the Australian and New Zealand (ANZAC) Corps at Gallipoli and in France. They were all able men, but they believed implicitly in the sanctity of military over civilian requirements in Britain's strategic fortress. Nevertheless, they were well aware of the Colonial Office's policy of advancing dependent territories towards responsible self-government and of improving standards of living; and they had colonial service officers at their elbows in the posts of colonial secretary, attorney-general and financial secretary to look after civilian interests. Sadly, colonial officials, however well meaning, can never really appreciate the true needs and wishes of the people, and always believe that they know best.

It took relatively little local pressure to persuade Smith-Dorien to propose the establishment of an elected City Council, which the Colonial Office authorized in 1921. He felt that the fortress's security would not be endangered since the officials and nominated members were to be in the majority and could outvote the elected members on controversial issues. The first City Council elections took place on 1st December 1921. In 1922 an Executive Council of four official and three unofficial members was appointed to advise the governor in running the civil affairs of the colony. The unofficial members were inevitably drawn from the ranks of the Millionaires who showed little sympathy for the plight of the working class.

While these small advances in local representation in government were welcome to the Gibraltarians, they were also seen to be totally inadequate. By 1925 the old bogey, which had torn the American colonies away from the mother country in 1776 – 'no taxation without representation' – reared its head in Gibraltar. The Governor, Sir Charles Monro, and his officials wanted to improve the basic city services – water supply, sanitation, road works and, most important of all, housing. This meant raising extra revenue by increasing rates and excise duties, which were absurdly low by United Kingdom standards. There was no income tax in Gibraltar, so it was the property owners and merchants who had to meet the increased bill and, quite naturally, they did not like it. Their objections were compounded by the fact that the non-elected majority in the City Council, who were keenest on improvements in municipal services, were British expatriates on three- to five-year overseas tours, known locally as *importados*, who did not pay rates anyway.

By February 1926, the elected councillors had decided enough was enough, and appealed to Monro for a reconstitution of the City Council to give it an elected majority. The ratepayers' and merchants' representatives would then have the voting power to fix the level of public expenditure and set the rates. Monro bluntly refused: there could be no question of allowing an elected majority – it could endanger the efficient working of the fortress.

In the past, the garrison had often been weakened by pestilences stemming from insanitary conditions in the city. He was not prepared to risk Gibraltarian *mañana* standing in the way of progressive administrative improvements. Indeed, such was the lack of confidence between the civil and military authorities that most municipal services were, and, until the 1980s still were, duplicated by the military, as were education, police and legal jurisdiction.

In 1929, a new and reputedly more liberal Governor, Sir Alexander Godley, arrived, and the local members of the City Council tried again for an elected majority, but, despite the new Governor's leanings, the times were far from propitious for further constitutional advance. Unemployment was high, homelessness was increasing and the soup kitchens were still in operation. Godley wanted to start a modest municipal housing scheme, for which he needed funds. His solution was to raise the duties on imported wines and to impose a new duty on perfume, which had become a lucrative commodity in the smuggling trade. The Exchange Committee and the Chamber of Commerce protested. Furthermore, they had the effrontery to petition for no further increases in duties and for a cut in public expenditure. Godley resisted local political pressure for an elected majority on the City Council not because he put the interests of the fortress first, but because he viewed the needs of the poorer citizens with greater concern than those of the men of substance.

By the time the next Governor, Sir Charles Harington, arrived in 1933, war clouds were gathering over Europe and in the Mediterranean where Mussolini was giving vent to his ambitions of acquiring a new colonial empire in Abyssinia. Admiralty and War Office interest in Gibraltar was increasing as was military expenditure, but the naval and military authorities on the Rock were also becoming more demanding. Harington was a strong, fair-minded man, who had held Lloyd George and Churchill in check during the Chanak crisis of 1922, and had successfully outfaced Mustapha Kemal when he tried to take his Turkish armies across the Dardanelles to attack the Greeks. Although

Harington sympathized with Godley's liberal ideas, his ability to extend them was sadly reduced by the growing international tension.

The Exchange Committee and Chamber of Commerce were not to be deterred by these factors. They came together with the Transport and General Worker's Union to maintain pressure for increased Gibraltarian representation in government. Quite fortuitously, they were given a lever with which to prize open the Governor's reluctance to accept Gibraltarian advice other than on City Council matters. Harington wanted to introduce death duties as a means of raising revenue. The Exchange Committee set up a subcommittee of C E Prescott (a notary public) and Sam Benady (later Leader of the Bar in the 1970s and 80s) to examine the new tax proposal. Their report again raised the cry of 'no taxation without representation'. After studying the Prescott/Benady report, Harington decided to go ahead with the imposition of death duties. Again the Exchange Committee reacted with vigour. It held an Extraordinary General Meeting on 30th July 1934, which resolved to petition His Majesty King George V, recording Sam Benady's view that:

> The crux of the whole matter was that the time had come that we should all have a larger representation in our own affairs, that is to say, at least an elected majority in the City Council (*Memoirs of a Gibraltarian*, by Sam Benady, p 21).

Sam Benady and Agustin Huart, head of the small TGWU, drafted the petition, but when their draft was considered on 2nd August 1934 by the Committee itself, it was opposed as unnecessary by several influential members. However, it was put to a large public protest meeting in true Gibraltarian style, and some 3,000 signatures were appended to the memorial before it was dispatched to London. It did generate a minor, short-lived, storm in Whitehall and a debate in the Westminster Parliament, but the British government's answer was still a firm 'No' to increased local responsibility in the fortress's government.

The chances of any constitutional advance diminished as

international tension grew in the run-up to the Second World War. The change of tone in Gibraltar was reflected in Harington's replacement in 1938 by General Sir Edmund Ironside (later Field Marshal Lord Ironside) with the additional responsibility of being British C-in-C (Designate) for the whole of the Mediterranean if war broke out. He was a great bull of a man, whose activities were centred upon strategic planning, military preparations and his own ambition to command the British Expeditionary Force if it went to France. He had little time left for local politics. Nonetheless, there was a silver lining in the gathering war clouds as far as Gibraltar was concerned. Unemployment and poverty diminished with the greater military activity and increased defence expenditure in Gibraltar. Mussolini had invaded Abyssinia in 1935; Hitler had reoccupied the Rhineland and the Spanish Civil War had begun in 1936; the German occupation of Austria and the Munich Crisis occurred in 1938; and Germany invaded Poland, starting the Second World War, in 1939.

When Salvador left Gibraltar for London in February 1935 to read law at the Middle Temple he was a young Spanish-speaking Gibraltarian, who was in no way anti-British and who was imbued with the twin ambitions of establishing his own legal practice in Gibraltar and of helping Gibraltarians less fortunate than himself when he returned to the Rock. He cannot have found it easy to settle down in the English environment, but the experience provided an essential counterpoise to his Gibraltarian upbringing, which was to enable him, in later life, to ride the English and Spanish horses so successfully in tandem. His initial understanding of the Spanish way of life became submerged in the Englishness surrounding him, and he began to understand more about the English mentality, making him ambidextrous in English and Spanish culture. Although the Conservative party was in power at the time in Britain, socialism was a fast-growing force in British politics. Its tenets reinforced Salvador's own radical instincts; and, although he probably did not know it at the time because he was not as yet finally set on a political career, they seem to have played a major role in shaping his future political thinking.

Indeed, his pre-war girlfriend – he was unofficially engaged to Leita Cazes, of a wealthy Gibraltarian family – used to refer to him as *mi novio el rojillo*, 'my fiancee, the little red'. Salvador was called to the bar of the Middle Temple on 26th January 1939 and read in the chambers of W A L Raeburn, a very senior barrister with a wide general practice, who was later appointed King's Council and acted as temporary judge of the High Court from time to time. With war clouds billowing in 1939, Salvador returned to Gibraltar in August, and set up his chambers. Initially in his home at 138 Main Street, he moved later to 215 Main Street and subsequently to Horse Barrack Lane. His intention was to develop a criminal and general practice, but within a fortnight of his return, Britain had declared war on Germany. He was called to the Gibraltar bar a few days later on 13th September 1939.

The outbreak of war threw all Salvador's plans into disarray; but the war also drew him step by step into the political arena. The minimal local representation, which had been won in Gibraltar's government during the 1930s, was swept away with the suspension of the City Council, and the reimposition of direct military rule by the Governor for the duration of the war. Although Salvador did not know it at the time, his life's work was to become the restoration of the Gibraltarians' voice in their own affairs, and its strengthening to the limits of full internal self-government set by the Treaty of Utrecht.

CHAPTER 2

THE FOUNDATIONS
OF POLITICAL INFLUENCE

The Birth of the AACR: 1939-44

They drew up some rules and when they were in draft form
they came to see me as a lawyer to help them with the rules.
That introduced me into the work that they were doing and
from then on I never looked back. (Sir Joshua's notes of October
1993 on the formation of the AACR)

The Gibraltar to which Salvador returned in August 1939 soon
stopped being a British colony advancing towards a degree of
internal self-government and became a fortress again, in which
the rights of its people were subordinated to military
requirements. The main fora in which Gibraltarians had a voice –
the City and Governor's Executive Councils – were suspended in
1940 for the duration of the war, and direct rule by the governor
and his three principal officials (colonial secretary, attorney-
general and financial secretary) was imposed under the overall
direction of the Colonial Office, Admiralty and War Office in
Whitehall.

The governor's Executive Council was later reinstated, but as it
was composed of his senior expatriate officials, sitting with three
nominated Gibraltarians, it could hardly be seen as representative.

The nominated members were all established and wealthy businessman: George Gaggero, Peter Russo and Edward Cottrell, each of whom was to be knighted in due course for their services to the Gibraltar government. The administration of the city was made the responsibility of a commissioner, who dealt directly with the officials who headed the municipal services, and with a locally appointed Board of District Commissioners, who were largely responsible for handling the evacuation of the civilian population and later its repatriation. The issue of Defence Regulations, based on those promulgated in the United Kingdom, became the Governor's means of bringing the Rock onto a war footing and managing its internal affairs. They were blunt instruments, but were accepted as one of the obvious necessities of war.

The first Commissioner was the Brigadier in charge of Administration, who held the post temporarily. He was replaced by A M Dryburgh, a Colonial Service official, who was an awkward uncooperative man and a heavy drinker. Lord Gort eventually sacked him, and he was replaced by Edward Cottrell in January 1943.

Within Gibraltar there was an exhilarating surge of loyalty to the Crown and a general desire to be of service once more to Britain and her Empire. There was no lack of volunteers for war work and for service on the many committees set up to advise and help the Governor in the transition from peace to war. Salvador became a member of the Managing Board of the Jewish Community, and had his first minor clash with the military authorities when he persuaded the Governor, on the Board's behalf, not to authorize the cutting down of the 200-year-old palm tree at the Line Wall Synagogue in order to clear fields of fire, and the digging of a gun emplacement in the old Jewish Cemetery at Jews Gate. He also joined the Gibraltar Special Constabulary on security duties. Shortly after he joined them, they were amalgamated with the Gibraltar Defence Force and he became a gunner on a 40mm Bofors anti-aircraft gun, sited on the Line Wall near the American War Memorial.

But behind all the exhilaration felt as Gibraltar resumed her war roles of convoy assembly port, fleet base and guardian of the western entrance of the Mediterranean, there was deep anxiety about the vulnerability of the civilian population. With Italy linked to Germany and Japan in the 'Pact of Steel', and with Franco's Spain favouring the Rome/Berlin Axis out of gratitude for Italian and German support during the recent Spanish Civil War, the possibility of the Rock being attacked from the air, if not by land and sea, was in everybody's mind. The film version of H G Wells's *War of the Worlds*, with its opening scene of the spire of St Martins-in-the-Fields crashing down, as bombs rained on Trafalgar Square, did much to turn exhilaration into anxiety. Everyone could see that Gibraltar presented a small but very vulnerable target.

That anxiety was not allayed by rumours of the top secret planning that had been going on since March 1939 within the Convent for the evacuation of the civilian population if the expected threat of attack became imminent. Little can ever be kept really secret in Gibraltar's closely knit community, and there was a general awareness of the probable need to clear the fortress's decks for action. In August 1939, the Governor, Sir Clive Liddell, took off the wraps and gave the City Council what was to be its last major task before its demise in 1940. It was to carry out the detailed planning and eventual execution of the evacuation of an estimated 13,000 'useless mouths' – useless, that is, in the defence of the fortress and naval base. The task of registering the potential evacuees and preparing for their dispatch, probably to Morocco, was given to a committee called the Evacuation Authority, headed by Edward Cottrell – the last chairman of the prewar City Council and a member of the Governor's Executive Council.

Salvador volunteered to help the Evacuation Authority and was soon immersed in the exacting task of compiling lists of families to be sent away, and of assessing their needs and means. Thus, he met a large cross-section of the population, and, more importantly from the point of view of his future political career, they got to know him. Always good-humoured and sympathetic, his quick brain and legal training helped him to sort out the genuine cases from the more bogus applicants for special treatment. His understanding of his fellow Gibraltarians grew apace and to some extent neutralized any anglicizing influences of his years of reading law in London. It brought him back into the Gibraltarian ways of thought and life, and gave him a feel for people's problems and anxieties, which was to stay with him all his life. A genuine plea for help would never go unanswered, but there was a reverse side to this generosity: he always found it difficult to sack incompetent subordinates if, by so doing, he would cause them personal hardship. As the first weeks of the war passed, it became clear that Italy and Spain were sitting on the fence, waiting to see how Germany fared before committing themselves. It seemed unlikely that the war would spread to the Mediterranean just yet, and this was partially confirmed when Franco declared Spain's neutrality on 6th October 1939. Evacuation planning was suspended much to the relief of the potential evacuees. Their relief was to be short-lived. Hitler's victories in the West in May 1940 made evacuation essential before Mussolini and/or Franco could declare war and start bombing the Rock. By 21st May, all the members of the Evacuation Authority, including the volunteers like Salvador, were at full stretch again, organizing the dispatch of the first batch of evacuees to Morocco in the small 1,200-ton *Gibel Dersa* and the 7,000-ton *Mohamed Ali Kebir*, which also carried Charles Gaggero and Doctor Jaime Giraldi to set up the Reception Authority in Morocco.

The agonizing evacuation of women and children, the old people and the infirm, and all those who had no active part to play in the defence of the Rock, is described in graphic detail by Tommy Finlayson in his book, *The Fortress Came First*. It was far from complete when Italy entered the war on 10th June and France capitulated on the 22nd with dire consequences for those Gibraltarian evacuees, who had already reached Morocco.

To ensure that French warships did not fall into German hands, the French navy was asked to sail its warships to British ports where they could either continue the war against the Axis or be demobilized and their crews sent home. At the French naval base of Mers-el-Kebir near Oran, Admiral Gensoul refused to join the Allies or demobilize his ships. Admiral Somerville's Force H, based on Gibraltar and comprising at that time the carrier *Ark Royal*, the battleships *Valiant* and *Resolution*, the battlecruiser *Hood* and all their attendant cruisers and destroyers, was ordered by Churchill to confront Gensoul. Somerville arrived off Mers-el-Kebir with Force H on 30th June. All the efforts of his negotiators failed to persuade Gensoul to change his mind. After a series of ultimatum deadlines had passed, Somerville was ordered by Churchill to open fire on his erstwhile colleague's fleet, still at its berths in Mers-el-Kebir harbour. His 36 salvoes destroyed or severely damaged all but one of Gensoul's heavy ships and killed 1,500 French sailors. French bitterness knew no bounds: the Gibraltarian evacuees in Morocco immediately became *personae non gratae* and were unjustifiably, but understandably, made to suffer the consequences. It so happened that a convoy of British freighters was approaching Casablanca at the time, carrying some 13,000 French soldiers and sailors who had opted not to join the Free French Forces after Dunkirk, and were being returned to French territory. To the French authorities in Morocco the convoy provided a godsent opportunity for getting rid of the Gibraltarians.

They paid no attention to the state of the ships, which their men had left in an indescribably filthy state, or to their unsuitability for carrying women and children back to Gibraltar or England. Using French Senegalese troops with fixed bayonets, they forced the evacuees onto the ships without any attempt to clean and provision them, and ordered the convoy out of Casablanca. The only practicable destination was Gibraltar where the ships could be cleaned, victualled and fitted out for the long sea voyage to England or elsewhere in the Empire.

The Governor, still Sir Clive Liddell, was in a quandary. Whitehall did not want the evacuees in England, which was under threat of invasion, and the search for somewhere else to send them was taking time. Time would also be needed to refit and victual the ships for a long sea voyage, or to send out other ships from

Britain to carry the evacuees to their final destination. On both counts, the evacuees' stay at Gibraltar was bound to be more than a few days. Sir Clive Liddell, for his part, did not want the evacuees disembarked in Gibraltar. Their original evacuation had been traumatic enough: to repeat the performance after a few weeks back in their homes on the Rock would be even more trying for him and for them.

Moreover, the Rock was already under sporadic air attack by French and Italian aircraft, and he did not have enough air-raid shelters for more women and children. He made the arbitrary decision not to allow any of the evacuees to land, but, as often happens with bad decisions, this one was soon overturned by events – and by the Gibraltarians themselves.

The announcement of his decision not to allow any of the evacuees to land quite naturally caused consternation and anger throughout Gibraltar. The menfolk of the evacuated families soon saw and heard about the grim conditions in which their women and children were being held on board, and there was a spontaneous mass protest in John Mackintosh Square on 11th July. Shops closed and the crowds seemed so threatening that troops were called out. Salvador wrote later:

> I have a vivid picture in my mind of the crowds of local men at John Mackintosh Square, where the kiosks are situated, standing right up against the lines of British troops with bayonets drawn – they had been sent out to control the crowds. Feelings were running very high, and it looked like the situation could develop into a riot. This was probably one of the first occasions when the local population had taken to the streets in an act of open defiance against a decision of the British government. (*Wartime memories. Gibraltar*, p 3)

A delegation led by Sam Benady and Antonio Baldorino, both City Councillors, presented the Governor with the people's case for allowing the families to disembark, and promised, in return, to ensure their peaceful re-embarkation when the time came for them to leave for England or elsewhere. In fact, Sir Clive was already under heavy pressure from the Secretary of State for the

Colonies to disembark the evacuees so that ships could be cleaned and refitted in the dockyard because there were no other ships available to be sent out for their onward journey. Sir Clive gave way, and the evacuees stayed on the Rock until their ships were ready to take them on to England.

Although the reversal of the Governor's decision was not entirely due to local pressure, an important precedent had been set: the Gibraltarians were no longer prepared to take the wartime draconian decisions of the Governor lying down if they saw them to be flawed and against their best interests, but they also saw that the Convent was prepared to accept reasoned argument and to listen to reasonable people. Unfortunately, most of the former Gibraltarian members of the City and Executive Councils, who might have provided constructive local civilian leadership, had left the Rock as evacuees or to join up in Britain, leaving a political vacuum. Only three members of the bar remained: Albert Isola and Peter Russo who had been appointed District Commissioners, and Salvador, who had enlisted in the Gibraltar Defence Force. The few remaining members of the original representative bodies – the Exchange and Commercial Library, the Chamber of Commerce and the TGWU – did form a loosely knit opposition group who were to serve Gibraltar well in the post-war era, but they remained individuals unwilling to join forces to challenge the establishment.

Salvador, aged 25, was too junior to provide the necessary leadership at this stage, but gradually made himself a reputation for standing up for what he considered right, and for getting things done by subtle persuasion. Although everything which had happened in Gibraltar since war was declared could be justified on military grounds, he sensed that there was something amoral about the treatment of the civilian population as flotsam of war. While he accepted that the British authorities in Gibraltar and London were doing their best to make the lives of the evacuees tolerable, his mind was already working towards ways of securing some civil rights for the inhabitants of the fortress, who, at that time, had virtually none. The fortress did, indeed, come first. It would not be long, however, before further arbitrary governmental decisions gave him the opportunity to provide some of the leadership that was lacking.

In the meantime, Salvador continued to work for the Evacuation Authority and to build up his own small legal practice. His mother, father and sister had left for Funchal in Madeira, at their own expense, but his two brothers stayed on in Gibraltar: one in the medical section of the Defence Force and the other in the fire brigade's administration. The British garrison was reinforced by up to some 20,000 men and was feverishly engaged in preparing to defeat Hitler's plan to attack the Rock (Operation Felix) from Spain if he could get Franco to co-operate. Franco, however, had an Achilles heel: Spain could not feed herself and was totally dependent on grain from North America, which the Royal Navy was deliberately allowing to pass through its blockade of Nazi-occupied Europe. Hitler could not provide alternative food supplies nor the inflated list of weapons and vehicles that Franco was demanding to enable him to enter the war. The deal fell through, and Franco declined to allow German troops to cross Spain to attack the Rock. By the end of 1941 the threat to the Rock from the land had faded away, but Gibraltar was soon to be given a new role in the war: to provide the forward launching-pad for the Allies' invasion of North Africa under the command of General Eisenhower.

One of the primary requirements for this new role was an all-weather bomber and fighter airfield to be built on the British half of the isthmus. A large force of Royal Engineers, including a company of tunnellers from the Royal Canadian Engineers, was deployed on construction work. The Canadians were civilian miners by profession and a very tough bunch to handle. When they got into serious trouble, which was not infrequent, they would demand civilian lawyers rather than military officers to defend them at their courts martial. As Salvador was the only freelance lawyer left on the Rock, he received most of the briefs to defend these Canadians. At the time he was about to be commissioned into the Royal Artillery as a gunner officer, but his successes at

Canadian courts martial led the Governor, Lieutenant-General Sir Noel Mason-MacFarlane, to cancel his commissioning and instead to give him leave of absence from the Gibraltar Defence Force to continue his legal work at courts martial. One example of his successes was his defence of two Canadians who had stowed away in a freighter bound for Canada. The ship was stopped in mid-Atlantic by the Royal Navy, and they were found and returned to Gibraltar. In spite of it being a clear case of desertion, Salvador managed to persuade the court that they had committed the lesser offence of absence without leave.

During his off-duty time, he was also able to undertake some defence work in the Magistrate and Sessions Courts in criminal cases, building up a substantial legal practice by the end of the war. On one occasion, he defended a sailor on a murder charge and successfully argued for its reduction to one of manslaughter. On another he defended two merchant ship captains, who in the view of Admiral Sir Andrew Cunningham, the Naval C-in-C Mediterranean, had lost their ships through negligence and should have their masters certificates withdrawn. Salvador argued successfully that the two losses were due to errors of judgement. Under the Merchant Shipping Act, errors of judgement did not warrant withdrawal of certificates. Thanks to Salvador, the two captains kept their certificates and returned to sea. He later became involved in the appeal against their conviction of the two Spanish saboteurs, Luis Lopez Gordon-Cuenca and José Martinez Muñoz, who were hanged in the Moorish Castle on 11th January 1944. He had the distressing experience of having to inform both men that their appeals to the Privy Council had been turned down, and of having to return their personal effects to their families after their execution. Such was Salvador's growing number of legal successes that he was appointed Deputy Coroner in 1941, a post he held until 1964. But his main interest lay in helping to generate political pressure for fairer treatment of the Gibraltarians, both those who stayed on the Rock – the worker bees as Mason-MacFarlane called them – and the evacuees in London, Madeira and Jamaica. There was an obvious danger of him falling foul of the military authorities for subversive preaching if there was a reactionary governor, who was unsympathetic to the aspirations of the Gibraltarians.

Fortunately, Sir Clive Liddell was replaced as governor in May 1941 by Lord Gort VC, a brave soldier and physical fitness fanatic, who was only concerned with making the Rock impregnable and had little interest in civilians. He was barely a year in Gibraltar before being sent to defend Malta, which was under siege and heavy Axis bombardment throughout 1942. He was replaced by the former deputy governor, Lieutenant-General Sir Noel Mason-MacFarlane, who had a diametrically different approach: the civilian population did matter to him, and, in consequence, he was to welcome rather than obstruct Salvador's early efforts to highlight the Gibraltarians' lack of rights.

Sir Noel Mason-MacFarlane was an interesting character. Known as Frank or Mason-Mac rather than Sir Noel, he held left-wing views, which was unusual for generals in those days. After the war he stood for Parliament and won the North Paddington seat from Brendan Bracken, Churchill's Minister of Information, for Labour. A fine fighting soldier, he had an acute brain, a realistic understanding of people and a gift for lucid expression. A natural linguist, who spoke most European languages, he had the panache and idiosyncrasy to inspire men, and the common touch to hold people's loyalty. He tended to be impetuous in espousing worthy causes, and this led him to take up the cudgels on behalf of the people of Gibraltar.

And cudgels were, indeed, needed to right successive wrongs inflicted, unknowingly or thoughtlessly perhaps, on the evacuees by Colonial Office and Ministry of Health administrators. The former were responsible for overall policy, and the latter supervised the actual housing and care of the evacuees. The wartime expansion and dilution of the staffs of these ministries, and the loss of many of their experienced official to the armed forces, led to unfortunate errors of judgement, which aggravated the inevitable misunderstandings that are bound to occur between people of different cultures and ways of life. Wartime restrictions and shortages of everything, from food palatable to Mediterranean people to adequate and warm housing for them, did not help. The first occasion for protest occurred in September 1940 and had nothing to do with crass administration. It had never been intended that the evacuees, who had arrived in England between July and October 1940, should stay there for long. The cold and damp of an English winter was expected to affect their health: London, where there was limited accommodation available, was being bombed; and housing outside London was already overcrowded with troops and London evacuees. The Colonial Office was therefore determined to send the Gibraltarian evacuees to the sunny British West Indies as soon as possible. Delays in putting this policy into effect were caused by shortage of suitable shipping and the time needed to prepare accommodation for them in Jamaica, Trinidad and Mauritius. As the weeks passed the evacuees made new lives for themselves in their relatively comfortable billets in Kensington and north London. Many found jobs, and few had any desire to go on another uncomfortable long sea voyage across the Atlantic. It was, however, their menfolk back on the Rock who started to worry first. They were horrified when they heard well-founded rumours that their families were about to be shipped to Jamaica. The U-boat war in the Atlantic was being waged unmercifully, and the chances of the ships carrying their loved ones being lost were far from negligible. It was time to protest again.

This time the protest was not generated by the accepted Gibraltarian leaders from the representative bodies. A group of dockyard and government clerical staff and workers banded together to carry their concerns to the Governor, still Sir Clive Liddell, who reported their disquiet to London. The evacuees were prepared to live through the English winter and to endure the German bombing of London, but they recoiled at the idea of boarding ships yet again with the great danger of being sunk at sea by German U-boats. Rather like the protest over Liddell's refusal to let the evacuees land on their way back from Morocco, events rather than the local protest stopped the move from London. The

City of Benares, carrying English children to Canada, was sunk with great loss of life, and this put an end to any further trans-Atlantic evacuation from Britain. Some 1,500 evacuees had in fact reached Jamaica direct from Gibraltar before the trans-Atlantic evacuations were stopped.

The leaders of the protest group were all experienced trade unionists. Albert Risso had been head of the workers' rights movement; Emilio Alvarez and Emilio Salvado were dockyard clerks; Antonio Morillo was a dockyard torpedo technician; Jimmy Keating was a high-grade dockyard foreman; Emilio Hermida was a clerical officer who later became treasurer of the post-war City Council; and Manuel Ghio was another union activist. After their apparently successful protest, they discussed the idea of forming a local association to look after Gibraltarian rights. They needed legal and political advice, and they took a decision which was to have a long-lasting impact on Gibraltarian politics. They turned to the energetic, politically aware and radical-thinking young lawyer, Joshua Hassan. They had drafted some rules, but had not been able to find a satisfactory name for their proposed association. To have suggested forming a political party in the wartime fortress might have incurred British opprobrium. Salvador vetted and largely redrafted their work in the form of a party constitution, and turned down their tentative suggestion that the name might be the 'Gibraltar Association' because it did not convey the idea of fighting for the establishment of civil rights for the people. After some considerable thought and discussion, he suggested the 'Association for the Advancement of Civil Rights'. The Gibraltarians had had precious little say in government before the war; they were unlikely to see much improvement during the war; but they had to plan ahead and lay the foundations for achieving a greater measure of Gibraltarian involvement in government after the war. The clumsiness of the title which Salvador suggested was mitigated by the exactness of its definition of the party's aims; and the initials AACR acquired a unique resonance about them.

Salvador entered this political work with great enthusiasm. As he says himself: 'I was part of the committee, attended all the meetings, and I prepared and redrafted most of the rules.' Indeed, this was the moment at which he conscientiously espoused a political career. A newly formed pressure group can only survive if there is a continuing demand for it; if it can gather enough active supporters; and if the political environment is favourable at the time. In the AACR's case, the never-ending grievances – real and imagined – of the evacuees in London, Jamaica and Madeira, provided the demand. A steady flow of letters from responsible senior citizens and from unhappy wives among the evacuees brought forward supporters in Gibraltar, who wanted something done to improve the living conditions of their relatives. And as it happened, the liberal 'Mason-Mac' became governor at just the right moment to provide a favourable political environment. The only discordant note came from the merchants and professional men, the majority of whom wished to avoid any association with an upstart workers' party, which might upset the *status quo*. They held back in suspicious but fragmented opposition to the AACR's efforts to express Gibraltarian frustration in a politically compelling way.

It was in June 1942 that Mason-Mac took over as governor from Viscount Gort. He was extraordinarily pleased to find the support that he needed in overcoming the conservatism of Whitehall, and he extended a hand of friendship to the radical, if not actually revolutionary, AACR. By September its founder members had taken Mason-Mac's and Miles Clifford's measure, and decided that the time was ripe 'to go public'. Albert Risso convened the inaugural meeting at the Prince of Wales Football Club premises on 18th September 1942. Before the meeting, he tried to persuade Salvador to accept nomination as the AACR's first president. Salvador refused this generous offer for good reasons. Writing later he explained:

> As he [Risso] had been the inspirer of the whole idea, he had been my inspiration and I looked to him as a man of the people, much older than me of course, honest and prepared to tell the workers unpleasant things about themselves if it were necessary. I did not want the AACR to start as a party created by just another

lawyer who was getting into politics. (Sir Joshua's notes: 15.10.93)

And so, despite all his background work, Salvador attended the inaugural meeting only as an observer, sitting in the body of the hall and not on the platform. When Emilio Hermida presented the rules to the packed meeting, he mentioned that they had been drawn up by a young local lawyer, who was sitting amongst the members. Such was Salvador's popularity among the Gibraltarians in general that he was cheered and chaired onto the platform. Nevertheless, he resisted all pressure from the floor to take over the presidency out of loyalty to Risso and because he believed that Risso, a worker himself, was more representative of the membership. Instead he allowed himself to be elected vice-president.

The Risso/Hassan partnership was a fortuitously happy one. Risso was a thoroughly honest and sincere man who was a foreman in the City Council garage where had proved himself an excellent mechanic. Rather shy and diffident, Risso was no demagogue. He came, in fact, from an upper middle class family like Salvador, his father being Gibraltar's vet. The two men's abilities and personalities complemented each other: Risso projected the worker image and was trusted implicitly by the party, while Salvador provided the intellect and rhetoric. Occasionally accused of making too few speeches, Risso made it clear that he had absolute faith in Salvador, who was the party's spokesman. There was no point in him repeating what Salvador was saying far more persuasively than he could ever do.

Risso, however, was no mere frontman: he was very much the leader and driving force of the party. Mason-Mac reacted to the emergence of the AACR with his characteristic enthusiasm for worthy causes. He sent an encouraging letter to the new association and invited its committee to the Convent to discuss how best the AACR could help the war effort. He gave them every encouragement to carry on their work of bringing the trials and tribulations of the evacuees to his notice; and he started to treat the association as a conduit between the government and the

Gibraltarians at home and overseas. The AACR committee, in their turn, expressed their intention of pursuing a campaign for the devolution of local government to elected Gibraltarians. Mason-Mac found little difficulty in supporting their aims.

Salvador, as a lawyer and one of the few competent English speakers in the early AACR, led the constitutional discussions with Mason-Mac and Miles Clifford, and as a result he became the equivalent of the party's chief executive as well as its spokesman and legal adviser. It was not until the Confederation of Labour was officially launched on 1st July 1947, and Risso became its first president, that Salvador took over as AACR president, a post which he was to hold throughout his active life in politics and in an honorary capacity after he retired. The AACR was to become Salvador's party, dedicated to bringing Gibraltar to the fullest practicable level of internal self-government within the constraints of the Treaty of Utrecht. However he still depended on Risso to maintain the workers' support for the AACR, while Mason-Mac's encouragement resulted in him eschewing confrontation with the British establishment in favour of co-operative persuasion in furthering Gibraltarian interests. Nevertheless, this did not stop British officers of the garrison, and later their wives, nicknaming him 'the Little Red' as his pre-war girl friend used to do.

In the autumn of 1942, the Rock was the scene of intense military activity as preparations were being made for the Allied invasion of French North Africa. Every square yard of usable space on and inside the Rock was stacked with ammunition and other war stores; every bit of parking area around the new airfield was crammed with fighter and bomber aircraft; and every billet capable of housing men was occupied by aircrew, sailors and troops. Eisenhower and his operational staff arrived in late October and set up their tactical command post in a headquarters deep inside the Rock. On 6th November, Force H put to sea to cover the landings on the Algerian coast which started at dusk next day, just as the news of Montgomery's victory over Rommel at El Alamein was flashing around the world. The Allied counter-offensive against the Axis had begun, and with it came hopes of reuniting Gibraltar's families before too long.

The new strategic airfield built across the isthmus and jutting out into the Bay of Gibraltar for the invasion of North Africa was to become a major bone of contention in the post-war dispute with Spain over sovereignty, and was to feature significantly in Salvador's final departure from office some 40 years later, after he had been the undisputed political leader of the Rock's people for all those years. Spain had emerged from her bloody civil war politically and economically emaciated, and had been in no position to protest about the construction of the airfield within the British half of the Neutral Zone on the isthmus. By the 1950s, however, Franco had gained enough confidence to protest about this infringement of the Treaty of Utrecht, which did not cede any of the isthmus to Britain – subsequent agreements had turned the isthmus into a neutral zone to reduce the likelihood of military clashes between British and Spanish troops.

Britain responded to Franco's protests by offering to take the matter of sovereignty over the British half of the isthmus, which she claimed by 'prescription' (ie over 200 years of continuous occupation), to the European Court of Justice at the Hague. Franco did not accept the challenge, fearing an adverse ruling by the court. Spain has continued ever since to claim that the airfield is on Spanish soil, and has tried to use the claim as a means of undermining Britain's title to the Rock. This became so evident after the signing of the Anglo-Spanish Airport Agreement in December 1987 that the unpopularity of Salvador's defence of its negotiation contributed to his decision to leave politics soon afterwards. Joe Bossano, his successor, has refused to implement it because of its implications for British sovereignty.

After the Allied invasion of North Africa, Risso, Salvador and the AACR committee decided that, although there was, as yet, no possibility of immediate repatriation of the evacuees because the Rock was still in the front line and working at maximum stretch as a naval and air base, supporting the Allied military operations in the Mediterranean – the capture of Tunis and the invasions of Sicily and Italy – they would press for a special leave scheme for husbands to join their families in London for about a fortnight. Only a few men in each workshop or government department could be away at any one time so ballots would have to be held in each to decide who should be allowed to join specific leave parties. Shipping was no problem: there was a steady stream of ships of all types plying between England and Gibraltar, feeding the vast Allied sea, land and air forces in North Africa and Sicily and returning home empty. Mason-Mac not only accepted the AACR scheme as both desirable and practicable, but gave the association the responsibility for carrying out the selection by ballot, which was held in public and with scrupulous fairness at the AACR's original premises at 2 Engineer Lane. The first Special Leave Party – 'Splea' party in official jargon – of 88 husbands left Gibraltar in July 1943; the second of 120 in October; and the third and last, as it turned out, at Christmas that year. The operation of the scheme brought about a close rapport between Salvador on the one hand and Mason-Mac and Miles Clifford on the other; and confidence grew between AACR activists and government officials. Salvador was starting to be accepted by most people on the Rock as the local spokesman on all Gibraltarian issues, but he was also, by force of circumstance, becoming the AACR's organizing mastermind. To carry out the Splea balloting fairly, he created a party organization, which he was to use later with telling effect for mounting massed protest marches and demonstrations when, as was to happen all too frequently, the AACR fell out with the government. The initial rapport between the government and the AACR was nearly destroyed soon after the first Splea party left for England in July 1943, thanks to what became known as the Marlborough House incident, which had started to generate political heat amongst the London evacuees at the end of May. They had never liked English cooking, although great efforts had been made to satisfy Gibraltarian tastes. Consequently, the practice had grown up of some evacuees taking their food to their rooms to recook it to their own liking, which was strictly against Ministry of Health fire regulations, but was winked at in most centres. At Marlborough House in Kensington, where Gustav

Bellotti, a pre-war City Councillor, was billeted with his family, the manager insisted on the regulations being obeyed. Bellotti, a self-important man who was prone to rush to litigation to get his own way, refused to comply and encouraged others not to do so either. He also sought legal assistance from Dr Newcome Wright, a crusading lawyer, who, with his wife, enjoyed fighting cases where there was a whiff of victimization.

The Ministry warned Bellotti that he would be evicted if he persisted in disobeying its regulations. Disobey he did, and so an attempt was made to evict him with the help of the police. The eviction was a fiasco. On Newcome Wright's advice, the other evacuees – mainly women – blocked the access to Bellotti's rooms by lying down in the corridors. Bellotti stayed put, was taken to court and, much to the Ministry's chagrin, won the first round although he was to lose the second when the Ministry appealed.

The Marlborough House incident was symptomatic of a growing sense of frustration among the evacuees, but it also triggered the issue of Gibraltarian civil rights for which Salvador and the AACR were committed to fight. Liaison between the evacuees and the Whitehall ministries was through Major Joseph Patron MC (later Sir Joseph Patron, first Gibraltarian Speaker of the Legislative Council), who had been appointed Evacuation Commissioner for London by the Governor. Patron chaired the Gibraltar Advisory Committee, consisting of nominated representatives from the various evacuee centres including Marlborough House. Each centre had its own liaison committee, again composed of nominated individuals. Major Patron was a hardworking and dedicated man, who gave outstanding service to Gibraltar throughout his life, but who was seen by some of the evacuees as a member of the British establishment and much better at conveying Whitehall's dictates to them than at fighting in the corridors of power for improvements in their living conditions. He and Bellotti were poles apart: Patron saw Bellotti as a troublemaker, who would never co-operate with anyone; and Bellotti considered Patron an unelected jumped-up jack-in-office, which was grossly unfair because Patron had dipped voluntarily into his own capacious pocket to help his fellow Gibraltarians.

After the attempted eviction, Bellotti and his collaborating malcontents set up a rival 'Provisional Executive Committee' to wrest the responsibility for Gibraltarian affairs in London from Patron, and sought the AACR's help to do so. This placed Risso and Salvador in some difficulty. If they supported Bellotti as most of their party wished, they might alienate the Governor and give the AACR an anti-British flavour, which could jeopardize the constructive relationship that they had just established with the government at all levels. However, when shorn of the Patron/Bellotti animosities, the Provisional Executive's case for replacing nominated committees by elected ones was so clearly in keeping with the AACR's political platform that they felt bound to try to negotiate a sensible compromise with Miles Clifford, the Colonial Secretary. Unfortunately, Bellotti did not help by demanding the resignation of Patron in a letter from his committee, dated 27th November 1943, which drew the terse comment from Mason-Mac that 'such letters were best ignored'. Clifford was equally sharp with Salvador a month later, annotating the margin of an AACR letter, which made extravagant claims about the effectiveness of Bellotti's committee and the uselessness of Patron's, with the single word, 'rubbish'. (Finlayson, p 115).

It was not until February 1944 that a meeting between the AACR, Patron and the Colonial Secretary took place. Salvador won the day with cogent argument, and agreement was reached that all non-representative or self-constituted bodies should be abolished and a fresh start made with a structure of properly elected committees. By then, however, the whole tiresome business had been overtaken by the much more important issue of repatriation. Italy had capitulated in September 1943, removing the Axis threat to Gibraltar for good and all. It was clearly safe to reunite families on the Rock if shipping and accommodation could be found for them.

Gibraltar was still a busy naval and air base with little or no spare accommodation for returning evacuees. Their numbers had been swollen to an estimated 20,000 souls by Gibraltarians who had previously lived in Spain and would not be able to return there, certainly as long as the war lasted, if ever. On the Rock, most of the evacuees' former dwellings were being used by the services for billeting and other military purposes. For instance, the whole of the Crutchett's Ramp area was taken over for military purposes.

The service commanders were adamant that little accommodation could be released until the war was over or the Chiefs of Staff in Whitehall agreed to a reduction of Gibraltar's military commitments, which seemed most unlikely.

Sadly for Gibraltar, Mason-Mac was sent off at short notice to head the British Military Mission to the new Italian government and later the Allied Control Commission in Italy. Before he left, he made it clear to the Colonial Office that, in his view, it was inconceivable that any Gibraltarian, who wished to return home, should be prevented from doing so by lack of accommodation. Temporary dwellings would have to be provided in hutted camps if need be. Regrettably, his successor was a dyed-in-the-wool military traditionalist.

Lieutenant-General Sir Ralph (Rusty) Eastwood, who took over in February 1944, was a firm believer in the primacy of military requirements and had little or no feelings for the civil population of the Rock. He was adamantly against repatriation until adequate accommodation and medical facilities could be provided for the returning families, and was not prepared to force the service commanders to release housing any quicker than they deemed reasonable from the military point of view. It had been easy enough to pack the evacuees off in 1940 when the Rock was under threat: it was to prove far more difficult and took infinitely longer to rehouse them when the threat to the Rock faded away. In the circumstances, the AACR had a clear mission to agitate for an accelerated return home, coupled with quicker release of requisitioned property, the construction of temporary housing for short term use, and the planning of longer-term building programmes. At critical moments in the long struggle to bring the people back, the AACR mounted well-ordered and peaceful mass demonstrations in the streets to protest about delays in repatriation. Salvador had already created the organization to do this as we have noted. With practical experience forced upon him by the need to make the AACR voice heard, he and Risso brought non-violent protest marching to a fine art. In mounting these demonstrations they were pushing in the same direction as the Whitehall ministries, who were bent upon sending the Gibraltarian evacuees back home as quickly as possible because Britain was having to accept refugees – particularly Poles and Jews – from all over Europe and housing for them was scarce. The repatriation issue became a contest between the AACR and Whitehall on one side with their feet firmly on the accelerator, and, on the other, 'Rusty' Eastwood and the Service commanders, with theirs on the brake.

Repatriation was handled for the Gibraltar government's Resettlement Board by the Repatriation Subcommittee, which met for the first time in December 1943. Urgency was brought to their deliberations by the renewed bombing of London in February 1944 in which one of the evacuee centres was hit, although mercifully there were no fatalities among the Gibraltarian casualties. The bombing brought an offer from Whitehall of three ships each able to carry 1,000 evacuees, but Eastwood maintained that he could not accept so high a rate of return and settled for a first batch of about 1,400, who reached Gibraltar to an emotional reception, largely organised by the AACR, on 6th April 1944.

In fact, the first batch had been lucky to get away when they did. As they left England, the whole repatriation scheme was stopped by security restrictions on all movement out of the UK, imposed to thwart German intelligence before the Normandy landings on 6th June. Worse was to come: on 13th June the V1 flying bomb (doodlebug) raids began on London, and six Gibraltarians had been killed and many more injured by mid-July. The AACR complained vehemently that they had warned the Governor that the Germans would answer the invasion of France with heavy bombing of London. Now that their prediction had been proved right, it was English women and children who were being evacuated from London to the country shires: what about the

Gibraltarians? On 4th July, Risso, Salvador and the AACR Committee members led an impressive mass protest march through Gibraltar to make the point that their families should be brought back to the relative safety of the Rock as soon as possible regardless of housing difficulties, or be sent somewhere else in the United Kingdom safer than London.

In the event, both options were used. AACR pressure, linked with Colonial Office persistence, resulted in the Governor being forced to accept a second batch of 3,000 evacuees, and the rest of the London evacuees were sent to the safety but discomfort of temporary camps in Northern Ireland, which were just adequate for summer weather but far from desirable for a Mediterranean people in the cold, wet and windy weather of Ulster's winter. By the end of 1944, only some 7,000 evacuees were back on the Rock; and, as Eastwood had predicted, many were living in grossly overcrowded houses or in transit accommodation. Neither he nor his Colonial Secretary, Stanley, could or would do as much as the AACR and the Colonial Office believed practicable to clear the wretched Northern Ireland camps before the remaining evacuees had to spend a second winter in them. Salvador, much against his own inclinations, was forced into open opposition to the Convent by Eastwood's and Stanley's attitudes.

With the Rock no longer under threat, it was time to start negotiations for a post-war constitution. Salvador had laid sound foundations for his future political influence. He was virtually leading the only political party in Gibraltar and had established himself as a young, forceful and charismatic leader: he knew his fellow Gibraltarians inside out, and they knew and trusted him. He was both the AACR's ideas and organization man. Although his command of spoken, as opposed to written, English was not one of his strongest points, he had a gift of inspired oratory in Llanito (Andalusian Spanish, spiced with Victorian barrack-room English), and could win the support of local political gatherings by his genuineness of purpose and the easily understood logic of his approach.

Under Salvador's guidance, the AACR had joined the Exchange

and Commercial Library, the Chamber of Commerce and the TGWU as the fourth of the local 'representative bodies'. But there was a difference: the AACR was not a meekly reactive and deferential group of worthies like the older institutions; it was a dynamic party with its own clear objectives of reestablishing immediate Gibraltarian participation in government, fighting for Gibraltarian rights, and one day achieving full internal self-rule. More importantly, its vice-president and future leader had shown the ability to vary his approach in subtle ways to suit the prevailing circumstances of the day. He had an intuitive feel for British thought processes, and for the limits of what they were likely to consider reasonable. He was thus able to work his way forward step by step with proposals seen as mutually beneficial to the colonial administration and the Gibraltarians, and hence acceptable to both. Later, he was to show that he had a similar grasp of the Spanish mentality. It was no accident that he became known in Gibraltarian political circles as *el pulpo* (the octopus): he had a tentacle in everything going on as self-government developed.

CHAPTER 3

SEEKING AN ELECTED MUNICIPAL AUTHORITY

1944-46

Elected Members of the First Post-War City Council:
J A Hassan (Elected Chairman)
Major J T Ellicott
A J Baldorino (Vice Chairman)
C McGrail
E L Alvarez
Lieutenant R J Peliza
O L Chamberland
(All were members of the AACR)

Italy's capitulation in September 1943 was not an unmitigated blessing for Gibraltar. It enabled the evacuees to start returning home, albeit in dribs and drabs, and it gave an incentive to those, like Salvador, who wanted to press ideas for post-war constitutional reform. But it removed from the Convent the one man, Mason-MacFarlane, who might have achieved more rapid repatriation and advance to internal self-government in full co-operation with the people of Gibraltar.

Mason-Mac's departure also had a critical effect upon Salvador's political thinking. Despite being radical and well left of centre by instinct, he had got on well with the Convent so far. His coming struggle with the militarily orthodox Eastwood and his unsympathetically conservative Colonial Secretary, R C S Stanley, was to turn him, at least temporarily, into a demandingly awkward politician. Sir Howard Davis, who was to become Gibraltar's first and only Gibraltarian Deputy Governor in the 1970s, who knew both wartime Colonial Secretaries described Clifford as 'having imagination without stability', whereas Stanley had 'stability without imagination'. Salvador himself recalled:

> Although he [Stanley] was always courteous to me, I never knew him well: he was very detached. (Sir Joshua's notes of 10.11.93).

Well before Mason-MacFarlane left to take up his appointment with the new Italian government, the AACR persuaded the other representative bodies to join them in discussions about the future shape of Gibraltar's constitution, so that they could present as near a united front as possible. In this they were given every encouragement by Mason-Mac, who appreciated that locally elected representatives would be far better placed to handle the city's affairs after the war than Colonial Office officials and Governor's nominees. He went further: he encouraged the Colonial Office itself to start planning post-war constitutional reform for Gibraltar as well.

In a letter to the Secretary of State for Colonies dated as early as 11th April 1943, Mason-Mac stated the case for increased local representation in government and pressed for an Advisory Council to be set up with six elected and six ex-officio members. He pointed out that apart from his own inclinations to associate the Gibraltarians more closely in their own government, the AACR, which had the support of at least three-quarters of the civilian population still on the Rock, was demanding a greater say in government through elected rather than nominated representatives. In one revealing paragraph, he says:

> I have met their committee more than once and they are, I think, fairly representative, well-spoken, and in many ways prepared to co-operate. I do not regard them as subversive in any way; we have so far discussed all points they have raised very amicably; and they have been very appreciative of my willingness to give them a

sympathetic hearing and my endeavours to meet, as far as lie in my power, their requests. There are, of course, no elected representatives of my people and I personally welcome the formation of this committee which enables me to keep more in touch with the popular feeling and local difficulties than I would otherwise be able to do. (PRO, CO.91/518/1)

Salvador and the AACR Committee took the lead in the discussions with the other representative bodies almost by default. Most of the active Exchange and Commercial Library members were already heavily committed, serving on commissions and committees set up by the City Commissioner to run what remained of the civilian administration; the Chamber of Commerce was blinkered by business considerations; and the TGWU was too small to have much influence. Moreover, the AACR was beginning to attract political activists from all levels of Gibraltarian society, who Salvador felt were jumping on the AACR bandwagon, which was clearly gathering momentum. New members like Sergio Triay, Lawrence Chamberland and Major Bob Peliza widened the party's political base.

Four clear Gibraltarian requirements emerged: the City Council must be reconstituted with larger locally elected representation than in pre-war days; the governor's nominated Executive Council should be replaced by an elected Legislative Council; both City and Legislative Councils should have built-in elected majorities; Governor's nominees should be abolished.

Mason-Mac would have had little difficulty in recommending such proposals to the Colonial Office, but the idea of elected majorities stuck in the gullets of Eastwood and the service commanders: in their view the security of the fortress was still paramount and required an 'official' majority in government, which took its direction from the Whitehall ministries and not from the local people.

Furthermore, the expatriate officials had grave doubts about the competence of Gibraltarians to run the city's internal administration, and were reluctant, like all colonial administrators, to believe that anyone but themselves could develop well-balanced and constructive policies. Through most of the official documents of this period runs a thread of doubt about Gibraltarian competence and the need to give them more experience in government administration before allowing them wider responsibilities.

Governor's nominees were naturally an AACR target because, although perhaps worthy as well as wealthy, they were grossly unrepresentative of the great majority of the people. Sir Arthur Dawe, Deputy Under Secretary at the Colonial Office with responsibility for Gibraltar's administration described them scathingly when he wrote:

> The central government is a complete autocracy rested on a Military Governor. The only unofficial element is a small group of unofficial members of the Executive Council. These councillors constitute a small commercial oligarchy. They are not in personal characteristics of a very high type and they naturally, on almost every question, find little difficulty in identifying the public interest with their private and commercial inclinations. (PRO, CO.91/88903, 14.12.45)

After considering all the constitutional arguments put forward by the AACR and the Governor, the Colonial Office proposed two bodies in which the casting vote would always lie with the officials: a new City Council with six popularly elected councillors and six officials and/or governor's nominees, chaired by one of the elected members; and an Advisory Council made up of the City Council sitting together with the colonial secretary, attorney-general and financial secretary, under the colonial secretary's chairmanship. The Colonial Office proposals were put to the committee drawn from the AACR and the representative bodies in January 1944 during the interregnum between governors. By that time, the AACR had virtually taken over the Exchange and Commercial Library, so Salvador was very much in the driving seat and persuaded the negotiating committee to turn down the offer for sound reasons. The Exchange and Commercial Library was eventually fully amalgamated with the AACR in January 1948. The City Council proposal might just have been acceptable as a first step, because it was to have an elected chairman; but an advisory council, chaired by the colonial secretary and without an elected majority, would be a façade. The real power would still rest with the Governor and his nominated Executive Council. The very word 'advisory' stuck in Gibraltarian throats as much as 'elected majority' was anathema to the expatriate officials.

For the moment, however, a head-on clash between the AACR and the Convent over constitutional reform was averted because the subject was still largely hypothetical. With Gibraltar still at full military stretch, serving the Allied war effort as a strategic air and naval base, there could be no question of constitutional change until these activities declined and a higher proportion of the evacuees had returned home to reconstitute the civilian population. Any lull there may have been in the incipient political struggle for constitutional reform was soon offset by a running battle, which developed between the Governor and the AACR over repatriation. Shortage of housing was the first and longest lasting reason given by Eastwood and Stanley for delaying repatriation despite constant Colonial Office and AACR pressure to accelerate it. The Resettlement Board was not allowed to bring back anyone who did not have a guarantee of accommodation in Gibraltar, and then only when shipping happened to be available. The 7,000 who were still in exile would have to wait for accommodation to be released by the services or for temporary camps to be built for them. The latter was unnecessarily delayed by the services' reluctance to provide suitable land for camps, despite their ownership at that time of 90 per cent of the Rock's surface. The early rush of repatriation was reduced to sporadic shipments by the autumn of 1944, when a new excuse for not clearing the Ulster camps any quicker emerged. Medical facilities on the Rock were deemed by the Chief Medical Officer to be overstretched and would break down altogether if any more evacuees were brought home before more nurses and doctors could be recruited. Recruiting extra medical staff in wartime was proving far from easy and would take time.

Eastwood made himself deeply unpopular by bringing Lady

Eastwood out to Gibraltar at a time when large numbers of Gibraltarian families were still separated. He made matters worse by ordering the renovation of the old Governor's Cottage at Europa (now Governor's Cottage Camp, near to the incinerator) as a hot weather retreat for himself and his wife. Despite their deep political antagonisms, Salvador confessed with typical generosity of spirit that 'Eastwood later developed a good relationship with me'! (Sir Joshua's notes of 10.11.93)

The medical argument was the last straw for the AACR. Its campaign for accelerated repatriation seemed to be thwarted at every turn by what seemed to be bureaucratic bumbling and lack of wholehearted co-operation from the colonial government. Salvador drafted a six-point resolution at the beginning of December 1944, demanding the immediate return of all evacuees from what were believed in Gibraltar to be the appalling conditions in the Ulster camps, and suggesting how the accommodation and medical problems could be solved. He presented the resolutions to a public meeting on 6th December before handing it to the Colonial Secretary. Regrettably, his efforts only widened the growing gap between the government and the AACR: the former considered the AACR suggestions impracticable and irresponsible as well as impertinent; the latter looked on the government as obtuse.

The rift in AACR/government relations was not helped by the public announcement on 30th December of the proposed re-establishment of the City Council and the creation of an Advisory Council on the lines already set out by the Colonial Office. Absolutely no attempt seems to have been made to meet the local demand for an elected majority in the former and for a Legislative Council instead of the latter. When it became clear in January that the AACR would not co-operate unless the City Council was given an elected majority, the Governor and Colonial Office gave way and allowed a seventh elected seat, giving a balance of seven elected members, including the elected chairman, to six officials and nominees. Nothing would, however, persuade the Governor to recommend modifying the Advisory Council proposals.

Salvador had won the City Council argument, but his acute political antennae warned him that trying to win a Legislative instead of Advisory Council might be a step too soon and too far. Confidence in Gibraltarian administrative abilities had to be established through their work in the City Council before there would be much chance of the British establishment agreeing to extend the principle of elected majorities from municipal to central government level. He persuaded the AACR Committee to accept temporary defeat over the Legislative Council, and to wait until the new City Council had been elected and was in office before taking up the cudgels once more.

To be fair to the three service commanders in Gibraltar, who were often accused of myopic intransigence, it was the service ministries in Whitehall which were mostly to blame. Their attitude was that Gibraltar was their fortress. The civilian population was the Colonial Office's responsibility. Only land and buildings, for which no further military use could be foreseen, could be handed over to the civil administration; and as the Cold War began to cast its shadow over military thinking the chances of any real estate becoming surplus to defence requirements diminished. Co-operation between the three services in Whitehall was difficult enough to achieve at the best of times: the addition of the Colonial Office made decision-making almost impossible and certainly far slower than it should have been. The local commanders on the spot had to shoulder the blame for Whitehall's failures to respond to Gibraltarian needs.

By the time Germany capitulated on 9th May 1945, new electoral lists had been prepared for the first post-war City Council elections, which were to take place on 24th July. In one of his periodic letters to the Gibraltar 'desk' in the Colonial Office, Stanley made an over-sanguine guess:

> . . . . it is unlikely that the AACR will secure more than four of the seven seats, in which case nothing very revolutionary is likely to happen as it can be assumed that the three non-AACR will vote with the official members against any irresponsible proposals. (PRO, CO.91/525/6 11.6.45)

Much to everyone's surprise, the AACR swept the board, winning all seven elected seats. Such was their success that at the next City Council election in December 1947 the AACR was returned unopposed. The credit for the AACR's success must go to Salvador, Sergio Triay and Lawrence Chamberland, who together organized the ingenious system by which the AACR directed its supporters to cast their four votes for specific AACR candidates so that all seven of its candidates were evenly covered and received the maximum number of AACR votes. Salvador's counting agent was Abraham Benatar. 'Bramy' became a great personal friend, who supported him throughout his political career although he never became a member of the AACR. His loyalty was to Salvador rather than the party. At the first meeting of the new Council on 1st August 1945, Salvador reaped the reward of all his hard work since the inception of the AACR. He was elected Chairman of the City Council, thus giving him a power base and platform of his own. Lawrence Chamberland, who was a Cable and Wireless employee and head of the Scientific Trades Union, became one of Salvador's principal lieutenants.

Just before City Council polling took place, an event occurred which should have brought Salvador even greater happiness than winning the election. In May, he married Daniela Salazar, a girl from northern Spain, who had been working as a secretary in Gibraltar during the evacuation period. They had two daughters born in 1946 and 1947, but their marriage was only to be happy for about ten years due to Daniela developing a distressing neurosis. It was to end in a controversial special divorce bill in 1969 as will be recounted in more detail later. Suffice it to say here that the months of 1969, while the controversy over the Hassan Divorce Bill was at its height, were one of Salvador's most difficult periods in local politics. The Rock's population being predominantly Roman Catholic, legislation for divorce on grounds other than adultery was not introduced until the 1980s. As there was no suggestion of adultery on Daniela's part, he cited cruelty and separation. It is a measure of his political popularity that he still topped the poll in the 1969 elections despite the electorate's aversion to divorce. His remarriage to Marcelle Bensimon that year gave him a consort who was to devote herself to his support in public and private life, and greatly assisted him throughout the latter half of his political career. For most Gibraltarians, 'Lady Hassan' is Marcelle rather than the late Daniela, who died in 1992; and his marriage to Marcelle has already exceeded the 17 years of his first.

Political success breeds success, but also rivals. Stanley was quick to note a right and left polarization in local Gibraltar politics, which had not made itself felt until the AACR's sweeping electoral victory. Members of the Chamber of Commerce and the wealthier families – the conservative right, who had represented Gibraltarian interests so far throughout Gibraltar's British period – began to resent the political progress being made by the young upstart lawyer, Hassan, who had won in two and a half years what the representative bodies of the inter-war years had failed to achieve in seventeen: a City Council with an elected majority. Their own positions and privileges as the Gibraltarian establishment were being undermined, and they did not like it. Albert Isola, for instance, as representative of the Chamber of Commerce during the Constitutional negotiations, advised the Governor not to allow an elected majority on the City Council lest power slip into the irresponsible hands of the lower orders, led by a leftist lawyer who could not be trusted.

Despite the prevalent dislike of the AACR in commercial circles, and the general unpopularity of the Governor and his Colonial Secretary, the right could not unite sufficiently to pose an effective opposition to Salvador's organized left. The establishment figures who did stand for election to the City Council did so, as they had always done, as 'independents'. Stanley, in a mood of frustration, noted the lack of establishment support for the government in the face of populist AACR pressure:

> It may not be fair to say that in Gibraltar every man's hand is against the government, but it is certainly true to say that few possess the desire or the courage to be seen arm in arm with it.

(PRO, CO.91/525/6, 11.6.45)

The sweeping AACR victory brought Salvador, as the leader of the left, problems of his own. He now had to ride two horses: the City Council where he must show administrative competence and responsibility; and the AACR committee, in which he had to vie with the more extreme radicals to maintain his position as their spokesman and mentor. He was so successful in chairing the City Council and running the municipal services that Stanley was forced to admit a modicum of confidence in Salvador's abilities. In a letter to the Colonial Office, dated 11th September 1945, he wrote:

> I do not view with alarm the fact that the elected unofficial majority are radical in complexion. The Council have, in my opinion, done well to decide that their meetings shall be held in public, for the knowledge that one's remarks may be reported in the newspapers is a healthy correction to irresponsible utterances. The extent to which further constitutional development will be possible depends very largely upon the attitudes of the Service Departments. One hopes there will be no impediment for the setting up of a legislative council, constituted in such a way as to provide all proper safeguards required by defence considerations. It would provide a valuable education in political responsibility for those who were nominated or elected members. The establishment of such a body would also serve to correct any tendency on the part of the City Council to endeavour to extend their authority beyond the limits of municipal responsibility. (PRO, CO.91/525/1, 11.9.45)

Stanley was keen to set up a Legislative Council for more personal reasons. He had at least one thought in common with Salvador: he could not abide the Gibraltarian nominees on the Governor's Executive Council, describing Patron, for instance, as a jellyfish. In his view:

> they behave [in the Executive Council] as if they were an unofficial opposition, and have ideas that they have responsibility to the 'people', but are the last persons that the 'people' would elect. (PRO, CO.91/525/6, 10.1.45)

Salvador saw them as opponents of the AACR and rivals in the post-war struggle for local political power. As an intuitive politician, he could brook no rivals and even at this early stage in his political career was already devising his own methods of political assassination. He was quick to appreciate that winning elections was the key to power and failure to do so was fatal to anyone however worthy. His first two targets were Joseph Patron and Peter Russo. He protested to the Governor in September 1945 about their nomination to the Executive Council on the grounds that Patron had been a disaster as Evacuee Commissioner in London, and Russo had received absurdly few votes at the recent City Council elections. They might be worthy, wealthy and experienced as Governor's advisers, but they could, in no way, be expected to represent the local population impartially on the Executive Council. Salvador's protest was successful in that neither joined the Executive Council immediately. Patron eventually did so in 1947, but Russo never did.

Riding the AACR horse was no easier than managing the City Council. The party had attracted political activists of all shades of opinion, making it difficult to impose party discipline; to agree a sensible constructive approach and to avoid gratuitous confrontations with the government. The Convent's lack of political sensitivity did not help, and led the AACR to increase its use of mass meetings, demonstrations and marches to generate pressure to correct popularly conceived injustices. Speeding up repatriation was the issue that continued to generate most heat, and was fuelled by a continuous stream of disgruntled letters of complaint about conditions in Ulster. There was also controversy over more routine issues like wage levels for government employees, trade union legislation, food rationing, future taxation, and, of course, housing, all of which led to political demonstrations of one sort or another organized by the AACR.

In carrying out his two roles – chairman of the City Council and *de facto* leader of the AACR – Salvador had to be something of a chameleon. As chairman, he looked and could play the part: his intelligence and legal gravitas, his neat black hair and dapper appearance, and his sober approach, all suited the leader of the municipality. As vice-president of the AACR, he had to be a man of the people and something of a rabble rouser. His extraordinary political charisma amongst the working people was based upon his palpable honesty of purpose, his willingness to take pains over individuals' problems and his ability to focus the feelings and aspirations of the majority. But he also had two other priceless assets: he wrote unimpeachable English and spoke compelling Spanish. In dealing with City Council business and negotiating with the Convent over constitutional reform, he could write the most lucid and persuasive papers in a simple elegant style, which could match the best of Whitehall's mandarins. And in AACR mass meetings and demonstrations, his high pitched tenor voice, fluent *Llanito* and logical approach, could sway a Gibraltarian crowd or audience as few other speakers could do. His oft repeated cry '*nosotros, el pueblo de Gibraltar . . .*' always brought him fervent acclaim.

It gradually became clear, however, that Salvador did not have the time to be the effective leader of both the City Council and the AACR, while, at the same time, building up his own successful legal practice. Fortuitously, Louis Bruzon was repatriated from Northern Ireland in September 1945. He had been one of Bellotti's most ardent supporters during the Marlborough House incident and had been chairman of the Provisional Executive Committee, which had tried to oust Patron. Nevertheless, he had done sterling work in making the evacuees' lives more tolerable in London and Northern Ireland. A man of great charm and keen sense of humour, who was an amateur playwright of some merit and an old friend of Salvador's, he put the Ulster evacuees' case in the strongest possible terms when he arrived back in Gibraltar. Joining the AACR, he was soon appointed its general secretary to relieve Salvador of much of the day-to-day organizational work and the correspondence with the Colonial Secretary. The two men got on extraordinarily well together because Bruzon, being a good professional civil servant and an able draftsman, kept out of the political limelight, leaving Salvador as the unchallenged policy maker, tactician and spokesman of the AACR. Bruzon's main contribution, besides helping Salvador, was to edit the AACR's party newspaper, *Luz* (the Light). Stanley was far less charitable about the AACR's activities than about Salvador's performance in the City Council. In his correspondence there are disparaging references to the party:

> Its president is one Risso, a pleasant plebeian, who is the dummy for Hassan, another lawyer and the brains of the organization. (PRO, CO.91/525/6, 9.4.45)
>
> The irritating and rather childish activities of the AACR have occupied a good deal more time than their intrinsic importance justifies. (PRO, CO.91/525/6, 15.9.45)
>
> The truth is that they are a completely irresponsible body although they have had the benefit of the brains of people like S P Triay and J A Hassan. (PRO, CO.91/525/6, 15.9.45)
>
> I am told that the unofficial members of the City Council met in camera before formal meetings take place and agree policy and take any direction from their Association's Committee. (PRO, CO.91/525/6, 15.9.45)

There was nothing reprehensible about preliminary AACR meetings. Any well-organized and disciplined party would do the same thing. Indeed, it became Salvador's standard procedure throughout his political career, and was reinforced by regular Sunday lunch-time meetings with his principal advisers at Doctor Jaime Giraldi's flat in Pitman's Alley.

Stanley's main worry was centred upon the activities of those he considered extremists like S P Triay, who he thought were intent on embarrassing the government at every turn. Sergio Triay was strongly anti-establishment and this made him too radical for Salvador's liking. He and his brother had been studying in London during the First World War. Their father, an official in the Port Department, wrote to them, begging them not to join up. His letter was opened by one of the censors, who leaked its contents. With wartime emotions running high in Gibraltar, the leak gave the Triays a totally unjustified reputation for disloyalty. During the

Second World War, 'S P' was evacuated and was employed by Nestlé in Switzerland and the United States, having been their lawyer in Gibraltar in the inter-war years. When he returned to Gibraltar, he joined the AACR and became one of its intellectual policy-makers. He broke away eventually to stand as an independent candidate for the first Legislative Council and was elected in 1953. He served with distinction on it, adding the perceptive insight of a good lawyer to their deliberations. Like all radicals, he had been an ardent supporter of the republican side in the Spanish Civil War, and was a keen advocate of less Gibraltarian hostility towards Spain. Paradoxically he was one of the earliest advocates of integration with Britain. He founded the Commonwealth Party, calling for dominion status for Gibraltar. He died in November 1954 at the early age of 53, only months after his new party's inauguration, bequeathing to two of his three sons, J J and J E Triay, his radical leanings and affection for Spanish culture.

Stanley also had suspicions that communist influences were at work in Gibraltar, but most colonial secretaries in other territories had similar fears as the collapse of Germany brought the Cold War in its wake. Looking for 'reds under the bed' was already a popular pastime among British as well as American officialdom. There may have been some members of the AACR who held extreme socialist views such as José Netto of the affiliated TGWU, but Stanley found no evidence of an active communist cell operating within their ranks.

As the Ulster evacuees began to realize that they were destined to spend a second winter in their dreary camps, the stream of letters of complaint multiplied and frustration grew among the AACR activists in Gibraltar. The autumn months were a period of political turmoil, culminating in the AACR deciding to send a delegation back to London to place before the Secretary of State for the Colonies, George Hall, their grievances about the lack of a Legislative Council, the slow rate of repatriation, and the unacceptable conditions of the Ulster camps. Before calling upon him they were to visit the camps themselves to build up their case for more rapid repatriation or the transfer of the evacuees back to better accommodation on the mainland. They were also to propose that responsibility for repatriation should be handed over by the Gibraltar government to the City Council, and that the service ministries should release 80 per cent of the land and housing which the military occupied within the city. The delegation was led by Albert Risso, who was accompanied by S P Triay, E J Alvarez, and Major Jack Ellicott. Salvador's duties as Chairman of the City Council prevented him from joining them, but such was his frustration with the Gibraltar government that he set the stage for the delegation's departure by handing in a memorial at the Convent for the Governor, signed by 7,000 Gibraltarians, which set out the people's grievances and was highly critical of Eastwood and Stanley personally: Eastwood because he had never visited the Ulster camps, and Stanley for what was seen as unreasonable stubbornness in meeting the AACR's responsible demands.

The Colonial Office must have done some very fast footwork to deflate the delegation's aspirations. Two days before it left for London on 7th November, HMG announced its intention to set up a Legislative Council in Gibraltar when the bulk of the population had returned home. It would not have the elected majority, which the AACR had been demanding, because the military requirements of the fortress, the strategic significance of which had been enhanced by the onset of the Cold War, had still to be safeguarded. It would have five elected and five official members, and the Governor would preside.

The announcement was naturally unwelcome to Salvador and the radical left because it meant they had lost, at least for the time being, the struggle for an elected local majority in the central government of the colony. The conservative right – 'the enemies of the elected majority' as Salvador called them – were secretly delighted: they had no wish to see the government dominated by AACR 'reds'. Stanley recorded:

> Among the Right there is scarcely veiled satisfaction at the fact
> that there will not be an elected unofficial majority in the

Legislative Council. (PRO, CO.91/525/6, 21.12.45)

The delegation's visit to London was only a partial success. They received an attentive hearing from the Secretary of State and soothing bromides from Colonial Office officials. Their prior visit to Ulster had shown the camps to be much improved and the remaining 3,000 evacuees in them far happier than they had been led to believe by the letters they had been receiving in Gibraltar. This did not, however, stop S P Triay issuing a damning report on the conditions as he saw them, which probably exaggerated the bad state of the camps. He also flew a kite about integration with Britain in the future which received little encouragement in London. So ended 1945: there were still some 5,000 evacuees waiting to return from London, Jamaica and Madeira; the City Council under Salvador's chairmanship was proving a remarkable success; and the establishment of a Legislative Council had been agreed, but without an elected majority. Eastwood was in no hurry to set it up in the face of continued AACR objections to its composition.

1946 was to prove another year of AACR agitation over repatriation. George Hall, the Secretary of State, visited Gibraltar at the end of January. The official Colonial Office's replies to the points raised with him by the AACR's November delegation to London had just been received, and were considered by Salvador and the AACR committee as highly unsatisfactory. Mr Hall personally rejected the AACR attacks on Eastwood and Stanley, and maintained that he was fully satisfied that they were tackling repatriation and other major issues 'with energy, drive and resolution'. He again turned down the suggestion that the City Council should take over rehousing evacuees on the reasonable grounds that providing new housing depended upon the military plans, which were already in train, to move troops out of the city southwards towards Europa, and because raising the money needed for renovating existing buildings and construction of new blocks of flats was beyond the City Council's capacity.

Salvador found himself in a difficult position during Hall's visit.

One moment he was briefing the Secretary of State as the responsible Chairman of the City Council, and the next he was playing the part of a radical politician, attacking the government in an apparently reckless way. Stanley gleefully records that the Secretary of State 'gave Hassan a dressing down' for his agitation against Eastwood and the Gibraltar government generally.

This was not so. Salvador met Hall as Chairman of the City Council just after he had led a demonstration protesting about the slowness of repatriation. Hall may have been annoyed to be told by Salvador not to be surprised that he was fighting for what he believed to be right. Nevertheless, the Secretary of State treated him with the utmost courtesy, and they met on equally friendly terms on later occasions during the visit. Salvador had demonstrated his ability to placate the British government when it was advisable to do so. If Hall had, indeed, upbraided Salvador as Stanley suggested, it was water off a duck's back as far as he was concerned. Before Hall returned to London, Salvador addressed an AACR public meeting in John Mackintosh Square, attended by some 5,000 people, and led a protest march through Irish Town to the Convent. All shops closed and the crowds lining the streets applauded as a document containing the meeting's resolutions was handed in for submission to the Secretary of State. The AACR unanimously rejected the Colonial Office replies to their memorial as unsatisfactory and unacceptable, and again demanded the acceleration of repatriation.

Just before the Hall visit, Salvador had been involved in an unfortunate clash with Eastwood over appointments of Justices of the Peace. Without consulting Salvador, since he had no statutory reason to do so, Eastwood appointed Antonio Baldorino, the City Council's Vice-Chairman, as one of a batch of the new JPs. Salvador took Baldorino's acceptance of the appointment without reference to the AACR committee as a gross breach of AACR rules, and as an affront to himself as the City Council's Chairman. Eastwood explained in a letter, now held on the Public Record Office files, that it was a matter of policy not to appoint busy barristers to sit on the magistrate's bench, but to use suitable public-spirited laymen. If Salvador replied, his letter is not on the file, but Stanley recorded that Baldorino was expelled from the AACR – still nominally a workers' party – for accepting the JP appointment. Stanley added, 'due to the personal pique of Hassan'.

Stanley could not know the full story. Baldorino had been a member of the TGWU and very active in helping the republican refugees, who came into Gibraltar during the Spanish Civil War. He had quarrelled with the TGWU and joined the AACR, who gladly accepted him for his experience as a pre-war City Councillor, and nominated him as an AACR City Council candidate for the 1945 election. He won his seat and was elected Vice-Chairman when Salvador was voted in as Chairman. Salvador got on reasonably well with him, but never entirely trusted his party political allegiance. It is hardly surprising, however, that the AACR committee demanded Baldorino's resignation from the party for flagrantly ignoring its rules, which stated clearly that he should have consulted the Committee first before accepting. Salvador's supposed pique was more in Stanley's mind than in reality, although it must be confessed that Salvador could be rather petty at times. He was eventually appointed a JP himself during General Anderson's governorship on 29th January 1949.

In the meantime, the repatriation battle went steadily on, waged largely between Salvador, Bruzon and Stanley. It rose to a crescendo in October when a new Secretary of State, Mr Creech-Jones, replying to a question in the House of Commons, stated that 2,100 evacuees were still in the Ulster camps and it was unlikely that they would all be home in under another two years. A general meeting of the AACR, organized by Salvador, was held on 12th November during which three resolutions, drafted by him, were carried unanimously: the two-year wait for repatriation to be completed was totally unacceptable; if the military authorities would co-operate in release of buildings, enough accommodation could be improvised for the last 2,000 evacuees;

> and . . . the evacuees are not repatriated immediately . . . only course open to Gibraltarians both here and in Northern Ireland

is to act in such a manner as to bring home to the government
once and for all the dreadful plight to which our evacuees have
been put purely for war reasons, but for which there is no
justification in lasting one more day. (Finlayson, *The Fortress Came
First*, p 184)

Salvador had right on his side. As Chairman of the City Council
he was well aware that empty or under-used accommodation did
exist if only Eastwood would seek powers from the Secretary of
State to requisition property and impose compulsory billeting on
those who were occupying houses too big for them. However, the
will to co-operate on the government side by using such draconian
measures was just not there: overstrained medical facilities
provided too ready an excuse for not taking extraordinary
measures to bring the last 2,100 evacuees back in anything more
than an intermittent trickle. The AACR threat of action to bring
home to the government the dire consequences of indecisive
action was never carried out. It was announced that Eastwood
would be leaving in February 1947, and he would be replaced by
Lieutenant-General Sir Kenneth Anderson, the former
commander of the 1st Army in Tunisia, who had seen a lot of the
Rock during the Allied landings in French North Africa and the
subsequent fighting for Tunis in 1943. An article by Rex North in
the *Sunday Pictorial* provided an apt epitaph for Eastwood:

Lieutenant-General Mason-MacFarlane . . . was a good soldier and
popular chief. His successor, Lieutenant-General Sir Ralph
Eastwood, who has just gone home, was probably a good soldier,
but certainly a bad Governor. Mason-MacFarlane got rousing
cheers from the local population when he left: the only people
who saw General Eastwood off were the Services, who had to.
(Finlayson, *The Fortress came First*, p 188)

Two small clouds, in biblical terms, 'no bigger than a man's
hand', had appeared on the Gibraltar's horizon during 1946. The
British Ambassador was withdrawn from Madrid in compliance
with the United Nations' resolution, calling for the political
isolation of Franco's fascist government of Spain; and the Colonial
Office unthinkingly included Gibraltar on the list of British

dependent territories, which it presented to the United Nations' Fourth Committee at the start of its deliberations on decolonization. Gibraltar should never have been included on the list because under the Treaty of Utrecht the Rock would be recolonized by Spain if Britain decolonized its people and gave up sovereignty. Franco was to exploit both events to Gibraltar's disadvantage in the coming years, and was to find Salvador a subtle and unflinching opponent.

CHAPTER 4

PRESIDENT OF THE AACR

The Return of the Last Evacuees
and the Birth of the Legislative Council
1947-1952

Elected members of the First Legislative Council (1950-53).

A R Isola (Indep)	2,022 votes
F Panayotti (AACR)	1,158
A J Risso (AACR)	1,112
J A Hassan (AACR)	1,009
J Patron (Indep)	567

On 20th March 1947, Gibraltar, rather than suffering a Shakespearian 'sea change', enjoyed one. On that day Lieutenant-General Sir Kenneth Anderson, accompanied by Lady Anderson, stepped ashore from the liner *Ascania* to take up his duties as Governor. The ship was also carrying just over a hundred evacuees home to Gibraltar from the Northern Ireland camps. During the voyage out in the *Ascania*, Sir Kenneth and Lady Anderson demonstrated the shape of things to come by visiting and talking with his Scottish frankness and sympathy to all the evacuees on board. It was clear from the very start of his tenure that the new Governor was assimilating Gibraltarian views and identifying himself with their problems.

As a broad generalization it can be said that governors come in one of two categories. They tend either to take Whitehall's side too slavishly from the Gibraltarian point of view, or to identify themselves with the Gibraltarians too closely for Whitehall's comfort. Eastwood had been an exception: he managed to alienate both Whitehall and the Gibraltarians! Anderson, like Mason-MacFarlane, belonged to the second category. He took the view that, as there were enough officials in the Whitehall ministries to speak for the British government, the governor's most important task was to present and argue Gibraltar's case with the Whitehall mandarins. Almost coincidentally with Anderson's arrival, Salvador's political position was strengthened by the events within the AACR, which led to his assuming its leadership *de jure* as well as *de facto*. Albert Risso had been heading an AACR subcommittee on workers' rights and had reached agreement on setting up a Gibraltar Confederation of Labour. When the Confederation was inaugurated on 1st July 1947, Risso became its first President, and Salvador succeeded him as President of the AACR. The AACR was now his party, and the only genuine political party in Gibraltar. As Chairman of the City Council and now leader of the AACR in his own right, he was in an immensely powerful position to influence government policy, but he was not, as yet, on the Governor's Executive Council. Nevertheless, he was not a man who could be ignored by Anderson nor by B T O'Brien, the Colonial Secretary. O'Brien had been Assistant Colonial Secretary in Cyprus and was married to a Cypriot. He was a middle of the roader, orthodox in his views, and a man who would try to avoid unnecessary confrontations. Salvador, who was to have a lot to do with him during the long negotiations over the Legislative Council, got on with him well, describing him as 'a learned type, serious, efficient and *simpatico*'. Salvador soon realized that the new Governor was a co-operative ally and not an enemy to outmanoeuvre. The principal political issues had not changed – speeding up the repatriation of the last 2,000 evacuees and setting up the promised Legislative Council – but there was a new willingness in the Convent to try to resolve them. The solution to the evacuee problem was new temporary and permanent housing. Although the redeployment of troops out of the City and the building programme itself were still the responsibility of the central government and not the City Council, a Planning Commission, comprising representatives of the military and civil authorities, was set up with Salvador as its Chairman, a post that he was to fill until 1969. A professional town planner was brought out from England to advise the Commission and to head its technical staff.

As Chairman of the City Council, Salvador was well aware that providing extra accommodation on the Rock was becoming increasingly difficult, however willing Anderson and O'Brien might be. By July 1947, repatriation had been reduced to a trickle by lack of accommodation on the Rock, and it was becoming clearer every day that passed that the Northern Ireland camps would not be cleared by the end of the year. The remaining evacuees would have to spend a third winter in Ulster unless something drastic was done about it. Building temporary hutted accommodation on the limited sites made available by the services, and modifying existing buildings to take more people, was being slowed by worldwide shortages of materials and fittings. Building permanent housing, although begun straight away, was even slower and would not help with the immediate repatriation problem nor with the existing overcrowding for some time. Both temporary and permanent building cost money, but this was not allowed to hamper progress. Some came from the Colonial Development Fund, but the lion's share was raised by the Gibraltar government.

It was clear to Salvador and the AACR committee that the drastic solution to ending the discomfort of the Northern Ireland camps, which they were seeking to do, was to persuade the Colonial Office to move the remaining evacuees back to London where life would be easier for them and the chances of gaining employment higher because of the post-war labour shortage in Britain. Quite fortuitously a new head of the Colonial Office Welfare Department, J L Keith, decided to make a thorough inspection of the camps to see for himself what all the fuss was about. His report was damning. It concluded that the camps were totally unsuitable for housing a colonial population and I am satisfied that they ought to be closed down at the earliest opportunity. I do not think that any local authority or government Department would be permitted to house people in similar conditions in this country and the continued retention of these camps exposes the Colonial Office to criticism to which there can be no reply . . . The provision of accommodation in England, and preferably London, must be pressed with vigour . . . (Finlayson, *The Fortress Came First,* p 195)

Keith's report was confirmed by the Executive Officer of the Resettlement Board in Gibraltar, D Lucas, who had also been sent to Northern Ireland to see whether the AACR complaints were exaggerated or not. With these two reports in his hands, the Governor cabled Whitehall:

Am frankly appalled at conditions in Camps as revealed in report by Head of Welfare Department . . . and fully confirmed by personal observations of my Resettlement Officer, and I trust that no efforts will be spared to secure transfer of maximum possible number [to England] before advent of winter. (Finlayson, *The Fortress Came First,* p 196)

The Colonial Office officials did act, and thought that they had obtained two suitable accommodation blocks in London – the Fulham Road Hostel and the Sussex Square Club near Hyde Park – which could take a thousand evacuees between them. The evacuees should be able to start leaving Ulster in November on a priority system. In anticipation of taking over these two buildings, the Colonial Office allowed Gibraltarian tradesmen from Ulster to start work on partitioning rooms to give families greater privacy and to increase the numbers of bed spaces. All seemed to be going well by mid-October.

Unfortunately, the Colonial Office was not the only ministry involved, or looking for accommodation for people in London. The Home and Foreign Offices were trying to find space for Poles, Jews and other displaced people from Europe, to whom Britain had offered temporary sanctuary. The Ministry of Works was involved in sharing out scarce building resources and the Treasury, as ever, was fussing over expenditure. An inter-ministerial battle started in Whitehall; no firm decisions could be taken; and the move from Ulster was delayed into December when Attlee's Cabinet discussed the matter. The Secretary of State for Colonies, Creech-Jones, lost the battle to keep Fulham Road and Sussex Square for the Gibraltarian evacuees. He was unable to stand up to powerful political personalities like Aneurin Bevan and Herbert Morrison, who foresaw a loss of votes in Fulham if a large number of Gibraltarians suddenly arrived in that marginal constituency. The Governor was instructed to make a further effort to find more accommodation on the Rock with the help of the services, who were told to be more co-operative.

As with Sir Clive Liddell's misjudged decision in refusing to allow the evacuees to disembark when they returned from Morocco in 1940, this Cabinet decision was equally flawed and eventually overturned by Salvador and his AACR committee's determined political pressure. The Governor made an immediate protest to London on 8th December, cabling the Colonial Office:

> Am appalled at unexpected opposition to move of evacuees to London. These unfortunate people are indeed being ill used and I must vehemently protest against attempt of Minister to cancel plans both personally and on behalf of government and people of Gibraltar. (Finlayson, *The Fortress Came First.* pp 201-202)

Three days later a delegation set off from Ulster with the AACR and Anderson's full support to demand an audience with the Secretary of State for Colonies, the ineffectual Creech-Jones. He ducked seeing them on the grounds that he was too busy with the crisis in Palestine. They were seen instead by his Under-Secretary of State on 12th December. By then a public announcement had been made by the Colonial Office, cancelling the transfer of the evacuees to London. All the delegation achieved was a tongue-in-cheek assurance that repatriation was to be accelerated by the services releasing more accommodation in Gibraltar.

There was fury in Ulster and Gibraltar at this rebuff. The AACR decided to organize a sit-in at the Fulham Road Hostel by the men already there getting the building ready for the arrival of the evacuees, and by reinforcements, who travelled over from Ulster at their own expense. In Gibraltar, a deputation, consisting of Salvador, Alberto Risso and Jack Ellicott, went to the Convent on 15th December to warn the Governor that they were repeating the threat, which they had made to Eastwood the year before, but had not used, of taking steps to impress the British government with the deep resentment felt by all classes in Gibraltar at this breach of faith.

Three days later all shops closed and a large crowd assembled in John Mackintosh Square during which Salvador put two resolutions to the meeting, which were passed unanimously. The first protested about the broken promises to transfer the evacuees 'from the inhuman camps in Northern Ireland' to England before winter; and the second supported the action already taken by the Governor on behalf of the evacuees, and urged him to take further drastic action to procure more military accommodation for them in Gibraltar. The demonstrators then marched, as usual, on the Convent, but this time there was a difference. When the Governor appeared on the balcony, he was greeted with loud applause! It was made quite clear that it was the British and not the Gibraltar government which was the target of the protest. (Finlayson *The Fortress Came First*, pp 203-205.)

Meanwhile, in Fulham Road, more and more reinforcements had arrived from Ulster. Creech-Jones came under pressure in the Commons from MPs supporting the Gibraltarian case and he wilted. Answering a loaded question from Sir Walter Smiles, Unionist MP for County Down, he announced that his officers were seeking accommodation for the evacuees outside London. And on 27th December, the Cabinet decision not to transfer the evacuees to England was quietly set aside, and Mr Keith was able to tell the 'squatters' in the Fulham Road Hostel that the Colonial Office was taking over the building for the evacuees. They had won thanks to Salvador's leadership, Gibraltarian stubbornness at Fulham Road, and Kenneth Anderson's support for the

Gibraltarian cause. Fulham has never lost its connection with Gibraltar. Many Gibraltarians, who decided not to return to the Rock, settled there, but have never lost their loyalty to Gibraltar. Their community spirit was reflected in the formation of the Gibraltar Group, led by Michael Mifsud and Albert Poggio, who organized fund-raising activities to provide charter flights to and from Gibraltar at affordable prices to keep families in touch with each other. It was not uncommon to see passengers boarding the Gibraltar Group charter flights carrying Gibraltarian delicacies such as calentita – a chick-pea flour flan – which is the Rock's national dish and incidentally one of Salvador's favourite breakfast dishes.

Indeed, Fulham became 'Little Gibraltar in England' with the 'Golden Eagle' Hotel near Fulham Broadway tube station as the community's principal meeting point. During the 1960s and 70s, they used to mount anti-Spanish demonstrations in support of Gibraltar when Franco's campaign to recover the Rock was at its height; Ivor Richards, Fulham's MP, became an active member of the Gibraltar Group in Parliament; Gibraltar's future politicians, Bob Peliza and Freddie Gache, who had business interests in London, were energetic supporters of the Gibraltar Group; and Joe Bossano, the future Chief Minister, formulated his 'Integration with Britain' policy while in Fulham. One of the 'Fulham Boys', who won most Gibraltarian acclaim, was Tony Macedo, Fulham Football Club's long-serving professional goalkeeper.

Back in Gibraltar, the services did do their best to release more accommodation, which included the temporary loan of the Naval Air Station at North Front. The Ulster camps were closed down on 21st July 1948, and the last of the evacuees wishing to return should have left Fulham Road by April 1951. Unfortunately, the explosion of the naval munitions ship *Bedenham*, which blew up in harbour while unloading on 27th April, did so much damage to housing that there was no option but to delay the completion of the repatriation until 24th August 1951. Some 2,000 of the original evacuees did not return: most of them had decided to settle in the United Kingdom for good. In Gibraltar, a shoehorn had been used to squeeze in all those who did want to return. In consequence, overcrowded housing became as acute as in pre-war days. Despite all the successful efforts that Salvador was to make during his years in office to win extra grants for new construction from the British government, the housing shortage was not to be solved satisfactorily until 1994, long after he had retired from politics.

Two events at the end of 1947 should be recorded. Women were at long last given the vote; and the AACR was returned unopposed in the City Council election on 5th December. Dorothy Ellicott, wife of Jack Ellicott, was the first woman to be elected to the City Council. She replaced her husband as one of the AACR members in the uncontested 1947 election when he retired from politics and she was elected to the Legislative Council in 1959.

No sooner had the repatriation battle with Whitehall been won at the end of 1947 than the New Year brought a new and unwelcome constitutional crisis, which looked to Gibraltarians like another breach of faith on the part of the British government. In the previous chapter, we recorded how the Colonial Office pre-empted the AACR's delegation to London in November 1945 by announcing the intention to set up a Legislative Council when the majority of the evacuees had returned to the Rock. It was to have five elected, three ex-officio and two nominated members. The proposal had lain in officials' pending-trays in Whitehall and Gibraltar throughout 1946 and most of 1947. Towards the end of that year, a Cabinet committee was asked to supervise the drawing up of the appropriate constitutional instruments to bring the Legislative Council into being.

In January 1948, some members of the committee, who knew a lot about constitutions but little about the fortress of Gibraltar and its people, began to question the need for three tiers of government in a city of 30,000 souls, including the military.

The critics had a point: was there any real need for a new tier between the City and Governor's Executive Councils? Why not widen the powers and increase the number of elected members of the City Council to take over many of the services like Medical, Education, Public Works, Housing and Town Planning, which were municipal in character, but because of military requirements were still the responsibility of the central and not the municipal authority?

In Gibraltar, the seemingly all-powerful service commanders did not welcome any extension of the City Council's remit. Despite the acknowledged success of Salvador's handling of the affairs of the City Council, they still did not consider the local politicians experienced enough to be given responsibility for areas of government that impacted on the defence of the fortress. The AACR were also opposed because Salvador's aim was to acquire a locally elected voice in the central government. He knew that military opposition was too strong, at that time, to allow the suggested widening of the City Council into what might become a national assembly where government policy could be properly debated; and, as long as the Governor was Chief Executive, his Executive Council was not the place for party political debate on major issues. A Legislative Council between the two, however, would provide the forum in which the Gibraltarian voice could be heard more clearly. The arguments between Whitehall and Gibraltar went on all summer, and were eventually resolved by Lord Listowel, Minister of State in the Colonial Office, flying out for face to face discussions in Gibraltar. Salvador and the AACR committee persuaded Listowel, a convinced socialist, that the creation of a Legislative Council was the only practicable way of increasing Gibraltarian voice in their own government. With Gibraltar's strategic importance growing every day as the Cold War verged on turning hot, it was no use trying to persuade the military to give way to the extent that the Cabinet committee had proposed. Nevertheless, experience with a legislative council might provide pointers to an amalgamation with the City Council in due course.

Salvador, however, failed in one respect. Listowel sided with the Governor and service commanders in refusing to allow an elected majority in the Legislative Council, which was to have, as originally proposed, five elected, three ex-officio and two nominated members with the Governor presiding and holding the casting vote.

Cabinet approval in principle was given in November 1948 and was made public the following January. Salvador's success in winning the Legislative Council was capped when Kenneth Anderson appointed him a Justice of the Peace on 29th January 1949 – an honour he had always coveted.

1949 was a year of consultations with the Convent, and between the Convent and Colonial Office, converting the Cabinet's agreement in principle into practical arrangements, including the mechanism by which voting was to be carried out by proportional representation. Salvador, as leader of the AACR, played a major role in these negotiations, which went on throughout the year and were without undue acrimony. He was statesmanlike enough not to continue pressing for an elected majority. His understanding of the British mentality warned him not to do so. The Cabinet had given its decision with some reluctance: to reopen the question would risk losing the Legislative Council altogether because there was still a feeling in Whitehall that Gibraltar was too small for three tiers of government, and military requirements must not be placed at risk. He must be content with half a loaf until working experience and events gave him the opportunity to seek further constitutional advance.

The establishment of the Legislative Council was authorized by the King's Order-in-Council on 3rd February 1950. The electoral rolls were then prepared, and the election was held on 8th November. The Duke of Edinburgh opened the first Legislative Council on 23rd November in the old Exchange and Commercial Library building in John Mackintosh Square, which was to become the House of Assembly in 1969. The result of the election was a personal disappointment to Salvador, who had misunderstood the proportional representation system of voting. After all his hard work arguing the case for an elected legislature, he came fourth in the poll and was behind Albert Isola (independent), F Panayotti (AACR) and Alberto Risso (AACR) – the votes are shown at the head of this chapter. This was because, thinking that his own vote was secure, he encouraged some of his supporters to vote for the weaker AACR candidates – he nearly overdid it! However, as the leader of the AACR, which had won three out of the five elected seats, he was accepted as leader of the elected members. There was, as yet, no government and opposition as such; just elected and official/nominated members.

Further disappointment was to follow. He topped the poll at the third City Council election in December that year, but the AACR lost two elected seats to independents: Peter Russo, the former District Commissioner, and Charles Povedano of the tobacco trade. The new City Council was composed of five AACR, two independents and six official members, leaving the AACR without a secure working majority. Salvador soon became aware that a conspiracy to deprive him of the chairmanship was being hatched by which Russo and Povedano would vote against further AACR dominance by joining the six official members when it came to electing the new chairman. Rather than be formally voted out of the chair, Salvador chose to resign on the day before the first meeting of the new Council. The coup succeeded and Peter Russo was elected Chairman instead of Salvador. Peter Russo, who tended to be the wild card in local politics, held the chairmanship for three years until the next election in 1953. His relationship with Salvador, which had never been very warm, at first turned icy, but then Russo began to find the work of the Council too exacting and gradually lost interest. He left Salvador to carry on essential business in committee, much to Salvador's delight because he could never bear to be left on the sidelines at any time and had to be at the centre of affairs. An effective working relationship grew up between the two men, and by the 1953 election they had become close friends. Salvador topped the poll again and, although Russo was also re-elected, no one tried to deny Salvador the chair of the third City Council. Russo was to cement their new found friendship by enabling Salvador to form a government after the 1964 Legislative Council election as we will see in the next chapter.

The question arises as to why Salvador had this apparent dip in popularity in the early 1950s. There was, of course, the natural determination on the part of his political rivals to cut him down to size before he could become too powerful. While he had the complete support of the working class, he was still viewed with suspicion by the middle classes and with hostility by the Establishment. Both were seeking to undermine the AACR and to stifle party politics as such on the Rock. In a small place like Gibraltar with its close family groupings, and where everyone knows everyone else's business – rumours and innuendos fly fast, inflaming prejudice, and can make or mar reputations more quickly and easily than elsewhere. Salvador, a Jew giving leadership to a predominantly Catholic community, had always had to contend with hidden prejudice until he became Gibraltar's accepted political leader in the 1960s. In 1950, the election results made him realize how far he still had to go to win that acceptance. He did not despair: he revised the AACR voting tactics and redoubled his efforts to achieve unchallengeable political leadership by drawing more of the middle classes into the AACR and making it an all-embracing national party. In this he was already having some success: able men who were to write their own names in Gibraltar's history, like Abraham Serfaty, Bob Peliza and Sol Seruya, were already members of the AACR, and most of the civil service were among its supporters although not, of course, as members.

The opening of the Legislative Council in November by the Duke of Edinburgh was to bring about fundamental changes in Gibraltarian political attitudes. Not only did people feel that they were, at last, on the road to Salvador's aim of internal self-government, but their internal political divisions began to change. The latter was not due to events in Gibraltar, but to the growing hostility of the Franco government in Madrid to the constitutional advances being made by the Gibraltarians. Franco saw that the Spanish claim to Gibraltar could be nullified – despite the provisions of Article X of the Treaty of Utrecht – if Britain, with the support of the United Nations, were to grant independence to the Rock's people, whom he considered were a riff-raff of fortress camp-followers of Spanish origins. He decided that he must pre-empt the process of creating a Gibraltarian state before it was too late. The Duke of Edinburgh's visit triggered a noisy renewal of the Spanish claim to the Rock. As had happened so often in the past, Spanish students were encouraged to attack the British Embassy in Madrid and consulates in other major Spanish cities, demanding the immediate return of the Rock to Spain. They needed little encouragement: their attacks got out of hand and they did extensive damage to British property and Anglo-Spanish relations. Moreover, on this occasion, the tone of the Spanish press suggested a more serious and longer term attempt, probably just short of military action, was to be made to 're-establish the territorial integrity of the Spanish realm'.

Until this sabre-rattling by Franco began, the internal political division in Gibraltar had been between Hassan's radical left and the commercially orientated interests of the right. As the Spanish threat gradually increased so the original division between left and right became blurred, and in its place came degrees of anti- and pro-Spanish political platforms. Instead of the relatively clear-cut left–right division in local politics, the differences became more of a spectrum of views on the Spanish issue with rabid anti-Spanishness, and hence pro-Britishness, at one end, and extreme advocates of appeasement of Spain at the other. Most of those at the pro-Spanish end of the spectrum had no wish to see the end of British sovereignty, but believed that co-operation with Spain was vital for the Rock's future prosperity.

During the life of the first Legislative Council, the left–right polarization in Gibraltar politics continued with the Spanish problem lying ominously in the background. As far as the elected members of the Council were concerned, foreign affairs, which included relations with Spain, were the responsibility of the Foreign Office. The Legislative Council was more concerned with the vexed question of taxation. With large numbers of evacuees still living in temporary Nissen huts, which were crumbling fast into piles of rusting corrugated-iron sheeting, and with gross overcrowding throughout the city, money had to be raised for new permanent housing. The Colonial Office insisted that the Gibraltar government should contribute one pound for every pound of grant aid given for construction of new housing. How should the money be raised? Only two sources of revenue were available: import duties and rates. There had been a highly unpopular and hence short-lived Trades Tax on business profits, but there was no income tax in Gibraltar – a tax generally accepted worldwide as the fairest of all and adopted by most European and Commonwealth countries. One of the first controversial measures presented to the new Legislative Council, and the last during Kenneth Anderson's time as Governor, was a draft income tax bill. The Council divided on left–right lines with the AACR supporting the introduction of the tax and non-AACR elected and nominated members opposed. The three officials member remained neutral in the debate which followed. The bill was then safely remitted to them for further detailed work on its contents, thus avoiding immediate political controversy in the last months of Anderson's tenure.

Anderson was given a great and heart-felt send-off by the people of Gibraltar when he said farewell to the Rock. The dour Scot, who had been called 'a good plain cook' by Montgomery during the Tunisian campaign, had turned out to be one of the best-loved governors in Gibraltar's long history, matching the achievements of Sir Humphrey Bland (1749-54) and Sir George Don (1814-31). He had fought grim battles with Whitehall on Gibraltar's behalf; he had brought the evacuees home and started the long process of rehousing them; and he had set up the first Legislative Council, giving the Gibraltarians some say in their central government as well as in City Council affairs. He and Lady Anderson so loved the Rock that they eventually came back to live the rest of their lives in Gibraltar. She worked tirelessly for Gibraltar charities and was appointed an MBE for her work. He died in 1959 and is buried in North Front Cemetery. She lived on in Gibraltar until 1983. She died that year in St Bernard's Hospital at the age of 83 and was buried alongside her husband.

Salvador found Anderson and O'Brien, the Colonial Secretary, co-operative and easy to work with. Salvador deserves the credit for creating the local political pressures that enabled Anderson to win his Whitehall battles; and it was his prescient arguments and persuasive powers that influenced Lord Listowel into agreeing to establish the Legislative Council, from which he was to be able to force further constitutional advances from the British government in the years to come. Those advances were to exacerbate the Spanish problem, but not just yet.

CHAPTER 5

Winning an Elected Majority on the Legislative Council and the Queen's Visit
1953-1961

Elected Members of the Legislative Council

1953-1956

J A Hassan (AACR)	3,435	
S A Seruya (Indep)	1,482	
A R Isola (Indep)	1,373	
S P Triay (Indep)	1,279	
J J Triay (Comwel)	1,263	
A J Risso (AACR)	130*	
A W Serfaty (AACR)	71*	
P J Isola (Indep)	671*	7th count
J E Alcantra (AACR)	136*	7th count

1959

J A Hassan (AACR)	3,420	1st count
S A Seruya (Indep)	1,815	1st count
P J Isola (Indep)	1,137	1st count
A Risso (AACR)	76*	2nd count
A W Serfaty (AACR)	39*	5th count
A J Baldorino Jr (TGWU)	920*	8th count
D Ellicott (Indep)	505*	9th count

* elected on subsequent counts

The 1950s were a transitional period in Gibraltar's history, during which the problems of post-war resettlement and regeneration of the economy tapered off, and constitutional advance and growing Spanish hostility became the main political issues. The last two were closely linked because fear of an emergent Gibraltarian state stoked Franco's determination to deter any further British delegation of power to the elected representatives of the Rock's local people. It was also the period during which Salvador became the Gibraltarians' undoubted political leader.

In May 1952, Lieutenant-General Sir Gordon Macmillan arrived as the Rock's new Governor. A Scot, like Anderson, he was perhaps less forceful but no less determined to fight Gibraltar's corner. He was one of the British army's natural gentlemen, whose good sense and charm of manner made him a true representative of the Crown in Gibraltar. Tragically, his children suffered from a hereditary form of blindness. Salvador found him easy to work with, and he became the Governor's closest Gibraltarian adviser. He described Sir Gordon as a great man.

It was right that Salvador should become Macmillan's principal Gibraltarian adviser. He was already leader of the elected members of the Legislative Council, Chairman of the City Council and President of Gibraltar's only coherent political party, the AACR. In the government reshuffle at the beginning of Macmillan's tenure, he joined the two nominated members, Peter Russo and Henry Coelho, in the Executive Council, in the place of Alberto Risso. There were two elected members in the Council, the other one was Albert Isola. Apart from a short three-year period from 1969 to 1972 when he was forced into opposition, he was to retain his seat on the Executive Council and on its successor, the Gibraltar Council, for 35 years, until he retired in 1987. In all those years, he had unimpeded entrée to the Convent and the ear of successive governors, giving him a uniquely powerful position to influence policy and events.

In Macmillan's first two years domestic affairs were dominant: pressing forward the building programme, and accelerating the moves to concentrate the garrison towards the southern end of the Rock; increasing the water and electric power supplies by installing distillers and extra generators; taking measures to strengthen the economy; and passing the controversial Income Tax Bill through the Legislative Council in April 1953 without undue controversy.

Salvador has often been accused of lacking economic ideas and management skills. He would himself be the first to concede that he was not a trained economist, nor an experienced businessman, but no one can gainsay the fact that Gibraltar's development went ahead and prosperity was regained during his years as Chairman of the City Council thanks in part, it must be admitted, to the British financial support for which he did most of the arguing. His success stemmed from being an admirable chairman of committees, who believed in consensus politics and acceptance of the hard political axiom that you cannot please all the people all of the time. Consensus or no, someone had to lead, especially among his Gibraltarian colleagues, most of whom were highly individualistic with strong ideas of their own. Salvador would listen closely to the views of the technical experts and to the arguments of his political supporters and opponents, and then use his depth of intellect and legal training to articulate an agreed policy, which he would then drive through with a degree of ruthlessness that lost him several influential AACR supporters, who found it difficult to work with him. Like most successful political leaders, he was a good judge of character, who usually put round pegs in round holes. This was not always possible in his early days because the talent available to him was limited, and it was more a case of deploying what was available to him to best advantage. As time went by he drew together an able political team, loyal to him, from which few deserted or were dismissed as failures. It is, however, generally acknowledged that Salvador's greatest strength lay in his extraordinary ability to judge the mood of the electorate with almost uncanny accuracy. His acute political antenna usually warned him of trouble ahead and enabled him to take evasive or defensive action in time.

The loss of Sol Seruya from the AACR's ranks in 1954 was an

example of both Salvador's alienation of able supporters and the acuteness of his political instincts. Seruya was a skilled entrepreneur, who had read economics and modern history at St Andrew's University in Scotland, and had studied at Madrid and Salamanca universities. He was thus bicultural and, like Salvador, understood both English and Spanish psychology and modes of thought. He had joined the Labour Party while in Britain and had left-wing views almost indistinguishable from those of Salvador. On his return to Gibraltar, he had done well financially by supplying the US 6th Fleet. He had joined the AACR in 1953, and as an economist and businessman could have been a great asset to the party. It was not to be: within a year he had left and was campaigning as an independent in the 1956 Legislative Council election campaign. A young and vigorous orator with an attractive, enthusiastic style, he built up a substantial following with his arguments for greater economic planning and management. Surprisingly, he came second in the 1956 poll, just below Salvador, but with only about half the number of votes.

The immediate cause of Seruya's departure from the AACR was an article in Spanish, which he wrote in *El Calpense* under the pseudonym 'Wellington', setting out his political philosophy. This rested on three pillars: the maintenance of British sovereignty; the need to diversify Gibraltar's economy so that it was less reliant on British defence spending; and the vital need for regional economic co-operation with Spain. Read today, the article seems inoffensive enough as far as Gibraltar is concerned. It pillories Spain for her crass coercive treatment of Gibraltar, which was bound to be counter-productive, whereas good neighbourliness would create prosperity on both sides of the frontier. Salvador had seen the article prior to its publication and had made some small amendments to it.

Nevertheless, the AACR central committee took strong exception to Seruya's insistence on regional co-operation with Franco's Spain, which was against AACR policy. Seruya was asked to retract the article, but, being a strong minded individualist, he showed his unwillingness to accept party discipline by publishing an English translation in the *Gibraltar Chronicle*. This was too much for the AACR central committee, who started internal disciplinary proceedings against him. Salvador's antenna warned him that the workers in general, and Alberto Risso's unions in particular, would not stand for any suggestion of co-operation with Franco's Spain in any guise – economic or otherwise. Knowing that the consensus within the central committee was firmly against Seruya, he let his expulsion from the party go ahead – some claiming that he did so to eliminate a potential rival. It was perhaps as well that Seruya went: sadly the two men could never have worked closely together even though their abilities complemented each other's so nicely. Seruya did become a very successful and popular Minister of Ports and Tourism in the Legislative Council of 1959-64 as an independent, but his political judgment was never fine enough nor were his supporters well enough organized to unseat Salvador at the polls. He and Salvador were bound to become bitter political rivals. Other much earlier departures from the AACR had been Sergio Triay and Major Bob Peliza. Triay, whose ideas for Gibraltar's integration with Britain were at the opposite end of the political spectrum from Seruya's, left in 1954 to form his own Gibraltar Commonwealth Party (GCP) through which he hoped to advocate the advancement of Gibraltar towards dominion status. Sadly he died the following month, leaving his son, J J Triay, to lead the party. J J won a seat in the 1956 Legislative Council election, but the GCP did not attract sufficient support to survive – it was ahead of its time.

Major Bob Peliza was an integrationist like Sergio Triay, who had been allowed by the military authorities to enter politics at the end of the war despite being a serving officer in the Gibraltar Defence Force. He won a seat for the AACR in the first post-war City Council election, but soon found himself at odds with Salvador and his colleagues, and also realized that politics and military service were incompatible. He resigned over local issues, but came back into politics in the 1960s and was to lead his newly formed 'Integration with Britain Party' (IWBP) against the AACR in the 1969 elections. He later became Chief Minister for a period of just over two and a half years in alliance with the Isola group. The unfortunate dip in Salvador's vote at the first Legislative Council election in 1950 was more than fully restored in the subsequent election in 1953. By then, the AACR had a clearer understanding of the proportional representation system and gave their supporters better instructions on how to cast their votes. He won it with 3,435 votes, while his nearest rival, Albert Isola, trailed behind him in second place with only 1,373 votes. With this substantial increase in popular support, Salvador was able to lead the elected members with greater political confidence in pressing for further constitutional reform. He drafted one of his most far-sighted AACR documents, setting out the path that he intended to tread in his quest for full internal self-government. Almost all his proposals were fulfilled within the next decade and a half. As it provides a fine example of his lucid and unabrasive approach to the British government, and as it is important in its own right as a policy document, it is given in full in Appendix 1.

In his paper's preamble, Salvador said:

> The Legislative Council has been in existence for nearly five years and the time is now ripe to take stock and see what further progress can be made in the way of constitutional development that will lead to the people being given full powers and responsibilities in civil matters. It is appreciated that progress towards this justifiable aim should be gradual and methodical . . .

He envisaged the City and Legislative Councils being merged eventually to form an elected Gibraltar Assembly. In the meantime, the constitutions of both Councils should be modified in ways that recognized 'the proved capacity of the people to manage their own affairs'. In the existing City Council only seven out of 13 councillors represented the local population, who paid two-thirds of the rates. The number of elected members should, according to this rate-paying criteria, be double that of the nominated members. In the Legislative Council an elected majority should be granted either by dropping two nominated seats or increasing the elected seats by two. And the Executive

Council should be replaced by a balanced 'council of ministers', which should consist of the governor as president, with three ex-officio members to represent the official side of the government and four members from the Legislative Council on the elected side, one of whom would be appointed 'chief minister'.

In anticipation of the introduction of a full ministerial system, all elected members of the Legislative Council should become 'Ministers associated with . . .' a specific government department but not responsible for it. In effect, they would be apprentice ministers, appointed by the chief minister, who would himself be chosen by the governor from the elected members. And finally, as it would no longer be appropriate for the governor to preside over the Legislative Council with an elected majority, he should be replaced in the chair by an independent speaker, and carry on his executive functions as governor in the proposed 'council of ministers'.

Sir Gordon MacMillan's tenure expired before Salvador had presented his paper officially to the Governor, but he had discussed it at length with MacMillan and his Colonial Secretary, Darell Bates. Bates, who had come from a Colonial Office post in Somalia, was a convinced supporter of decolonization throughout the Empire. He and Salvador were 'on the same wavelength', and Bates's advice was invariably constructive and helpful. It was for this reason that most of Salvador's proposals were gradually accepted by the next Governor, Lieutenant-General Sir Harold Redman, who arrived in July 1955 and retained Bates as Colonial Secretary. It was during MacMillan's time that Salvador first came into contact with members of the Parliament in Westminster. In 1954, he led the first Gibraltar parliamentary delegation to London, and in the following January hosted the first United Kingdom parliamentary delegation to Gibraltar. This was the start of a very fruitful liaison, which lead to the development of the Gibraltar Parliamentary Group in Westminster. The Group was to serve Gibraltar well in the years to come.

General 'Dixie' Redman, as he was known in the army, was a rather colourless but hyper-efficient staff officer with a clear brain but no experience of anything comparable to Gibraltar politics in which compromise rather than confrontation is sought, although it often looks very much the reverse. He had served in Gibraltar earlier in his career as an up-and-coming but unpopular brevet major, and had been upset by not being invited to join the prestigious Royal Gibraltar Yacht Club. He made an unfortunate start as Governor, which helped indirectly to accelerate the official presentation of Salvador's constitutional reform proposals. Two months after he took over, the acting Financial Secretary, John Hayward, proposed a 10 per cent *ad valorem* import duty on specific luxury items such as cars, cameras, cine-projectors, wireless sets, watches, clocks and, surprisingly, razor blades, as an 'emergency measure' to ensure stability in Gibraltar's finances in the face of continuing Spanish economic harassment since the Queen's visit in 1954 described later in this chapter. Razor blades were on his list as enough were imported into Gibraltar to shave all the inhabitants of Andalusia with a large profit to the smuggling community.

It transpired in July that income collected from taxes was better than expected. Salvador and the elected members believed that there should, in fact, be a decrease rather than an increase in taxes, and that a decision should be deferred until the usual budget session in November. In any case, he believed that Hayward was setting about raising the money in the wrong way. He should be negotiating with the Colonial and Foreign Offices for a subvention as they were responsible for failing to stop the Spanish harassment. Gibraltar should not be expected to pay for a failure in British foreign policy.

Redman, however, supported Hayward and insisted on bringing in the new import duty straight away. The elected members raised an immediate cry that this was 'dictatorship not democracy'. Redman, as president of the Legislative Council, allowed an immediate debate on the specific issue, at the end of which the five elected members and one of the nominated members, Peter Russo, voted against the measure, defeating it by six votes to four. Even the Governor's casting vote could not save the acting

Financial Secretary's bill. Redman was totally inexperienced in handling Gibraltarian issues. Instead of adjourning the debate for further informal discussions behind the scenes to reach an acceptable compromise and thus avoid confrontation, he used the Governor's special reserve powers – as he had every right to do – to force the measure through the Council then and there. Led by Salvador, all the elected members walked out in protest. They were not prepared to be dictated to in matters of finance by the new Governor, who seemed to be acting like Sir Robert Gardiner, the detested, self-righteous, 19th-century incumbent, who had ruined 'trade' with Spain in his time.

Public protests gathered momentum, and on 2nd August all shops closed for an hour in the evening while a crowd of some 3,500 people assembled in John Mackintosh Square and followed Salvador and the other elected members to the Convent where they handed in a protest, demanding intervention by Whitehall to overturn the apparently unconstitutional use of the Governor's reserve powers. When this demand was rebuffed, Salvador and his elected colleagues resigned their seats in the Legislative Council on 30th September. Such was the political outcry in Gibraltar and dismay in Whitehall that the Secretary of State for the Colonies, Lennox-Boyd, flew out from London on 8th October to scold both sides and to review the changes needed to prevent a similar occurrence in the future. Salvador led his colleagues in presenting their case to him in no uncertain terms. They were not concerned so much with the tax as the Governor's use of his reserve powers to bulldoze through a relatively minor bill without even referring to Whitehall first. This was not the democracy that the AACR had been fighting for: it was a return to military dictatorship! Redman was convinced that he would be recalled. Lennox-Boyd supported him in public but laid down that in future the Governor's reserve powers were not to be used without reference first to the Secretary of State. He also insisted that in matters of finance the Standing Finance Committee of the Legislative Council must be consulted before proposals were finalized. As a sop to the merchants, who were the real instigators of this unhappy affair, he reduced the duty from ten to eight and a half per cent. Salvador and the other members, who had resigned their seats, were re-elected unopposed at the subsequent by-election. But the most important effect of his visit was to speed up the AACR paper on constitutional reform.

Salvador presented his reforms paper in October 1955. Redman persuaded Whitehall to authorize his first two proposals – the increase in the numbers of elected members in both the City and Legislative Councils almost straight away. The elective seats were increased from five to seven for the Legislative Council elections of September 1956, giving the Council its elected majority and meeting Salvador's medium-term objective of gaining real influence in the central government of the Colony. Redman generously recognised Salvador's hard, unrelenting but always constructive work on constitutional reform by recommending him for the CBE, which he received in the Queen's Birthday Honours List of 1957.

It took Redman rather longer to win agreement to the appointment of a speaker to preside over the Legislative Council instead of the governor. He won through in the last few months of his tenure in early 1958 so that the change could be made in the interregnum between governors. The worthy Major Patron (later Sir Joseph), who had so irritated the evacuees and the AACR when he was Commissioner for Evacuees in London during the War, was appointed the first Speaker on 27th June 1958. He was by then a much respected senior citizen and above local political infighting. It was to be another year before Salvador's proposal for a Council of Ministers was put into effect in a watered-down form, by the new Governor, General Sir Charles Keightley, after the 1959 election. Instead of being made ministers, each elected representative was titled 'Member associated with . . .' a specific government department; a 'Council of Members' was established; and Salvador became 'Chief Member', in effect heading a future local government, which was 'under training' to gain administrative experience.

Incidentally, Redman was very shoddily treated by the British government at the end of his tenure. The first that he knew of his relief was an article in *The Times*, saying that the former supreme commander of the ill-fated Suez operation was to be governor and C-in-C Gibraltar. It appeared that Redman was of no significance: all that mattered in Whitehall was finding a suitable post for Keightley. A simpler explanation of this discourtesy was a failure in communication between Whitehall ministries, but it was grossly unfair to Redman, who had become a highly respected Governor after surviving the reserve powers incident. His greatest achievements were winning agreement in Whitehall for carrying forward the constitutional advance three steps further along Salvador's envisaged road to internal self-government. Salvador again headed the poll in the 1959 election with 3,420 votes – almost double Sol Seruya's 1,815 votes, who came second again. New and younger faces had begun to appear among the candidates: Peter Isola and Dorothy Ellicott were successful as independents, but Aurelio Montegriffo (AACR), who was to become one of Salvador's most trusted ministers in due course, failed at his first attempt. R J Pilcher, the father of Joe Pilcher, the Minister for Tourism and the Environment in Joe Bossano's government in the 1990s, also failed.

Salvador's proposed transformation of the Executive Council into a Council of Ministers was set aside for the time being, and so was the introduction of the title of 'chief minister'. Nonetheless, Salvador could be justifiably proud of the speed of constitutional advance that he had engineered since 1950 when the first Legislative Council was opened by the Duke of Edinburgh. He was also gratified when the chairmanship of the City Council was brought into line with English practice and was raised to the status of mayor. Salvador became the first Mayor of Gibraltar with all the dignity appertaining to such a post. Sadly, his marriage was beginning to break up just when he most needed the support of a loyal and sympathetic consort. Daniela left him on two occasions for a time, and her frequent absences from important social functions became a topic of local gossip, which – as the polls showed – was doing him surprisingly little political damage because there was genuine public sympathy for him in his unhappy marriage to a psychiatrically disturbed wife. Nevertheless, Daniela created a weakness in his political armour, which his rivals would try to exploit when it came to his divorce in 1969.

I have departed from strict chronology in this chapter to separate Gibraltar's constitutional advances and internal affairs from the Queen's visit to the Rock in 1954 and its impact on Anglo-Spanish-Gibraltar relations. We will now look at both.

Throughout the early 1950s, Spanish hostility had been growing in step with each constitutional advance granted to the people of Gibraltar. Spain's international confidence and economic prosperity were also growing. Due to NATO's Cold War strategic need for greater depth in Europe and for US air bases in the Iberian peninsula, Spain's political isolation had been eased, and she had been allowed to join the Western community of nations, despite the continuing Franco dictatorship. Her new-found status was consolidated during 1953 by the successful completion of negotiations with the Americans for the use of Spanish air bases. However, she had not been admitted to the United Nations, and so she could not, as yet, use that forum to bring pressure to bear on Britain to return the Rock.

The death of King George VI and the coronation of Queen Elizabeth II in June 1953 gave Spain a pretext to reopen the Gibraltar question bilaterally. Gibraltar was included in the Queen's post-coronation tour of the Commonwealth, and as soon as the itinerary was announced, the Spanish Ambassador in London, the Duque de Primo de Rivera, protested to the Foreign Office, warning of the 'profound displeasure that this visit to the so-called "Crown Colony" for obvious reasons, would arouse in the Spanish people.' (*1st Spanish Red Book*, p 57) The Foreign Secretary, Anthony Eden, sharply rejected the Ambassador's *démarche*. To have done anything else would have suggested that Spain had a right to interfere in Gibraltar's affairs. The first Spanish Red Book on Gibraltar described the recent constitutional advances as pseudo-decolonization, and stated disingenuously:

> The British objective could not be clearer: to whitewash, before
> the United Nations Organization to which Spain did not then
> belong, the colonial façade she had built up around a military
> base, in order to continue thus, uncriticized, to assure her future
> domination of it.
> Spain had no other path open to her but to try to defend, alone
> and within the bounds of strict respect for international law, the
> rights that the Treaty of Utrecht had granted her. (*1st Spanish Red
> Book*, p 59)

The Spanish Ambassador was again rebuffed on 12th January
1954 when he made a final attempt to have the Queen's visit
cancelled. Spanish student riots were staged once more in Madrid
and other major cities, this time doing considerable damage to
British property, for which the Spanish government subsequently
apologized; and on 19th April, the Foreign Ministry in Madrid
started its preliminary moves in what was eventually to become
Gibraltar's 15th siege. The Spanish consulate in Gibraltar was
closed and three restrictions were imposed at the La Linea
frontier: Spaniards without work permits were no longer allowed
to cross into Gibraltar; no new work permits were issued; and the
Spanish customs post at the frontier was downgraded to what the
Spaniards termed a 'police and control' post. At the same time, a
torrent of abusive and tendentious reporting was let loose in the
Spanish press and radio programmes, demanding the return of
the Rock to Spain. The Spanish government justified these
restrictions on the grounds that the Treaty of Utrecht forbade
communication with Gibraltar by land. They were now intent on
showing that the authorization of such communication in the past
had been an act of grace on the part of the Spanish government,
which they had every right to rescind if they so wished. In fact, it
had been no such thing: the frontier had been opened during the
Napoleonic Wars, when the Spanish line of fortifications across
the isthmus had been blown up by British Sappers from the
Gibraltar garrison. Spain had never felt strong enough to close it
again for any length of time while Britain was the world's
superpower. In the light of Spain's new-found confidence and

Britain's relative decline, the Franco government decided to try twisting the British lion's tail.

The Queen's two-day visit with the Duke of Edinburgh and their two children, Prince Charles and Princess Anne, to the Rock, which started on 10th May 1954, was a resounding success and demonstrated the colony's heartfelt loyalty to the Crown. For weeks prior to the visit preparations had been going forward: decorating houses, shops and offices; erecting welcome arches across the streets; installing flood-lighting; and turning the Rock into a dazzling display of red, white and blue. When the big day came – one of the greatest days in Gibraltar's history – the streets were packed and heartfelt cheers and applause erupted spontaneously along every foot of the route taken by Her Majesty.

The only sour note came from across the frontier. There had been several parades in the nearby Campo de Gibraltar, and in major cities throughout Spain of blue-shirted falangist youths, screaming for the return of the Rock to Spain. However, during the actual visit, the military governor of the Campo forbade all demonstrations and disturbances and the Spanish government closed the frontier to prevent any untoward incidents for which they might be considered responsible. Security in Gibraltar was tight, but as one London newspaper commented, the fervid loyalty of the 27,000 inhabitants was the greatest guarantee of the Queen's safety.

Salvador, as Chairman of the City Council, was responsible for organizing and managing the ten events on the civic side of Her Majesty's programme, all of which exceeded expectations and did him great credit. For the first time in Gibraltar's history, an elected representative of the people – Salvador – was privileged to address the reigning sovereign. The highlight of the visit was the luncheon for 57 guests in the Assembly Rooms with Her Majesty seated between the Governor and Salvador. The Queen described the event 'as a landmark in your history', and Salvador in his reply said:

> We are justifiably proud that our beloved Rock should be the final stepping stone in your triumphal journey through the

Commonwealth and Empire. (*Gibraltar Chronicle*, 12th May 1954.)

He presented Her Majesty with a painting of the Rock by Gustavo Bacarisas, which hung in Buckingham Palace for many years in rather an obscure place until Salvador arranged for its return to Gibraltar as a piece of Gibraltar's history. It then hung for a time in the Convent, and is now on public display in the Gibraltar Museum.

The visit ended with a royal review of some 3,000 servicemen at North Front, which made a fitting finale to the Queen's tour of the Commonwealth and Empire. For his part in making arrangements for the visit to Gibraltar, Salvador was appointed a Member of the Royal Victorian Order (MVO, later renamed LVO – Lieutenant of the Order).

The Spanish frontier restrictions were not lifted after the visit, but were taken by most Gibraltarians as just another piece of petty Spanish spite, which they had had to put up with so often in the past, and which had never lasted for very long. Even though the Spanish government in far off Madrid was being awkward, the Spanish people were as friendly and as charming as ever. There seemed to be no need to worry unduly about Franco's rhetoric from El Pardo, or about the student demonstrations. The Gibraltarians had heard and seen it all before. The Queen's visit increased their confidence in Britain and the future.

The Gibraltarian assessment of the shallowness of this initial Spanish threat was borne out by events. While Franco made speeches, offering a 'lease-back' solution whereby the Rock would be returned to Spanish sovereignty and its military facilities would be leased back to Britain, officials of the two governments were working hard behind the scenes to improve Anglo-Spanish relations for the economic benefit of both countries.

It was not an easy task because Franco's utterances infuriated British ministers and the Gibraltarians even more so. In one speech he referred to them as 'natives' when he announced with misjudged magnanimity:

The return of that fragment of our nation to the mother country

will not only cause no loss to the natives, but will guarantee the
legitimate interests of the population, to whom it offers a
magnificent and better future. (*1st Spanish Red Book.* p 60)

Looking across the frontier into impoverished Andalusia, few
people in Gibraltar took him seriously. Franco's words, however,
illustrated the difference between the Spanish and British
approaches to the Gibraltar controversy. Franco's primary interest
was regaining lost territory and national dignity; the wishes of the
'natives' were of no real concern to him: to Britain, it was the
wishes of the people that mattered most as she set about
decolonizing her wideflung empire in accordance with United
Nations' resolutions.

Britain studiously ignored Franco's public bluster, and both
governments made strenuous efforts to understand the other's
point of view in private. By 1959 a new spirit of friendship had
been born and the Spanish Foreign Minister, Don Fernando
María Castiella, paid an informal five-day visit to London at the
end of August. Negotiations began for the mutual abolition of
tourist visas – a matter of great interest to Spain as her government
wanted to make it easier for British tourists to visit the country.
Britain insisted that an agreement could not be signed as long as
the Gibraltar frontier restrictions remained in force. Spain
countered with the claim that the Campo was a restricted military
area and so a special regime was needed at the La Linea crossing
point. In the end Spain agreed to modify the restrictions to allow
all British passport holders, including Gibraltarians, to cross the
frontier to and fro once a day, but maintained her restrictions on
her own nationals, excusing this by claiming that Spain's economy
could not stand them shopping freely in Gibraltar. In return for
this partial gesture of good will, Castiella was invited to make a
formal visit to London for talks with Selwyn Lloyd, the British
Foreign Secretary. The visit took place in July and did much to
restore Anglo-Spanish relations in general. With both countries
wishing to avoid any unnecessary friction, they skirted round the
Gibraltar issue. The same thing happened when Lord Home,
Selwyn Lloyd's successor, paid a return visit to Madrid in May 1961.

On both occasions, the British side asked for a return to the pre-1954 regime at the frontier, but did not press the issue unduly. The Spaniards, having made the excuses that the Campo was a military zone and that their economy would suffer if Spaniards were able to shop freely in Gibraltar, could hardly be expected to recant entirely. And so the modified restrictions stayed in force and were argued about at diplomatic level until the whole situation was changed by the United Nations Committee of 24 placing Gibraltar on its agenda for discussion in September 1963. Spain, at last, had a forum in which she had high hopes of winning international support for the return of the Rock to Spain through the process of decolonization. Throughout this period of argument with Spain over the 1954 frontier restrictions, Salvador and the other elected members had no responsibility for foreign affairs. The Foreign Office handled all communications with Spain through diplomatic channels, keeping the Governor informed and seeking his advice when necessary. The Governor, in his turn, kept his Executive Council informed and sought their advice too: or that was the theory.

General Sir Charles Keightley was not a man who had often sought advice from anyone in his life. Overwhelmingly ambitious and ruthless in pursuit of his military career, he had been a very young corps commander during the Italian campaign, and after the war had been C-in-C of three of the major British military commands: BAOR, the Far East and the Middle East where he had been the Supreme Anglo-French Commander for the ill-fated Suez operation in 1956. He was pompous and egocentric without much time for local Gibraltar politics, nor for local views. There was little advice that Salvador, as Chief Member, was asked to give or could contribute other than assessments of the effects of the frontier restrictions on Gibraltarian morale and economy. But all this was about to change as the Spaniards started to exploit their membership of the United Nations, and Keightley was replaced by a much more relaxed Governor, General Sir Dudley Ward, who took over in July 1962. The 1950s had seen Salvador pull steadily ahead of his political rivals in popular esteem, and rightly so. He had joined the Governor's Executive Council; he had handled the Gibraltarian side of the Queen's visit with sureness of touch; he had become the first mayor of Gibraltar; he had won the long-sought elected majority in the Legislative Council, and become its Chief Member; and he had topped the poll in three successive Legislative Council elections with increasing majorities. On the death of Albert Isola QC, he applied for and was granted silk on 15th December 1961, becoming one of the only two QCs in Gibraltar, the other being his cousin, Sam Benady. So far his career had centred upon internal Gibraltar politics. In the 1960s, he was to be hustled at short notice onto the world stage to fight for Gibraltar at the United Nations. From that moment onwards he became an international politician engrossed in Gibraltar's confrontation with Spain.

CHAPTER 6

THE UNITED NATIONS
AND THE LANSDOWNE CONSTITUTION
1962-1965

Members of the Legislative Council elected in September 1964

J A Hassan (AACR)	4,603	1st count
P J Isola (Indep)	1,822	1st count
S A Seruya (Indep)	916	1st count
P G Russo (Indep)	878	1st count
A Risso (AACR)	52	2nd count
L W Triay (Indep)	366	3rd count
A J Baldorino (Indep)	507	8th count
A V Stagnetto (Indep)	327	10th count
Mrs M Chiappe (AACR)	52	12th count
A P Montegriffo (AACR)	38	12th count
A W Serfaty (AACR)	35	12th count

The first half of the 1960s were momentous and challenging years for the Gibraltarians, who found themselves at the mercy of an unbalanced triangle of political forces. There was the United Nations' pressure for decolonization of all dependent territories administered by the old colonial powers, and two grossly divergent British and Spanish interpretations of the meaning of the word 'decolonization'. And in the background hovered the shadow of the Treaty of Utrecht, barring Gibraltar's road to the full independence intended by the founding fathers of the United Nations. In the last months of the Second World War, Britain had fully supported the principle of post-war decolonization. Spain had had no hand in drafting the United Nations Charter because she had been outlawed as a military dictatorship and close associate of the defeated Axis powers. In accepting the decolonization provisions of the Charter, Britain had laid down for herself certain rules which she intended to follow in the emancipation of her own dependent territories. No territory would be rushed prematurely towards independence to please the anti-colonialist Americans or Nehru's non-aligned Afro-Asian bloc. She would give her colonies their freedom when they were ready and able, in her view, to stand squarely on their own feet politically, economically and militarily. The speed with which each colony or protectorate would advance to self-government would vary enormously since it would depend on the abilities and wishes of its people.

Until 1960, when Harold Macmillan made his famous 'Winds of Change' speech in Cape Town, the speed of colonial emancipation was judged by the Colonial Office and the governors of the dependent territories. Macmillan's speech reflected Britain's acceptance of the fact that she could no longer afford to act as an imperial power. It heralded an acceleration of the planned conversion of her Empire into the Commonwealth, and the decision to let the local political leaders in each territory, instead of the Colonial Office, decide the speed at which it could reach a self-sufficient and secure independence without a British presence. Gibraltar was a special case in three respects: her primary *raison d'être* was as a fortress; her people were European and far more able to manage their own affairs than any of the other dependent territories, but had not been allowed to do so because of the military factor; and even if she had been granted internal self-government any earlier, she would have been prevented from getting independence by the Treaty of Utrecht, which required Britain to offer the Rock to Spain if she was ever to give up possession. When Gibraltar was placed on the agenda of the United Nations Committee of 24 due to Spanish pressure in 1963, the Foreign and Colonial Offices were confident that

Britain's enlightened decolonization policy was unimpeachable, but that it might be advisable to show clearly that the decolonization of Gibraltar was on course by setting in train further steps towards internal self-government, for which Salvador was already pressing. They were, however, misjudging Spain's ability to interpret the decolonization clauses of the United Nations Charter in an entirely different and obtusely adverse way; and they underestimated the international support that Spain would be able to muster for her interpretation.

In the United Nations' decolonization Resolution 1514 (XV) there are three relevant paragraphs. The British view was, and still is, that decolonization means giving the people of a dependent territory the freedom to rule themselves according to the wishes of the majority. This view is supported by Resolution 1514 (XV)'s paragraphs 2 and 5:

> 2. All people have the right to self-determination; by virtue of that right they freely determine their political status and freely pursue their economic, social and cultural development.
> 5. Immediate steps shall be taken, in Trust and Non-Self-Governing Territories which have not yet attained independence, to transfer all powers to the peoples of those territories, without any conditions or reservations, in accordance with their freely expressed will and desire, without distinction as to race, creed or colour, in order to enable them to enjoy complete independence and freedom.

Spain's contention was that Gibraltar was a piece of Spanish territory and not a people that had been colonized by the British, and that it should be decolonized by handing it back to Spain regardless of the wishes of the present inhabitants, who were nothing more than camp-followers of mixed race, working for the British base, and who had no right to acquire Spanish soil. Spain's view finds its support in a legalistic misinterpretation of paragraph 6:

> 6. Any attempt aimed at the partial or total disruption of the national unity and territorial integrity of a country is incompatible with the purposes and principles of the United Nations.

This paragraph was torn out of context by Spain. It was intended originally to protect the integrity of colonies and protectorates from predatory neighbours as they moved towards independence, and not to force the return of a territory, which had been the home of a people for over 250 years, to a former colonial power. It is worth noting that Spanish speeches and documents rarely mention paragraphs 2 and 5. They concentrate exclusively on paragraph 6 – the basis of their supposed case.

Thus the series of battles, which were to be fought in the United Nations during the 1960s, were over the relative importance of the wishes of a people as opposed to possession of the Rock on which they lived. Britain had every reason to expect that, in the latter half of the 20th century, people would come first in the minds of all fair-minded diplomats. Sadly, fair-mindedness was not an outstanding attribute of the United Nations' membership. As we shall see, Britain and Gibraltar were to be bitterly disappointed by the support Spain managed to acquire for her inhumane territorial claim. She could not only count on the votes of the Hispanic bloc, but also on those of most of the newly independent Afro-Asian states whose knee-jerk reaction was to oppose anything that favoured the old imperial powers: Britain, France and Holland. Spain was no longer classed as an imperial power because she lost her empire so long ago, largely due to British influence in the South American wars of independence!

General Sir Dudley Ward arrived to take over as Governor in June 1962. He was a straightforward honest-to-goodness soldier, who had risen from the ranks. He had been an employee of Cable and Wireless in Gibraltar in the 1920s before enlisting in the army. In the Second World War he had risen to command the 4th Division with distinction in Italy, and continued to rise, through the strength of his personality and military abilities, to be C-in-C of the Rhine Army and then C-in-C Middle East Command in the 1950s. He was happy to represent Her Majesty in Gibraltar and to support the Gibraltarian cause, but the nuances of constitutional reform, let alone the intricacies of the argument with Spain, were barely within his comprehension. He left all that to Salvador and

Darell Bates, who was still Colonial Secretary. Well before Spain engineered Gibraltar's inclusion in the United Nations' agenda in 1963, Whitehall became aware through diplomatic channels that Castiella was developing the Spanish case for confrontation with Britain over sovereignty of the Rock, using paragraph 6 of Resolution 1514 (XV) as the basis of his argument. To reinforce the British case, based on paragraphs 2 and 5, the Colonial Office was only too willing to speed up Gibraltar's advance to full internal self-government, thus meeting her decolonization responsibilities as far as the Treaty of Utrecht would allow. To go any further would be tantamount to abrogating sovereignty and enabling Spain to claim first refusal under the last clause of that treaty. Gibraltar, in effect, would merely become a Spanish instead of a British colony – hardly what the United Nations had intended.

In Gibraltar, the establishment of a Council of Members in 1959 – with Salvador as Chief Member and each elected member of the Legislative Council being associated with a government department – had served its purpose as a training expedient by 1962, when Sir Dudley Ward became Governor. Responsibilities were becoming more and more confused as some members began to flex their muscles in their departments, and as directors, who were mostly expatriate Colonial Service appointees, found themselves in invidious positions *vis-à-vis* their political apprentices, who wished to have more say in the policies of their departments. The dividing line between 'association with . . .' and 'responsibility for . . .' was too nebulous for practical purposes, and led to frustration and friction between strong-minded members, who sought political kudos by bending the rules, and equally forceful directors, who would not allow them to do so. Salvador and his Council of Members were finding themselves 'neither fish nor fowl'! They had political responsibility without executive power in central government, and the voters were expecting more of them than they were being allowed to deliver. The change of governor was an opportunity for reviewing the workings of the Council of Members. The review was put in hand during the autumn of 1962, and was led by Darell Bates on the official side as

Colonial Secretary, and by Salvador as Chief Member and leader of the AACR on the elected side. They concluded that the time had come to introduce a proper ministerial system with members responsible for departments, and the Council of Members becoming the Council of Ministers with Salvador as Chief Minister. They stopped short of recommending the amalgamation of the Legislative and City Councils, and the introduction of a Westminster-style House of Assembly with government and opposition, but the idea was already being discussed informally.

There were two good reasons for stopping short of a Westminster confrontational-style of government. Firstly, Gibraltar was deemed to be too small for such a complex system; and secondly, there were not enough able men who were prepared to enter Gibraltar politics to provide a proper spread of ministerial appointments. It seemed more appropriate for each elected member, of whatever political persuasion, to be made responsible for a department appropriate to his or her interests and abilities. A member would be representing the Gibraltarian point of view and requirements to the expatriate director of his department, and not a party view.

There were several reasons for the dearth of able Gibraltarians in local politics, even though most of the Rock's inhabitants enjoy setting Gibraltar to rights. Participation in government was a meanly paid, part-time activity. The development of party politics meant that most elected members had to be convinced politicians; imbued with a desire to lead and help their fellow Gibraltarians despite the financial consequences; and be possessed with a desire for power and influence. Making money had greater attractions for most Gibraltarians than winning public notoriety and opprobrium in politics. There was also the lack of middle and upper class confidence in being able to win enough support in the face of AACR opposition, which monopolized the working-class vote to an extent that would-be non-AACR candidates assessed their own chances of election as being too low to make the effort worthwhile. No political party has succeeded in Gibraltar unless it was seen as left of centre.

Negotiations with Whitehall went on for almost a year with the Colonial and Foreign Office mandarins ever conscious of the need, as they saw it, to demonstrate to the United Nations that the decolonization of Gibraltar was being pressed forward at a responsible pace, and that they were 'washing whiter than white' in meeting the decolonization requirements enshrined in the United Nations' resolutions. For this to be convincing, they appreciated that there might be advantage in having a recognized local political leader to speak for Gibraltar and to give the Gibraltarian point of view as to the Rock's future. Who better than Salvador? Two birds could be killed with one stone if Salvador were to be knighted: he deserved the accolade for his great services to Gibraltar over the past twenty years; and no one had done more to bring Gibraltar forward from direct military government of the pre-1945 days to the almost full internal self-government of the 1960s. Dudley Ward met little opposition in Whitehall when he recommended that Salvador should be knighted and recognized as the Gibraltarian's first locally born political leader. The announcement of Salvador's promotion to Knight Bachelor came in the 1963 Queen's Birthday Honours List, giving him increased status at home and abroad. He could represent, if need be, the Gibraltarian view in New York when the Committee of 24 opened its September session to examine the progress being made in the decolonization of Gibraltar, in which Spain, although not a member of the Committee of 24, had applied and had been granted permission to intervene. During the summer months of 1963 this examination was casting very few shadows before it in Whitehall. There were far larger and more pressing problems demanding attention. The repercussions of the 1962 Cuban missile crisis had not yet died away; Harold Macmillan's government was on its last legs; the confrontation with Indonesia had just begun in Borneo; Cyprus was again in turmoil; and there were the first signs of revolt in Aden. Preparations for Gibraltar's examination at the United Nations could not, and did not, receive the attention in Whitehall that it deserved. In any case, the officials concerned felt confident that

Britain had no case to answer: her decolonization record was exemplary. In the post-war anti-colonial environment, it seemed in Whitehall that the Spanish territorial claim was most unlikely to succeed against the wishes of the indigenous people – the Gibraltarians.

It was very late in the day when Whitehall woke up to the need to prepare full briefs for the British representative on the Committee of 24. Salvador had always listened avidly to Spanish political broadcasts and perhaps was the first to realize the dangers of Spain being allowed a hearing before the Committee, and for no Gibraltarian voice to be heard in rebuttal. At Salvador's prompting, Darell Bates agreed to press the Foreign Office to request the chairman of the Committee of 24 to allow Gibraltarian representatives to put their case as well. And so it came about that with only a few days left for the preparation of the Gibraltarian case that Salvador and Peter Isola set off for New York. The Committee had already started its meetings on Gibraltar on 11th September before they arrived.

There was some controversy about who should actually go to New York with Salvador to give a balanced Gibraltarian view. Sol Seruya had what appeared to be a better claim to go with him than Peter Isola. He had come second in the 1959 election, well ahead of Isola, who came third. He was Member for Port and Tourist affairs with trading experience and a firm grasp of economic issues, which would be useful in presenting Gibraltar's case, whereas Isola was another lawyer like Salvador and was Member for Education, which was a less relevant portfolio than Seruya's. However, what probably made Bates back Isola was the simple fact that Salvador and Seruya were both Jews, which could have had an adverse effect on some anti-semitic members of the Committee of 24, and would have given the Spaniards a gratuitous wild card: under Utrecht, no Jew or Moor was allowed to reside in Gibraltar!

Soon after the examination started in New York on 11th September it became clear that it would not be a British walkover. The British representative, Cecil King, gave a short opening report on the economic and constitutional progress being made in

Gibraltar, and ended saying:

> The people of Gibraltar, through their freely elected leaders, have emphasized that they wish to retain a close association with Britain and they already enjoy a large measure of responsibility for their internal affairs under the present Constitution. The British government, for its part, is always ready to consider proposals for change put forward by the people of Gibraltar or their elected representatives. (*1st Spanish Red Book*, pp 318-9)

The Spanish representative, Don Jaime de Pinies, followed with a long rambling and emotional speech, in which he claimed that under the Treaty of Utrecht Britain had had no right to turn the fortress, first, into a British colony on Spanish soil in 1830, and then into a non-self-governing British territory in 1946. Britain had done all this while Spain had been too weak to do more than utter useless protests, which the British, in their high-handed way, had just ignored. Gibraltar and its Campo were indivisible geographically, economically and culturally, and should be reunited within the Spanish realm as Resolution 1514 (XV) paragraph 6 laid down. Spain was willing to discuss the reunification of Gibraltar and its Campo, taking full account of the interests of the inhabitants. In his final peroration he said:

> ... the Spanish people hope confidently that the United Nations will actively help to eradicate [colonialism] from this part of Western Europe, in the same way and measure, and with the same sense of urgency, as it has carried out the process of decolonization in other countries. Public opinion in Spain is united, without exception of any kind, including all our inhabitants within and outside Spain, and they confidently hope that the United Nations will be able to do justice to such an equitable claim. We are in favour of decolonization, but for all. We want respect for our rights; our honour demands this, and when we mention the sacred words, we Spaniards are touched to the very roots of our being. We have waited 250 years, and now the time has come to seek a solution. (*Ibid*, pp 333-4)

During the early days of the examination the representatives of Uruguay, Iraq, Tunisia, Venezuela, Syria and Cambodia made impassioned speeches, supporting Spain's demand for the restoration of her territorial integrity and advocating Anglo-Spanish negotiations to bring this about. All were former colonies or protectorates of Spain, France or Britain and would vote against Britain whatever arguments were presented. Only Denmark and Australia supported the British case until 19th September, when Gibraltar's representatives were invited to intervene as 'petitioners', to put the Gibraltarian view. Salvador and Peter Isola were well aware of the grave responsibility which they carried on behalf of their people, and of the hostile atmosphere prevailing in the Committee of 24. Ever since the Suez debacle, when Britain gave way to American anti-colonialist pressure, it had become fashionable in the international community to denigrate everything British. Macmillan's 'Wind of Change' speech was seen as marking the rout of imperial Britain and not the fulfilment of her planned and responsible withdrawal form empire. Every British political move was seen as a devious effort to hold onto her colonies, and to preserve her military bases. Despite the very short time available for preparation, and the hostility of the Committee, Salvador made a brilliant speech, which is so important that it is reproduced in full in Appendix 2. He made a number of crucially compelling points. First, he stressed that he and Peter Isola had come to New York on their own initiative; they were an exclusively Gibraltarian delegation, expressing the views of the whole of the people of Gibraltar; and that he himself was the Chief Member of Gibraltar's Executive and Legislative Councils, head of its biggest political party, the AACR, and unanimously elected Mayor of Gibraltar. Although Isola was his most bitter and able opponent in local politics, they were united and at one with the people on the question of Gibraltar's future. Both the Hassan and Isola families had been well-established on the Rock for over 200 years.

Having made it clear that his was the authentic voice of the Gibraltarians, he went on to question the whole basis of the Spanish case:

> Spain has asked on many occasions that Gibraltar should be returned to it. Now the Spanish representative seeks to achieve this objective under the guise of a passionate abhorrence of colonialism. We do not question Spain's dislike of colonialism, but we do most emphatically maintain that its application to Gibraltar is completely irrelevant. (*Ibid*, p 352)

Defining colonialism as subjugation, exploitation of resources, social injustice and political deprivation, he proceeded to demolish each in turn as far as Gibraltar was concerned.

Nothing could be further from the truth than to suggest that the people of Gibraltar were subjugated by a foreign power. They were the descendants of people who, of their own free will, settled in Gibraltar after it had been conquered, and accepted that the requirements of the fortress must come first. With the decline of Gibraltar's strategic importance over the past 40 years, the Gibraltarians had become an emancipated community with a mind of their own and the right to determine their own future.

Gibraltar's resources, other than its military importance, had certainly not been exploited: quite the reverse, the people of Gibraltar derived economic benefit from the presence of the British armed forces on the Rock. Moreover they gained much from British administrative expertise, judicial independence and responsible legislature, which characterize government at its best.

Socially, the level of education was very high; there was no distinction of class, race or religion; the courts were impartial; and, indeed, Gibraltar had achieved one of the very first objects of the United Nations Charter – its faith in fundamental human rights, in the dignity and worth of the human person, and the equal rights of men and women.

And most important of all, although Gibraltar had not yet achieved full self-government, it was well on the way to doing so. After describing the steady growth of representative government since 1945, he said:

> It must, I think, be evident to all you gentlemen that although Gibraltar is still, formally, a 'Crown Colony', in spite of the fact that the word 'colony' and its cognate expressions have been

expunged from all local institutions, nothing could be further away from the generally accepted interpretation of 'colonialism' than the situation in Gibraltar today. (*Ibid,* p 357)

He then attacked the Spanish claim:

Do not let us delude ourselves. We all know the true reasons why Spain has raised this matter in this Committee. And I, my colleagues, and the people of Gibraltar, knowing the Spanish character as we do and the Spaniard's regard, above all else, for his honour, not only understand his attitude towards Gibraltar but respect him for it. But, gentlemen, the people of Gibraltar also have a high regard for their honour. The land in which they live is their birthplace and was the birthplace of their forebears – for no less than 250 years. (*Ibid.*)

What then were the wishes of the people of Gibraltar? The decolonization resolution gave three options to emergent non-self-governing states: sovereign independent status; free association with an independent state; or integration with an independent state. Unfortunately, Gibraltar was too small for the first; the third was impracticable for several reasons, not the least of which was the loss of political identity that integration would lead to; so it was a free and close association with Britain to which the Gibraltarians aspired. This he said was:

. . . the free choice of the people of Gibraltar, and I, their spokesman before this Committee, am entitled and empowered to say this with the full backing of the whole people of Gibraltar. (*Ibid,* p 360)

Pointing out that no community could exist for over 250 years without creating its own individuality, culture and way of life, Gibraltar had no wish to be swallowed up by Spain, Britain or anyone else. While Gibraltarians had a desire to be true friends of Spain, they also appreciated the Spanish wish to 'recover peacefully what by conquest they had gained and by conquest they had lost'! The people of Gibraltar had had nothing to do with these conflicts and should not be made to give up what they hold most dear in order to reverse an accident of history. Salvador ended his speech saying:

> The Committee of 24, representing as it does the big and the small nations, will strengthen their prestige as upholders of the rights of colonial peoples by reaffirming the principle of self-determination, thereby allowing us to continue the way of life which we have freely chosen for ourselves. (*Ibid*, p 361)

Peter Isola followed, confirming that he did not, indeed, see eye to eye with Salvador on internal affairs; nevertheless, he endorsed, on behalf of all Gibraltarians who were not of Salvador's political persuasion, everything that he had said. He then described, in graphic terms, the Gibraltarians' greatest fear: being 'sold down the river' in bilateral talks between Britain and Spain, carried on behind their backs. To offset this fear, Gibraltarians placed their faith in the United Nations Charter, but he continued:

> We never thought, in all sincerity, that we would have to come post-haste to New York to claim for ourselves the right of self-determination. We never thought that it might be suggested in this Committee that the future of our people, our Gibraltar, should be discussed by two great Powers without reference to our fundamental rights in this matter. We never thought, and we do not think, that this Committee could ever countenance such a suggestion. (*Ibid*, p 362)

He then turned to the question of sovereignty, making the crucial point, which is still valid today:

> Gibraltar, as the Committee is aware, is a British possession. We do not doubt it; we do not dispute it. But what the people of Gibraltar say is that, whatever the juridical position may be, Gibraltar belongs to the people of Gibraltar and to no one else. We can only protest strongly at the suggestion that it is a piece of Spanish soil over which Britain has sovereignty. It is a piece of Gibraltar's soil and, by right and by virtue of the Charter, it belongs to us and to us alone, and only we should be allowed to decide its future. (*Ibid*, p 363)

After repudiating the Spanish contention that Gibraltar was a cancer in Spain's economy and that Gibraltar's economy was based on smuggling, he ended with an appeal:

> We in Gibraltar are confident and know that this Committee will
> do nothing that will prejudice our position, will not agree that
> one form of imperialism – if one likes to call it that – should be
> supplanted by another form of imperialism by another country. It
> is we, and we alone, who must decide our future. We trust that
> the Chairman and the other members of the Committee will
> reflect on that position. (*Ibid*, pp 364-5)

The Australian representative, Mr McCarthy, gave Salvador and
Isola Australia's fullest support. After demolishing the flimsy
historical arguments put forward by the Hispanic bloc as based
upon 'tiny and chosen fragments' of history, he pointed out that
Salvador's and Isola's words were fundamental to the debate:

> . . . for theirs are the voices of the people of Gibraltar, not the
> voices of the United Kingdom, not the voices of Spain (*Ibid*,
> p 368)

The Spanish representative had the last word. In another long
and largely irrelevant speech, he maintained that the Gibraltarians
were not 'passive subjects of colonialism, but the active
instruments in the perpetuation of that system'. Spain, however,
had no intention of treating them as the British had done the
original Spanish inhabitants of the Rock, whose descendants still
lived in exile across the frontier at San Roque. Spain offered them
'a magnificent future in the Spanish realm', and would respect
their interests when the Rock was returned to Spain. What more
could they want?

The Chairman of the Committee, Mr Coulibally of Mali, at last
realized that the Spanish case might be flawed and the Gibraltar
problem was more complex than he had been led to believe.
Salvador and Peter had influenced him by making two crucial
points: the Rock was inhabited by a people who had a right to self-
determination; and it was neither Spain's to acquire nor Britain's
to relinquish – it belonged to its people, the Gibraltarians. The
two sides, however, were too far apart for a consensus resolution to
be drafted before the 1963 General Assembly opened on 20th

September. Coulibally, therefore, adjourned the Gibraltar debate until the next year's session.

Salvador and Peter arrived back in Gibraltar to a hero's reception that has never been surpassed. All Gibraltar crowded into the streets to shower congratulations on them as they drove through the city, standing in the back of an open jeep. Salvador's powerful political reputation had been further enhanced, and he was now seen to have international standing: and Peter's was made for him overnight. They had propagated the Gibraltarians' claim to be treated as a people for the first time. If the United Nations had been a level playing field on which objectivity could win, their efforts in New York might have swung world opinion in their favour.

Regrettably, Lake Success has never been level and unbiased: voting is based on national interest and prejudice. The Hispanic bloc were deaf to anti-Spanish argument; the Afro-Asians would not vote for any resolution that favoured the old colonial powers; and in the post-Suez era only Britain's closest allies would vote in her favour. Strong though the Gibraltarian case was, the pro-Spanish lobby determinedly resisted the acceptance of the legitimacy of the Gibraltarians as a people.

As soon as the adjournment was announced, the Foreign Office tried to persuade the Spanish government to co-operate in pressing for the Gibraltar issue to be withdrawn from the Committee of 24's agenda so as to avoid further damage to Anglo-Spanish relations. Diplomatic exchanges began in November 1963 in Madrid, and were brought to a climax in March 1964, when the British side accepted that while Spain had no rights in Gibraltar, she did have interests in Gibraltar that Britain had no wish to injure. As evidence of her sincerity, the proposals for further constitutional advance in Gibraltar were sent to the Spanish Foreign Ministry with a request that Madrid should specify what her interests were so that steps could be taken to protect them. In reply the Spanish government rehearsed all their old arguments about its rights under Utrecht, but did not define what they were. They made it quite clear, however, that they were opposed to giving the Gibraltarians any increased responsibility for the internal affairs of the Rock, and objected to any changes being made before the United Nations resumed its debate on Gibraltar in the autumn. While the British government was quite prepared to make sensible modifications to its constitutional proposals to protect genuine Spanish interests, it was not prepared to abandon them or even delay them until after the second United Nations debate. To have done so would have been tantamount to acknowledging that Spain had rights in Gibraltar. After a series of discussions in London between Lord Lansdowne, the Minister of State for Commonwealth Relations and Colonies, and a Gibraltar delegation of elected members of the Legislative Council led by Salvador, the 1964 Constitutional Conference under Lansdowne's chairmanship started in Gibraltar on 7th April. The outcome was announced three days later.

In the introductory paragraph of the announcement, there was an important statement of policy insisted upon by Salvador:

> All the unofficial members of the Legislative Council made it clear that they did not seek independence nor any control of defence or foreign policy, and that it was their wish and that of the people of Gibraltar that Gibraltar should always remain in close association with Britain. They sought, however, certain modifications to the constitution to give the people of Gibraltar fuller control of internal affairs. (*Ibid*, p 381)

The constitutional changes that had been agreed increased the number of elected members of the Legislative Council from seven to eleven; eliminated nominated members; Salvador became Chief Minister; elected members were given responsibility for government departments and became ministers; the Council of Members became the Council of Ministers; and the Governor's Executive Council became the Gibraltar Council with five officials, including the governor, and five ministers, including the chief minister.

The governor, in consultation with the chief minister, would allocate ministerial portfolios, and the chief minister would direct government business in the Legislative Council as its leader. The colonial secretary would cease to be a member of the legislature and would become the permanent secretary to the government of Gibraltar.

One major issue was left unresolved: the future of the City Council. Lord Lansdowne considered that the suggestion of amalgamating it with the Legislative Council needed further study, which should be carried out during the life of the next Legislative Council, which was to be for five years. Its election would be held on 18th September 1964.

It was during this intense period of constitutional negotiation that Daniela finally left Salvador on 4th March 1964 and did not return. He made up his mind that his marriage had broken down irreconcilably and that he must seek a judicial separation from her in the Supreme Court after the statutory period of three years, on grounds of desertion and cruelty. It was during those three years that he met Marcelle Bensimon, a Jewess from Larache in Spanish Morocco, who had come to Gibraltar in the early 1960s to help refugee Moroccan Jews, who were making their way to Israel, using Gibraltar as a stepping stone. She was a graduate nurse, who had trained in Spanish Morocco and Spain, and had been nursing in Switzerland. She was working at the White Rock Jewish refugee camp when Salvador met her in 1965. Their friendship blossomed, and, as we shall see later, she was eventually to become the second Lady Hassan.

Before the 1964 elections could be held, Anglo-Spanish relations took a nasty turn for the worse.

Negotiations had been going on for some time between Sir Douglas Home's Conservative government and the Franco regime for a joint naval construction programme. In June, questions were asked in the House of Commons about the desirability of dealing with a fascist regime, and whether Franco had agreed as a *quid pro quo* for naval co-operation to give up his claim to the Rock. Franco felt that his dignity had been besmirched by these exchanges in the Commons, and reacted by breaking off negotiations. When coupled with Spanish objections to the new Lansdowne Constitution for Gibraltar, this debacle sent Anglo-Spanish

relations tumbling to a new low. The Gibraltar debate reopened
in the Committee of 24 that autumn in a strained, if not hostile,
atmosphere.

Salvador was fully occupied during the summer of 1964
campaigning for the September elections, and preparing for the
United Nations debate. For the latter, he organized and led the
drafting by a committee, composed of all the elected members of
the Legislature, of a short, well-argued and telling pamphlet called
The Future of Gibraltar, which was sent to all the members of the
Committee of 24 together with an album of photographs of
Gibraltar. Once again, as this is a crucial statement of Gibraltarian
policy, its conclusions are reproduced in full in Appendix 3. The
most important paragraphs read:

> It is a matter of fact that sovereignty over Gibraltar is at present
> exercised by Britain. The Spanish claim to sovereignty has been
> brought before the Committee of 24. It has been stated that the
> British have a colony on Spanish soil and an attempt has been
> made to suggest that the people of Gibraltar are Spanish in their
> outlook and traditions and desire unification with Spain.
> The soil of Gibraltar should belong to no one but the people of
> Gibraltar and the people of Gibraltar do not desire to be united
> with Spain. (*The Future of Gibraltar,* p 11)

In the September Legislative Council election, which was fought
on relations with Spain rather than the usual left/right issues,
Salvador and Peter Isola – the heroes of New York – came first and
second in the poll, but Salvador had well over double Isola's votes
(4,603 to 1,822). Sol Seruya slipped to third place with 916 votes
– half Isola's vote. Unfortunately for Salvador the AACR's sixth
candidate, Ernest Mor, was not elected, and so Salvador was left
without an overall majority. Isola tried to form a government from
the six successful independents but failed. Then, thanks to
Salvador's old friend, 'Bramy' Benatar, acting as an intermediary,
Peter Russo, who had been elected as an independent, repaid his
political debt to Salvador by agreeing to support him in forming
an AACR government. And so it came about that Salvador was
called by Sir Dudley Ward, the Governor, to become Gibraltar's

first Chief Minister. The turnout at the poll had been a record at 76.24 per cent.

Ten days later, Salvador and Peter Isola flew to New York for the resumed debate on Gibraltar, which began on 22nd September. It proved to be a dialogue of the deaf, which would be dreary to recount in detail and tedious to read. The debate lasted 16 days and centred on the issue of the existence or otherwise of Gibraltarians as a people. Spain contended that there was no such thing as a Gibraltarian. Britain, with Salvador and Isola speaking impressively, insisted that the people of Gibraltar had lived, bred, prospered and often suffered acute hardship on the Rock for over 250 years and were certainly a united people with their own distinctive way of life, culture and traditions. Britain would defend, with all necessary means, their right to full internal self-government and self-determination within the limits of the Treaty of Utrecht.

Spain tried to trump the presence of Gibraltar's leaders by putting up the mayors of the Campo towns and an eminent Spanish historian to present the Spanish case. It was a pointless exercise, which Salvador had little difficulty in ridiculing. The mayors were unelected Franco appointees, speaking from government briefs. They could not speak for the people of the Campo with the same authority and authenticity as Salvador and Isola, who had been elected so recently as the Gibraltarian representatives.

Salvador concentrated upon overturning the Spanish refusal to acknowledge the existence of Gibraltarians. His most telling point was:

> We are not an indigenous people colonized by outsiders, nor are we an imported population of the colonizing power. We are a people, like many other modern countries, not the least of which is the United States, who have grown up by lawful and legitimate immigration. (*Ibid*, p 427)

Peter Isola condemned the viciousness of the anti-Gibraltarian campaign in the Spanish media, and then attacked the Spanish contention that only paragraph 6 of Resolution 1514 (XV) need be considered, because, in the Spanish view, there were no indigenous people on the Rock:

> Can this Committee really tell our people against their own wishes and desires expressed to you by Sir Joshua Hassan and myself, their elected representatives, that they are to be freed from British colonialism, to which they have not objected, and handed over to Spanish colonization, to which they have openly protested. However hostile may be the attitude of this Committee to the United Kingdom or friendly towards the interests of Spain, can that of itself determine the future of our people? (*Ibid*, p 439)

The Spanish representative, still Pinies, reiterated *ad nauseam* the camp follower argument:

> They [Salvador and Isola] came not only to request protection of the interests that Spain has at all times been ready to consider and respect, but actually to assert that the 17,985 persons encamped around a British military base, and protected by Great Britain's military power, constituted a population with a juridical personality or status, and possessing every right over the Territory of their residence, including the right of self-determination . . . . Never in the history of the process of decolonization has an attempt been made with greater effrontery to deceive the international community in the United Nations. (*Ibid*, p 443)

There were two new elements in the debate. The first was a warning by Pinies that if Spain did not get her way, she would cut off Gibraltar from the Spanish mainland and treat all Gibraltarians as *personae non gratae*. The second was less serious as far as the Gibraltarian economy was concerned. The Soviet representative intervened in the debate, opposing the Spanish case. He laughed at Spain's contention that Gibraltar was a threat to Spanish security, and he refused to countenance the return of the Rock to the colonialism of Franco's 'fascist' regime. By far the most important issue in Soviet thinking was the liquidation of Western military bases. The Soviet Union wanted a demilitarized and decolonized independent Gibraltar. He did not say how this was to be brought about, but in making his case, he put forward a new argument, which Pinies was to seize upon and use in future debates. He maintained that Salvador and Isola were mere British stooges put up to perpetuate the British military hold on the Rock for the benefit of NATO. Their wish to stay British was nothing more than a devious British ploy to keep control of the western entrance to the Mediterranean. At the end of the debate, a consensus was drafted and passed, inviting Britain and Spain to find a negotiated solution for the decolonization of Gibraltar in accordance with Resolution 1514 (XV), but without limiting it to paragraph 6 as Spain wanted. Britain was thus at liberty to insist on her interpretation of decolonization, enshrined in paragraphs 2 and 5, which made paragraph 6 irrelevant. Cecil King, the British representative, had the last word when he announced that:

> . . . the United Kingdom government, although not prepared to discuss with Spain the question of sovereignty over Gibraltar, and while not departing from its view that it was under no obligation to consult with Spain on matters concerning Gibraltar, was nevertheless always willing to discuss with the Spanish government the maintenance of good relations between the two countries and the elimination of friction. (*Ibid*, p 112)

This was all too much for Madrid. Castiella's elegant plan for winning back the Rock through the United Nations was unravelling because the British were ignoring the pro-Spanish Committee 24 as far as the real issue was concerned – the transfer of sovereignty. Counter-productively, Castiella decided to turn the economic screw on the Gibraltarians once more, thereby giving the British government a valid reason for refusing further talks with Spain under duress. Exports from Spain into Gibraltar were stopped, and British passports issued in Gibraltar or in British consulates in Spain were refused. As few Gibraltarians had United Kingdom issued passports, they were effectively barred from crossing the frontier. Castiella's ingenuous reply to diplomatic protests was that Spain was only imposing justifiable anti-smuggling measures common on all international frontiers. He brought matters to a head on 18th November by demanding the negotiations called for in the United Nations consensus. The

British ambassador in Madrid replied sharply that while Britain might be willing to talk, she would not do so under duress: frontier restrictions must be lifted first. The frontier restrictions were undoubtedly damaging the Rock's economy, but were also bringing wide political support for Gibraltar in Westminster, Whitehall and Fleet Street. The Gibraltar lobby was given wholehearted support on both sides of the Commons. The normally tightfisted mandarins in Whitehall were preparing to 'sustain and support' Gibraltar financially with a willingness that they had never shown before. And the British press was equally committed to the Gibraltarian cause, being particularly incensed by Spanish expressions of injured innocence in accusing the Gibraltarians of being the aggressors!

Before the constitutional reforms of 1950 it would have been for the governor and his expatriate officials to deal with the economic effects of Spanish harassment. With the rapid advance towards full internal self-government, the burden of dealing with the internal effects of the restrictions fell squarely upon the shoulders of Salvador and his ministers, who also had to play the leading role in maintaining the morale of the people. There was only an ill-defined line between internal and external affairs for which Salvador and the governor were respectively responsible. Thanks to Salvador's long experience in working with the Convent, there was very close co-operation between the two, and between them and the Whitehall ministries.

A senior economic adviser to the Colonial Office was sent out to recommend the steps which should be taken to reorientate the Rock's economy, including the accommodation of over a thousand Gibraltarians who had previously been living in Spain. His visit led to Salvador and Isola flying back to London on 24th November for discussions on Gibraltar's immediate needs. They met the Colonial Secretary, Arthur Greenwood, and were assured of Britain's full and determined support.

Greenwood was true to his word. In February, he sent out his Under-Secretary of State, Mrs Eirene White, to explore what further needed to be done; and by May Salvador was able to announce the development of a 'master plan' for reorientation of the economy. In his view, Gibraltar should be made as self-sufficient as possible whether Spain lifted her frontier restrictions or not. He paid another visit to London with Peter Isola on 22nd July at which a financial support package of £1.2 million was agreed with the Minister of Overseas Development, Mrs Barbara Castle. While most of the diplomatic haggling, which went on during the winter and spring of 1964/5, was handled by Whitehall with the Governor being kept informed, and he, in his turn, keeping Salvador in the picture and seeking his advice on the Gibraltarian reaction to events, there was one important foreign affairs venture which was left to Salvador to handle discreetly by himself. The manager of the construction firm building the Gibraltar Casino became friendly with Salvador, and told him that he had influential friends in Madrid, who could arrange for him to meet a representative of General Franco to see whether anything could be engineered by personal contact to ease the ever-increasing Spanish frontier restrictions. Sir Dudley Ward saw no objections to such exploratory talks; and Salvador was not averse to talking to anyone as he was crystal clear in his own mind how far the people of Gibraltar were prepared to go to end frontier restrictions. Moreover, he wished to impress on the Franco regime, as he had tried to do at the United Nations, that the Gibraltarians were not British stooges: they had a clear identity and policies of their own.

Salvador had two meetings with a Señor Lumbrera in a Tangier hotel. Lumbrera's aim, Salvador recalls, was to enable Spain to recover sovereignty over the Rock by offering the Gibraltarians all manner of treaties and promises for their future happiness within the Spanish realm. Salvador told him bluntly that sovereignty was not for discussion. The Gibraltarians wanted no change; the British government supported them and knew their wishes, which it respected; and the Gibraltarians had no desire to become Spanish however attractive the carrots dangled before them. What might seem heaven to Spaniards, brought up throughout their long history under autocratic regimes, would be purgatory for people whose democratic way of life had been shaped by the *Magna Carta* of 1215.

Nothing came of these meetings except a congratulatory letter to the Governor from the Secretary of State, which Darrel Bates copied to Salvador:

> I feel that the discussions which Sir Joshua has had have been most useful in emphasizing that the policy of Her Majesty's government in the recent White Paper (Comnd. 2623) has the backing of the people of Gibraltar. If you see no objections I shall be grateful if you will convey my appreciation to him on the tactful way in which he handled these talks and of the firm stand he has taken in making it clear to Sr Lumbrera the wishes of the people of Gibraltar and the policy of Her Majesty's government. (Copy held with Hassan notes of 27.5.94.)

As Spanish intransigence grew, Salvador and Isola decided that there was no point in carrying on with confrontational party politics. All their energies and those of the other elected members of the Legislature should be pooled in the fight against Spain. On 8th July, they had formed a coalition government with Isola as Deputy Chief Minister to carry Gibraltar through the economic crisis gratuitously imposed on Gibraltar by Spain. Ever since 1704, few things have united Britons and Gibraltarians more firmly than Spanish attempts to recover the Rock. Sir Dudley Ward's tenure as Governor came to an end in June 1965. Sadly his first wife, Beatrice, had died in 1962. Towards the end of his tour, he remarried Joan de Pechell, who had been working as the welfare officer at the Royal Naval Hospital. Salvador and Dudley were the best of friends and on the most amicable terms, but it was Salvador with the co-operation of Darell Bates – formerly the colonial secretary whose position was now renamed 'permanent secretary' – who steered Gibraltar through the difficult storms of the early phases of the Spanish restrictions with a deft and unobtrusive hand. Salvador's successes at the United Nations in 1963 and 1964 had brought the name 'Gibraltarian' into international usage, although not general acceptance and certainly not by Spain. He became a recognised actor on the world stage, and the living symbol of the flaw in Castiella's case for the return of the Rock to Spain. He was the proof that the Gibraltarians did exist and could not be ignored, however much Castiella might wish to do so. Under Salvador's subtle leadership, which melded well with British thinking, the people of Gibraltar were not prepared to compromise their rights as a people in the cause of amicable Anglo-Spanish relations, nor surrender to Spanish coercion.

CHAPTER 7

CONTINUING SPANISH COERCION
AND THE REFERENDUM
1965-1967

The Gibraltar Coalition Government, 1965-69

J A Hassan	Chief Minister
P J Isola	Deputy Chief Minister
S A Seruya	Economic Development
P G Russo	Housing
A Risso	Labour and Social Security
L W Triay	Port and Trade
A J Baldorino (Jr)	Post Office
A V Stagnetto	Public Relations
A W Serfaty	Tourism
* Mrs M Chiappe	Education
A P Montegriffo	Medical Services

* Resigned: E Alvarez (AACR) won by-election, May 1967

1965 was the year in which the British and Gibraltar governments realized that Spain's diplomatic, political and economic offensives to recover the Rock were not going to crumble as they had done so often in the past as internal divisions and *mañana* sapped Madrid's determination to succeed. Franco was sure that Gibraltar was ripe for picking, but he did not think that it was worth a war with Britain. Castiella, the architect of the Spanish decolonization ploy and a determinedly obstinate Basque, was utterly convinced that his twin-track offensive, forcing negotiations upon the British while coercing the Gibraltarians, was paying dividends. Certainly he had converted the bilateral Anglo-Spanish dispute into a United Nations issue with significant international support for Spain's view that Gibraltar was a British fortress on Spanish soil, and that the present inhabitants, whom she claimed were not a people in the true sense of the word, had no right to determine the future of the Rock even though it was their homeland.

Views in Westminster and Whitehall should change, or so Castiella hoped, with the advent of Harold Wilson's Labour government with a reputation for anti-colonial inclinations. It was a vain hope: most Labour governments had proved themselves to be just as, if not more, imperial than the Tories. Harold Wilson promised to respect the wishes of the Gibraltarians, and under his direction Eirene White and Barbara Castle developed the 'sustain and support' policy to neutralize the effects of Castiella's frontier restrictions.

Nevertheless, Castiella's hopes were not entirely without foundation. There was a growing feeling among officials in Whitehall, if not among the politicians in Westminster, that Britain's refusal to negotiate under Spanish duress might be counter-productive in that Britain's case could be damaged internationally; and that reorienting and sustaining Gibraltar's economy would certainly be expensive. Many of Britain's closest allies made it clear that they thought that she was not helping the Gibraltarian cause by refusing to talk to Spain.

Salvador was well aware of the dangers of negotiation with Madrid, and the majority of the Gibraltarians were equally suspicious of London because they knew all too well that their needs were usually subordinate to maintaining friendly Anglo-Spanish relations. Knowing the Spaniards far better than any Whitehall mandarin could ever do, Salvador realized that no amount of logical argument would cut much ice with Castiella, who had sunk too much of his own political capital into his plan for recovering the Rock and could not pull back even though he might perhaps see logic in doing so. On the other hand, Salvador also appreciated the British propensity for compromise. He believed that Gibraltar's safety lay in a twin-track policy of his own: developing, in close co-operation with British ministers, a greater degree of economic self-sufficiency for the Rock; and stiffening the British government's backbone when dangerously attractive compromises were suggested by Spain. Without Salvador's subtle influence with successive governors and British ministers during the mid-1960s, Gibraltar might, indeed, have been sold down the river by default as Spanish pressure continued to mount, especially in the United Nations.

The Gibraltar issue was brought up at the United Nations General Assembly in the autumn of 1965 in the form of the usual resolution urging Britain and Spain to find a negotiated solution. Much to the surprise of Spain and to the chagrin of the Gibraltarians, Britain did agree to re-open negotiations without preconditions and without exempting discussion of sovereignty. Salvador wrote a strong letter of protest direct to the Prime Minister, Harold Wilson, because the Gibraltar government fully supported the policy of 'No negotiations under duress' and had no wish to see it overturned. Harold Wilson replied rather lamely that pressure in the United Nations had caused the change, but he reaffirmed his policy of support for Gibraltar in which he said there was no change.

The Foreign Office hoped that this seemingly significant gesture of goodwill on Britain's part would encourage the Spanish government to lift the frontier restrictions. Every Gibraltarian could have told the 'know-alls' in Whitehall that such gestures would be interpreted by Madrid as a sign of weakness, and that the screw would be tightened once more in order to break Gibraltarian resistance. However, both Whitehall and Madrid were miscalculating: Madrid thought that Spain was winning and so had no reason to reciprocate the British goodwill gesture; and Whitehall underestimated Gibraltarian determination to resist the mix of Spanish political and economic coercion, and so were perhaps over hasty in offering to negotiate with a fascist government without reservations.

During Whitehall's preparation for the new talks, Salvador was invited to London to advise the Foreign Secretary, Michael Stewart, on the Gibraltarian view on what was negotiable and what was not. The Foreign Office knew from informal diplomatic exchanges that Castiella would be proposing a lease-back of the military base to Britain once the Rock had been returned to Spain, and the establishment of a specially favourable status for its inhabitants when they entered the Spanish realm. Salvador made it abundantly clear that these proposals should be rejected out of hand since they involved a change of sovereignty, which his people would never accept. Gibraltar wished to remain British, and with British political and economic support would resist Spanish coercion with the same stoicism that Gibraltarians had always shown when the Rock had been threatened in the past. With the Gibraltarian position thus firmly established, it was decided that the British delegation's counter-proposals would be based simply upon meeting the stated Spanish reasons for imposing the frontier restrictions in the first place: dislike of the constitutional advances towards full internal self-government, which had started in 1950 with the establishment of the elected Legislative Council; and objections to the continuing existence of the frontier fence, which had been an irritant to Spain since its erection in 1908. The Foreign Office was helped in formulating its counter-proposals by the Constitutional Committee set up in Gibraltar after the 1964 election, under the chairmanship of Peter Isola, to report on the desirability of amalgamating the Legislative and City Councils, and to recommend the constitutional changes that would be needed to give Gibraltar full internal self-government in close association with Britain and without prejudicing British sovereignty. The Isola committee favoured the amalgamation of the two Councils. All that would be needed to meet the Spanish demand for reversion to the pre-1950 municipal style of internal self-government would be to call the new combined council the City Council instead of the House of Assembly; the chief minister would become mayor; and the ministers would be councillors. Many people in Gibraltar felt that the 1964 style of government was too complex in any case, and that a municipal local government was more appropriate. If the price for lifting frontier restrictions was reversion to a municipal format without loss of internal self-government, it might be well worth considering.

Removing the frontier fence would only be a cosmetic political gesture, because an airfield perimeter fence would still be needed and it had to run across the isthmus only a few yards south of the existing fence, which was old and needed replacement anyway. However, the fence could only be taken away if its removal was not construed as a diminution of British sovereignty over the southern half of the Neutral Zone on the isthmus – a proviso which was to cause immense trouble in the 1980s and 90s.

Other sweeteners might be added: the return of the Spanish consul to Gibraltar; allowing Spanish military aircraft and warships to use Gibraltar's base facilities, provided operational and administrative control remained firmly in British hands; and increasing Anglo-Spanish co-operation in anti-smuggling operations.

The Anglo-Spanish talks, which began at Admiralty House in London on 18th May 1966, were not only polite and courteous dialogues of the deaf, but also talks between two delegations that might have come from different planets. There was no real comprehension between Anglo-Saxon and Latin minds and their thought processes. Words with the same Latin roots meant different things to Britons and Spaniards. For instance, to the Spanish, the word 'negotiation' means finding a way towards a specific objective, which has already been agreed. Castiella believed that the United Nations had specified the objective: the return of the Rock to Spain. All that was required in the Anglo-Spanish talks was deciding the route to that objective, bearing in mind the interests but not the wishes of the Gibraltarians. To the British, 'negotiation' means finding a solution acceptable to both sides without a specified objective – talks about talks laced with hard bargaining. Michael Stewart had no intention of working towards a transfer of sovereignty; he wanted to win the lifting of restrictions by meeting Spanish complaints as far as it was possible to do so without impinging on sovereignty and with Gibraltarian consent.

With typical Spanish obtuseness, Madrid could not resist tightening the screws before each of the five rounds of the 1966/67 Anglo-Spanish talks. Before the first round began, Madrid tried to curry favour with the Soviet Union by dredging up a complaint about Britain turning the Rock into a NATO base, thus placing southern Andalusia at risk from a Warsaw Pact nuclear strike on the fortress. Spain had no wish to take such risks on behalf of NATO, a military alliance to which she did not belong. She conveniently ignored the presence of US military bases in Spain, which were far more likely nuclear targets. The Spanish Foreign Ministry sent a letter to all NATO powers, stating her objections to their using Gibraltar for military exercises and as a base. The letter was not sent to London on the specious grounds that it might jeopardize the coming talks, but a clear warning was given that if the talks did not go Spain's way, clearance for British aircraft to continue to overfly Spain on their way to and from Gibraltar would be refused.

At the first round on 18th May, attended by Michael Stewart, the Foreign Secretary, Castiella started the talks off personally by presenting the Spanish case in a long omnibus paper, which took all morning and much of the afternoon to deliver. It was a compendium of all his speeches to the Spanish Cortes, and those of de Pinies at the United Nations. They were drawn together in a way that seemed to lead logically to a proposal for replacing Utrecht with a new convention of four articles. The first would restore the territorial integrity of the Spanish realm, which he claimed was the agreed objective of United Nations. The second would lease-back the military installation of the fortress to Britain. The third would guarantee the rights and interests of the Gibraltarians within the Spanish realm. And the fourth would be agreement to the signing and registration of the convention under the auspices of the United Nations.

If the strength of a case is in inverse proportion to its length, Castiella had a very weak case! His paper was 36 pages long: in fact, he became so tired reading his lengthy diatribe after lunch that he had to ask one of his aides to read the latter half of it for him. In it he made the fundamental error – perhaps due to prompting by the Soviet Union – of assuming that Britain's true reason for retaining the Rock was military, but camouflaged by her moralistic insistence on honouring the wishes of the Gibraltarians. In his view, offering Britain the continuing use of the fortress, coupled with fair terms for the Gibraltarians, was an elegant solution to the problem, which the pragmatic British should find hard to refuse. It was no such thing: Michael Stewart agreed to study Castiella's proposals carefully, but then and there proceeded quietly – he was by nature a quiet and self-effacing man – to reject each controversial section of the Spanish case, ending up by saying:

> Without going into details of the proposals, I must take up one. You spoke of measures to protect the inhabitants, and measures that would be registered with the United Nations in regard to their rights. Now inevitably one asks oneself: how certain in practice would such guarantees be? It would be much easier for us to approach that question with confidence if at the outset of detailed discussions Spain herself showed her regard for the ordinary human feelings of these people by removing some of the restrictions.
> That is probably as far as it is reasonable for me to go now. These are important and serious proposals. I made it on the one hand clear that I think these now could be considered; that our officials could examine them. On the other hand there was much in your statement with which I could not agree, and I repeat again that I believe that it would greatly help if there could be a removal of restrictions. (Cmnd 3131, Nov 1966, p 40)

What, however, pleased Salvador and the people of Gibraltar most was Stewart's robust reiteration of Britain's right under Utrecht to sovereignty over the Rock in perpetuity and without any limitations whatsoever. The second round of talks began at official level without the presence of ministers on 12th July, at which the British counter-proposals were put. In Gibraltar, Sir Gerald

Lathbury, the new Governor, had worked through them with Salvador and Isola some days before. Neither political leader liked them because, knowing the Spanish mentality, they believed that such relatively minor concessions would only stoke Spanish ambitions and lead to a further tightening of restrictions rather than the reverse, as indeed was to happen. However, as the proposals gave nothing away on sovereignty, both Salvador and Isola told Lathbury that the Foreign Office had Gibraltarian consent.

The Spanish delegation expressed immediate disappointment that their own 'generous offer' had not been accepted at once, and made no real attempt to examine the British counter-proposals, reiterating instead the well-worn record that decolonization of Spanish soil could not be dependent upon Gibraltarian wishes. What irritated the Spanish delegation even more was the statement that the removal of the frontier fence would be without prejudice to British sovereignty over the southern half of the Neutral Zone. In subsequent exchanges, the British side maintained that their right to sovereignty was based on the internationally recognized right of prescription (ie long usage): they had occupied the area since the 18th century. The Spanish delegation argued that prescription was invalid because Spain had continually protested, but had never been militarily strong enough to eject British forces from the Neutral Zone. Their immediate response to the British announcement of *de facto* sovereignty over the southern half of the isthmus on which the Gibraltar airfield stands, was to carry out their threat of banning all British military aircraft flights over Spain from 4th August 1966. They also withdrew all female labour permits and stopped fresh produce entering Gibraltar from the Campo. Before the third round, scheduled for 6th September, could open, there was a debate on Gibraltar in the Commons on 11th August, in which a wide cross-section of MPs of all parties showed their distrust of the government's handling of the negotiations and jeopardizing Gibraltar's future. Using his membership of the Commonwealth Parliamentary Group, Salvador was able to enlist and brief a large number of Gibraltar supporters and well-wishers from among the MPs, including Edward Heath, Lord Boyd-Carpenter, Sir 'Freddy' Bennett, Sir Ian Orr-Ewing, Sidney Silverman, Julian Amery, Nigel Fisher and many other men of political influence. They all tried to make Harold Wilson reiterate the British promise to respect the 'wishes of the Gibraltarians'. He refused on the grounds that such a statement could prejudice the current Anglo-Spanish talks. All he would do was to reaffirm British government policy set out in the Gibraltar White Paper of April 1965:

> The policy of Her Majesty's Government is clear. Great Britain has at no time renounced her title to Gibraltar or failed to defend her position there and will not do so now. She has no desire to quarrel with Spain but she will stand by the people of Gibraltar in their present difficulties and take whatever measures may be necessary to defend and sustain them. (Cmnd 2632 of April 1965, p 12)

The Gibraltar Group had to be satisfied with this assurance, but, thanks to Salvador's lobbying, the government had been warned that any weakness that it showed on Gibraltar would stir up a political hornet's nest. It could ill-afford another crisis of confidence in its handling of colonial affairs after its bungled withdrawal from Aden and Ian Smith's unilateral declaration of independence (UDI) for Rhodesia.

The discussions in the third round of the respective negative written replies from both sides to the original Spanish proposals and the British counter-proposal were overlaid by acrimonious debate on the legality or otherwise of overflying restrictions and Britain's claim to sovereignty over its half of the isthmus. No discernible progress was made: indeed, the isthmus argument put the two sides even further apart.

As usual, the Spanish government took steps to foul the atmosphere before the fourth round of talks, scheduled for 10th October, by finally abolishing the customs post at La Linea. On the British side, the over-gentlemanly Michael Stewart had been replaced as foreign secretary by the ebullient, no-nonsense, George Brown, who decided that neither side was likely to accept the legal arguments of the other. When the fourth round opened he cut further wrangling by proposing that both sides should put the legal issues to the International Court of Justice at the Hague.

The Spanish delegation refused on the grounds that the Gibraltar problem was political, stemming from the United Nations decolonization resolutions, and was not amenable to legal adjudication. The United Nations – a higher body than the International Court of Justice – had directed Britain and Spain to settle their differences and to decolonize Gibraltar as quickly as possible: reference to the Hague would take years if not decades to reach a decision. With Spain refusing the challenge, the talks were temporarily postponed for the autumnal United Nations diplomatic shadow dancing to take place.

Unfortunately, the Franco government had let popular expectations of a British surrender to Castiella's forensic skills to rise too high. When the Spanish delegation returned empty-handed, anti-British rioting broke out on 30th October all over Spain, coupled with attacks on the British Embassy and consulates during which considerable damage was done to British property. The riots were self-defeating: next day a debate on Gibraltar took place in the House of Commons during which Spanish sympathizers were swept away by a wave of pro-Gibraltar sentiment. Speakers like Sir Alec Douglas Home and Edward Heath were still highly suspicious of Harold Wilson's intentions, and gave further dire political warnings of the political damage which would flow from any sign of weakness in the face of Spanish coercion. Goaded by irate members of the Commons, Fred Lee, the Colonial Secretary, flew out to Gibraltar post-haste for discussions with Salvador, his ministers and the business community on an enhanced aid package. He agreed to another tranche of £600,000 and promised more as soon as the Gibraltar government could define what additional aid was needed.

Welcome though the promises of further aid might be, it was, in fact, the Gibraltarians themselves under Salvador's inspiring leadership, who did most to reorientate the economy of the Rock to withstand further Spanish economic coercion. The heroes of

1966 were the women of Gibraltar who, despite losing their Spanish maids, abandoned their almost Victorian lifestyle confined to their homes, looking after their families, and went out to take jobs to keep the economy from collapsing. The trade unions accepted that men should be encouraged to moonlight to fill the many gaps in the labour market; the business community sought and organized alternative sources of supply principally in Britain, Holland and Morocco; and negotiations were begun with the Moroccan government for additional labour once the Spanish workers were stopped from crossing the frontier, which was so obviously in Madrid's mind despite the damage that it would do to the economy of the Campo.

Although few people realized it at the time, the Spanish coercion had one important positive effect. It united all Gibraltarians and consolidated their identity as a people. Before the Spanish offensive started, they had been uncertain as to whom they really were. They saw themselves as British, but they knew that their forebears had hailed from all over the Western Mediterranean as well as from Britain. Now they knew for certain, thanks to Salvador and Isola hammering home the message at the United Nations, that they were British Gibraltarians and the Rock was their home. They were a people in their own right with an indomitable spirit, which they were about to show as Spanish aggravation grew in intensity.

In December, Salvador and Isola crossed the Atlantic once more to take part in the Gibraltar minuet, which this time was danced by the United Nations Fourth Committee, responsible for trusteeship matters. The anti-British atmosphere had got worse because the Hispanic and Afro-Asian blocs felt that they had the United Kingdom on the run. Most of Britain's colonies had been or were about to be granted their independence in the next few years, and Denis Healey, Wilson's Minister of Defence, was edging towards recommending total withdrawal of British forces from East of Suez. One more concerted effort they thought would see Gibraltar returned to Spain.

The debate, which was a replay of all the old records, turned into farce when the more rabid anti-Gibraltarian members tried to stop Salvador and Isola presenting the Gibraltar case on the grounds that they were nothing more than agents of the administering power sent to ensure the maintenance of the fortress in British hands. In the end, the Chairman granted Salvador and Isola fifteen and ten minutes respectively to put Gibraltar's case. Salvador used his fifteen minutes to highlight the increasing Spanish economic coercion and the virulence of the Spanish press campaign, which were hardly in keeping with Spain's stated desire to give the Gibraltarians a far better future within the Spanish realm. He then reiterated the three options allowed to a colonial people in the United Nations Charter: integration with a sovereign state; independence; or free association with a sovereign state. The Gibraltarians had no wish to integrate with anyone let alone Spain; Gibraltar was too small for total independence; and so the Gibraltarian choice was free association with Britain. He confessed that a movement was starting in Gibraltar for full integration with Britain, but the Gibraltar government and official opposition were against integration because of the probable loss of Gibraltarian identity. He then listed the rights which Gibraltarians already enjoyed and wished to preserve (see Appendix 4).

Peter Isola, in his ten minutes, also castigated Spain's hostility to the Gibraltarians and asked the Committee to remain impartial in this Anglo-Spanish dispute. The Gibraltarians were only observers in it, but were the victims of Spanish coercion. Nevertheless, they had been working hard to make the process of the decolonization of Gibraltar, as they understood it, a success. He himself was heading the Gibraltar Constitutional Committee, which was developing ideas as to:

> ... the form of constitutional development that should take place in Gibraltar without, of course, any change of British sovereignty with a view to insuring permanently, for the people of Gibraltar, the rights which the Charter of the United Nations wishes to see given to colonial people. (*2nd Spanish Red Book*, p 777)

The extraordinary ignorance, bias and hostility within the Fourth Committee were shown when Salvador was cross-examined by Mr Jouejati of Syria. He was chided for having allowed Harold Wilson to meet Ian Smith in HMS *Tiger* at Gibraltar to persuade him to reverse Rhodesia's UDI; and for having accepted and worked with men 'like Gerald Lathbury, whose colonial record in Palestine in '45 and '46 is well known', and Charles Keightley, the general in command of 'the British aggression against Suez'. Salvador had every right to lose his temper when the Saudi Arabian representative, Mr Al Rachach, accused him quite irrelevantly of having three loyalties: to Gibraltar, to Britain and to Zion. Salvador was rebuked for the intemperate language of his reply, but he was fully justified in using what the Uruguayan representative called 'an improper tone, in a voice perhaps too passionate'. (*Ibid*, p 778-789) After the usual behind-the-scenes wrangling, a consensus resolution was drawn up, which regretted the delay in Gibraltar's decolonization and urged Britain and Spain to continue their search for an agreed solution, 'taking into account the interests of the people of the territory'. It was abundantly clear, however, that the Committee accepted the Spanish interpretation of decolonization; that members considered Salvador and Isola little more than British stooges; and above all that every British argument had only one aim in view – maintaining her military grip on the Strait of Gibraltar.

Despite the hostility of the majority of the Committee, Salvador and Isola had made an important impact which was reflected in the resolution. The Committee was even-handed enough, as Isola had asked, not to lay the blame for the delay in negotiations at Britain's door; no mention of paragraph 6 of resolution 1514 (XV) had been made to the exclusion of paragraphs 2 and 5 as Spain had hoped; and it had underscored the 'interests of the people', although the British delegation would have preferred 'wishes of the people'. When the resolution was put to the vote, many people were surprised when Lord Caradon, the British permanent representative to the United Nations, who had listened to the debate with great interest and respect, voted for it. In explaining his vote, he made it clear to the Committee that Britain understood 'interests' to embrace 'wishes': only the people themselves could decide where their true interests lay.

The 1966 United Nations session ended without significant change in the position of the two sides, but the battle lines were more clearly defined. The return of a rocky peninsular to Spain was still seen by the majority of the United Nations as more important than meeting the wishes of a people who had lived on it for two and a half centuries. The reasoning behind the majority view was entirely emotional: the urge to liquidate one of the last remaining symbols of British imperial power. The existence and wishes of the Gibraltarians had still not been imprinted on the minds of the world community. Ways of doing this would have to be found by Salvador and his colleagues in the Gibraltar government and by the Foreign Office in Whitehall. In Gibraltar, as Salvador had warned the Fourth Committee, a new pressure group led by Bob Peliza, advocating integration with Britain as a means of giving the Rock long-term political and economic stability, was gathering support. In the early 1960s, Peliza had set up a small study group to look into the desirability and practicability of integration with Britain. It included Joe Bossano, who had recently gained a BSc in Economics at Birmingham University and was full of ideas about integration, and Maurice Xiberras, a radically minded civil servant, and later school teacher, with equally strong views on integration, who, despite the ban on government employees dabbling in politics, had made a much publicized speech at an Old Grammarians' dinner, advocating integration rather than Salvador and Peter Isola's call for close association with Britain, a term that he considered meaningless.

Initially they drew little support or even interest. They were ostracized by the established politicians and by the business community as political simpletons; ignored by the *Gibraltar Chronicle*, whose editor refused to print their letters; barred from holding meetings in John Mackintosh Hall and shunned by the Catholic Church. Salvador and the AACR were virulently against them not just because they were trying to become a rival political party, but on an important matter of principle: integration would, in the end, destroy the Gibraltarian identity – the very thing that Salvador had been fighting so hard and so long to generate and enhance. All the constitutional advances, which he had and would achieve in the future, were aimed at giving the Gibraltarians the opportunity to handle their own affairs as a recognized people. The hardships involved in withstanding the current Spanish hostility were overwhelmingly worthwhile if they led in the end to freedom in association with Britain.

Peliza's integrationist pressure group eventually hit the headlines thanks to a letter that he wrote to Fred Lee, the Colonial Secretary, in November 1966 after the breakdown of the fourth round of the Anglo-Spanish talks. In it he advocated integration as the only sure way of dispelling Gibraltarian fears of losing their right to stay British. He drew parallels with Britain's offers of integration to Malta and Rhodesia, which were, in fact, never taken up. His letter achieved notoriety by being referred to in the Commons, and as a result the *Chronicle* at long last began to publish IWBP letters. The 1966 United Nations debate and further frontier restrictions, which agitated public opinion in Gibraltar, gave Peliza enough political support to enable him to turn his pressure group into a political party – the Integration with Britain Party (IWBP) – with Joe Bossano as its secretary. It was officially launched on 24th February 1967.

The launch of the IWBP gave Gibraltar three political parties, each of which advocated one of the three United Nations options for decolonization. Salvador, the AACR and most of the independent members of the Legislature advocated free association with Britain; Bob Peliza and the IWBP backed integration; and there was a small group led by J E Triay, which believed in coming to an arrangement with Spain, although not necessarily becoming part of Spain. The idea of integration with Britain began to gain increasing support across the political spectrum. Moreover, the IWBP were well to the left of the AACR, which had moved towards the centre during its 22 years in power. In Joe Bossano, who was to become the TGWU leader of the public sector workers in 1974, Salvador found he had a political rival who could seriously damage the AACR by drawing away the some of the working class vote, which Alberto Risso had previously been able to deliver for the AACR.

The emergence of the IWBP as a political force widened the debate on how to react to the continuing Spanish offensive, but it did little to advertise the need to acknowledge the existence of the Gibraltarians and their wishes to the world at large. Quite who originated the idea of holding a referendum to test their wishes, and indirectly to publicize their existence, is uncertain, but it was Judith Hart, the minister of state in the new Commonwealth Office, who espoused the idea and drove it forward. She invited Lathbury, Salvador and Peter Isola to come to London in February, and again in March, to discuss the idea and to prepare the British position for the fifth round of talks with Spain, which Britain had agreed should be reopened on 18th April 1967.

Nothing changed: Madrid again muddied the waters by another tightening of the screw. On 12th April, Madrid declared, on grounds of national security, a tight air exclusion zone for civil as well as military aircraft over Spanish territory and waters adjacent to the Rock, making the use of the airfield as restricted, if not as dangerous, as possible. In a statement in the Commons the next day, Herbert Bowden, the Commonwealth Secretary, postponed the fifth round of talks as an immediate response and to allow for diplomatic exchanges on the subject. Britain appealed to the International Civil Aviation Authority, but that technical body refused to act because it had no power to deal with political issues. The air exclusion zone became effective on 14th/15th May.

Meanwhile, in Gibraltar, Bob Peliza's IWBP had been gaining significant political support. An opportunity to test it came on 23rd May. Salvador confessed later that he had made one of his few casting errors. After the 1964 election, he had appointed Mrs Chiappe, a school teacher, to be Minister for Education. The other teachers made her life such a misery with their unreasonable demands that she felt that she could not carry on and resigned her seat on the Legislative Council. In the by-election that followed, Peliza stood for the IWBP against Emilio Alvarez of the AACR. In the straight fight and on a high 55.8 per cent by-election turn out, Alvarez just beat Peliza by 145 votes: the IWBP was clearly a coming force, with which the AACR would have to reckon.

The fifth round of talks started on 5th June. They were short-lived: arguments over the air exclusion zone ensured that this would be so. The British delegation soon realized that the Spanish ploy was to attack two objectives with one stone: to inflict further damage on the Rock's economy with the air exclusion zone; and to advertise Spain's objections to the British claim to sovereignty over the southern half of the isthmus, on which Gibraltar's airfield lay. The stone did not strike either target squarely: techniques were soon developed for landing British commercial aircraft on the airfield runway despite the tight turns involved and the difficulties of avoiding the pockets of air turbulence that surround the Rock; and Britain again offered to put the whole sovereignty issue, including the isthmus, to the Hague, which Spain steadfastly refused to do.

Fed up with all this pointless procrastination, Judith Hart, a great supporter of Gibraltar, rose in the House of Commons on 14th June 1967 and announced the British government's intention to hold a referendum at which the people of Gibraltar would be invited to say which of two courses would best serve their interests:

A) To pass under Spanish sovereignty in accordance with the terms proposed by the Spanish Government to Her Majesty's Government on 18th May 1966 [for Castiella's plan; see Appendix 5] or,

B) Voluntarily retain their link with Britain, with democratic local institutions and with Britain retaining its present responsibilities.
(Cmnd 3325, June 1967, p80)

If the majority favoured the first alternative, Britain would open negotiations with Spain accordingly. If the latter was their choice, Britain would regard it as a free and voluntary relationship of the people of Gibraltar with Britain. Discussions on appropriate constitutional changes would follow. The United Nations, the Commonwealth and Spain would be invited to send observers, and Spain would be allowed to put its proposals publicly to the people. Voting would not be until early September to allow time for the electoral register to be prepared, listing only Gibraltarians. The questions had been prepared with immense care during the February and March visits to the Commonwealth office by the Gibraltar team – Lathbury, Salvador and Isola. The permanent under-secretary, Sir Arthur Galsworthy, played a leading role in the negotiations between the British and Gibraltar governments, but the subtle wording of alternative B owes much to Salvador's drafting. It encapsulated his political philosophy and gave him the trigger for further constitutional reform if B was favoured.

Britain notified the United Nations and Spain of her intentions, and invited observers to attend the referendum. The Spanish lobby was still strong in New York. The Committee of 24 decided that the referendum was contrary to its current Gibraltar resolution, which denied the Gibraltarians any say in the Rock's future. In its view, the referendum was yet another ploy to delay the decolonization of Gibraltar. The Spanish government was not even prepared to take up the offer of being allowed to put its 'generous' package to the Gibraltarians. There was one important dissentient voice in Gibraltar: the eminent lawyer, J E Triay. He sponsored a petition, asking that holding the referendum should be reconsidered, or, if it had to be held at all, that the questions should be redrafted to provide for a negotiated solution, which he said:

> . . . tends to be excluded by the terms of the Referendum which, as now drafted, presents the Gibraltarian with the very confrontation with Spain which his leaders have expressed so often a desire to avoid. (Cmnd 3735, August 1968, p 35)

The opposition that his petition generated in Gibraltar was such that he had to appeal to the referendum administrator, Robert Fowler, for police protection, which was provided. Judith Hart stuck to her guns with Salvador's full support despite the umbrage displayed by the world community. The referendum went ahead in an excited, but very orderly way on 10th September 1967. The famous result, which hardly needs repetition here, was 44 votes for Spanish sovereignty and 12,182 votes to stay in free association with Britain, out of an electorate of 12,757. Salvador could not have been more delighted with the result, which gave him a mandate for the further constitutional reforms he had in mind. The Spanish press and foreign ministry had to find an excuse for their dismal showing. The *2nd Spanish Red Book*, published in 1968, comments:

> Many observers of international politics wondered how it was possible to describe as a manifestation of democracy this Gibraltar Referendum which was held under the vigilant guns of Her Majesty's warships. (p 231)

In fact, the naval operations, which provided this excuse, were only a routine minesweeping exercise, carried out by 11 small vessels from England and four from Malta with a destroyer acting as a support ship.

Neither Spain nor the Committee of 24 accepted the relevance of the result, but it confirmed Britain's contention that the Gibraltarians had no wish to pass under Spanish sovereignty. It should have ended the whole tedious wrangle, since people are more important than territory – at least in the Anglo-Saxon mind. Castiella, however, would not give up; and was about to become really nasty.

For Salvador, 1967 was a year of political triumph and domestic unhappiness. Politically, he had been vindicated by the result of the referendum, and he had triggered further constitutional reform. Domestically, he had decided to seek a divorce from Daniela, when the three-year separation point was reached in March 1967. The problems of that divorce will be looked at in the next chapter: it was to be far from straightforward.

CHAPTER 8

THE 1969 CONSTITUTION AND THE START OF THE 15TH SIEGE
1968-1969

The 1969 election result:

J A Hassan (AACR)	7,086	Leader of the Opposition
P J Isola (Isola Group)	5,688	Without Portfolio
R J Peliza (IWBP)	5,495	Chief Minister
M Xiberras (IWBP)	5,414	Labour and Social Security
A W Serfaty (AACR)	3,956	Opposition
A P Montegriffo (AACR)	3,872	Opposition
E J Alvarez (AACR)	3,817	Opposition
M K Featherstone (AACR)	3,691	Opposition
A J Gache (Isola Group)	3,566	Information, Port, Trade and Industry
I Abecasis (AACR)	3,461	Opposition
C Anes (IWBP)	3,406	Public Works and Housing
J Caruana (IWBP)	3,405	Medical and Health Services
L Devincenzi (IWBP)	3,283	Education and Recreation
W M Isola (Isola Group)	3,031	Tourism and Municipal Services
J L Hoare (AACR)	2,921	Opposition

Not elected:

A V Stagnetto (Indep)	2,815
F Gonzalez (IWBP)	2,564
J Gonzalez (AACR)	2,478
A J Baldorino (Indep)	1,927

The referendum cleared the decks in two respects. Whatever Spain and her supporters had to say about the irrelevance of its result to the Anglo-Spanish dispute, it showed beyond all reasonable doubt and to the world at large that the people of Gibraltar had no desire to become part of the Spanish realm, and wished to stay in close association with Britain while becoming as independent as was practicable for so small a state. And, secondly, and almost more importantly from Salvador's point of view, it gave him his mandate to reopen the constitutional issue, which had lain fallow in Whitehall's pending trays since the 1964 constitution was introduced, although the Isola constitutional committee had been at work considering what the next steps should be.

Whitehall had not followed through on further constitutional advance since 1964 because the British government wished to give the Anglo-Spanish talks some small chance of success. This forbearance had been in stark contrast to Madrid's policy of heightening coercion. Quite understandably, Gibraltar's electorate found this 'turning of the other cheek' to Spain abhorrent, and, to some extent, this frustration rubbed off on their local leaders, Salvador and Peter Isola, who had supported, at least in public, most of the Foreign Office's policies. The internal Gibraltarian political debate on the Spanish issue widened perceptibly as Bob Peliza's integrationists gained electoral ground from this frustration, and J E Triay's collaborationist ideas received a reluctant hearing among the business community. The elation engendered by the referendum gradually dissipated during the autumn of 1967, and a mood of frustration took its place. The idea of gaining lasting security through integration instead of free association with Britain held attractions for a growing number of the electorate, although, as Salvador frequently pointed out, it would mean the loss of a measure of Gibraltarian identity. However, as other people remarked, the Scots, Welsh and Irish had managed to retain strong national identities within the United Kingdom: why not the Gibraltarians? In any case, most Gibraltarians had been brought up to consider themselves British, although they had doubts about this being really so. Joining the English, Scots, Welsh and Irish as citizens of the United Kingdom had strong emotional attractions, which Salvador, thanks to his acute awareness of Gibraltarian feelings, was wise enough not to challenge directly, leaving it as an alternative if free association proved politically and constitutionally impracticable. The reverse was true of J E Triay's Spanish-oriented policies: they remained anathema to the electorate and so could be attacked with impunity.

Frustration was evident too on the Spanish side of the border. Locally, the frontier restrictions were an example of cutting off your nose to spite your face. The economy of the Campo, such as it was, went into steep decline with rising unemployment, despite the Spanish government's attempts to industrialize the area artificially. The good life promised to both the Gibraltarians and the inhabitants of the Campo seemed as far away ever. The oil refinery built at the head of the Bay of Gibraltar in the early 1970s brought some extra employment whilst it was being built, but very little once it was in operation. The same applied to the stainless steel rolling mills on the Palmones river. High-rise blocks of flats built on the Spanish half of the isthmus remained half-empty until the frontier reopened in the mid-1980s; and the ship yard built near La Linea has never been used to this day.

At national level in Madrid, Castiella's frustration was understandable. Spain seemed to have won all the United Nations debates on Gibraltar and was utterly convinced that her claim was unimpeachable. And yet he could not drive his advantage home because the devious British paid no noticeable attention to either the Committee of 24, Fourth Committee or even the General Assembly. The British government treated United Nations' resolutions as mere recommendations and not as mandatory instruments. It was not prepared to be ordered around by a bunch of irresponsible former colonies, who were keen to flex their muscles by ganging up against Britain. Misguidedly, Castiella continued developing the economic siege of Gibraltar with the assiduity of a torturer of the Spanish Inquisition. By doing so he only increased Gibraltarian and British determination to resist his efforts to regain the Rock. By the autumn of 1967, the Gibraltar issue had been distilled into a demand by Spain that the

Gibraltarians should not be allowed any say in the decolonization of a parcel of 'Spanish soil', and the British counter that there could be no change of sovereignty over the Rock against their wishes, which had been amply demonstrated in the referendum.

Believing that the extraordinarily favourable result of the referendum gave it the initiative, the Foreign Office proposed on 20th October that the Anglo-Spanish talks should be resumed on the basis of improving relationships over Gibraltar, but excluding the issue of sovereignty: Spain refused. A month later the Foreign Office tried again: this time Castiella asked for a postponement until after the United Nations General Assembly, which was due to meet in December 1967, had considered the latest resolution on Gibraltar, drafted by the Committee of 24 under Spanish pressure on 1st September, ie before the referendum. In it, the Spanish lobby had managed to narrow the options down by specifically stating that decolonization was to be carried out in accordance with paragraph 6 of Resolution 1514 (XV), restoring the integrity of the Spanish realm, and ignoring paragraphs 2 and 5, which supported 'decolonization' of people rather than territory.

Salvador and Isola again put the Gibraltarians' case in New York with the result of the referendum to back it, but they made little impact on the closed minds of the General Assembly, which were more interested in divesting Britain of a military base than doing justice to the local population. Lord Caradon (formerly Sir Hugh Foot, governor of Cyprus), was Britain's permanent representative at the United Nations. His socialist credentials were as far beyond doubt as those of his brother, Michael Foot, the revered Labour leader. He spoke and voted determinedly against the Committee of 24's resolution, and was aghast when the General Assembly passed it by a substantial majority (73 for, 19 against with 24 abstentions). In a short speech in which he rejected the resolution, he said:

> Throughout the debates of the Fourth Committee both this year and before, we have emphasized that there are two basic principles which we cannot betray: first, the principle that the interest of the people must be paramount, and, secondly, that the

people have the right freely to express their own wishes as to their future.

. . . we shall not be deterred, nor shall we be deflected from carrying out our obligations. Again therefore I say that my Government could not accept a Resolution which sought to take sides in a territorial dispute between two member states, and at the same time sought to ignore the freely expressed wishes of the overwhelming majority of the people concerned. (Cmnd 3735, August 1968, p 50)

In conversation, he let it be known that he considered the passing of the resolution as 'unworthy of the United Nations and a disgrace to its committees'. Salvador was even more outspoken, saying:

Abuse of fact, distortion and deliberate lies have won the day. Gibraltar is ready to resist being handed over to Spain, and the Gibraltarians are not going to be deterred by any more restrictions from the Spanish. (Morris and Haig, *The Eternal Triangle*, p 37)

Flushed with what he described as a 'glittering victory' at the United Nations, Castiella demanded on 12th January 1969 a reopening of talks in Madrid, suggesting 18th/20th March for them. In his letter, Castiella tried to be conciliatory in a backhanded sort of way:

The Spanish Government would like to remove from the negotiations the idea of a struggle between nations in which there could be victors and vanquished and believes that the restitution of Gibraltar to Spain is an inescapable fact of our time which, if carried out by means of sincere dialogue, will benefit the permanent interests of both peoples. (Comnd 3735, August 1968, p 51)

This time, it was the British side that fortuitously fouled the atmosphere before the talks began. On 4th February, Lord Shepherd, minister of state in the Commonwealth Office, arrived in Gibraltar for discussions with Salvador, Peter Isola and all those who had been involved in formulating the Gibraltarian requirements for the next constitutional advance. No secret was made of his visit nor of its purpose. Madrid protested immediately it was announced in the House of Commons, but to no avail. In consequence, when the March talks did start, they broke up after two days of acrimonious exchanges. The Spanish delegation was only prepared to discuss the implementation of the latest United Nations' resolution, which had been firmly rejected by Lord Caradon in New York; and the British side vainly tried to coax the Spaniards into accepting that the frontier restrictions were doing the Spanish case more harm than good, and must be lifted before there could be any progress in normalizing Anglo-Spanish relations.

Although Peter Isola chaired the constitutional committee, Salvador was still closely involved in its deliberations, and it was he who persuaded Sir Gerald Lathbury, the Governor, to invite Lord Shepherd out to the Rock for face to face discussions with Gibraltar ministers and the business community about constitutional matters and the economy. When asked how it was that he had put so much effort over so many years into the successive revisions of the Gibraltar constitution, Salvador explained that his interest in constitutional law had been fired by Mr W A L Raeburn, whose chambers at 5 King's Bench Walk he had joined after passing his bar finals and being called by the Middle Temple, on 26th January 1939. He occupied the desk recently vacated by another student practitioner, David Marshall, who was also to become a prominent politician in his own country as Chief Minister of Singapore, and role model for Salvador.

In the early 1950s, when Salvador was about to become Chief Member in the Gibraltar Legislative Council, he visited London by happy coincidence at the same time as Marshall. Both men were there for constitutional talks with ministers and officials in Whitehall. Marshall had already briefed their old master, W A L Raeburn, and also Professor Ivor Jennings, the greatest expert at that time on constitutional development, on Singapore's case. Raeburn invited Salvador to dinner to meet Marshall and Jennings, proud to have been the tutor of two pupils, who by then had become the leaders of their peoples at opposite ends of the earth. At that time, Singapore was further advanced constitutionally than Gibraltar, and so could provide useful precedents. Both were essentially fortress colonies, although Singapore was far larger and had the vast wealth of a world trading centre. Marshall was able to advise Salvador on ways and means of making progress in their mutual problem of squeezing increasing measures of internal self-government out of the reluctant Colonial Office. They met subsequently on several occasions and corresponded to exchange ideas. Marshall's friendship was of immense value to Salvador, particularly in preparing his important constitutional proposals of October 1955 (see Appendix 1).

Gradualness was the key to successful constitutional advance. Whitehall had to be convinced at each stage that the security of the fortress could not be endangered by any irresponsible action of the local government if its powers were to be increased, and that there were enough men of the right calibre to handle the next stages in the devolution of power. A two way street of confidence had to be built between the Governor and his Chief Minister. By the time Lord Shepherd arrived in Gibraltar, Salvador had served seven governors. They had come to respect him as Gibraltar's undoubted and highly experienced political leader, and in return he gave them the ideas and arguments that they needed to pursue the constitutional advances which he wanted and which Whitehall would never have initiated of its own free will unless goaded by Gibraltar. Salvador was the perceptive, tactful and ever practicable goad.

Lord Shepherd's visit and the quick breakdown of the March talks in Madrid gave Castiella another excuse - not that he needed one - to twist the coercive screw once more. Claiming that Britain was basing her case on the Treaty of Utrecht, he declared that Spain would do so too. The treaty declared that there was to be no communication by land between the Campo and the Rock, and so he warned that the frontier gates would be closed on 6th May to all but the 5,000 Spanish workers, who still had work permits, and to Gibraltarians with special passes. Tourists and other visitors would have to use the Algeciras ferry.

In the meantime, Gibraltar was to be shaken by what became known as the 'Dove' affair or riot. On 1st April, a letter with a strong Gibraltarian nationalist flavour was published in the *Chronicle*, signed by 'The Doves' - J E and J J Triay, A C Ocaña, Joseph Coll, Charlie Cruz and Albert Falquero, the majority of whom were directors on the board of the Chamber of Commerce. In it, Salvador's coalition government was accused of political bankruptcy, and a demand was made for a Gibraltarian negotiated settlement with both Spain and Britain, the latter being accused of being 'purely defensive, and patently passive'. The thrust of the letter was contained in its second paragraph:

> It is an appeal to those of us to whom the word 'Gibraltar' and 'Gibraltarian' signifies and represents a character and a way of life which is our own. Because it is our own, and because the Gibraltarian is a socially mature adult, the responsibility for the preservation of this way of life and for the survival of the Gibraltarian in the final analysis is ours and ours alone. (Report of the Commission of Inquiry, 1st August 1968, Appx C.1)

These sentiments were unexceptionable, but the idea that the Gibraltarians could negotiate a replacement for the Treaty of Utrecht with the Spanish government, which did not even acknowledge their existence as a people, let alone allow them have any say in the future, as Madrid saw it, of 'a piece of sacred Spanish soil', was totally naive.

Nevertheless, the Doves thought that they had evidence to the contrary, although they did not reveal this in their first letter. Their crime in the eyes of the electorate was not naivety, but their apparent pro-Spanish attitudes. That afternoon, Salvador called all the elected members of the Legislature together, and drafted with them a response from his coalition government, which appeared in the *Chronicle* next day. Their letter, quite rightly, doubted the possibility of a negotiated settlement, and challenged the Doves to produce specific proposals, which were likely to succeed.

Feeling soon began to mount against the Doves. J E Triay had already lost most of his political credibility by speaking on the radio and petitioning formally against holding the referendum. Such was the outcry about the Doves' first letter that A C Ocaña publicly dissociated himself from his colleagues, who were compelled by public resentment to resign from the Chamber of Commerce. But worse was to come. On 4th April, the Doves' reply to the government's challenge to produce specific proposals was published in the *Chronicle*. Their ideas for constitutional reforms to bring about an autonomous Gibraltar were not very different from those already being negotiated by Salvador with the British government. But they suggested, again naively, that they could win Spanish co-operation and friendship without any change of sovereignty, which, in their view, rested with the people of Gibraltar and with no one else. Three flags would be flown over the Rock - the Union Jack, the Gibraltar City flag and the Spanish flag. They were not suggesting a condominion, but would allow the Spanish flag to be flown as a symbol of their autonomous Gibraltar having had its origin in Spain's acceptance of their proposed replacement of Utrecht by a new Anglo-Spanish Convention.

In their enthusiasm to show that such a minor cosmetic gesture would bring about a settlement with Madrid, they then revealed:

> We went to Madrid to ascertain whether they [their proposals] were acceptable to Spain and we were assured by the Foreign Minister Sr Castiella himself that they were. Will the Government now take this matter up and pursue these investigations further?
> (*Ibid*, Appx C.3)

The fat was truly in the fire: the fact that the Doves had been in Madrid was resented by most people as much as their suggestion that the Spanish flag should fly over the Rock. Gibraltarian anger flared to white heat when, during the night of 5th April, the Spanish television service broadcast a commentary on the Doves' proposals, in which it was stated that their ideas would be acceptable to Spain, but only after a transfer of sovereignty, and that the Doves had been so informed!

Before dawn, Dove cars and property had been daubed with paint, and next morning there was general excitement in the Piazza where people were congregating to buy lottery tickets and to discuss the Spanish TV snub to the Doves, but no more than that. The police were expecting some relatively minor incidents, perpetrated by anti-Dove activists. The possibility of mob violence in Gibraltar had always seemed so remote that it was not in any policeman's mind on 6th April. The police had had little or no training in riot control, and there were no plans for or training in army/police co-operation if a political protest got out of hand. Calling in the army was almost unthinkable to Salvador and his ministers, who believed that everything should be done to avoid endangering the good relations that existed between the people and the garrison, which was there primarily for British strategic purposes and not for internal security duties within the colony. Moreover, there was an understandable psychological barrier to calling on the garrison for help. He and his AACR colleagues had been trying with considerable success since the war to demonstrate their competence in government: calling out troops to help in dealing with their own people would be an admission of failure.

At about 9.30am, political hotheads well known to the police but considered harmless and unlikely to be able to attract much support, began haranguing the crowd in the Piazza, demanding that Doves be deported or hanged as traitors. How wrong the police were in their assessment. Shouting at the top of their voices, they gathered a small crowd around them, which grew as more and more people arrived to see what was going on. The crowd started to cheer and egg on the protesters. There had been some rowdy anti-Dove scenes in the pubs during the night spurred on by the Spanish TV programme. Some of the tougher elements in Gibraltarian society were still in a destructive mood next morning and provided the rabble rousers with a hard core of rioters prepared to attack the Doves and their property if the government took no action against them.

Some twenty or so of the most determined Dove opponents set

off for the Convent gathering supporters on the way. By the time they reached the Convent, they had a couple of hundred people following them of whom about 50 were intent on rough justice for the Doves, the rest being interested spectators mainly out for the fun of a protest march. The crowd was noisy but orderly. Sergio Gustavino who was among the group who had started it all in the Piazza, was invited into the Convent with a small delegation in the time-honoured fashion of protest marches in Gibraltar. The Governor heard their views on the deportation of traitors and assured them that he was consulting London on what action should be taken. Apparently satisfied, the crowd began to disperse, but a small mob of men, still bent on violence, returned up Main Street hurling abuse at Dove business premises, but, as yet, doing little or no physical damage. The violence started with the overturning of an Allied Bakeries van, owned by Albert Falquero and Charlie Cruz, in Irish Town where the Triays had their residences and legal chambers.

Overturning the van, and a little later a Dove-owned bus, seemed to embolden the mob, which set about systematically targeting and damaging any Dove property which the police had been unable to reach ahead of them. The Commissioner of Police foolishly tried to lob two tear gas canisters, which was all he had with him, into the crowd. It was far too little and only infuriated the mob, turning it against the police. The Commissioner had to escape into a nearby house from which he was rescued much later.

When Salvador heard what was going on, he decided that he had to intervene to stop the mayhem. Word went round that he would address the people from the balcony of the City Hall at about 1.30pm. A crowd of about a thousand congregated in the Piazza, of which only about ten ringleaders and by now some 200 toughs comprised the hard core of the destructively inclined mob. Salvador's first attempt to speak from the balcony was drowned out by excited shouting for the expulsion of the Doves, and for the dismissal of the Commissioner of Police. Handed a loudhailer, he was a little more successful and invited a delegation from the mob to meet him in his committee room. He came out onto the balcony again with some of the delegates, but could not be heard when he tried to address the crowd, so he took the bold decision to go down with some of his ministers into the crowd to mix with and talk to them face to face. Waving away the police escort, he waded in amongst the mob and succeeded in persuading them to disperse, which they did by about 2.30pm.

Salvador's success was short-lived. Some of the mob had not gone to the Piazza and had carried on attacking Dove property. The pubs were open, and gangs of men reformed to carry on the attacks during the afternoon. The worst and most spectacular incident was the burning of J E Triay's yacht, berthed off the Canneries wharf, and the most extensive damage was done to the widely scattered premises and vans of Allied Bakeries. Enraged though the mobs were at what they deemed was Dove treachery, they only damaged Dove property and there was no looting. Moreover, the police were never attacked deliberately, although several suffered minor injuries in scuffles.

In the Convent, the Governor was in a difficult position. Information coming from the police was sketchy. He had plenty of troops if he needed them, but he was not prepared to call them out unless the Commissioner of Police requested him to do so and the Chief Minister agreed. By about 3pm rumours of further damage being done after Salvador had, as he thought, persuaded the mob to disperse, reached Lathbury, who warned the deputy fortress commander to move troops down to HMS Rooke, the naval barracks, in case intervention became necessary. He summoned the Permanent Secretary, the Flag Officer Gibraltar the Attorney-General and Salvador to the Convent. Both the Governor and Salvador were anxious not to involve the garrison, but the ultimate decision lay with the Governor.

At first, reports suggested that the police were regaining control, but with the burning of J E Triay's yacht it became clear to Lathbury that the police needed help. He sent out military officer patrols to assess the situation. By 4pm he was satisfied from their reports that the situation was deteriorating fast. He phoned the Commissioner of Police and told him bluntly to make up his mind whether he needed military assistance or not. The Commissioner quickly agreed that he did, and Salvador, with greatest reluctance, swallowed the bitter pill of military intervention. Despite there having been no pre-planning or training in army/police co-operation, the action of the troops was quick, discreet and effective. Unarmed except for pick helves for use as batons, they quickly took over guarding the mob's most likely targets and sent Land Rover mounted patrols into the city. It was enough of a show of force to dampen enthusiasm for any further violence amongst the mobs, who gradually dispersed to avoid arrest.

There was some suggestion at the time that the systematic way in which Dove property was attacked pointed to there having been some pre-planning and organization behind it. The commission of inquiry examined this possibility, but concluded:

> We are satisfied that the disturbances were not the result of an organized conspiracy. The evidence indicates that there had been discussions among certain sections of the Gibraltar population, largely the rougher elements of the working class, and especially the 'taxi-driver' element, about the activities of the Doves and reprisals which might be taken against them. But the disturbances themselves appear to have been spontaneous, arising out of the tense political situation and resentment against the Doves, inflamed by Gustavino's eloquence. (*Ibid*, p 30, para 160)

The greatest mistake made by the police through lack of experience in riot-control was not to have arrested the ringleaders more quickly. Had Gustavino been arrested for incitement to riot before the march on the Convent, events might have taken a less violent turn. As it was, the whole affair supplemented the referendum result in confirming the grass-root determination of Gibraltarians to have no truck with Spain and to support Salvador's government in opposing the Dove faction.

Castiella's announcement of the imposition of tighter land frontier restrictions in strict accordance with the provisions of Utrecht brought Salvador and Isola back to London towards the end of April for a week's discussions on the 'sustain and support policy' and on constitutional reform. At their meetings with George Thomson, the Commonwealth Secretary, they went over the contingency plans, which had been maturing for some time, for the replacement of Spanish labour with Moroccans; for British military assistance in maintaining essential services such as power, water supply and sewerage if Spanish labour was suddenly withdrawn; and the unobtrusive reinforcement of the garrison, naval guard-ships and air defence fighters. On 6th May, the Spanish government did, as they had said they would, close the land frontier to all but Spanish workers. Next day, George Thomson removed any doubts that still lingered about the Wilson government's Gibraltar policy by declaring forthrightly during a House of Commons debate on Gibraltar:

> HMG will never betray the rights of the people of Gibraltar to determine where their own interests lie. I give the assurance that in no circumstances will Britain surrender sovereignty over Gibraltar against the wishes of the people of Gibraltar. We will protect and support them whatever the threats that are brought to bear on them. (Hansard, 7th May 1968)

In this statement lay not only confirmation of the 'sustain and support' policy, but also the seeds of the ultimate wording of the famous preamble to the 1969 Constitution. George Thomson followed through with a two-week visit to the Rock to plan the way ahead with the governor, Salvador and the other members of the Legislative Council. On his arrival, Salvador presented him with a memorandum containing four crucial points as an agenda for talks on further constitutional advance promised in the referendum questionnaire:

> 1. Gibraltar should cease to be a Colony and be accorded a new political status which would contain a reference to Britain's permanent and exclusive sovereignty.
> 2. Gibraltarians should be exempted from the provisions of the Commonwealth Immigration Act of 1962.
> 3. Gibraltar's affairs should be transferred from the Commonwealth Office to the Home Office.

4. Britain should declare an intention not to exercise her rights under the option clause of the Treaty of Utrecht without the consent of the people of Gibraltar expressed through a two-thirds majority in a referendum. (Morris and Haig, p 41)

Salvador's realization of the need to steal some of the IWBP's clothes before the next election is evident in points two and three. George Thomson met point 2 with an assurance that 'all Gibraltarians who want to come to Britain will be able to do so'. He met the others by agreeing to the setting-up of a constitutional conference under Lord Shepherd, which would be held in Gibraltar in July.

The Shepherd Constitutional Conference, which lasted from 16th to 24th July, did not start very auspiciously. Shepherd came out with a team of advisers, who comprised the British delegation. Inadvisably, he opened the conference by saying that the new constitution must not conflict with the Treaty of Utrecht, which was self-evident, but he then went on to say that nor should it have the effect of worsening Anglo-Spanish relations! Nothing could have been more tactless in the circumstances with Spain again tightening the economic garrotte around Gibraltar's neck. Here was the head of the British delegation declaring publicly what every Gibraltarian had always feared - and still do to this day - that Anglo-Spanish relations carry more weight in Whitehall than Gibraltar's political and economic well-being.

Salvador was quick to take him up on the issue, saying in his opening remarks:

> . . . it is most unpalatable to be told at this crucial stage that we, who have been on the receiving end all the time should not, by any new constitution that we may work out together, make Anglo-Spanish relations any worse than they are . . .
> . . . let there be no doubt that this aspect of the deliberations is uppermost in the minds of the people of Gibraltar today and in the days that will follow. It will be a sad day for Gibraltar if at the end of these talks some acceptable formula has not been found. (*Ibid*, p 42)

His remarks clearly made an impact on the British delegation since the rest of the conference was both cordial and successful. The two sides had done a great deal of work refining their ideas over the previous four years and they were not too far apart in their concepts. The outcome was sensibly ingenious and was unique to Gibraltar, reflecting as it did the continuing, though diminishing, military needs of the fortress and the essential rights of the civilian population.

The fundamental decision was to amalgamate the Legislative and City Councils to form a single House of Assembly, which had been debated at the Lansdowne Conference of 1964 but left for further study. There were to be 15 elected members plus two officials – the attorney general and the financial secretary. To form a government, a party or coalition would have to win eight seats.

The uniqueness of the agreed constitution lay in its division of powers. In most British colonial constitutions the powers of the governor are defined: the local government is responsible for all else. The reverse was to be the case in Gibraltar. The local government's powers were defined in a 'List of Defined Domestic Matters' for which it was to be responsible but which excluded anything that might have a conceivable impact on the security of the fortress: the governor remained responsible for everything else, which included the royal prerogative, foreign affairs, defence and ensuring 'good government' and economic stability.

To the Gibraltarians, however, and to the Spaniards as well, the most important aspect of the Shepherd Constitution was the crucial preamble, in the drafting of which Salvador led the AACR, IWBP and the Isola Group, though not the Doves, in playing an active and constructive part. Bob Peliza and the IWBP legal adviser, Sir Frederick Bennett, are often given the credit for devising the formula, as is Lord Shepherd himself, but the truth is that it was the product of a combination of many minds and drafting skills both in Gibraltar and Whitehall, which led to the wording acceptable to the Parliament in Westminster and the Legislative Council in Gibraltar. In the long discussions, chaired by Lord Shepherd in Gibraltar, Salvador had Aurelio Montegriffo and Abraham Serfaty in the AACR team; Bob Peliza brought in Maurice Xiberras from the IWBP; and Peter Isola represented the Isola group of independents.

The final version of the preamble was in two parts, enshrining: first, British sovereignty; and, second, the paramountcy of the wishes of Gibraltar's people:

> Whereas Gibraltar is part of Her Majesty's dominions and the British Government have given assurance to the people of Gibraltar that Gibraltar will remain part of her Majesty's dominions unless and until an Act of Parliament otherwise provides, and furthermore that Her Majesty's Government will never enter into arrangements under which the people of Gibraltar would pass under the sovereignty of another state against their freely and democratically expressed wishes. (1969 Gibraltar Constitution)

The preamble was a triumph for those who drafted it, and for Salvador as Chief Minister, whose balanced input to the debate had been crucial. It was equally a triumph for the people of Gibraltar, who deserved this granite-like reassurance of British support in the face of deepening Spanish hostility. It has, indeed, acted ever since as Gibraltar's 'safety net' in the continuing struggle with Spain over her claim to sovereignty over the Rock. Much to Spain's annoyance Britain had formally given the Gibraltarians the veto in the Anglo-Spanish dispute, which Spain had tried to deny for so long and was to go on doing. The preamble signalled to Spain that Gibraltar was far from ripe for the picking as Franco had thought and Castiella still believed. With the specific assurances set out in the preamble, the people of Gibraltar were now even less likely to give in to Spanish coercion or to the anti-British antagonism of the Hispanic and Afro-Asian blocs in the United Nations.

Madrid did not read 'the writing on the wall' and reacted with accustomed hostility to the further enhancement of Gibraltarian powers of internal self-government. Castiella protested to U Thant about Britain's flagrant disregard for the United Nations' resolutions on Gibraltar, but the British reply on 6th August was bluntly robust. United Nations' resolutions were recommend-ations and not mandatory. As Britain had mandatory obligations to the people of Gibraltar under Article 73 of the Charter, she was not prepared to act on the subordinate 4th Committee's 'diktats', which ran contrary to the provisions of the Charter.

Spain could not take these rebuffs lying down. She once more engineered a further tightening of the United Nations' resolution on Gibraltar at the December meeting of the General Assembly. A deadline for decolonization of the territory, using the Spanish interpretation of decolonization, was set for 1st October 1969. Lord Caradon rejected the resolution, saying that it was happily so far removed from possibility as to be incredible, and Britain would not accept it.

Sir Gerald Lathbury's tenure as Governor came to an end on 1st January 1969 before the new constitution was actually finalized in Whitehall. He had given his wholehearted support to Gibraltar's cause throughout his three and a half years in office, doing everything that he could to squeeze financial help out of the British treasury and backing Salvador in his quest for further constitutional advance. One thing he did not have to worry about was maintaining the morale of the people: Spain did that for him by the obtuseness of Castiella's restrictions. Their forebears had suffered far greater hardships during the sieges of Gibraltar by the combined forces of France and Spain, and they were not to be cowed by economic restrictions and vitriolic propaganda. As the riots showed, few Gibraltarians wished to be associated with the Doves.

Salvador was sorry to say goodbye to Gerald Lathbury. They had worked well together, and they had a common bond in having to face difficult marital problems. Lathbury's own marriage had broken down before he had been appointed governor, but Lady Lathbury agreed to accompany him out to Gibraltar to act as his hostess during his tenure. It was not a happy time in the Convent since not only was their relationship extraordinarily difficult, but she also spent a great deal of her time in Spain, using the Algeciras ferry to get there. They were eventually divorced after they had left Gibraltar. He remarried later and went to live in Spain near Alicante where he could enjoy his hobby of birdwatching.

Admiral Sir Varyl Begg, the first sailor to be appointed Governor and C-in-C of the Rock, arrived on 17th January. Admiral Earl Mountbatten, who was chief of defence staff, had been pressing for the integration of the three armed services, and, although he did not succeed in this, he did bring them closer together. One of his measures was to appoint tri-service commanders in each of the overseas commands. The Near East Command in Cyprus had a general as C-in-C; the Middle East Command in Aden had an air marshal; and as the Far East Command in Singapore was being wound up, which should have had an admiral as C-in-C, the navy was given Gibraltar as its share of the defence patronage – hence Admiral Begg's appointment. Each of the C-in-C appointments was to be rotated between the three services. Begg's successor, for example, would be an airman. For the first four months of his tenure Sir Varyl and Tom Oates, the new permanent secretary, who had replaced the long serving and able Darell Bates, were preoccupied with finalizing the details of the new constitution with Whitehall and Salvador's coalition government, and with facing up to Spain's final twists of the coercive garrotte. The constitution was published early in May and received the Royal Assent on the 30th of that month. The date of the first general election for the new House of Assembly was set for July. Madrid lost no time in completing the economic investment of the Rock. On 8th June the last of the Spanish labour force were stopped from crossing the frontier and joined the ranks of the Campo's growing army of unemployed; on 22nd June the frontier gates were finally closed on the Spanish side to all comers; and five days later Spain stopped the Algeciras ferry, thus breaching their own interpretation of the Treaty of Utrecht whereby communication with Spain was always to be allowed by sea. The 15th siege of the Rock had begun, and was to prove the longest.

While these final Spanish coercive measures were being imposed, there was a further upsurge in Gibraltarian unity and defiance of Spain, which could not be matched in the coalition government because electioneering for July was already under way. It was the first election to be fought on genuine party lines. In previous elections it had been the AACR party organization against a number of independents without party machinery, each with his own personal policy and dependent upon his political charisma. This time it would be a fight between two organized parties, Salvador's AACR and Bob Peliza's IWBP, with a number of independents thrown in to complicate the arguments and the voting. In the coming election the electorate would be faced with two clear alternative policies for Gibraltar's way ahead, to which there was no easy answer and on which there was unlikely to be a clear-cut verdict. The Isola group of independents would probably hold the balance of power. Put in its simplest terms the question was, did the people support Salvador's policy of working towards full independence in 'free association with Britain', or did they prefer Bob Peliza's 'integration with Britain'?

Salvador was totally committed to his concept of 'free association' for which he had fought so hard and so often at the United Nations and in Whitehall. As one of the AACR Committee put it, 'Gibraltar with but not under Britain'. Salvador, however, refused to endorse some of the younger AACR members' cry of 'Gibraltar for the Gibraltarians'. He knew that this was impracticable. Instead he stressed the loss of Gibraltarian identity which might result from integration.

Peliza symbolized the Gibraltarian dream of being part of the United Kingdom. He articulated the deep-seated desires of most Gibraltarians, who had always wanted to be treated as truly British and not just as colonial subjects of the British Crown. Spain's implacable hostility tended to help the integrationists. In the choice between maintaining the fullest possible Gibraltarian identity, which Salvador advocated, and Peliza's policy of seeking integration, it seemed to many electors that the chances of greater political security and economic stability, which might flow from integration, could outweigh some loss of Gibraltarian identity.

The Isola group tended to side with the AACR in favouring 'free association', but their support was ambivalent as later events were to show. The Doves decided that discretion was the better part of valour and did not enter the campaign.

It was not, however, political rivalry that broke up the Hassan/Isola coalition. Sadly, it was Salvador's divorce bill that caused an irreparable personal breach between the two leaders, who had worked so closely together at the United Nations and in their coalition government. As in most Roman Catholic countries, divorce was not recognized at the time in the laws of Gibraltar, except on grounds of adultery, which were no part of the original Supreme Court case for Salvador's judicial separation from Daniela on grounds of desertion and cruelty. As the judicial separation, which he had been granted in 1967, did not enable him to start a new life with Marcelle Bensimon, he gave serious consideration to leaving Gibraltar and setting up a legal practice in England so that he could eventually divorce Daniela under English law and marry Marcelle. His closest friends and political colleagues such as Aurelio Montegriffo and Abraham Serfaty were aghast at the idea of his services being lost to Gibraltar and to the AACR, and persuaded him to seek a bill of divorce in the Legislative Council as had been the practice in England in the 19th century and was still used in Canada. As divorce was permissible in the Jewish community, and there was already a growing body of opinion that divorce should be legalized in Gibraltar, Salvador accepted their advice and approached the Governor, still Sir Gerald Lathbury, for his views on the use of the Canadian precedent in Gibraltar.

Fortunately, Gibraltar's Attorney-General, Sir Kenneth Roberts-Wray, was an eminent constitutional lawyer with a distinguished career in the Colonial Service, and was thus well equipped to deal with this delicate case. He advised the Governor that a bill of divorce could be presented to the Legislative Council, but that the Governor's assent could not be given to it without the prior consent of the Secretary of State, Anthony Greenwood. This was because of the well-worn Colonial Office practice of restricting governors' powers in its overseas territories through royal instructions, which listed measures that required the secretary of state's prior consent rather than subsequent approval. Any law affecting divorce was on this list. Nevertheless, Sir Kenneth advised that the consent was unlikely to be withheld since the Jewish community accepted divorce. However, the possibility had to be faced that there might be, and, indeed there was, criticism among the Catholic community and others, that the Chief Minister was seeking special privilege beyond the normal reach of the ordinary citizens.

Salvador was still reluctant to proceed with a divorce bill since he was not entirely convinced that the Secretary of State's consent would be given once the bill had passed through the Legislative Council. He took up the matter with his old friend Sir Arthur Galsworthy, the permanent under-secretary of state at the Commonwealth Office, who had been so helpful to him in drafting the referendum questionnaire two years earlier. He asked Sir Arthur to seek the likely views of the Secretary of State – that is of the ministry – before going any further. Sir Arthur replied in a long and friendly letter, showing genuine concern for Salvador's future happiness, but saying that he did not see any prospect of the Secretary of State approving the bill. His staff had researched precedents in other colonies where there were marked religious differences among the population, as in Cyprus, and in other dependent territories, and had come regretfully to this inevitable but disappointing conclusion.

Salvador's friends within and without the government and the Legislative Council urged him not to give up. The acute political instincts, possessed by most Gibraltarians, suggested to them that the Secretary of State was hardly likely to override a bill blessed by the local Gibraltarian legislature, which had no vital political significance outside Gibraltar. Salvador, at last, agreed to take the risk, knowing the Governor and Attorney-General, as well as the Gibraltar Legislature, would support him.

The Hassan Divorce Bill was presented by Anthony Baldorino (Jr), an independent, on 1st January 1969, just as Lathbury was leaving. Salvador himself, of course, took no part in the proceedings at any time during the Council's deliberations. Under normal circumstances it should have been a simple case of confirming the Supreme Court's original findings that there had been an irreparable breakdown of the marriage, and sanctioning the divorce. But the circumstances were not normal in two important respects: with a general election due within months, there was the temptation to make political capital out of the case, which Salvador's political opponents could not resist; and there was also the underlying ground swell of political disquiet over the issue of divorce in Gibraltar with the pro- and anti-divorce lobbies seeking support from the case for their arguments.

Aurelio Montegriffo moved the second reading in April. He argued that as Gibraltar was essentially a Roman Catholic community, which abhorred divorce, it was preferable to cater for the exceptions among the other faiths rather than to attempt to change the law even though there was growing pressure to bring Gibraltar's law into line with English divorce laws. It should be open to non-Catholics to bring in private members' bills as Salvador was doing. Peter Isola and Sol Seruya, Salvador's main political opponents, took Daniela's side and complained at once that the second reading should not have been allowed to go ahead without Lady Daniela being properly represented. Salvador had an old friend, who was one of London's leading 'divorce' silks, Joe Jackson QC, to represent him, whereas Daniela had only her own local solicitor, Bernard Vaughan, to put her case. Proceedings were, therefore, adjourned for a month while Vaughan sought and briefed a silk for Daniela.

In the meantime, a select committee, chaired by the Attorney General, was appointed to scrutinize the bill and to report back to the Legislative Council. The members were Aurelio Montegriffo, Guy Stagnetto and Anthony Baldorino. Vaughan obtained Geoffrey Hollis Crispin QC to represent Daniela, but he took an inordinately long time preparing his case, which included having copies made of the Supreme Court tapes of the original ten-day separation proceedings. Joe Jackson, on Salvador's behalf, objected to further delays on the reasonable grounds that the breakdown of the marriage was not in question. A motion put forward by Peter Isola for a further two months' adjournment was defeated, and on 31st May the Hassan Divorce Bill was passed by the Legislative Council. Sir Peter Russo, Aurelio Montegriffo, Albert Risso, Emilio Alvarez, Guy Stagnetto, and Anthony Baldorino voted in favour, believing that Daniela had been given ample time to brief her defence Counsel; the Attorney General, Financial Secretary and Louis Triay abstained; and Peter Isola and Sol Seruya voted against on the grounds of undue haste and objection to the composition of the select committee, which they considered biased in Salvador's favour.

Hollis Crispin did not endear himself to Salvador and his colleagues when he stated publicly that it was his view that Daniela should have cross-petitioned for divorce on grounds of admitted adultery by Salvador. He had filed a discretionary statement before the Supreme Court hearing, admitting adultery, but Daniela had refused to use it either out of spite or out of financial considerations. Joe Jackson responded by calling Crispin's views 'Victorian': by modern standards it had been a trivial disclosure by Salvador himself, and Daniela saw it as of no importance since it occurred outside Gibraltar. Crispin also irritated the Catholic anti-divorce lobby by arguing that the best course of action by the Legislature would have been to change the law, giving the man in street equal access to divorce. This did eventually happen, but not until 1984 when the Divorce Ordinance eventually came into force. Salvador's friends were delighted when they were proved right in their assessment of the Secretary of State's reaction when the bill was sent to him for consent. On 25th July, only a fortnight later and just five days before the general election for the new House of Assembly, the Governor, now Admiral of the Fleet Sir Varyl Begg, called Salvador to tell him of the Secretary of State's approval. Sir Varyl commented, 'This is what the people want, isn't it?'

This was certainly so: Arthur Greenwood had seen no reason to oppose the wishes of the Gibraltarian electorate's representatives in the Legislative Council. Sir Varyl's remark was prophetic as the results of forthcoming election were to show.

The case and controversy surrounding it, and about divorce in general, had filled the local press and media for weeks. To avoid further unwelcome publicity, Salvador and Marcelle were married quietly at the registry office early on election morning and then went off to continue their election campaign. The media's attention was so taken up with reporting the election that the news of their marriage did not break until after the poll was closed.

At the election, there were a record number of 19 candidates, and there was a high turnout of 71.4 per cent. For the first time, voting was to be by direct voting instead of proportional representation. Each elector had eight votes so that he could cover the eight candidates needed to form a government. The new system, however, was not too well understood by the electorate or the party organizations. Instead of using all eight votes on the candidates of one specific party, some electors used, say, six on the party of their choice and two on personalities whom they trusted in other parties or independents.

When the results were declared, it was immediately evident that the divorce controversy had done little damage to Salvador's standing with the electorate. He was given another clear vote of confidence. He topped of the poll once more with 7,086 votes to Peter Isola in second place had 5,688. Sol Seruya did not stand for election. He could see no political future for those who sought economic collaboration with Spain. He left for Israel to become director of the United Israel Appeal in Jerusalem, and later became Israeli Ambassador to the Philippines.

Unfortunately for Salvador, the eighth of his AACR candidates, Francis Gonzalez, was not elected due to some AACR supporters scattering their votes instead of blockvoting, leaving the AACR without an overall majority and with a need to form a new coalition government. The IWBP won five and the Isola Group three seats. Salvador, however, had the largest number of elected members, so the Governor asked him to try to form a government. No member of the IWBP was ever likely to support the AACR; and such was the enmity created by the Divorce Bill that Salvador and

Plate 1. A recent photograph of Sir Joshua (Salvador) Hassan.

Plate 2. Salvador at the age of three.

Plate 3. Greeting Her Majesty the Queen in 1954; on the left are HRH the Duke of
Edinburgh and Mr Chiappe, the City Engineer.

Plate 4. A.W. Serfaty demonstrates a Japanese mini-camera (a novelty in
those days) to Her Majesty; the Duke of Edinburgh and Salvador look on.

Plate 5. Greeting Her Majesty the Queen, and the Duke of Edinburgh, in 1954.

Peter Isola were no longer on speaking terms. In any case, Peter's financial problems prevented Salvador offering him a portfolio. The other two elected members of the Isola group, Willie Isola and Alfred Gache, refused Salvador's offers of ministerial appointments, and so the Governor sent for Bob Peliza.

Although the Isola group was essentially right-wing and Peliza's IWBP was well left of the AACR, Isola found, in theory, enough common ground with the IWBP to form what was, in practice, little more than an anti-Hassan coalition. Peliza became Chief Minister, and Salvador had to accept being the Leader of the Opposition for the first and only time in his long political career. Peter Isola could not hold any ministerial post because of his financial problems. Thus it came about that the first Gibraltar government with full responsibility for internal affairs, and faced with the threat of an indefinite Spanish siege, was made up of men with no governmental experience of any kind. Peliza had been on the first City Council for a short time in 1945, and Willie Isola had been a city councillor for a number of years, but the rest had only enthusiasm and reforming zeal to guide them.

CHAPTER 9

THE PELIZA INTERLUDE
AND THE BIG LIE ELECTION
1969-1972

The Peliza/Isola Coalition Government of 1969-72

Major R J Peliza	Chief Minister
M Xiberras	Labour and Social Security
Major A J Gache	Information, Port, Trade, and Industry
J Caruana	Medical and Health Services
W M Isola	Tourism and Municipal Services
Miss C Anes	Public Works and Housing
L Devincenzi	Education and Recreation
P J Isola	Without portfolio

The rough justice of Salvador's demotion to Leader of the Opposition after receiving such an overwhelming personal vote of confidence from the electorate could have made him an embittered man. It did nothing of the sort. Every black cloud is said to have a silver lining if only it is sought. Salvador found several personal, professional and political streaks of silver in the darkness of his demotion. Laying aside, albeit temporarily, the cares of office, he was able to spend more time with Marcelle. In the two and a half years that he was out of office, 11/18 Shorthorn became a happy home. Their first daughter was born on 27th September 1973, and their second, Marlene, on 15th March 1976. In Marcelle, Salvador now had a consort who gave him unstinting support in his political life. Without her encouragement, he might well have given up politics on several occasions. Their partnership grew ever stronger as the years went by with Marcelle becoming a formidable opponent of anyone who challenged her husband unfairly. 'How can they say such things?' was often on her lips in times of political crisis when unkind and unthinking things were said about Salvador by his opponents.

Professionally, Salvador had more time to devote to his legal work. How he had managed over the last 25 years of often intense political activity to hold his chambers together as a profitable practice is surprising. In theory Gibraltar politics was only a part-time occupation, and members of the Legislature were paid accordingly: half an upper grade civil servant's salary! Again in theory, Salvador worked in his chambers during the morning and in the Chief Minister's office in the government Secretariat or the Mayor's Office in the City Hall in the afternoon. In practice, his sense of duty made him find time for political work at any time of the day or night, and his practice had to bear the consequences. The break as Leader of the Opposition – again in theory – should have given him more time to devote to his practice. In fact, this proved another illusion: his political work increased with his determination to recover the leadership of Gibraltar at the first opportunity.

Politically, the break from being Chief Minister gave him time to rethink AACR policies, and to reorganize and reinvigorate his party with the primary aim of returning to power through creating an effective opposition to the Peliza/Isola coalition. For the first time since 1945 there was a clear divide between government and opposition policies. The old left–right split had long since closed: only a left-of-centre party was electable. Xiberras has described the party differences aptly: Salvador's slogan was 'Give Spain a hope' whereas Peliza and all the IWBP demanded 'Give Spain no hope'. But they both stood on the common ground of the non-negotiability of sovereignty. The great divide came over ways and means of raising the 15th siege and giving Gibraltar security and stability despite the continuing hostility of Spain. The AACR stood for close association with Britain, achieved by flexibility of approach to Spain and co-operation with Whitehall. The IWBP sought integration with Britain, coupled with an inflexible rejection of any concessions to Spain and an intuitive suspicion of Whitehall's longer-term intentions. Since the Franco/Castiella campaign to regain the Rock began in 1954, it had been tacitly assumed that the Foreign and Colonial Offices in London and the Hassan/Isola team in Gibraltar would eventually win through with the twin-track policies of negotiations with Spain and 'sustain and support' of Gibraltar by Britain until success was achieved. Some concessions might have to be made to enable Spain to lift her ill-considered and counter-productive frontier restrictions without loss of face, but no suggestions for change in sovereignty would be countenanced.

The IWBP had two reasons for challenging these comfortable assumptions: doubts about Her Majesty's government's true intentions over the Rock's future, and ambitions to see standards of living and social legislation in Gibraltar brought more into line with that of the United Kingdom, which so many Gibraltarians had tasted as evacuees during the war. Their doubts sprang from the instinctive conviction that Whitehall was secretly intent on selling Gibraltar down the river as part of its general policy of withdrawal from old imperial commitments, and to improve Anglo-Spanish relations. In the IWBP view, the only sure way of achieving security and stability was by actual integration with Britain rather than ill-defined close association with her. Integration would automatically bring improvements in Gibraltar's quality of life. There need be no further negotiations with the Spaniards, and certainly no concessions need be given to them as a price for lifting frontier restrictions. In short, IWBP policy was integration with Britain and no concessions to Spain. Salvador was painted as a compromiser, prepared to back Whitehall in making fatal concessions, which, in the end, might slide the Rock by sleight of hand into the Spanish realm despite the objections of the Gibraltarians.

Salvador's policy was, indeed, one of sensible compromise on any matters where there was mutual benefit to both sides, but without any flexibility whatsoever on the issue of sovereignty, which was just as non-negotiable to the AACR as it was to the IWBP. He was prepared to examine all proposals for solving the Anglo-Spanish impasse, and to meet anyone – Spaniard or otherwise – with influence or ideas for ending the siege, provided British sovereignty was not impaired in any way. He maintained his objections to integration on the grounds of the inevitable dilution of Gibraltarian identity, which he had fought so hard to establish, and on the practical difficulties of devising a sound political, economic and administrative plan for realizing the IWBP's dream. His close working relations with British ministers, officials and governors over a quarter of a century made him realize that integration was most unlikely to be acceptable to the British government even as a possible option.

The IWBP generated its political support from three groups of electors. The first was from a large number of people, like Bob Peliza himself, who were loyal servants of the Crown and more English than the English. To them, becoming genuine citizens of the United Kingdom was a dream which had hitherto been considered impracticable, but now seemed well worth pressing for to trump the Spanish claim to sovereignty. The second group was more significant in terms of AACR votes. The working class, which had been the AACR's original mainstay when Salvador was pressing for the advancement of civil rights, now had an attractive political alternative in Joe Bossano's ideas of fighting for parity of pay, standards of living and social legislation enjoyed by the United Kingdom's workers. The struggle for civil rights had largely been won: parity was coming to be seen as a new popular objective. If Salvador did nothing to harness this new trend, AACR support would dwindle. And the third group were those who, for one reason or another, were determined to end Salvador's long reign irrespective of policy arguments, and who would vote for the IWBP or any other party that stood a chance of driving his AACR out of office.

If Salvador was to return to power, he had to staunch the haemorrhage of working-class support. He had to make it clear that the AACR was still essentially a workers' party, which had their interests at heart. He won agreement to renaming it the Gibraltar Labour Party. AACR was not dropped, but was coupled with the new title, and his party became the GLP/AACR. It was, however, more often referred to as the AACR than the GLP.

But he had to do more than make cosmetic changes. New blood was needed to provide charismatic AACR candidates for grooming for the next election. Adolfo Canepa, a very able but austere schoolmaster, and Horace Zammitt, an ebullient ex-policeman, joined Aurelio Montegriffo, Maurice Featherstone, Abraham Serfaty, Isaac Abecasis and Colonel Hoare as new members of the team, which set about putting over the AACR case with vigour, and supporting its constructive opposition in the House of Assembly. Perhaps Salvador's most effective weapon was his use of the press to give wide publicity to his attacks on the government as Leader of the Opposition. Montegriffo and Featherstone were particularly effective as journalists writing in the *Gibraltar Evening Post*; and Francis Gonzales, the AACR candidate who had failed to win the eighth AACR seat at the election, made amends as a useful press correspondent. Their articles did much to keep the AACR policies in the forefront of the minds of the electorate, and made the press generally pro-AACR. Salvador also had a body of publicly silent but effective supporters amongst the majority of civil servants, who had been implementing his policies for most of their working lives and did not like change. In a small place like Gibraltar where everyone knows everyone else, their personal views made an impact, although they were not allowed to take an active part in politics. Their dislike of their new and inexperienced political masters, who quickly demonstrated their ignorance of administration and their radical socialist credentials, was soon working in the AACR's favour.

The most important policy aspect of Salvador's preparations for his fight back at the next election was his development of his theme of 'the right to our land' as a direct counter to Peliza's integrationist philosophy. He had begun using this slogan in the early days of the struggle with Spain at the United Nations when the Spanish representative had differentiated between the territory of the Rock and its people. It was slightly unfortunate that he used the word 'land' instead of the more expressive 'homeland' because, in the early 1970s, Sir Varyl Begg was fighting one of the perennial battles with the Ministry of Defence over the vexed subject of Crown lands in Gibraltar for which the Gibraltar government was expected to pay exorbitant prices when it was surplus to defence requirements. Many expatriates in Gibraltar and officials in Whitehall were confused as a result, but this hardly mattered as they had no votes. What did matter was Salvador's ability to make the electorate see that owning their own Gibraltarian homeland was more attractive than Peliza's ideas on integration. Like Waterloo, winning the political battle would be 'a close-run thing'. Only the election itself would prove how successful or otherwise he had been in arguing his case.

The groundwork for Salvador's return to power was being well laid with the enthusiasm and ruthlessness that always characterized his destruction of political opponents. Nevertheless, it must have been galling for him to see Bob Peliza flying off in his place for consultations in Whitehall with all the attendant publicity; and equally irritating to observe that Peliza seemed to establish himself in the Governor's confidence quite quickly, and to enjoy a happy honeymoon period with the electorate. In Sir Varyl's papers there is a note on his assessment of the Peliza administration:

> The new ministers – whilst of varying ability – were keen, ready to learn and full of reforming zeal. With the sole exception of Xiberras, the Minister for Labour and Social Security, who had to give up his Government teaching job before standing for election, they all had other jobs. Peliza turned out to be an able leader. Xiberras, the brains of the outfit and a doctrinaire Socialist, soon displayed a compelling urge to restructure the Gibraltar society. ... The new team, however, was not without abilities. Gache, the Minister for Information, Ports and Trade, soon became the object of attack by the local Press (mainly pro-AACR) because of

his frequent absences in the United Kingdom where he has business interests, and Devincenzi, Minister for Education, turned out to be something of a lightweight, leaning excessively on his colleagues. Caruana, Minister for Health, and Miss Anes, Minister for Housing, settled to their tasks well, and William Isola put his previous City Council experience to good use in handling tourism and municipal affairs. (Begg Papers, 10.4.70)

Sir Varyl deserves some sympathy in having to face the early and most difficult years of the 15th siege with a new local Gibraltar government which was not only inexperienced but was also trying to operate the new 1969 Constitution in which the responsibilities of the former Legislative and City Councils were merged into one House of Assembly, and the posts of their supporting civil servants were amalgamated as well. It was not easy to assess Gibraltar's future requirements because several basic assumptions were soon shown to be false. For instance, instead of Gibraltarian morale slumping when the implications of the blockade sunk in as the Spaniards hoped, and some of the expatriate British officials feared, it became increasingly resilient as the weeks, months and years passed. The Spanish government hopefully offered Gibraltarians full Spanish nationality if they settled in Spain, expecting large numbers to desert the besieged Rock. Their offer was laughed to scorn by the people, and ridiculed in the Gibraltar press. Very few took it up.

More importantly, the economy did not collapse when the Spanish labour force left the Rock. Much to most people's surprise, the reduction of income from tourism was offset to some extent in the economy by the combined effects of stopping the wages of the Spanish workers draining off into Spain, and by an increase in wages within Gibraltar, caused by the shortage of labour, which created a psychological 'feel good' syndrome amongst the Gibraltarian workers without any fear that the new money would leak away into Spain.

Lord Shepherd visited Gibraltar again early in September 1969 to set the parameters for a revised 'sustain and support' package with the new Peliza government; and Peliza led an IWBP delegation back to London at the beginning of December to present Gibraltar's requirements for countering the Spanish blockade. The outcome was highly satisfactory. A financial package of some £4 million – a large sum in those days – was agreed, to be used mainly for housing; and the Ministry of Defence released a large area of reclaimed land on which the Varyl Begg estate was eventually built. Other measures included temporary housing for the imported Moroccan workforce; the first phase of the comprehensive schools building programme; additional medical facilities; and port development. A further £100,000 was granted to pay for technical assistance in overcoming the effects of the Spanish siege measures. There was little in Peliza's performance so far that called for rigorous opposition from Salvador. There was, however, an as yet undetected wages time-bomb ticking away under the 'feel good' syndrome, which was not destined to explode until after Salvador had regained power.

The origins of this future industrial unrest lay in the wage and salary levels negotiated between public and private sector employers and unions at the biennial pay-structure reviews, recently carried out by an arbitrator, A I Marsh. With a closed frontier and a restricted and inadequate labour force, the pre-siege balance of negotiating power between employers and unions was swinging in the latter's favour, although this was not yet generally evident. As long as the cost of living remained reasonably stable, there was no cause for alarm. Joe Bossano, having only quite recently returned to Gibraltar, had not sought election as an IWBP candidate in the 1969 election since he lacked the necessary public support as a relatively unknown personality at that time, so he began to build a political power-base by working for the TGWU as well as acting as secretary for the IWBP. He could see that with no effective yardstick for wage settlements available, parity with United Kingdom might be turned into the Gibraltar wages and salaries criteria by steady and unrelenting union pressure.

While Bob Peliza was interested in the IWBP's primary aim of integration to neutralize the Spanish claim, Joe Bossano, the IWBP's Secretary, was more intent on advancing the secondary aim of winning parity by any means available, and Maurice Xiberras was the political tactician who sought to use both strands of IWBP policy to best advantage. As a graduate in economics, Bossano saw that he might be able to carry through the IWBP's secondary aim of parity quickest by using worker dissatisfaction with the inevitable rises in the cost of living caused by goods being shipped in at increased cost from overseas. The cost of living crisis, however, was, as yet, some way off and so integration stood alone at the top of the IWBP's political agenda. Bossano's successful espousal of the parity issue was, in due course, to make him Salvador's most dangerous political rival. During Lord Shepherd's September visit, Peliza had told the minister of state that seeking negotiations for integration was the policy of the new Gibraltar government, and he claimed that it had the full support of the electorate. Shepherd replied bluntly that Her Majesty's government were not prepared to accept integration proposals in the foreseeable future. In spite of this rebuff, Peter Isola moved a motion in the House of Assembly in November calling for official talks with the British government on the subject, which was carried by a majority vote. The AACR abstained because they could not win agreement to an amendment designed to preserve Gibraltarian status. Peliza reiterated his government's claim to 'real United Kingdom citizenship' during his December visit to London and was again rebuffed.

In the meantime, 1st October, the United Nations' date for the conclusion of Anglo-Spanish negotiations for the handover of the Rock to Spain, had come and gone without British compliance or any awkward incidents. Tension did rise locally, but the presence of an increased number of British and Dutch warships, including a commando carrier, carrying out exercises in waters near Gibraltar, reassured the Gibraltarians and certainly angered, if not deterred, Madrid. Spain made no attempt to impose the United Nations' resolutions by force, but, as a gesture of continuing malevolence, cut all Gibraltar's telephone and telegraph links passing through Spain. The probability of this happening had been foreseen and alternative routes established. Only the local lines to the Campo could not be substituted.

The passing of the 1st October deadline demonstrated to the world in general, and to Franco's government in particular, the barrenness of Castiella's Gibraltar policy. Castiella had, indeed, invested too much of his personal political capital in it to be able to survive its failure. In any case, Franco was keen to win acceptance of Spain as a member of the Western Community by joining the European Community and NATO, but to do so he would need British support. In a Cabinet reshuffle, the reputably Anglophile López Bravo replaced Castiella. He was well aware that coercive policies were unlikely to work with the British; nor were the blasts of anti-British and vicious anti-Gibraltar propaganda, which always accompanied Spain's affrays in the United Nations, anything but counter-productive. He began a rethink of Spain's Gibraltar policy, and raised hopes in London and Gibraltar that Spain would, at last, accept that Gibraltar was not ripe for the picking as Franco had originally thought, and that the key to the future of Gibraltar lay, quite properly, with the Gibraltarians whatever the Treaty of Utrecht might say.

Knowing the British propensity for seeking compromise solutions to intractable problems, Bravo persuaded Franco's cabinet to try a softer and more co-operative approach. The vicious anti-Gibraltarian press campaign was stopped; the United Nation's Secretary-General was informed that Spain would not be raising the Gibraltar issue at the December 1969 session; and diplomatic channels would be used to further the dialogue with Britain rather than formal talks between national delegations, which had hitherto led to unhelpful confrontations. The new British Ambassador, Sir John Russell, was cordially received by Franco, and everything seemed set for constructive diplomatic exchanges between London and Madrid: the British hoping to find a way of enabling Madrid to lift the 15th siege without loss of face; and the Spaniards trying to present a package of sweeteners to persuade the Gibraltarians to accept a change of sovereignty with good grace, if not enthusiasm. Bravo, however, was a lone soft-liner in the falangist cabinet, the majority of whom were still ardent supporters of the hard line on Gibraltar, as were most of the officials of the foreign ministry, who had worked so hard and for so long to make a success of Castiella's policy. Bravo's softer approach was very much on trial, and he was unable to win support for any lifting of frontier restrictions without the promise of a major concession on sovereignty from the British side, which, under the new 1969 Constitution, Britain was unable to give without Gibraltarian agreement. The Rock was no longer Britain's to give away, nor Spain's to acquire: it belonged to its people, the Gibraltarians.

The possibility of Spain ending the 15th siege received a surprisingly mixed reaction in Gibraltar. It had become a matter of honour not to seek better relations with Spain. People with close relatives in Spain, whom they wished to visit, would not say so for fear of being branded as 'doves'. And the Gibraltarian workers, being much better off as a result of the withdrawal of the Spanish work force, had no wish to suffer a drop in their living standards through the Spaniards returning. Neither of the main political parties welcomed the possibility because they knew that Spain had not abandoned her claim to sovereignty and would extract some damaging reciprocal concession from Britain before actually ending restrictions. The price might well prove too high for the Gibraltarians to stomach while seeming eminently reasonable to the compromise prone mandarins in Whitehall.

There were three potential concessions, which the Foreign Office put to the Governor. The first suggestion was a reduction in the garrison, which had been reinforced in 1967 after the United Nations set 1st October 1969 as the deadline for the Rock's hand-over to Spain. Sir Varyl robustly rejected the idea as military madness while Spanish frontier restrictions lasted.

The second suggestion was the internationalization of the airport, opening it to Spanish civil and military use. There was already a proposal being examined for lengthening the runway to take Boeing 707s, but this was turned down as uneconomic. The

RAF had no need for extra length to take their military aircraft so were disinclined to foot the bill, which would, therefore, fall on the Gibraltar government or Overseas Development funds. As the Tridents and BAC 1lls, flown by British commercial firms, could land on the existing length, the enormous cost of some £5-10 million could not be justified at that time for the relatively few 707s likely to use the runway. The issue would be raised again when Salvador returned to power and wished to increase the tourist traffic to help the siege economy.

Internationalization of the airport was a very different matter. Sir Varyl opposed it strongly on two grounds, which are still valid today: British and Spanish air controllers would never be able to work in harmony in an area that had been disputed for so long; and it would jeopardize British sovereignty over the southern half of the isthmus. Writing to the Foreign Office on 5th December 1971, he said:

> Joint administration of a civil/military airfield must surely place a great strain on the patience and tact of the officials concerned even when the administering countries are in close alliance, have common objectives and well established goodwill. But when the proposed joint administrative co-operation would present only a first step towards re-establishing goodwill over Gibraltar and would be staged on an open and disputed frontier, the very site of bitter discord extending over 267 years, I have the gravest doubts whether it could be made to work. (Begg Papers, 5.12.71)

He adds his objections to endangering sovereignty in his conclusions:

> It also seems to me that any arrangement for joint administration of the airfield would imply a dilution of British sovereignty and restraints on British jurisdiction . . . (*Ibid*)

The third suggestion was the old chestnut of dismantling the frontier fence, the case for which was as easy as ever to demolish as being pointless since the airfield would still need its perimeter fence, which stretched across the isthmus only a few yards to the south. The main objection, however, was the risk of Spain using its demolition as a means of diluting British sovereignty and jurisdiction over the isthmus.

Thanks to Sir Varyl's forthright opposition none of these suggested concessions were put to the Spaniards. Sir John Russell accepted that in any case they were unlikely to lead to a lifting of restrictions unless there was a fundamental change in Spanish policy. So far, there had only been a replacement of the hard line approach of Castiella by Bravo's softer line, and the Franco government's objectives remained unaltered. In these circumstances, Madrid was likely to pocket the concessions and ask for more without lifting any of the frontier restrictions. Moreover, under the 1969 Gibraltar Constitution, Britain was bound to consult the Gibraltar government on these proposed concessions, which it was certain to oppose. The internationalization of the airfield was anathema to the Gibraltarians, as it is today, and for the same reasons: dilution of sovereignty and unworkability of joint control.

Throughout 1970, '71 and '72, overtly friendly diplomatic minuets were danced in London and Madrid in the quest for a formula that would allow substantive Anglo-Spanish negotiations to take place with some hope of success. All the well tried steps were rehearsed yet again: lease-back, condominion, autonomy within the Spanish realm, the precedents of Andorra, Lichtenstein and Monaco, and so forth. Sir Alec Douglas Home, the Foreign Secretary, had informal discussions with Bravo in Luxemburg in June 1970; at the United Nations in October 1971 after visiting Gibraltar a month earlier; and in Madrid in February 1972. Cordiality abounded in the *nuevo clima* of Anglo-Spanish relations brought about by Bravo's efforts, and was given impetus by the common ground of Britain's and Gibraltar's imminent entry into the European Community, and Spain's application to do so as well. Phrases like 'thinking together' and 'working together' to find a novel solution to the age-old problem of the Spanish claim, perhaps within the growing unity of Europe, were bandied about, but without any quantifiable success.

Gibraltar's principal political leaders – Peliza and Salvador –

were kept informed by the Governor of what was being discussed and were asked for their reactions at every stage. Under the new constitution relations with Spain were a part of foreign affairs and *ipso facto* non-defined matters outside the remit of local ministers, but Sir Alec Douglas Home gave categorical assurances when he met the members of the House of Assembly in September 1971 that the established custom of the Governor consulting the chief minister and leader of the opposition on Gibraltar's relations with Spain would be continued.

Howard Davis (now Sir Howard, the only Gibraltarian so far to be appointed Deputy Governor) was directed by Sir Varyl Begg to draft a paper for dispatch to the Foreign Secretary, setting out the Gibraltarian view of the diplomatic probing, which had been going on in Madrid and London. One of its paragraphs gives the full flavour of the those days:

> The modern Gibraltarians despite their multi-racial background now have an intense pride in being Gibraltarian ('our land' is the current slogan) and a strong desire to maintain their British institutions and freedoms . . . They have been constantly told that, if they play things in a low key, improved Anglo-Spanish relations would in due course usher in a period – the key to future progress – when the Gibraltarians and Spaniards would again learn to live together. They have accepted this; they note the signs of improved Anglo-Spanish relations – the visits and so on but they do not observe any lifting of restrictions and they do not sense any change in Spanish thinking or intentions concerning Gibraltar: and they are fearful of where this process will lead them . . . They cannot discern how a happy solution to their predicament may be brought about . . . They are not yet at the end of their tether by any means and they have certainly not reached a point when in their view the sovereignty of their 'homeland' is up for negotiation. (Begg Papers, 7.3.71)

The Governor invited Peliza and Salvador to a confidential meeting to discuss the Davis draft. As he was barely on speaking terms with Peliza, Salvador asked to see the Governor separately because he feared that at a joint meeting Peliza might be 'tempestuous and uncontrolled', and he did not trust him not to misrepresent what was said. Sir Varyl persuaded Salvador to change his mind and out of deference for the Governor he did so with unfortunate results.

During the joint meeting, Sir Varyl asked the two political leaders, 'What if the Spaniards offer a thousand-year lease?' Salvador replied that anything which came from Spain that would not lead to total sovereignty over the territory would be worth looking at. Peliza refused even to consider any such proposal, and excitedly accused Salvador, quite unjustifiably, of being in favour of the 'lease-back' solution. Sir Varyl drew Peliza's attention to the fact that Salvador had said nothing of the sort. Although these talks were strictly confidential, there should be no misunderstanding of what Salvador had said, which was in keeping with his public position of exploring every suggested way out of the current impasse.

Despite the confidentiality of the talks with the Governor, Peliza could not resist going public on the issue. He accused Salvador of being prepared to accept the lease-back solution. Salvador asked the Governor to make a statement to say that he, Salvador, had never agreed to lease-back and had only accepted that it should be examined. Sir Varyl declined to intervene on the grounds that the discussion was confidential and that he must not interfere in local politics. Salvador protested in writing that he thought he was being very badly treated. His relations with the Governor were soured; and quite understandably so because, in effect, Sir Varyl, by not rebutting Peliza's claim, was strengthening the IWBP hand in the key political argument over concessions to Spain.

Other influences were at work. Negotiations for Britain and Gibraltar to join the European Community were in their final stages, and Spain was applying to join as well. Many people felt that a solution to the Gibraltar problem might be found within the creation of a truly united Europe. How it would come about was not clear either in London or Madrid, but the possibility brought on a new effort to find an acceptable way of enabling Bravo to persuade the Franco government to raise the 15th siege since it

Plate 6. Salvador with Harold Wilson.

*Plate 7. The young Salvador at a dinner of the
Association of Labour Mayors in 1954.*

*Plate 8. Salvador with Sir Winston and Lady Churchill during
their visit to Gibraltar in 1961.*

*Plate 9: Greeting HRH Princess Margaret with Lieutenant-General
Sir Harold Redman, in 1957.*

Plate 10. Addressing the Committee of 24, with Peter Isola sitting on his left.

Plates 11 & 12. A triumphant election night.

Plate 13. With HRH the Duke of Edinburgh at the Victoria Stadium
in the late 1950s.

Plate 14. A bevy of Gibraltar QCs. From left to right: AB Serfaty, Sir Alfred Vasquez,
Guy Stagnetto, Sam Benady, Sir Joshua Hassan.

Plate 15. A recent photograph of Sir Joshua Hassan with Sir Edward Heath; Albert Poggio looks on.

Plates 16 & 17 (below and facing page). The Forces' farewell to Sir Joshua, on his retirement, 25 April 1988.

Plate 18.   Salvador when he became a QC.

was becoming pointless within the ambiance of a united Europe which might make the sovereignty issue irrelevant – or so it was felt in the early 1970s. Sir Alec Douglas Home met Bravo for talks in October 1971 and February 1972, and agreed to meet again in July 1972. These talks were watched with great suspicion by the integrationists in Gibraltar. It seemed all too clear that Britain had a golden opportunity to slip Gibraltar into Spain under the cloak of European unity. So wild did the speculation become, especially amongst Gibraltar's trade unions, who were virulently anti-Spanish and more particularly anti-fascist, that Sir Varyl Begg invited a delegation from the Gibraltar Trades Council to the Convent for a briefing on the international situation.

José Netto, who was district officer of the TGWU, led the delegation. Sir Varyl explained the strategic Cold War reasons for Spain to be readmitted to the Western community nations despite her fascist dictatorship, and pointed out the decline in the military importance of the Rock and its dockyard that would occur once Spain was admitted to NATO and the EC as she surely would be in a few years' time. Any attempt to bring pressure to bear on the British government by mounting strikes in the dockyard would be counter-productive. In his papers there are his pencil notes for the meeting:

> Responsible trade union officials should understand that while Gibraltar was useful the dockyard was not essential to British or Western defence; and that contrary to what was often said in Gibraltar, HMG received no payment from NATO for the use of the Gibraltar base – or indeed for any of its bases.
> It was ludicrous for the unions to get into conflict with HMG [over pay and conditions] and at the same time to press HMG to be hostile to Spain in the EEC context. There was no British interest, political, economic or military in having bad relations with Spain – quite the contrary. There were countries in NATO and the Western Alliance who would like to see Spain in NATO and in the EEC: it seemed almost inevitable that Spain one day in 10, 20, 30 years' time and purged of Fascism, would take its place in the European Community. (Begg Papers, 2.6.72)

After the meeting, some members of the delegation such as Michael Feetham, the taxi drivers' leader who later became a minister in Joe Bossano's administration, made public statements on their version of what had transpired coloured by their own points of view. Being sold down the river in the torrent of EEC negotiations was a very real fear created by Sir Varyl's briefing of the union leaders, and, indeed, did much to strengthen union members' support of the IWBP at the expense of the AACR. Netto was reported as saying that the issue preoccupied him more than any internal matter, and it might become necessary for the union to take the lead in getting the political parties and other bodies in Gibraltar to unite and demand from HMG a categorical statement of their present and future intentions regarding Gibraltar in view of the divorce between Anglo-Spanish relations and the Gibraltar issue. (Begg Papers, 16.6.72)

Coincidentally with these two unfortunate affairs involving the Governor – the meeting on Howard Davis's paper and the union briefing – Peliza was beginning to have doubts about the loyalty of Major Gache, the Isola group member of the government, holding the portfolio of Information, Port, Trade and Industries. Gache, as the Governor had observed in his earlier summary of ministerial abilities, was having to spend too much time away in London looking after his own business affairs and was neglecting his ministerial responsibilities in Gibraltar. He wanted to exchange portfolios with Willie Isola, the Minister for Tourism, since this would enable him to visit England as part of his ministerial duties. Willie Isola was not prepared to give way, nor was Peter Isola prepared to make him do so. Peliza then made a series of political misjudgements. He believed Gache, unable to get his way, was on the point of precipitating an election by resigning from the government, which was probably true; but he also believed that he could tar Salvador with a pro-Spanish brush in an election by using his 'lease-back' slander as his main weapon, and union disquiet over Gibraltar's ill-defined future in a United Europe. On 22nd May 1972, he took time by the forelock and asked the Governor for a dissolution of the House of Assembly on the grounds that he had lost confidence in Major Gache. He was assuming that a ground swell of electoral support for his policy of making no concessions to Spain would sweep the IWBP back to power.

Peliza was making the biggest mistake of his political career. The electorate did not fall for what the AACR dubbed 'the big lie' about Salvador being willing to make unwise concessions to Spain. In a small place like Gibraltar, the local grape vine is quick and remarkably accurate, and Peliza's interpretation of what was said at the Governor's meeting was largely discounted. Other less dramatic factors, however, were to lead to Salvador's return to power.

The 1972 election, which was held on 23rd June, was the first truly two-party poll held in Gibraltar. There were no independents standing: the three Isola group members joined the IWBP. Both parties entered eight candidates. The AACR took the first eight seats, and the IWBP the last seven with one of their candidates, Mrs A Smith, not being elected. Salvador once again headed the poll nearly 500 votes clear of Peliza, Xiberras and Isola. Canepa, Salvador's new recruit, came second in the poll, and Joe Bossano, who stood as an IWBP candidate for the first time, came a modest fifth among the IWBP candidates. The results were:

Hassan	(AACR)	5,001
Canepa	"	4,770
Montegriffo	"	4,713
Abecasis	"	4,712
Featherstone	"	4,681
Serfaty	"	4,670
Zammitt	"	4,604
Hoare	"	4,571
Peliza	(IWBP)	4,516
Xiberras	"	4,502
P Isola	"	4,496
W Isola	"	4,411
Bossano	"	4,382
Caruana	"	4,369
Devincenzi	"	4,361

With only the two parties competing, efficient block voting was one of the keys to success. Salvador's regeneration of the AACR party organization and block-voting techniques gave it the edge over its less experienced rival; his choice and grooming of candidates proved that he was still a good judge of their political worth; and his achievement of a favourable press throughout his two and a half years in opposition was perhaps decisive. Above all, the electorate showed their preference for his concept of a Gibraltarian Gibraltar under the Crown rather than Peliza's integrationist ideas.

Soon after the election, Bob Peliza had to leave for England for family reasons. He retained his seat in the House and returned to Gibraltar to take part in all debates, but leading the IWBP from England was clearly impracticable. He handed over the party to Maurice Xiberras, who had come second to him in the IWBP section of the poll, and Xiberras took over as Leader of the Opposition as well.

Salvador picked up the reins of office with a reinvigorated team, who, with two exceptions, served him until his retirement fifteen years later. Isaac Abecasis was badly hurt in an unfortunate car accident outside the Casino and had to resign, and Colonel Hoare, who did not seek re-election in 1976.

An apt tailpiece to this 'big lie' election was provided in a letter from the Governor, dated the day after the election, in reply to a critical pre-election letter from Salvador. After congratulating him on his personal success as well as his party's, Sir Varyl referred to his failure to rebut Peliza's distortion of the 'lease-back' meeting:

> I would only say in reply that my earnest desire to preserve the principles of confidentiality, impartiality and fair play has caused me great anxiety over the past three weeks. If I got the solution wrong as your final paragraph suggests I am sad: but at least I take comfort from the fact that no one today can possibly say that any action on my part affected the election to the advantage of your party. Your success at the polls has self-evidently been achieved by you and your colleagues alone. (Letter attached to Hassan notes of 27.5.94)

Salvador commented:

Needless to say that after I formed a government I got on very well with Sir Varyl Begg. (Hassan notes 27.5.94)

CHAPTER 10

RETURN TO POWER
AND INDUSTRIAL UNREST
1972-1976

The House of Assembly, 1972-76:

Government:

Sir Joshua Hassan	Chief Minister
A W Serfaty	Tourism, Trade and Economic Development
A P Montegriffo	Medical and Health Services
M K Featherstone	Education
A J Canepa	Labour and Social Security
I Abecasis	Housing
Col J L Hoare	Public Works and Municipal Services
H J Zammitt	Information and Sport

Opposition:

Major R J Peliza	IWBP
M Xiberras	IWBP
P J Isola	IWBP
W M Isola	IWBP
J Bossano	IWBP
J Caruana	IWBP
L Devincenzi	IWBP

Salvador's return to power as Chief Minister did not usher in a period of political and economic calm. The 'big lie' was not expunged by the election result and rumbled on with the IWBP reviving it at every favourable opportunity; and the fuse on the time-bomb of industrial unrest was getting ever shorter with IWBP encouragement. It was to explode within two months of the new AACR government taking office.

The 'big lie' and industrial unrest were indirectly connected. The former was centred on the increasingly futile talks with Spain and the latter on equally obstinate negotiations with Whitehall. The interconnection between the two was the impact of the news of strikes in Gibraltar on Madrid's estimates of the effectiveness of their frontier restrictions on Gibraltarian morale. The very fact that they were occurring sent a wrong signal to the Franco regime, suggesting that the Gibraltarians were, at long last, rebelling against their 'colonial masters'. In reality, both the main political parties were intent on demonstrating their anti-Spanish credentials, and 'dove' tendencies were as unpopular as ever.

The IWBP's regeneration of the 'big lie' was based upon suspicion and misconstruction of Salvador's motives during a new spasm of Anglo-Spanish talks between Bravo and Sir Alec Douglas Home, which began a fortnight after his election victory. The imminent entry of Britain and Gibraltar into the European Community, set for 1st January 1973, and Spain's clear intention of applying for membership, had provided a new dimension to the stale Anglo-Spanish dialogue on Gibraltar, and had caused a new flurry of diplomatic activity. The idea that the pack-ice, which was gripping the current dialogue, might somehow be thawed and broken up by the warmth generated by common membership of the EC, was gaining credibility in London and Madrid. It seemed logical to most people in the 1970s that arguments over sovereignty would become less relevant in the context of a united Europe. The idea chimed in well with British wishful-thinking that closer relations with Spain could lead to lifting the frontier restrictions as a gesture of good will and mutual respect amongst real friends. Madrid, however, saw only an opportunity to exploit the apparent absurdity of Gibraltar remaining a potentially hostile British fortress on Spanish soil when the old nation states of Europe, whose rivalries had fostered the need for it in the first place, were on their way out.

Sir Alec invited Bravo to London for exploratory talks on 9th July 1972. Bravo was keen to improve on Castiella's offer of a special status for the Gibraltarians within the Spanish realm, giving them virtual autonomy, but only if sovereignty was transferred as the United Nations directed. While Bravo was warned that any package that even hinted at a change of sovereignty was most unlikely to be acceptable to the Gibraltarians and hence to the British Cabinet, who were constitutionally bound to respect Gibraltarian wishes, the two men agreed to meet again for a 'working meeting' in November after further soundings had been made in Gibraltar, London and Madrid.

The Governor and Salvador were called to London in early August for briefing on the content of the Home/Bravo talks, as they were also to be summoned before and after all their subsequent talks. Sir Alec told them that Bravo was always clutching a document, which he referred to as his very favourable constitution for an autonomous Gibraltar within the Spanish realm. Sir Alec saw the document at each 'working meeting', but neither read it nor accepted a copy since he did not wish to give any impression of willingness to negotiate. Salvador confirmed that such proposals, whatever they might be, would be totally rejected by the people of Gibraltar if they involved change of sovereignty. The Bravo proposal, or as little as was known about them, seemed to him no more attractive than 'the glittering future' offered by Castiella ten years earlier at the beginning of his diplomatic assault on the Rock in the United Nations.

When Salvador returned to Gibraltar, he confirmed the unacceptability of Bravo's ideas in a letter to the Governor in which he added his own on the way forward:

> The only way in which some real progress might be made . . . would be to shelve the question of sovereignty for a period and to discuss ways and means of attempting to restore normal relations. Adamant though the Spaniards might be on this, I believe it is worth repeating it to them once more, at the same time as it is made known to them that there is no prospect that their proposals, which are quite unrealistic, would be acceptable in

their present form. (Begg Papers, 23.9.72]

Xiberras, as Leader of the Opposition, also wrote to the Governor restating the IWBP's uncompromising view that there must be no concessions to Spain; ties with Britain should be strengthened; and Britain should exercise the veto on Spain's entry into the EEC until the 15th siege was raised. Xiberras also complained that the Opposition were not being kept fully informed on the Home/Bravo talks.

There was some truth in Xiberras's last complaint. Ever since Peliza's breach of confidence over the 'lease-back' proposal, Sir Varyl had decided that he must sup with the IWBP with the proverbial long spoon, and be circumspect as to what information he could risk giving to Xiberras without raising further suspicions that a deal was being struck with Spain behind Gibraltarian backs. Restricting the information given to Xiberras was less of an advantage to Salvador than it might seem. Salvador could not divulge information given him in confidence by the Governor or Foreign Office officials to counter further embroidery of the 'big lie' by the opposition. The IWBP could and did use mere rumours and speculation in their attacks on Salvador's policy of examining all new ideas that might enable Spain to lift restrictions without loss of face.

Salvador, through long association with governors at the Convent, knew that to use confidential information for local political purposes was the surest way to end consultation on the Spanish question. Under the 1969 Constitution there was no need for the governor to keep the chief minister, let alone the leader of the opposition, informed. Anglo-Spanish relations as foreign affairs were non-defined matters and hence the sole responsibility of the governor. Sir Alec had, however, assured Salvador that the FCO would always keep him informed through the Governor of the exchanges with Madrid. Regrettably, Salvador's absolute respect for confidentiality was soon to lead him into a personal confrontation with the Spanish Ambassador in London, as we shall shortly see.

Soon after Salvador's return from London, a quite unexpected mini-constitutional crisis arose. During the evening of 16th August a Moroccan military helicopter landed at the Gibraltar airport. On board was Lt-Colonel Ankrane, the Deputy Commander of the Moroccan Air Force, together with an officer aide and the helicopter crew of three other ranks. The two officers sought asylum. Ankrane had been directing an abortive attempt to assassinate King Hassan of Morocco by shooting down his aircraft as it came into land. They had commandeered the helicopter for their escape when the plot failed. The question arose as to who held jurisdiction for granting asylum – the Governor or Salvador's government.

Sir Varyl Begg did not hesitate and pre-empted any attempt by Salvador to claim local government jurisdiction. The fugitives had landed on an RAF operational airfield. In his view, this gave him undoubted jurisdiction and he ordered the men to be taken into military and not civil custody. Realizing that the Moroccan workforce in Gibraltar might cause trouble, and not wishing to offend so important an ally as King Hassan, upon whom Gibraltar depended heavily for supplies as well as labour, the Secretary of State backed Sir Varyl and ordered their immediate return to Morocco. This caused public outcry in Gibraltar because their return was tantamount to the death sentence. Salvador, however, had the good sense not to challenge the Governor, who had the Secretary of State behind him, on an issue of no vital importance to Gibraltar. Ankrane was tried in Morocco and shot. Appeals by Ankrane's wife against the British decision not to grant her husband asylum caused considerable embarrassment, and led to her taking her case to the European Court of Human Rights. The British government settled for a considerable sum out of court.

Four days later the time-bomb of industrial unrest exploded in a general strike called by the TGWU and supported by the IWBP. The leader of the strike was a young worker/priest, Father Bernard Linares, who had entered public life in Gibraltar as chaplain of the Young Christian Workers. He had come fresh from Rome at the time when Pope John XXIII's Vatican Council was instilling new ideas into its young priests of becoming directly involved in social action. Linares – young, dedicated and keen – had seen that the trade unions in Gibraltar had become part of the establishment as loyal supporters of the AACR, thanks to Alberto Risso's long and close association with Salvador. The TGWU's relationship with the AACR was akin to the linkage between the Labour Party and the TUC in Britain. Linares believed that if social progress was to be made, he must break TGWU subordination to the AACR, and give his young Christian workers a radical anti-establishment sense of mission.

Linares's vehicle for social reform was the Young Christian Workers' magazine, *Social Action*. He made a charismatic impact upon his young followers, amongst whom he found and enthused many would-be militants. Throughout 1970 and 1971 they steadily infiltrated the TGWU committees, and had gained control of its Executive Committee by the end of 1971. This led, as Linares hoped, to the AACR severing its political links with the unions, thus removing Salvador's moderating influence and allowing the young extremists to gain the upper hand with unhappy results. The measure of Linares's success was the startling increase in TGWU membership from 1,900 at the end of 1971 to 4,860 by the time of the general strike eight months later in August 1972.

Linares's relationship with Salvador quite naturally became very strained. Linares saw him as a political enemy, and the enmity was all the more embarrassing because Salvador was a life-long friend of his father. By organizing political marches, Linares usurped what had been Salvador's prerogative and also alienated many of the Catholic community, including the conservative Bishop Rapallo. Salvador generously avoided exploiting Linares's difficulties with the local Catholic hierarchy. Despite their political differences, there was never a personal feud between them, and in later life after Linares had ceased to be a priest and had become a successful school teacher, rising to be headmaster of the Boys' Comprehensive School, the two men became great friends.

The ostensible cause of the strike was the growing mismatch

between wages and the rising cost of living, but there were political anti-AACR and anti-Spanish undertones based upon continuing union belief in the 'big lie', which José Netto, the TGWU's District Officer, had been so worried about after the briefing meeting with the Governor before the 1972 election. At the post-election biennial wages review, the union side demanded a £5 to £6 wage increase for industrial workers, and IWBP irresponsibly gave wide publicity to its alleged intention to implement such an increase if they had been re-elected. The official employers (Ministry of Defence, Property Services Agency and the Gibraltar government) told the union negotiators that such a large increase was more than Gibraltar's fragile economy could absorb as long as Spanish restrictions lasted.

Salvador and the local Gibraltar government were in a difficult position. Only a fraction of the public sector workers were in their employment: the great majority were on the payrolls of Whitehall ministries, whose negotiators had the hard-nosed officials of the British Treasury breathing down their necks. Salvador could not direct his negotiators to settle without Whitehall concurrence, but it would be Gibraltar that would suffer from consequential union strike action.

After some desultory and half-hearted negotiations in Gibraltar, at which the official employers made a not ungenerous offer, José Netto called out on strike those industrial workers, who could most disrupt essential municipal services. These services in Gibraltar, however, were not so easy to disrupt because of the duplication of the civil and military facilities. On the military side contingency plans had been well laid for keeping electricity, water and sewage flowing in the military systems with the help of servicemen flown out from England. On the city side, industrial action by Gibraltarians to disrupt their own municipal services was deemed by management to be utterly unthinkable. If such a thing were to occur, the managerial and non-union members of the workforce were expected to be able to keep essential services running for the short time that industrial action was likely to last. The military plans worked relatively smoothly, and, on the civil side, the essential municipal services were kept going for the first 24 hours. Then a wave of hostile picketing and outright intimidation started at the King's Bastion power station, forcing the managerial staff to quit. At Salvador's request, and with the agreement of the Gibraltar Council, a military team took over the station and successfully maintained the city's power supplies, but then Netto, in retaliation, declared a general strike, which lasted for a week before loss of earnings eroded the militants' enthusiasm for further confrontation. Any tendency to violence was contained by the police: there was no need to call out troops to support them.

The August 1972 general strike proved to be only the first round in the long struggle for parity of wages with the United Kingdom, which Xiberras, Linares and Bossano were developing. For the time being, however, political interest within Gibraltar swung back to the Spanish question with the Home/Bravo 'working meeting' taking place in Madrid on 27th November 1972. Again it was a friendly dialogue of the deaf, the final communique blandly stating that the talks had not yet reached a stage at which formal negotiations might begin. The two sides were to have another working meeting in May 1973.

When Salvador saw Sir Alec after the November 'working meeting', he offered to meet a Spanish representative on any matter considered worthwhile, and he might thereby be able to find out more details of Bravo's proposed Gibraltar constitution without generating suspicion of secret negotiations. And so it was arranged that as the political leader of one of the new member states of the EC, Salvador should pay his first visit to Brussels in February 1973 to get to know the British EC delegation and familiarize himself with the European Commission environment. During this visit, the Foreign Office would arrange a secret off-the-record meeting with a senior Spanish delegate to the EC in Brussels.

Salvador travelled to Brussels accompanied by Joe Pitaluga, the Administrative Secretary, and an official of the Overseas Development Agency (ODA), who was not told the real reason for the Brussels trip and was with them merely to lend credibility to the EC familiarization excuse for Salvador being in Brussels at all. The Spanish representative turned out to be Ambassador Arguelles, a retired diplomat of great prestige, who had been Spanish Ambassador in Washington, and was sent by Madrid specially for the secret meeting. Salvador and Pitaluga met him at the Hotel *Los Amigos* in Brussels, having given the ODA official the slip.

The meeting lasted for about five hours. Arguelles stressed that he had no authority to commit the Spanish government; and Salvador made a similar disclaimer and said that he was mainly interested in probing Spanish thinking. The talks were friendly and resulted in Salvador leaving the Ambassador with a copy of his paper on the 'rights we want preserved', which he had used in the United Nations' debates. In return Salvador received a copy of Bravo's proposed Gibraltar constitution, which Sir Alec had been unable to read or accept.

The Bravo proposals, which were deemed by Salvador to be so totally unacceptable to most Gibraltarians as to be absurd, can be distilled down to seven main points: Gibraltar would have autonomy within the Spanish realm for legislative, judicial, administrative and financial purposes; Gibraltarians would become Spanish nationals, but would not have to renounce their British citizenship; the 1969 Constitution would be retained in a suitably amended form; the Spanish penal and police laws would be introduced for internal and external security; there would be a Spanish governor appointed by the Spanish head of state; the senior members of his executive council would be Spaniards or Gibraltarians with Spanish nationality; and the official language would be Spanish while the use of English would be safeguarded.

These proposals were not very different from those put forward by Spain in the United Nations and at the time of the referendum, and had been rejected out of hand on both occasions. They had also been repeatedly turned down by Whitehall as unlikely to be acceptable to the Gibraltarians, but Madrid wanted to confirm that this was really so by approaching Salvador directly. They got their confirmation: Salvador ridiculed them.

By the time the May 'working meeting' was due, Bravo's credibility within the Franco government was in terminal decline. When he could not report any significant progress after that May meeting, at which Julian Amery, the new Minister of State at the Foreign and Commonwealth Office, replaced Sir Alec Douglas Home, he joined Castiella in retirement as yet another disappointed Spanish Foreign Minister who had failed to recover the Rock. Lopez Rodo, a hardliner in the Castiella mode, was appointed in his place and Madrid's relations with Gibraltar went back to square one.

One of Rodo's first acts was to pick up where Castiella had left off by complaining to the Secretary-General of the United Nations, Kurt Waldheim, that in the last four and a half years the British government had made no effort to fulfil the United Nations resolution on the return of the Rock to Spain. The Spanish government was obliged to take further steps to encourage compliance. On 6th August, yachts and other vessels, registered in Gibraltar, were forbidden entry into Algeciras, thus cutting the last tenuous link with Spain. And on 29th October, the Spanish minister at the United Nations reopened the debates on Gibraltar, which Bravo had abandoned. The 'thinking and working together' of the Home/Bravo period turned into open confrontation with Rodo doing the sabre-rattling. The General Assembly duly passed another worthless resolution, pressing Britain and Spain to make fresh efforts to resolve their differences: worthless because it did not face up to the paramount need to meet the 'wishes' of the Gibraltarians and not just their best 'interests', which Spain maintained were fully covered by the generous offer of autonomy within the Spanish realm.

Out of deference to the United Nations, a British delegation met Rodo's team for new 'exploratory' talks in Madrid at the end of May 1974. Sir John Killick, who led the British 'explorers', claimed that his expedition had been 'useful', but in reality they only found out that the Spaniards had taken several paces backwards in their thinking. All the old Castiella arguments were redeployed about there being no such people as Gibraltarians; about civilians on the Rock being just part of the fortress and having no right to any say in the future of a piece of Spanish territory, which they had never possessed; and about Britain using respect for their 'wishes' as a stratagem to hold onto the fortress, which controlled the western entrance to the Mediterranean. There were no further talks for the time being, but the Gibraltar issue was the subject of a two-page special report in *The Times* on 30th September 1974, in which the British and Spanish cases were set out, but without the Gibraltarian point of view being adequately covered. Salvador countered with a letter on 14th October, making the Gibraltarian case. He ended by saying that the Spanish government made much of the generosity of its special regime for Gibraltarians once sovereignty passed to Spain, but no details had been disclosed. This gratuitous throw away line was to have unfortunate repercussions for Salvador.

Ten days later, on 23rd October, the Spanish Ambassador in London, Dr Manuel Fraga Iribarne, launched a counterblast in *The Times*, pointing out that details of the special regime were known to the British government, and early in 1973 had been given to:

> a distinguished Gibraltarian who is a prominent figure in the public life of the Rock. That he did not think it proper to make it known to his fellow citizens is hardly Spain's fault. (*The Times*, 23.10.74)

This could only refer to Salvador's meeting with Ambassador Arguelles, the Spanish Foreign Office representative in Brussels, in February 1973. Moreover, Fraga let it be known to Gibraltarians, who visited him in London, that Salvador had received a very generous offer from the Spanish government for a change in the Gibraltar constitution, which he was keeping from the people because it was so good that he was frightened that they might accept it!

Salvador countered with another letter to *The Times*, dated 12th November, to which the Foreign Office did not object, confirming that he had received the proposals, but he had not released them, firstly, because they were no better than the terms offered by Castiella before the 1967 referendum when they had been rejected out of hand by the Gibraltarian electorate, and secondly, because he believed that he was bound to respect the diplomatic confidentially of his talk with Arguelles.

The reaction in Gibraltar was that Salvador should have found a way of making the details of Bravo's proposed constitution public much earlier, and some people wondered how he could have maintained such farcical proposals confidential for so long. This was more in sympathy than criticism. His defence was that he had to maintain confidentiality, but, when Fraga breached it, the Foreign Office agreed that he was free to publish the details, which he had done.

In fact, when Salvador and Pitaluga had arrived in Brussels before the Arguelles talks, they had been well received by Sir Michael Palliser, the head of the British mission to the EC, who drew up a defensive brief for use in the event of news of the meeting leaking out. Ambassador Arguelles thought the precaution quite unnecessary, little expecting that his own side would let him down.

The Times's diplomatic correspondent, Mr Rendel, with whom Salvador had been dealing, reported in the paper that the Spanish Embassy had made 'acid comments' on Salvador's disclosures. Later, he told Salvador that the Embassy had used 'any nasty or vulgar insult that you can imagine'. [Hassan's letter to the author of 8.7.94 gives an account of the whole of the Fraga affair].

This was all grist to the IWBP, who trumpeted the correspondence as proof of the 'big lie' and that Salvador was, indeed, collaborating with Whitehall in plotting to sell Gibraltar down the river! Xiberras entered *The Times* correspondence columns as well with a long letter complaining that Sir Alec Douglas Home's assurance of close consultation with both political parties in Gibraltar on discussions with Spain, given in amplification of the 1969 Constitution, was being flouted by the Governor. He said that his protests to the Governor and the

Foreign Secretary had been in vain. What else, he asked, had happened at Brussels, and had any other meetings taken place of which he was unaware? Not surprisingly, his letter elicited no reply from the British, Spanish or Gibraltar governments, who had no wish to carry on the Anglo-Spanish dialogue entwined in local Gibraltar politics in the pages of *The Times*.

In any case, the IWBP was in no fit state to profit by Salvador's disclosures. It was beginning to disintegrate through internal divisions and rivalry between Xiberras and Bossano. Xiberras was keen to pursue the will-o'-the-wisp of integration despite its repeated rejection by Whitehall. He was, in reality, driving into a political cul-de-sac. He believed that the best way forward was through a local cross-party constitutional conference, which the House of Assembly agreed to set up, to examine ideas for developing closer political and economic links with the United Kingdom. Salvador was happy to support its establishment since any ideas worth pursuing would most probably chime in well with his concept of close association rather than integration with Britain.

Bossano was keener on pursuing the struggle for wages parity: a steep but climbable mountain track and no cul-de-sac like the road chosen by Xiberras. He had no real faith in integration *per se* since he realized that it was anathema to Whitehall. By this time, he was not only a member of the House of Assembly, but also an established union leader. As branch officer of the TGWU public sector workers, he had a power base of his own and could discard the IWBP when he no longer needed it. He had ambitions to lead a party of his own, which did not help in his relationship with Xiberras, who felt he was not entirely loyal to the IWBP. He was, in truth, too strong a personality and with his stark political views, he could not act as second fiddle to anyone.

The old Isola group of independents, who had thrown their lot in with the IWBP, were not really interested in either integration or parity. This did not help party unity, and the strains of the unnatural alliance between the IWBP and the Isola group, brought about to form Peliza's anti-Hassan government after the

1972 election, were becoming all too obvious to the electorate.

It has been suggested that the furore in *The Times* had been deliberately engineered by Salvador to help his case for more financial aid under the 'support and sustain' policy. This is nonsense: the hard-nosed officials in the British Treasury were hardly likely to be swayed by a minor political row over diplomatic confidentiality.

Nonetheless, it might be fair to argue that Salvador's loyalty to the British government's Gibraltar policy, and his strict preservation of confidentiality, did endear him more to Judith Hart, the Minister for Overseas Development, than Xiberras, who was still pressing for economic, if not political, integration with Britain. British ministers and officials had confidence in Salvador with whom they had worked for three decades.

The 1975-8 aid package of £7.7 million was announced in public on 13th November 1974, only a day after Salvador's second letter to *The Times*, so he must have known that the package had already been agreed before he gave the controversial details of the Brussels meeting. It was a generous package, which he had every right to be pleased to have negotiated.

In the meantime, Admiral of the Fleet Sir Varyl Begg had been succeeded in October 1973 by Marshal of the Royal Air Force Sir John Grandy, the first airman to hold the appointment. Sir Varyl had borne the heat and burden of the first four years of the 15th siege. He was a hard man and not easy to work with; nevertheless, he was equally hard on Whitehall, the corridors of which he had known so well as chief of naval staff. He had carried through the further reorientation of the Rock's economy; negotiated the introduction of the Moroccan workforce; and encouraged the British Treasury to authorize a reasonable level of financial aid. He tended to be over sensitive to criticism of military demands associated with the Cold War. His memorial in Gibraltar is the Varyl Begg housing estate, built on naval reclaimed land towards the north end of the harbour, which he persuaded the Ministry of Defence to release for civilian housing.

Sir John Grandy was a very different character. Salvador found him rather aloof at first, and above the strife of local politics. He was very much Her Majesty's Representative in Gibraltar and looked it. Nevertheless, Salvador soon found him easy to work with and they became great friends. He could not have arrived at a worse time. The Anglo-Spanish dialogue had turned sour under Lopez Rodo; Gibraltar resolutions were again being bandied about in the United Nations; and to make matters worse, the cost of living in Gibraltar was still escalating with food prices rising at an annual rate of 20 per cent in the spring of 1974. The consequent industrial unrest was to plague Sir John for most of his four-year tenure.

The 1974 biennial wages review, which began in September, was an acrimonious affair with José Netto and Joe Bossano placing the TGWU demand for parity firmly on the table, backed by threats of industrial action if their demands were not met. Bernard Linares had abandoned politics. Fearing an IWBP takeover of the TGWU led by Bossano, he had tried to form his own union called the Gibraltar Workers Union, but he failed to obtain negotiating rights from the official employers due to intense opposition from the powerful TGWU in London as well as in Gibraltar. The central office of the TGWU, backed by Netto and Bossano in Gibraltar, had proved too much for the well intentioned, but politically inexperienced, worker/priest.

As José Netto's command of English was minimal, Joe Bossano, the Public Sector Workers' branch officer and thus the principal union officer pressing for parity, took the lead. Salvador was once again in a difficult position. With Whitehall ministries – Ministry of Defence, Property Services Agency and the Treasury – paying a much larger proportion of the wages bill than the Gibraltar government, he could not settle the dispute alone, and yet it was Gibraltar and not Whitehall that was to suffer the disruptive industrial action that accompanied the negotiations and was more vicious than in Netto's earlier general strike. Go-slows, working to rule, blacking goods and individuals, sudden power cuts, picketing, demonstrations and other irritants just short of a general strike were used to intimidate the official employers. Even the Convent suffered several months of picketing. There were three good reasons why Salvador could not negotiate a separate agreement for the Gibraltar government workers. Breaking ranks with the other official employers would have enabled Bossano not only to divide and rule, but also to establish a wages spiral beloved by trades unions the world over. He would also have been accused of using 'support and sustain' money to featherbed his own workforce. And most crucial of all, Gibraltar's frail siege economy could not have sustained the extra wages burden of around £12-16 per head per week for its own workers.

Fortunately, Xiberras and Bossano were not united on policy. Xiberras was intent on using the pressure for parity, or equivalence as he called it, as part of his integrationist case. He abhorred the industrial violence being advocated and pursued by Bossano. Nevertheless, Bossano was leader of the union 'shock troops' and had his way. At times, Salvador and his ministers went in fear for their own safety from union militants.

Negotiations finally broke down early in October. With the help of the London TGWU headquarters, a Gibraltar delegation set off for London, and reached agreement for an interim pay award while an official inquiry into the parity claim was set up. The official employers offered interim increases of between £3.40 and £6; Bossano demanded £10 across-the-board for all workers. When this was rejected, industrial action was stepped up and a one-day general strike was called for 4th December, which hastened the arrival of the parity inquiry team led by the experienced industrial trouble-shooter and arbitrator, Sir Jack Scamp.

Bossano convinced the Scamp team that acceptance of the yardstick of parity with United Kingdom wage levels was the only realistic way of settling pay disputes in the closed economic environment of Gibraltar with its shortage of indigenous labour. Scamp recommended in June 1975 that 80 per cent of UK levels was right for Gibraltar and should be phased in progressively. Bossano was far from satisfied, but by May 1976 he had accepted that half a slice was better than none for the time being. He continued to exert industrial pressure for 100 per cent parity, which he won eventually for his public sector workers in 1978, and he acquired a left-wing political 'sainthood' from his supporters for his efforts, which was never to be forgotten. His success put him on the road to becoming Salvador's main political rival with a power base in AACR's original constituency of the working classes.

Two events occurred in 1975 which wrought sea-changes in Gibraltar's internal and external politics. In September, Roy Hattersley, the new Labour government's Minister of State at the Foreign and Commonwealth Office, visited the Rock on a familiarization trip and made his name in Gibraltar by verbally closing the integration option, thus inflicting a grievous wound on Xiberras's IWBP; and in November Franco died, giving hope of a major change in Spain's Gibraltar policy. The post-IWBP and post-Franco eras were about to dawn.

Roy Hattersley's two days in Gibraltar were epoch-making. The local Constitutional Committee was in the final stages of completing its deliberations on its recommendations for forging closer political and economic links with Britain; and political campaigning was just beginning for the next House of Assembly elections, due in a year's time, in September 1976. Hattersley was convinced that integration ideas should be snuffed out once and for all, and he said so in unmistakable terms at his press conference and in interviews on TV and radio. While the Labour government would honour the preamble to the 1969 Constitution, it held that integration was neither practicable nor desirable, and that it would not be accepted by the Westminster Parliament. Xiberras quite naturally reacted with undisguised fury. Not only was Hattersley pre-empting consideration of the Constitutional Committee's findings, but he was also diminishing the IWBP's chances of winning the 1976 election. He wrote to the Governor, protesting about what he saw as a British minister interfering in Gibraltar's internal affairs. Sir John Grandy tried to placate him by pointing out that Hattersley had given a personal view, resulting from his visit, and had not been making an official statement of British government policy. Xiberras was not to be placated: he and the other IWBP members walked out of the House of Assembly in protest and stayed away for most of October. Bossano saw the futility of pursuing integration any further and resigned from the IWBP in November, but remained in the House as an independent. Salvador could not be anything but pleased to see the Opposition sliding so determinedly towards its own self-destruction.

Franco's death on 20th November and King Juan Carlos's accession to the Spanish throne two days later did not mean that Gibraltar's troubles were over. Indeed, in his accession speech, the King emphasized that Spain would continue her efforts to regain sovereignty over Gibraltar, but later signalled that methods of achieving this objective might change by ordering telephone communications to be restored between the Rock and the Campo over the Christmas period.

Three months later, in March 1976, the new Spanish Foreign Minister, José María Areilza, was invited to London to meet James Callaghan, who had succeeded Harold Wilson as British Prime Minister. Callaghan restated the British position that there could be no change of sovereignty against the freely and democratically expressed wishes of the Gibraltarians; and Areilza suggested that the new Spanish democracy might be more flexible over the Gibraltar issue. True to the British belief that generating Anglo-Spanish friendship was the best way of bringing about an amicable Gibraltar settlement, Callaghan welcomed democratic Spain's application to join the EC without insisting upon the lifting of fascist Spain's frontier restrictions. It was a lost opportunity and gross misjudgment of the Spanish character for which Gibraltar has had to pay ever since! Although later, Margaret Thatcher threatened to bar Spain's entry into the EC unless the frontier was opened, the prime opportunity of prizing Gibraltar free, when Spain was politically at her weakest, was missed.

In June, Salvador and Xiberras flew to London to present the Constitutional Committee's proposals for closer ties with Britain. The IWBP suffered a fatal blow. The British government refused to consider further constitutional change to avoid any risk of spoiling the growing warmth in Anglo-Spanish relations. By 7th September, even Xiberras's confidence failed him after the Hattersley Memorandum was published, officially ending any last lingering hopes of the integrationists. He could not muster enough candidates for the coming general election, so he resigned and the IWBP passed into history. He himself stood as an independent at the election, which was held a fortnight later on 23rd September 1976.

The 1976 election was fought primarily, as in 1972, on alternative policies towards Spain. With the recent creation of a democratic Spain, the range of options had suddenly widened in men's minds if not in practice, and brought forward a record number of candidates. The AACR deployed its well-tried team with only one change: Major Frank Dellipiani replaced Colonel Hoare. Salvador stood sensibly on his own record, and wisely advised against any hasty moves to reopen negotiations with Spain until her democratic institutions were more fully established and fears of military or right-wing coups had subsided. Conversely, he was not prepared to bring pressure to bear on Britain for further measures of decolonization until the effects could be seen of Spain becoming an EC partner. Bossano formed his own party, the Gibraltar Democratic Movement (GDM), to replace the IWBP as the main opposition party. He managed to field the eight candidates, including himself, needed to form a government. They were all newcomers with ambitions to enter Gibraltar politics. He would have liked to enlist trade unionists, but could only find three suitable candidates from their ranks – James Brooking, Joseph Victory and Joseph Gingell. The other four – Reggie Valarino, Brian Perez, Gerald Restano, and George Mascarenhas had centre or centre-right leanings with no common bond between them other than opposition to Salvador and the AACR. Thus the GDM was a hotchpotch akin to the old-style independents with Bossano instead of Peter Isola as their leader.

There were nine genuine independents: Xiberras, Peter Isola and Peliza, each with established political reputations; J E Triay, Tito Benady and Eric Ellul advocating closer association with

Spain; and Peter Isola, Willie Isola and Major Gache being individualists.

Once again Salvador topped the poll with a large majority over Xiberras and Bossano in a 74.8 per cent poll; and the AACR won the eight seats needed to keep them in office.

The results were:

J A Hassan	(AACR)	7,225
M Xiberras	(Indep)	6,029
A J Canepa	(AACR)	5,916
H Zammitt	(AACR)	5,293
J Bossano	(GDM)	5,021
A P Montegriffo	(AACR)	4,883
F Dellipiani	(AACR)	4,494
I Abecasis	(AACR)	4,454
A W Serfaty	(AACR)	4,364
M K Featherstone	(AACR)	3,757
P J Isola	(Indep)	3,608
R Peliza	(Indep)	3,383
R Valarino	(GDM)	3,368
B Perez	(GDM)	2,969
G Restano	(GDM)	2,447

The unelected were:

GDM: J Victory, G Mascarenhas, J Brooking, and J Gingell.

Independents: C Isola, W Isola, J E Triay, E Ellul, T Benady, and F Gache.

Bossano, with the second largest party, the GDM, replaced Xiberras as Leader of the opposition.

Thus it became Salvador's responsibility to lead Gibraltar in the dramatically changed circumstances brought about by Franco's death and the rebirth of Spain as a democratic constitutional monarchy. No one could tell how long the Spanish metamorphosis would take or whether any political stability achieved would last. The chances of a right-wing coup could not be discounted, and the very fear of one would make Spanish politicians chary about inducing one through being soft over Gibraltar. Madrid still found it hard to stomach the idea of raising the 15th siege even with Franco gone.

CHAPTER 11

THE STRASBOURG PROCESS
1977-79

House of Assembly in 1976:
Government:

Sir Joshua Hassan	Chief Minister
A J Canepa	Labour and Social Security
H J Zammitt	Housing and Sport
A P Montegriffo	Medical and Health
Major F J Dellipiani	Municipal Services
I Abecasis	Postal Services
A W Serfaty	Tourism, Trade and Economic Development
M Featherstone	Education and Public Works

Opposition:

J Bossano	Leader of the Opposition
Dr R G Valarino	
J B Perez	
G T Restano	

Independents:
M Xiberras
P J Isola
Major R J Peliza

When Salvador took up the reigns of office once more, he was faced with external and internal political vacuums. Externally, the new Spanish government had not yet had time to develop a new Gibraltar policy, although there was much talk about it in the newly elected Cortes, and among the local municipal authorities in the Campo. Internally, the Gibraltar opposition was fragmented and ineffective; partially winning the parity battle had largely allayed industrial unrest; the integrationist campaign had run into the sands of the Hattersley Memorandum; and there were high hopes of economic improvements which might flow from the new democratic regime in Spain. During the first half of 1977, political interest within Gibraltar was centred upon attempts to restore the two-party system of government, which had been lost with the collapse of the IWBP.

There were four political personalities who might find a unifying formula, which could bring coherence to the opposition. Maurice Xiberras had come second to Salvador in the recent general election poll and had a large personal following amongst the electors, but had failed to hold his IWBP together after the Hattersley debacle. The highly experienced Peter Isola had always sought power and had the ability to lead a party, but he was still precluded from holding ministerial office. The trade union activist, Joe Bossano, whom Salvador recognized early as a serious future rival, already had solid backing amongst the public service workers, but his hastily created, chameleon-like, GDM needed time in which to grow into a genuine alternative government-in-waiting. And in the wings, there was the dove element led by J E Triay, who had boldly formed the new 'Party for the Autonomy of Gibraltar' (PAG) soon after the 1976 election to take advantage of the birth of democratic Spain. Triay was 'a voice crying in the wilderness' as far as the electorate were concerned. Nevertheless, Salvador never underestimated his abilities and political charisma amongst those members of the business community who had suffered most from the frontier restrictions and wanted to come to an arrangement with Spain. Moreover, his oft-used links with Madrid made him a threat to Salvador's control of the way people looked on Spain.

Instead of developing into a political force, with which Salvador would have to reckon, Bossano's GDM was soon disintegrating through its own contradictions, and helped, no doubt, by a mix of

AACR, press and general public criticism, which encouraged his non-trade union members to desert. The first signs of internal tension broke surface on Armistice Day 1976, when Bossano refused to lay the Leader of the Opposition's traditional wreath at the Cross of Sacrifice on the grounds of his pacifist beliefs. Gerald Restano, the most right-wing of his non-trade union colleagues, laid it instead.

As the days went by, the three GDM members of the House began to feel more than uncomfortable about Bossano's radical policies. Within nine months, Dr Valarino crossed the floor of the House in August 1977, followed shortly afterwards by Restano, and Perez, and finally by Mascarenhas. With the GDM having only one member, Bossano himself, left in the House, Xiberras, as leader of the independents, took over once more as Leader of the Opposition, and began to form a new party of his own, the Democratic Party of British Gibraltar (DPBG), with much the same policies as his defunct IWBP of working for closer links, although not actual integration, with Britain. His supporters in the House were Peter Isola, Bob Peliza and Gerald Restano. Dr Valarino joined the AACR government as Minister for Municipal Services; and Brian Perez supported the government without obtaining a portfolio. In the consequential reshuffle of portfolios, Dellipiani, who had surrendered Municipal Services to Valarino, took over Education, leaving Featherstone with Public Works.

In gathering his new DPBG together (its formation was not announced until June 1978), Xiberras sought to tap those who wished to oppose Salvador and yet were not part of Bossano's trade union clique. His driving political motives were, firstly, to expose what he saw as Salvador's cosy relationship with British ministers, which he believed could lead to an Anglo-Spanish deal behind Gibraltarian backs to slip the Rock into Spain either as a condominion or by lease-back; and, secondly, to press for full British citizenship instead of Overseas British citizenship, which was being proposed in the Green Paper on citizenship. He did not have long to wait before he had several opportunities to make his presence felt at international level during what became known as the 'Strasbourg process'.

The Anglo-Spanish dialogue was revived in late 1976 by the emergence of two young and ambitious politicians as foreign ministers in London and Madrid: David Owen and Marcelino Oreja. David Owen was a surprise appointment to Foreign Secretary, made by James Callaghan: he was young, inexperienced and believed he could solve the thorniest international problems through face to face meetings. He hoped to persuade Salvador to meet the Spaniards halfway with some condominion-style solution; and he tried to encourage Oreja to lift the frontier restrictions as a preliminary sweetener for the Gibraltarians to make negotiations for such a solution feasible. He seems to have had little real appreciation of the depth of Gibraltarian resentment of any suggestion of concessions to Spain on sovereignty.

Oreja was an Anglophile like Lopez Bravo, but also like Bravo he was not a free agent and was ground between the lower millstone of the demands of the people of the Campo for an immediate lifting of frontier restrictions to help their economy, and the upper millstone of doctrinaire opinion in political, official and military circles in Madrid, which refused to countenance any weakening over Gibraltar. Oreja met his Campo critics first with a speech at San Roque in February 1977, in which he promised to seek a formula for returning the Rock to Spain, thus ending frontier restrictions. Then on 12th July, the upper millstone began to turn. The Spanish government declared to the Cortes that the re-establishment of the territorial integrity of the Spanish realm was still one of its primary foreign policy objectives. Whether he liked it or not, Oreja could not propose an end to the 15th siege without substantial concessions by Britain on sovereignty. In fact, little had changed as far as Gibraltar was concerned with the advent of democracy in Spain. David Owen visited Madrid in September to invite the Spanish Prime Minister, Adolfo Suárez, to visit London in October. He was at pains to point out that the British government would not make raising the Spanish blockade of the Rock a precondition for British support for Spain's entry into the EC and NATO. His view was that one good turn deserved another, and, as the Spaniards were gentlemen, they were expected to respond to the British gesture by lifting restrictions on Gibraltar of their own accord. He was to be bitterly disappointed.

Just before Suárez's visit to London in October, he was embarrassed by a one-day strike and noisy demonstrations at the frontier by the people of La Linea, who demanded the opening of the gates and the ending of the siege. As in Franco's day, these local demonstrations in far-off, backward Andalusia made little impact on the hardliners in Madrid.

Suárez's visit to London brought two substantial gains for Gibraltar. Not only did Suárez recognize the existence of the Gibraltarians as a people with rights of their own, but he also agreed to Gibraltarian political representatives attending future Anglo-Spanish talks on Gibraltar, but only as part of the British delegation and not as a third party. He stated bluntly that lifting restrictions could not be a gradual process: it must be part of a 'global' package. Suárez's principal contention was that the whole Gibraltar question could be solved within the parameters of Spain's new democratic and 'regionalized' constitution, which was being drafted to give the Basques and Catalans a large measure of autonomy within the Spanish realm. Gibraltar could be given a comparable, though perhaps a more independent status, through 'a negotiated statute respecting the identity, culture and special characteristics of the Gibraltarian people'. This offer was unlikely to appeal to the Gibraltarians any more than Castiella's or Bravo's version of the same theme. The only perceptible change was that Gibraltar would have autonomy within a democratic Spain rather than a fascist dictatorship.

Following the now established practice, the Governor, Chief Minister and Leader of the Opposition were summoned back to London early in November for briefing on the Suárez visit and for consultations on the way ahead. Salvador was accompanied as usual by Joe Pitaluga as his personal aide. David Owen sprung an immediate surprise on Salvador by asking to see him privately. They met with only Ewen Fergusson, Owen's private secretary, present.

The Foreign Secretary started this private meeting by suggesting that there was a need for Salvador to have contacts with the new Spanish ministers, who seemed to be more flexible in their approach and might be persuaded of the advantages to Spain of lifting frontier restrictions if it were put to them by a Gibraltarian. He proposed a clandestine 'cloak and dagger' approach, but, after his experience with Ambassador Arguelles in Brussels, Salvador was chary of secret meetings, which could so easily become public knowledge. He replied that he saw no difficulty whatsoever in meeting Spanish ministers quite openly, and could see no reason to dramatize the affair. The first step should be a straightforward approach to see whether Oreja was, indeed, prepared to meet a Gibraltarian team. Owen was satisfied with Salvador's reaction, and the diplomatic machine went into action.

Back in Gibraltar, Salvador told the House of Assembly that he had proposed to the Foreign Secretary that the time was now ripe for reopening Anglo-Spanish talks, this time with Gibraltarian representatives in the British delegation. He had been adamant in London that the talks should only be exploratory in nature and without commitment on either side. The House endorsed his proposal unanimously.

Oreja also welcomed a meeting, which was to be held at Strasbourg on 24th November 'in the margins' of the Spanish negotiations for entry into the EC. It took place in a small building next to the UK's EC Commission's offices, and lasted two and a half hours – long enough for the two sides to get to know each other personally but not much more than that. The room was so small and cramped that it was possible for Salvador to see the scribbled notes passed to Oreja by his hardline Foreign Ministry official, Solano.

On two occasions Salvador saw a curt note, saying 'corta' (end the discussion), being passed, which seemed to have had little or no effect on Oreja's enthusiastic perorations! Salvador claims that he and Xiberras had a bipartisan approach to the meeting as he had had with Peter Isola at the United Nations. While this may be true as a generality, Xiberras still believed that Salvador and the Foreign Office were intent on finding ways of slipping the Rock unobtrusively closer towards Spain. He saw his first duty was to be on guard against any concessions on sovereignty being made to Spain as sweeteners by either Owen or Salvador.

The declared aim of the meeting was to find ways of re-establishing good neighbourly relations between Gibraltar and Spain. Salvador's main preoccupation was to drive home the inhumanity of the frontier restrictions, which were fascist in origin and their continuation was a disgrace to new democratic Spain. Oreja was more interested, as his prime minister had been in London, in putting over the merits of the new Spanish constitution, which he claimed would fully protect Gibraltar's 'interests'. As usual, he ignored the fundamental issue of their 'wishes', and there was, once again, no real meeting of minds.

Nevertheless, all those present felt it was worth continuing the Strasbourg process – Anglo-Spanish talks with Gibraltar ministers present – in Paris in March 1978 in the hope that some common ground for improving relations might emerge. Despite Suárez's statement during his London visit that lifting restrictions could not be piecemeal, tentative proposals were made to look into the possibility of setting up a number of joint working parties at local level to study what could be done to alleviate hardship caused to citizens on either side of the frontier, which had been Salvador's main theme at the meeting. The first three working parties would perhaps study reopening the Algeciras ferry, restoring land communications, and restarting the payment of pensions to former Spanish workers, who had contributed to the Gibraltar pension funds.

This first meeting in the Strasbourg process did seem to have some effect on Oreja's thinking. Telephone links with the Campo were restored permanently at Christmas time, 1977. On 24th January 1978, Javier Ruperez, the foreign policy adviser to Suárez's political party (UCD), visited the Rock via Tangier for long and constructive consultations with Salvador, who was now seen in Madrid as one of the key players in the Gibraltar confrontation.

Indeed, Strasbourg had changed the whole basis of Gibraltar negotiations from a bilateral struggle between Britain and Spain into a triangular match in which the Gibraltar government was, at last, recognized by Spain as having a legitimate and crucial part to play.

Having made the usual hardline speech on Gibraltar to the Cortes on 11th January, Oreja's line in a speech to foreign journalists on 30th January had noticeably softened, thanks no doubt to the Ruperez/Hassan talks. He discoursed on dropping dependence on Utrecht and looking at Gibraltar in the present-day context. This seemed to infer that Spain was now depending on her entry into the EC and NATO to provide a sensible answer, which it might well have done if Europe had quickly become a replica of the United States. Unfortunately for Oreja, his softer line on Gibraltar was soon embarrassed by the Organization for African Unity claiming that the Canary Islands should be granted independence from Spain as states of 'African character'; and King Hassan of Morocco also observing publicly that the return of Gibraltar to Spain would mean the return to Morocco of the two Spanish enclaves on the Moroccan coast, Ceuta and Melilla.

When arrangements were being made for the Paris meetings set for 15th March 1978, Salvador asked for morning and afternoon sessions so that he could talk to Oreja personally over lunch. The talks were as usual cordial but made no real progress: the Spanish claim and the Gibraltarian refusal to accept Spanish sovereignty made this inevitable. The setting up of the working parties had been proving difficult, and despite the endorsement given to them by the Paris conference all three were constantly delayed by Spanish prevarication until 17th July.

Only Salvador could claim any success in Paris. When he met Oreja in the lunch break, he complained bitterly at the harshness of the division of families caused by the closure of the frontier. Oreja responded by appointing Esteban Bravo as a confidential liaison officer between Salvador and himself to whom Salvador could talk 'as if he were talking to Oreja himself'. Bravo was to play an active part over several years as a 'runner' between

Salvador and successive Spanish foreign ministers. [Personal account of Strasbourg process: Hassan, 7.9.93.]

Sir John Grandy's tenure as Governor ended in April 1978. He was succeeded by General Sir William Jackson (one of the joint authors), whom Salvador quickly noted was the first governor to be younger than himself. A sapper and thus imbued with the history of the Rock and its people, he had been C-in-C of Northern Command and then joined the Army Board as Quartermaster-General. He was also a member of the Cabinet Office Historical Section, writing the last three volumes of the official history of the Mediterranean campaigns, in which he had fought as a young officer and had visited Gibraltar on several occasions, although he had not served on the Rock.

At one of his early meetings with Salvador, Sir William made three points. First of all, there were quite enough people in London to present Whitehall's point of view to Gibraltar, but there was only one person in Gibraltar, himself as Governor, to speak for Gibraltar in Whitehall. His first task was to strengthen Gibraltar's voice in the British corridors of power. His second task was to find a way to break the 15th siege. And his third was to increase the sense of Gibraltarian identity and to give Gibraltar greater self-confidence. He hoped that there would be far more Gibraltarians and many fewer British expatriates in senior posts by the time his tenure as governor ended. Salvador had seen so many governors come and go that he took such aspirations with a pinch of salt, but offered his ready co-operation to the new Governor, who was clearly as left of centre in his political views as Salvador. But he did warn him to be careful about the way he talked about increased Gibraltarianization. While people might like to see more Gibraltarians heading government departments, they would be worried by the resultant weakening of British links. The more cynical would see it as a preparatory step to a British withdrawal and the Rock reverting to Spanish sovereignty with an established Gibraltarian government.

With the Whitehall departments' acceptance of 100 per cent parity in the latest round of wage negotiations, industrial peace seemed assured and the Spanish question again came to the forefront of Gibraltar's affairs. David Owen wanted to engineer another meeting with Salvador without Xiberras, whom he deemed an 'abominable no-man', being present. The opportunity came with an invitation to Salvador to attend Sir Gerald Lathbury's memorial service on 3rd July, which enabled him to fly to London without raising Xiberras's suspicions. David Owen agreed to see him at the Foreign Office at 10am before the service for which Salvador would have to leave the FCO by 11am. Much to Salvador's annoyance he was kept waiting until 10.45am before being ushered into the Secretary of State's office, and then the short meeting was what Salvador has described as a 'stormy fiasco'.

David Owen said that he wanted more support from Gibraltar ministers for a rapprochement with Spain, and then unwisely added: 'I will have to push you along'. Salvador's curt reply was: 'No sir; I will not be there if you do. You will have to push the people of Gibraltar yourself.' The effect was electric: David Owen realized that he had met his match! There was far less inclination in the FCO thereafter to take Salvador's support for granted, but it also raised suspicions in Salvador's mind of the unwelcome effects of Spain's entry into the EC on Whitehall thinking. An unimpeachable excuse might emerge from the new European relationships for Britain to renege on the preamble to the 1969 Constitution!

The first meeting of the Strasbourg working parties had been set for 17th July in London, and it had been intended to announce the date at the beginning of the month. On 5th July, cables arrived from Sir Anthony Acland, British Ambassador in Madrid, reporting that Oreja was getting cold feet about the working parties. First, he wanted no early announcement of the meetings, which he said should be low-key; secondly, he wished to discuss pensions first, before the Algeciras ferry; and, thirdly, he would not be able to meet David Owen in New York in September to review progress as had been scheduled for some time.

The Governor, with Salvador's concurrence, sent a strongly worded signal to the FCO deploring the Spanish request for no announcement and low-key meetings because this would undermine the credibility of the Strasbourg process in the eyes of the international as well as the local Gibraltar press. There was no objection to dealing with pensions first as long as the Algeciras ferry was also discussed, otherwise it would appear that Spain was only interested in squeezing money out of Gibraltar. The reopening of the ferry was far more important to the economies of both the Campo and Gibraltar. The Gibraltar House of Assembly would not agree to a penny of their pension funds being paid in Spain until the ferry was reopened.

For once, Madrid accepted that there was no way out. They agreed that the teams could meet in London on 17th July, but warned that their delegation was not ready to do more than listen to what the British side had to offer. Robin O'Neill, the Deputy Governor, led the British team, supported by Joe Pitaluga. It was all very friendly, but lacking in any real substance. Both sides handed over position papers and agreed to study them before meeting again in October, thereby keeping Strasbourg alive, but only just.

In the meantime, the old fear of Gibraltar being sold down the river welled up in Salvador's mind. The Owen 'I must push you' incident still rankled. Then the new Governor started his programme of making Gibraltar more Gibraltarian by flying, with FCO's permission and Salvador's tacit agreement, the Gibraltar City flag over the Convent. It was flown on the gaff below the Governor's flag (the Union flag defaced with the Governor's crest), as in a flagship, where the Admiral flies his flag at the masthead with the national flag on the gaff. The same format was used at the Convent. Salvador's initial reaction was one of pride that Gibraltar's own flag should be given such prominence, but, on second thoughts and with the help of Gibraltarian cynics, he began to suspect that it might be part of a deliberate ploy to reduce the significance of the Union Jack to Gibraltar. His anxiety was increased when the Financial and Development Secretary opposed a project for building a new power station and water distillation plant on the North Mole on the grounds that before long Gibraltar would be able to buy both power and water from Spain. It all seemed too ominous for comfort. Salvador believed, with some justification, that Gibraltar was being pushed too fast and too far in the tidal wave of enthusiasm for a united Europe. At his weekly Friday afternoon 'cosy' with the Governor, Salvador asked Sir William point-blank whether there was, indeed, a hidden agenda for getting rid of the Rock. Sir William could assure him that no such policy existed although he confessed that there was a body of opinion in Whitehall which would be happy to be rid of the Gibraltar anachronism and believed in a policy of 'nudging by neglect'! He felt that the most dangerous thing was the absence of any well-developed Gibraltar policy in the FCO.

He himself had failed to find one during his initial briefings before sailing out to Gibraltar. The only fixed point was honouring the preamble to the 1969 Constitution: everything else was pragmatic reaction to events as they forced themselves upon the lowly Gibraltar desk officer in the Southern European Department of the FCO. He could assure Salvador that although healthy Anglo-Spanish relations were seen as more important than the affairs of Gibraltar, there was no inclination to sacrifice the Rock on the altar of supposedly growing European unity. There was, however, a deliberate ploy to preempt Gibraltarian affairs from fouling Anglo-Spanish relations. Any real initiatives would have to come from Gibraltar. He, as Governor, intended to seize every opportunity to put forward new ways ahead.

With Salvador's help and advice, he had already stirred the FCO into persuading Madrid to accept the first meeting of the Strasbourg working parties in London. He had gone further by suggesting to the FCO his own solution to the Gibraltar problem. A new agreement should be drawn up, which accepted the validity of both the Spanish claim and the right of the Gibraltarians to self-determination, and which allowed Spain to test Gibraltarian opinion by referendum every 30 years. As soon as the Gibraltarians decided that they wished to join Spain, Britain would surrender sovereignty. Whether the time interval should be 10, 20, or 30 years would be subject to negotiation, but from the point of view of maintaining stability 30 seemed the right answer. After the hostility bred by frontier restrictions, the people of Gibraltar were unlikely to change their minds in less than a full generation.

It was all easier said than done. The FCO and the British Embassy in Madrid handled all Gibraltar's external affairs. The Governor could only advise, coax and goad. It was not until almost the end of November that Oreja could be cajoled into accepting the second round of working party talks, which were held in Madrid on 14th December with predictable results. Robin O'Neill again led the Gibraltar team. He summed up his frustration:

> It was like negotiating with an East European country – wooden and inflexible. There is still a great gulf between the UK and Spanish understanding of each other's positions, which can only be bridged by talking, but we will have to talk for a long time to get our self-determination stand into their thick skulls. [Jackson Diaries for 16.12.78]

Minimal progress was made. Technical sub-groups were set up on pensions and telecommunications. There was no progress on the Algeciras ferry, which Madrid had earmarked as a blackmailing card to induce the formal Anglo-Spanish negotiations demanded by the United Nations. This being so, the reopening of the ferry was a very long way off: it is still not running in 1995! However, telephone communications with the Campo were again restored over Christmas and not disconnected thereafter.

1979 was an anxious and frustrating year for Salvador. General election campaigns in Spain, Britain and Gibraltar created an atmosphere of change and uncertainty. The announcement of the Spanish elections for 1st March came first, along with press reports that Felipe Gonzalez's socialists (PSOE) might just win. In Britain, the reverse was happening: Jim Callaghan's Labour government was tottering to its close with Margaret Thatcher's Conservative opposition well ahead in the opinion polls. And in Gibraltar there was, as yet, no reason to expect the early election which eventually occurred in February 1980.

Salvador's anxiety about British intentions was exacerbated at the beginning of January by the Governor probing his views on the latest FCO suggestion for driving the Strasbourg process forward. David Owen was keen to make dramatic progress before the Labour government was forced out of office, which seemed increasingly likely. He wanted to offer substantive ministerial talks in exchange for lifting frontier restrictions. As sweeteners to Spain, he also wanted to 'internationalize' the dockyard, naval base and airport, possibly as NATO facilities so that Spanish ships and aircraft could use them. The talks would not overtly embrace the sovereignty issue, but, in Foreign Office jargon, it might be alluded to obliquely.

Salvador would have none of it. He made it quite clear to Sir William that he could not be associated with the Owen proposals. He knew that Xiberras would object vehemently and would have the electorate solidly behind him. This was especially so after the recent brutal murder of Madrid's military governor by the Basque terrorists ETA. The majority of Gibraltarians wanted to have nothing to do with the new democratic but unstable Spain, and preferred the isolation of the Rock, their safe and peaceful home.

Gibraltarian antagonism towards Spain was not eased by a visit on 13th January by the PSOE's shadow foreign minister, Luis Yañez, who saw Salvador and Xiberras, and then held an over-frank press conference at which he expressed the view that the frontier restrictions were wrong, but, nevertheless, it was not the right time to lift them. The PSOE wanted Gibraltar back just as much as all other Spanish political parties. He was sure that the Gibraltarians would much prefer to be part of a socialist Spain than continuing to suffer the deprivations of a closed frontier. Spain was a different place now, which Gibraltar could join without fear of losing its autonomy. Press comment next day was vitriolic.

Despite the Governor reporting fully on Salvador's and Xiberras's opposition to the proposal of ministerial talks in exchange for an open frontier, David Owen decided to press ahead and asked to see Salvador without Xiberras on 24th January. There would be no combined Hassan/Xiberras meeting with him until after the Spanish elections when it was clear who would be in power in Madrid. Xiberras protested vigorously through the Governor and Owen agreed to see him with Salvador provided he could see Salvador alone a day or two earlier. Like all affairs of mice and men, the planned meetings were thrown into disarray by the death of Salvador's mother-in-law, which compelled him to return to Gibraltar without meeting David Owen, and to withdraw from public affairs until the period of mourning was over.

In the meantime, Joe Bossano, who was not privy to, but was aware through rumour, of the Owen proposals, decided to try to influence events by mounting anti-Strasbourg rallies and a march on the Convent to express Gibraltarian misgivings. If the Spaniards were to be persuaded to lift the siege, they would want concessions. Rather than give anything, Bossano's followers preferred to stay under siege: their jobs would not be taken by Spaniards, who were often willing to accept lower wages. His rallies were well attended, but his Convent march on 3rd February fizzled out in pouring rain!

Before Salvador and Xiberras left again for London, the Governor had taken the precaution of advising the Foreign Secretary on how to handle both men. They should be asked for their advice rather than risk any repetition of the 'I will have to push you' incident. Owen took this to heart, and both Salvador and Xiberras returned to Gibraltar well pleased with the forthright advice they had given to the Foreign Secretary. David Owen had espoused the Governor's referendum idea and had persuaded the Cabinet to agree that Spain must be offered the opportunity to test Gibraltarian opinion at set intervals of seven to ten years. Salvador suggested 20 to 25 years was more practicable. He also insisted that not a penny from the pension funds would be forthcoming until the Algeciras ferry was restored and restrictions on landing and take-off flight-paths at the airport were at least eased. Towards the end of the interview, the Foreign Secretary introduced ideas for linking Spain's EC entry with the lifting of frontier restrictions – a policy which the FCO mandarins had been trying to avoid for fear of fouling Anglo-Spanish relations. The phrase coined was that the continuing of frontier restrictions would be 'inconceivable' when Spain joined the EC. Furthermore, Spain was to host the 1980 Helsinki Human Rights Conference. It seemed equally inconceivable that she would be able to do so with much credibility as long as a glaring breach of human rights existed in her own back yard. But although inconceivable to the British mind, nothing was inconceivable in the Spanish conscience as far as the Rock was concerned.

The whole Strasbourg process was soon overtaken by events, but Owen's discussions with Gibraltar's political leaders were not a waste of time. Although he was never able to use his newly acquired insight into Gibraltarian thinking, the FCO officials, who attended the meetings, were strongly influenced by them. More importantly, the talks restored Salvador's confidence in British intentions and in the Governor. There was no plot to sell Gibraltar down the river: only a difficult balancing act for the FCO to perform. The best interests of Gibraltar were often at variance with the requirements of the British Ambassador in Madrid, who was more concerned with the wider scenario of Anglo-Spanish relations, and who tended to see events through Spanish eyes.

Adolfo Suárez won the Spanish general election on 1st March 1979 so it looked as if Oreja would be able to carry on with the Strasbourg process. It was not to be. On 28th March, Jim Callaghan lost a crucial vote of confidence in the House of Commons, and on 1st May, Margaret Thatcher became Britain's first woman Prime Minister with Lord Carrington as her Foreign Secretary. When asked about the future of the Strasbourg process, Lord Carrington replied that he knew nothing about it as he had played no part in its creation or development. He wanted to think afresh about Gibraltar before opening new talks with the Spaniards. It would be some time, however, before he would be able give Gibraltar his full attention. Thus, the Strasbourg process died unmourned as David Owen left the FCO.

Little perhaps pleased Salvador more at this period than his sweeping victory on 2nd March over Bossano in the House of Assembly. As usual, Bossano had tabled a motion condemning the Strasbourg process, which was defeated by 14 votes to one. It was to be one of many Bossano attacks on subsequent negotiating 'processes'. Salvador was always willing to talk to Spaniards in his quest for an honourable solution, which he could put confidently to the electorate.

Meanwhile, Bossano was building his own political platform opposing any softening towards Spain.

CHAPTER 12

THE LISBON AGREEMENT
1979-82

House of Assembly after the 1980 Election:
Government:

Sir Joshua Hassan	Chief Minister
A J Canepa	Economic Development, Trade, Labour and Social Security
M K Featherstone	Public Works
I Abecasis	Tourism and Postal Services
H Zammitt	Housing and Sport
Major F J Dellipiani	Education
Dr R G Valarino	Municipal Services
J B Perez	Medical and Health Services

Opposition:

P J Isola	Leader of the Opposition
G T Restano	
Major R J Peliza	
W T Scott	
A T Loddo	
A J Haynes	

J Bossano	Independent

The Spanish and United Kingdom elections were over, but it would take some time before the new governments would be ready to lock horns again over Gibraltar. Oreja stayed on as Spanish Foreign Minister and was keen to restart the Strasbourg process in which he had invested much of his political capital and he wanted to see some return on it. Lord Carrington, on the other hand, had bigger fish to fry: the international crisis created by the Russian invasion of Afghanistan; the cruise missile deployment arguments in NATO; and the struggle for Rhodesia, which looked ripe for settlement. These matters would hold his attention for some months, leaving little time to devote to Gibraltar. In the middle of June, he advised Oreja that he would not be able to meet him for preliminary discussions until the United Nations session opened in New York in September. In the meantime, he made Sir Ian Gilmour, the Lord Privy Seal and Minister of State in the Foreign and Commonwealth Office, responsible for Gibraltar's external affairs; and he authorized officials to continue seeking a basis for substantive ministerial meetings on Gibraltar in the autumn.

Sir Ian Gilmour visited the Rock on a familiarization tour in mid-July. He created a very favourable impression with his genuine care for and understanding of Gibraltarian feelings, and for the robustness of his arguments in their support. His constant reiteration of the 'inconceivability' of Spain entering either NATO or the EC without lifting restrictions was music to local ears, and showed that the Labour Party's refusal to link the two – entry into the Western Community and frontier restrictions – had no place in Tory thinking. The screw was to be turned at each stage of Spain's NATO and EC entry negotiations in much the same way as Spain had tried to coerce Gibraltar during the United Nations' decolonization debates of the 1960s.

Quite unexpectedly Gibraltar was faced with a general election of its own. In the middle of August, Maurice Xiberras was forced to leave politics, following the breakup of his marriage. He resigned his seat in the House of Assembly, and handed over the leadership of the opposition and of the DPBG to Peter Isola. Salvador was left to decide whether to hold a by-election or to ask the Governor for a dissolution of the House of Assembly and a general election. He decided on the latter because a general election was due in any case by September 1980 so a by-election would be a waste of tax-payers' money. Salvador's only worry was timing.

There were several factors to be considered. The FCO and the Governor wanted it as early as possible in order to give Gibraltar recently elected representatives at the new Anglo-Spanish talks that they hoped would start by the turn of the year. Peter Isola also saw advantage in an early date. Salvador, however, hesitated for one overt and two covert reasons. Overtly, he was worried about the next budget: if it was likely to be an unpopular one, he would ask for an early dissolution; but, if the financial situation was improving as much as he thought, he would delay the poll for as long as the Constitution would allow.

The two covert reasons also called for maximum delay, and were surprising but relevant to his political sensibilities. First, he wanted to give Peter Isola enough time to consolidate his position as leader of the opposition, and to strengthen his DPBG. By doing this he would ensure that J E Triay was squeezed out and could not become leader of the opposition, which would have polarized Gibraltar politics into pro- and anti-Spanish lobbies instead of the current division between different degrees of opposition to the Spanish claim. It is worth noting that at this time he viewed J E Triay as a greater threat to his position than Joe Bossano. The latter had abandoned his efforts to form an 'across-the-board' political party under his own leadership and was building a new 'Gibraltar Socialist and Labour Party' (GSLP) with his election candidates drawn from amongst his trades union supporters.

The second covert reason, and perhaps the most influential, demonstrates his humanity and loyalty to old colleagues. There was draft legislation almost ready to be tabled in the House of Assembly for the provision of pensions for long-serving members of the House of Assembly. There were several AACR members whom he would have liked to retire to bring in younger blood, but he would not do so unless he knew that they had an alternative source of income. He decided that he must see the pension legislation through before asking the Governor for a dissolution so that they were not embarrassed financially.

After much toing and froing, in which the Christmas period had to be taken into account, the election date was fixed for 6th February 1980 – just within the constitutional time limit. The AACR had a surplus of suitable candidates so Salvador was able to retire Aurelio Montegriffo and Abraham Serfaty, who had served him so well since the foundation of the AACR and who were now assured of ministers' pensions. Serfaty went on to become an excellent Mayor of Gibraltar. Since Dr Valarino and Brian Perez had crossed the floor of the House from Bossano's failed GDM, Salvador decided they must present themselves for re-selection as candidates by the AACR Committee. Both were re-selected; and the AACR eight-man team for the election became: Hassan, Canepa, Abecasis, Valarino, Featherstone, Dellipiani, Zammitt and Perez.

Thanks to Salvador delaying the election for as long as possible, Isola did have enough time to gather together eight candidates. Bossano's very recently formed GSLP could only field six, including himself, who were all politically inexperienced and relatively unknown trade union colleagues of his. J E Triay's PAG presented a meagre two candidates besides himself – Tito Benady and Peter Triay. There were also two independents, Dr Cecil Isola and Eric Ellul. The campaign was mainly fought on television, radio and in the press. It was a very dull affair with an AACR victory a foregone conclusion. The only interest lay in who would lead the opposition in the new House – Isola, Bossano or Triay – and what their relative positions would turn out to be in popular esteem. Salvador was not faced with any real challenge and could be said to have underplayed his hand. Sparse public interest was reflected in a correspondingly low poll of 65.32 per cent as against the usual 70 per cent. The votes cast for the 15 members elected were:

Hassan	(AACR)	4,970 votes
Bossano	(GSLP)	4,906
Canepa	(AACR)	4,563
P Isola	(DPBG)	4,201
Peliza	(DPBG)	3,857
Restano	(DPBG)	3,601

Abecasis	(AACR)	3,478
Valarino	(AACR)	3,352
Featherstone	(AACR)	3,138
Dellipiani	(AACR)	3,131
Zammitt	(AACR)	3,105
Perez	(AACR)	3,089
Scott	(DPBG)	2,831
Loddo	(DPBG)	2,814
Haynes	(DPBG)	2,810

This result was significant in two ways. First of all, Bossano came second in the poll with only 64 votes less than Salvador, showing his greatly increased personal popularity, but none of his GSLP candidates was elected to support him. He was still a political leader without a party, whom Salvador could denigrate but no longer ignore. Secondly, J E Triay's PAG occupied the bottom three places in the whole of the poll, and so could be denigrated and ignored. Bossano and not Triay became Salvador's nightmare. Peter Isola emerged as the undoubted Leader of the Opposition with five of his DPBG elected. He posed no significant threat to Salvador as a future chief minister because of his financial problems.

Well before the election campaign had started officials in London, Madrid and Gibraltar had begun their task of preparing a formula, which might provide a replacement for the Strasbourg process. Oreja and Carrington did meet as planned 'in the margins' of the United Nations' 1979 session in New York on 24th September. Carrington stated firmly that the British pledge to the people of Gibraltar was an immovable datum point in any discussions on the future of the Rock. What was needed was a facesaver for Spain to lift restrictions as early as possible if Britain's signature was ever to adorn Spain's EC accession treaty. Oreja noted the threat and replied that Spain would lift restrictions on two conditions: that Britain would enter into substantive talks on 'Gibraltar's territorial status'; and that the frontier fence was removed. The latter was mere window-dressing to enable Oreja to claim a significant, although quite useless, political advance: the airfield perimeter fence would still seal off the British half of the isthmus just a few yards further south.

Lord Carrington agreed to study Oreja's proposal. He hoped they would be able to meet again in Brussels in November. In the meantime, officials could continue preparing the ground. One of the officials was the Governor, who had served in various policy-making directorates in Whitehall on and off for some 15 years. In his view, it was essential to seize the initiative on behalf of Gibraltar: Whitehall on its own tended to come up with grey 'lowest common denominator' proposals! He and Salvador had been invited to the opening of the Royal Engineers' new Gibraltar Barracks complex at Minley in Surrey on 27th September so it was arranged for them both to visit the FCO next day for a briefing on the Carrington/Oreja meeting and to discuss the way ahead.

The FCO meeting with the Permanent Under-Secretary, Sir Michael Palliser, in the chair, was a success. It was agreed that the Governor, in conjunction with the head of the Southern European Department of the FCO, should draft model British and Spanish declarations, which might be used to seal a deal between Carrington and Oreja when they were able to meet. These would be sent to Sir Anthony Acland in Madrid to discuss with Spanish officials. The drafts produced by the Governor were:

> Spanish Declaration: In view of the Spanish Government's application to join the EEC and accede to the Treaty of Rome, communications by sea, land and air will be restored between Gibraltar and Spain.
> British Declaration: HMG are prepared to discuss the future of Gibraltar in the context of the EEC. There can, however, be no change in the status of Gibraltar without the freely and democratically expressed wishes of the people of Gibraltar. (Jackson Diary, 7.10.1979)

The Governor's original idea of allowing Madrid to test Gibraltarian opinion at intervals of about 20 to 25 years was dropped early on for two reasons: Spain was not willing to risk a series of rebuffs; and Gibraltar would suffer from repeated phases of political instability. The FCO wanted to delete the words 'in the context of the EEC', but the Governor advised against this because 'to discuss the future of Gibraltar' without the EEC qualification could imply discussion of sovereignty.

Both Salvador and Peter Isola were given every opportunity to comment on these preliminary drafts and on the many subsequent changes of wording and expansion of the texts. They often asked for amendments, which were usually accepted by the Southern European Department of the FCO. They did not disagree with the idea of the two joint declarations, but were sceptical, as they had every right to be, about the Spaniards agreeing to anything so positive, which gave them nothing in return. The declarations were to undergo many changes in detail but not of substance over the next few months. Indeed, the drafts, which were eventually amalgamated into one combined document, were to provide the foundation upon which the future Lisbon and Brussels agreements were eventually based.

One piece of encouraging news came from the FCO in September. Anglo-Spanish relations seemed to be improving to the extent that a royal state visit to London by King Juan Carlos was being proposed for June, and a tentative suggestion was being studied in Whitehall for the Queen to visit Gibraltar during her 1980 Mediterranean tour. The Governor seized the opportunity, with Salvador's help, to make a strong case for her to do so: the Gibraltarians needed reassurance on the sovereignty issue before the forthcoming substantive Anglo-Spanish ministerial talks; they deserved a royal visit after withstanding thirteen years of siege; the visit would be an imaginative way of setting the seal on the restoration of normal Gibraltarian relations with Spain and would fix a target date for completion of negotiations; and the Queen should not visit Madrid without coming to Gibraltar as well.

By October 1979, pressure was again building up in the Campo for an immediate opening of the frontier. Demonstrations, riots and a general strike occurred in La Linea, and every effort was being made by Andalusian representatives in the Cortes to speed up the lifting of restrictions. As early as July 1979, the Cortes had voted for the gradual easing of the siege in exchange for British concessions. It was a welcome but useless gesture. As Salvador frequently pointed out to journalists and others, Gibraltar had nothing to give but goodwill in exchange for the ending of Spain's unilaterally imposed coercive measures.

In Madrid, views on a united Europe were as divided as they were in London with pro-Europeans and Euro-sceptics existing in all political parties. The pro-Europeans were bringing pressure to bear on Oreja to demonstrate in EC circles how democratic, civilized and worthy of acceptance into the Western European family Spain had become by ending Franco's Gibraltar folly. The Euro-sceptics were conversely keen to keep the siege going to ensure a British veto on Spain's entry, which seemed increasingly likely. Margaret Thatcher was already known for her ruthless defence of British interests. It seemed unlikely that she would countenance Spain's accession before frontier restrictions were lifted. These pressures persuaded Oreja to ask on 18th October for a resumption of Strasbourg type meetings, and a fortnight later he was pressing for an Anglo-Spanish ministerial meeting. He was rebuffed because Lord Carrington was too deeply involved in chairing the Lancaster House Conference on Rhodesia to be able to pay any attention to Gibraltar. However, officials on both sides remained active, and just before Christmas Sir Anthony Acland was authorized to present a developed version of the two declaration proposal to Oreja, whose reaction was not unfavourable. He had two sticking points, both concerned with placating his hardliners. He must have 'negotiations' and not just 'talks'; and mention of 'the Gibraltarians' right to self determination' should be avoided. Neither seemed unsurmountable problems to the British side, but it would not be Acland who was to resolve them.

Acland's tenure as ambassador ended in the New Year, and he was replaced by Richard Parsons. Whereas Acland epitomized the FCO policy of giving Anglo-Spanish relations priority over the Rock's affairs, Parsons was to prove a stout friend of Gibraltar, who went to great lengths to find ways of enabling Madrid to save face. Paradoxically Parsons, the Governor and the FCO officials, who were aiming so resolutely at ending the siege, were, in fact, working against the instinctive wishes of the majority of Gibraltarians. An opinion poll, conducted by Eddie Campello's newspaper *Vox*, showed that 90 per cent of the people did not want the frontier opened. They were frightened of being taken over by what they aptly termed 'osmosis' – the infiltration of Spanish capital, businesses and labour, leading unobtrusively to an eventual Spanish social and political takeover. Moreover, there seemed to be a measure of security to be had behind the closed gates, which shut out the evils of an unstable Spain and the world in general.

As political life in Madrid returned to normal after the Christmas break, accounts of the Oreja/Acland meeting, circulated by the Foreign Ministry to other interested ministries, came under intense criticism from both pro-Europeans and hard-liners because they seemed to show a hardening of the British position, in that, unlike the former Labour government, Carrington's team were intent on playing the trump card of refusal to sign Spain's treaties of accession to NATO and the EC unless the 15th siege of Gibraltar was lifted. The situation was made worse by the increasing hostility of France to Spain's entry into the EC. Spain badly needed British support to offset French obstruction, but even this did not stop Madrid cancelling King Juan Carlos's proposed visit to London in June and placing in jeopardy the tentative ideas of the Queen's visit to Gibraltar during her Mediterranean tour in 1980. Oreja did not convey his reply to Acland's points to Richard Parsons, as might have been expected, but to Lord Carrington through the Spanish Ambassador in London, the Marqués de Perinat, who was an inflexible hard-liner as far as Gibraltar was concerned. The reply was almost childish in maintaining the old Castiella line, and showing that there was still no meeting of minds despite months of hard work by officials behind the scenes. It was time for Lord Carrington, who was successfully over the Lancaster House Conference on Rhodesia but not its tricky aftermath, to take off the gloves.

On 8th February, Richard Parsons was instructed to deliver Carrington's tough uncompromising reply to Oreja personally. Perinat's outdated and inflexible note could not serve as a basis for negotiations, and, if his line was maintained, stalemate would ensue. He would, however, be prepared to meet Oreja in Lisbon on 10th April during the meeting of the Council of Europe. He hoped that the Spanish side would be in a more constructive mood. Both Salvador and Peter Isola were gratified by the Secretary of State's strong line when the Governor briefed them on the exchanges.

Lord Carrington's stiff letter to Oreja made its intended impact in the ministry of foreign affairs in Madrid. Richard Parsons was able to collaborate closely with Durand, the second most senior foreign ministry official, who was to be the Spanish negotiator, and with Oreja's private secretary, in preparing the draft declarations to be tabled at Lisbon. Throughout March the drafts were refined between Parsons, Durand, the FCO and the Governor, who sought Salvador's and Isola's advice at each stage. There was the inevitable horse-trading, the most important of which was the British acceptance of the word 'negotiations' instead of 'talks' in exchange for the restrictions being lifted by 1st June instead of 'gradually' as the Cortes had demanded. In the end, the two declarations were grafted into one finely balanced document.

In anticipation of the Lisbon meeting, the Cortes debated Gibraltar on 22nd March with many deputies seeking to shackle Oreja. All the old arguments were rehearsed, and there was a glimmer of realization that the frontier would have to be opened if Spain was to enter the EC. But what infuriated the people of Gibraltar as they read the press reports of the debate in the Cortes, was the repeated assumption that Gibraltarians would be better off with Spain protecting their interests rather than Britain. Several speakers still seemed to think that there was no frontier at all at La Linea. According to them, the Gibraltarians and the inhabitants of the Campo were one people and Spanish at that! Salvador was quick to respond with a robust and highly popular reply on TV and radio, forcefully making the point that it was the people's wishes that mattered, not just their interests; and the Gibraltarians were not Spanish and had no wish to become Spanish.

The day before the Lisbon meeting, the Governor received the final text of the proposed agreement with direction to put it to Salvador and Isola, and to request them to avoid 'rocking the delicately balanced boat' by last-minute quibbles over wording. Its aim, he was to remind them, was to enable Spain to lift the 15th siege without loss of face and without endangering Gibraltar's interests. He was also directed to ask them to show some gratitude to Spain if restrictions were, indeed, lifted. They had shown none when the telephone links with the Campo had been restored, and this had irked Madrid. Salvador was equally irked by being directed by the Governor as to the line he should take. The Governor's diary records:

> As Salvador left my office, he gave me a broad hint that he did not like being given direction on what he should say. I hoped that I had been tactful, but obviously not tactful enough. (Jackson Diary, 9.4.80)

Both of Gibraltar's political leaders were in a relaxed mood when they went through the text with the Governor. The Spanish TV and radio broadcasts were so raucously Castiella-like in tone that they assumed the chances of success at Lisbon were minimal. They need not fuss unduly over the text, which ran:

> 1. The British and Spanish Governments desiring to strengthen their bilateral relations and thus to contribute to Western solidarity, intend, in accordance with the relevant United Nations Resolutions, to resolve, in a spirit of friendship, the Gibraltar problem.
> 2. Both Governments have therefore agreed to start negotiations aimed at overcoming all the differences between them on Gibraltar.
> 3. Both Governments have reached agreement on the establishment of direct communications in the region. The Spanish Government has decided to suspend the application of measures at present in force. Both Governments have agreed that future co-operation should be on the basis of reciprocity and full

equality of rights. They look forward to the further steps which will be taken on both sides which they believe will open the way to closer understanding between those directly concerned in the area.

4. To this end both Governments will be prepared to consider any proposals which the other may wish to make, recognizing the need to develop practical co-operation on a mutually beneficial basis.

5. The Spanish Government, in reaffirming its position on the re-establishment of the territorial integrity of Spain, restated its intention that in the outcome of the negotiations the interests of the Gibraltarians should be fully safeguarded. For its part the British Government will fully maintain its commitment to honour the freely and democratically expressed wishes of the people of Gibraltar as set out in the Preamble of the Gibraltar Constitution.

6. Officials on both sides will meet as soon as possible to prepare the necessary practical steps which will permit the implementation of the proposals agreed above. It is envisaged that these preparations will be completed not later than 1st June.

Salvador accepted the agreement as the best obtainable in the face of Spanish dogmatism. Isola said that the word 'negotiation' in paragraph 2 would cause him trouble because of its association with change of sovereignty in Gibraltarian and Spanish minds. The Governor reassured him that paragraph 4 limited negotiations to those of a mutually beneficial basis. This phrase indirectly excluded discussion of a change of sovereignty as it would only be of benefit to Spain. Moreover, there was also the safety net of the preamble of the 1969 Constitution, which was reiterated in paragraph 5.

10th April was a long and anxious day waiting for news from Lisbon. The two foreign secretaries should have met at 5.30pm, but the Council of Europe meeting overran. The unbelievable news that the text had been agreed did not reach the Convent until 8pm. Gibraltar and its political leaders went into a state of shock. For many Gibraltarians the worst had happened: the frontier was to be opened by 1st June – or so the agreement said! Parsons and Durand had done such excellent ground work before the actual meeting in Lisbon that both Carrington and Oreja were ready to sign the agreement without further haggling. Carrington said after the meeting that he could not understand what all the fuss had been about: agreement was reached with so little acrimony. He was soon to find out.

In Gibraltar there was acute anxiety in every walk of life. The Governor's diary entry for 11th April paints the picture:

> Gibraltar is a turmoil of uncertainty. What does it all mean? Why have the Spaniards given in so easily? What has HMG given away in return? Where is the snag? What are they up to? It cannot be good! If it's good for Spain, it must be bad for Gibraltar! And so on and so on. (Jackson Diary 11.4.80)

Salvador and Isola had been so taken by surprise that they gave uninspiring explanatory addresses on TV, realizing that they were both implicated in bringing about what many people did not want. Joe Bossano leapt in quickly to make the most of the situation. He arranged a mass meeting for 13th September in Casemates Square, which was to be followed by a silent march of protest to the Convent. His intention was to exploit the electorate's shock and aversion to the frontier being opened by thumping home his theme that there was nothing to negotiate about. He hoped for a crowd of about 3,000; Salvador estimated that he would be lucky to gather 500; and in the event about 1,500 turned up. Bossano's speech was telling but moderate, and the march on the Convent was orderly and restrained. The Governor accepted a GSLP petition that there should be no negotiations on sovereignty, and agreed to forward it to Lord Carrington. The crowd were informed of this by Bossano, whom the Governor allowed to speak from the Convent balcony. The crowd dispersed peacefully, and Bossano's status as a responsible politician was enhanced.

The most telling thing about the whole demonstration was the high proportion of middle class families in the crowd. Most of the rowdies, who usually gathered to enjoy any form of political demonstration, stayed away. Bossano had sensed the mood of the people more accurately than Salvador. This is the moment which historians may perceive as the beginning of Salvador's political decline. It was no fault of his: the hard fact was that a real rival had emerged, whose political philosophy of resistance to the Spanish claims became increasingly popular among the electorate, many of whom did not trust Salvador's close association with the seemingly never-ending diplomatic wheeling and dealing between London and Madrid. Bossano appeared to be the man most likely to thwart any attempt by Whitehall to sell Gibraltar down the river.

As mentioned earlier, Salvador has often been accused of following public opinion rather than leading it. While this is generally an unfair criticism, he did fail to provide political leadership on the night that the Lisbon agreement was announced, and allowed Bossano to seize the initiative. The closeness of the vote between Salvador and Bossano at the recent general election was a warning of the relative decline in Salvador's political popularity. After Lisbon, his trumpet sounded with a less certain note. He was no longer the unchallenged leader of the Gibraltarians: Bossano offered the electorate a credible alternative. Salvador's first plan to draw some of Bossano's more extremist teeth failed, but arrangements were made for Bossano to see Sir Ian Gilmour a few days later.

The London visit was a great success in that it gave Salvador and Isola renewed confidence in British ministers, in the Gibraltar group of MEPs and in the Lisbon agreement. Their euphoria was clearly reflected in their TV and press interviews on their return to Gibraltar, offsetting to some extent their dismal performances on Lisbon night.

The unfortunate Oreja received a very different reception when he returned to Madrid. He was deemed to have exceeded his brief by the Spanish cabinet and by most of the Madrid government ministries, particularly the army, marine and air departments, which were especially hostile to the agreement. He was forced by his colleagues to seek British interpretations of various phrases favourable to Britain in the agreement, which all took time. The standard British reply was that such questions would be settled during the post-Lisbon negotiations and should be placed on the agenda for the first meeting, which was set for 9th June in London. Salvador, strongly supported by Isola, was adamant that no negotiations at all should take place before restrictions were lifted.

Trying to bring the Spanish government to implement Lisbon was like playing snakes and ladders on a board with far more snakes than ladders. During the two-and-a-half-year struggle over implemention, Gibraltar hit nine snakes wearing the gold and red livery of Spain, and one adorned with the Union Jack! The first two snakes can be put down to unrealistic administrative estimates of what could be done by 1st June. Thereafter, the rest were attempts by Spain to renegotiate the agreement covertly via the back door.

The first snake was a request from Madrid to delay opening the gates for vehicles due to lack of time to make the necessary administrative arrangements. Salvador dug in his heels when the Governor put Oreja's request to him. He and Isola would not attend the 7th June meeting unless the gates were fully opened. Indeed, he was so annoyed with the negative attitude of the various Spanish ministries concerned with making practicable arrangements at the frontier that he soon began to doubt Spanish sincerity. He refused to continue spending money on preparation of car parks and other traffic arrangements on the Gibraltar side of the frontier. He was to be proved right. 1st June passed with no opening of the gates even for pedestrians. A new date of 30th June was set for the opening of the frontier and the first ministerial meeting, but the second snake's head appeared in the way. Oreja asked for British help in dealing with his opponents. Could Britain not promise him in advance of negotiations some obvious concession like removing the frontier fence? Gibraltar had already agreed to Spaniards seeking work in the city and to Spanish companies buying property. Salvador was not prepared to countenance any further pre-negotiation concessions. Oreja was left empty-handed, but had his face saved for him by a visit to Spain by US President Jimmy Carter, which killed the 30th June date for him. Why this was not foreseen earlier in Madrid, when the new date was being fixed, it is difficult to understand, but it did cover up Oreja's inability to gain a consensus in government circles on an opening date.

Before the third snake's head appeared, the Gibraltarians were to suffer a disappointment, which hurt them deeply. When the itinerary of the Queen's 1980 Mediterranean tour was finalized, she was shown as visiting Morocco, Algeria and Tunisia, passing through the Strait of Gibraltar in the royal yacht *Britannia*, but not calling in to visit Gibraltar. Protests from the Governor and Salvador down the political spectrum to the lowliest charitable bodies in Gibraltar resulted in only one change: the Queen would fly over instead of transiting the Strait in *Britannia*. The FCO was adamant that persuading Spain to implement the Lisbon agreement was difficult enough without giving Madrid an excuse to jeopardize what had been achieved so far by allowing a royal visit to the Rock at this difficult time. Sadly, it proved to be the right decision.

The third snake had real substance. Oreja was dismissed on 9th September before he was able to bring the Spanish cabinet to set a new date. His political credibility was exhausted, and he was replaced by Perez-Llorca, who met Lord Carrington in New York a fortnight later. The stumbling block now was a demand by Spain that her workers should be treated as EC citizens in Gibraltar before Spain actually signed the Treaty of Rome. Carrington rebuffed him and chided him for Spain's failure to honour her word given at Lisbon. Carrington's words had little impact in Madrid where numerous hard-liners blocked the way towards setting a new date. Fresh diplomatic minuets were danced in London and Madrid until 29th January 1981 when the fourth snake brought all progress, such as it was, to a halt.

The Suárez government resigned over the controversial Spanish divorce bill, and Calvo Sotelo, Spain's former representative at the Council of Europe in Strasbourg, formed a new CDU government, retaining Perez-Llorca as his Foreign Minister. Nothing changed in Madrid as regards Gibraltar policy, but Spain was entering a worrying period of instability with the military clearly hovering in the wings ready to intervene if there was the least threat to what they saw as the integrity of the realm. Reopening the Gibraltar frontier might have risked a military coup, if it was not handled astutely, and so Calvo Sotelo had to approach the Lisbon agreement with circumspection. He was not prepared to hurry matters along however much Richard Parsons might press Perez-Llorca for a new opening date.

Fears of military intervention became a reality within a fortnight of Sotelo taking office. The whole world was regaled on its TV screens with live coverage of Colonel Tejero holding the Cortes to ransom at gunpoint. The coup was badly planned and it failed, but it underlined the frailty of Spanish democracy. The people of Gibraltar were delighted that the frontier had not been opened on 1st June. They were even more grateful when a series of political assassinations in Madrid that summer reinforced their feeling of security behind their closed frontier. For the next ten months, no Spanish government could have reached a consensus for opening the frontier: internal opposition and the risks of reaction by the military were too high. This did not inhibit Parsons and Perez-Llorca from seeking new ways forward, usually based upon the latter's pleas for help to sway the Spanish cabinet with further British concessions. When the Governor put Perez-Llorca's successive pleas to Salvador, he rejected them out of hand as matters to be brought up in the formal negotiations, which could not start until frontier restrictions were lifted.

On a number of occasions Parsons reported that Perez-Llorca had said that the decision to open the gates was imminent. Whenever the Governor briefed Salvador on these reports, the latter was almost invariably sceptical and unimpressed. His intelligence of the true situation in Madrid, culled from talks with Bravo, his link-man to Perez-Llorca's office, pointed in the opposite direction: a consensus on opening the gates was as far off as ever. It was not that Perez-Llorca was deliberately stringing Parsons along, but he underestimated the opposition, whereas Bravo did not and was proved right on each occasion – nothing happened. The sixth snake was the small but emotionally charged affair of the royal invitations to the Prince of Wales' wedding at the end of July. The King and Queen of Spain accepted, but when it was announced that the royal honeymoon would start from Gibraltar, their acceptances were withdrawn by the Spanish government amid a wave of acrimony in the British and Spanish media. For once Salvador was able to turn a Spanish snake into a ladder to the great advantage of Gibraltar. The British Nationality Bill was passing through Parliament with Gibraltarians still styled citizens of 'British Dependant Territories (Gibraltar)'. Salvador, with Isola's wholehearted support, and the sterling work done in the UK by Bob Peliza, galvanized the Gibraltar lobbies in both the Commons and the Lords in a bid for full British citizenship, using the sympathy for Gibraltar generated in Westminster, although not in Whitehall, by the Spaniards' failure to implement the Lisbon agreement and their behaviour over the royal wedding.

The Gibraltar lobby in the Commons only just failed to have the bill amended, but prepared the way for a vigorous assault on it in the Lords by the strong force of peers in the Gibraltar Group. In the Lords, an amendment was carried giving Gibraltarians the right to United Kingdom citizenship. Rather than lose the whole bill by putting it back to the Commons, the government accepted the amendment on 27th October, and Gibraltarian dreams became a reality; much to the chagrin of Madrid and intense joy in Gibraltar. Gibraltar's luck seemed to be changing. The start of the royal honeymoon on the royal yacht, *Britannia*, was a resounding success. Salvador's arrangements were a great credit to Gibraltar, whose people rose to the occasion in a hysteria of loyalty. The couple arrived with the Prince piloting the aircraft of the Queen's flight and were transferred to a small open Triumph 'Stag' loaned by Bramy Benatar. It was the only suitable open car on the Rock, the back seat of which was raised to give the crowds a better view of the couple. As they drove through Main Street to *Britannia*'s berth in the dockyard, they were almost drowned in confetti thrown from the windows as well as from the cheering crowds on the packed pavements. There was red, white and blue bunting and Union flags everywhere. When *Britannia* sailed away that evening, a vast armada of small craft escorted her into the

Mediterranean. There were no demonstrations by Spanish fishermen or by the people of La Linea as had been feared. The Spanish people had been mesmerized by the wedding on TV two days earlier: they had no wish to disturb the happy couple on their honeymoon.

Gibraltar's change of fortune did not last long. As if seeking revenge for its defeat in the Nationality Bill, the large snake, flying the Union Jack representing Whitehall ministries, was already sliding into position on the board. On 24th June, the Rock was shaken by the announcement by John Nott, the Defence Secretary, stemming from his recent defence review, that Chatham, Portsmouth and Gibraltar dockyards would be run down and closed by 1983, and that the Rock's airport would be civilianized.

Many people in Gibraltar had seen the closure coming, but this was no consolation for the thousand or so workers who would be losing their jobs. The plain fact was that with a smaller navy there was already too much dockyard capacity of the wrong sort. Rapid technological changes in the use of advanced electronic systems, gas turbine engines and revolutionary hull design needing no mid-life refits, required totally different and very expensive dockyard testing and repair facilities, which could only be provided for a few yards with a high through-put of ships. It would not be economic to modernize the small Gibraltar yard to take the new classes of warships. If it was decided to keep the yard open for political reasons, it would only be able to handle orthodox vessels like the fleet supply ships. Unfortunately, Gibraltar's current bread and butter came from refitting the aging Leander class of frigates, which were nearing the end of their useful lives and would be replaced by more modern ships that were beyond Gibraltar's existing capabilities without expensive modernization.

Salvador was the least surprised by this decision. Since the early 1970s, the Admiralty had been trying to close the dockyard as uneconomic. Judith Hart, Minister for Overseas Development, had been keen to set in hand a study in depth of what alternative employment might be found for the workforce and other measures that would fill the yawning gap made in the Rock's economy. As it happened, David Owen had just become Foreign Secretary and was just starting soundings, which were to lead to the Strasbourg process. He wanted Salvador to meet some Spanish go-betweens, but Salvador refused unless the possibility of the dockyard closure and Judith Hart's study was kept secret. He could not face the Spaniards with such a bombshell ticking away. His point appears to have been taken because he heard nothing more of the study, and could only assume that the Admiralty were stopped for political reasons by the Labour government. Unfortunately, the Conservative John Nott was inadequately advised by the FCO on the repercussions of closure while the Rock was still under siege.

Salvador grasped the essentials of the Whitehall's problem very quickly, but was astounded, as was the Governor, at the timing of the announcement. It was almost inconceivable that the British government should close Gibraltar's main source of employment and income with the frontier still closed and Spain prevaricating over implementing the Lisbon agreement. So serious would be the damage to the Rock's economy and to Gibraltarian confidence that the resignation of the Chief Minister seemed more than likely. If the British government did, indeed, support its Minister of Defence, then Salvador and his ministers could not carry on, and reversion to direct military rule was almost unavoidable. Fortunately, the Governor appreciated from his long experience in Whitehall that defence review decisions can be challenged successfully before they are put to the Cabinet's Defence and Overseas Policy committee, presided over by the prime minister, where the final decisions are made for Cabinet approval or otherwise. He advised Salvador to put any precipitate thoughts of resignation aside and to concentrate on the political battle to reverse or modify the Ministry of Defence's decision in Gibraltar's favour.

It is hardly surprising that John Nott's dockyard announcement rekindled in Salvador's and many other Gibraltarians' minds the suspicions of a Whitehall plot to slide Gibraltar unobtrusively into

Spain. The mandarins seemed to be knocking away yet another chock holding Gibraltar on the slipway! As usual it was nothing of the sort: it was an example of Whitehall inter-ministerial bargaining at its worst. Defence reviews are carried out on a strict need-to-know basis. The case for closing the Gibraltar yard was militarily unimpeachable; and under Treasury rules the Ministry of Defence was only allowed to spend taxpayer's money on strategically essential measures. The Gibraltar yard could not be classed as such, so if the yard was to be kept open as part of the sustain and support policy, some other ministry – obviously the FCO – must pay. The FCO had not reacted in time or with sufficient vigour in presenting its political objections to closure, and any way had no money in its votes to pay to keep the yard open. The impasse was complete, but Lord Carrington persuaded the Cabinet to defer the closure decision for further examination with a full political input.

In Gibraltar, the Governor reacted swiftly, and with Salvador's full support, set up a consultative committee composed of the three principal political leaders – Salvador, Isola and Bossano – and representatives of the Chamber of Commerce, shipping interests and the dockyard management with the Financial and Development Secretary, Reg Wallace, as its secretary. Its task was to seek alternative ways of filling the hole in the economy if the navy did pull out, which certainly seemed inevitable. Eminent outside consultants were brought in to advise the Committee on the most practicable way forward. They concluded there appeared to be only two solutions: commercialization, or the FCO to pay the navy's overheads to go on using the yard for naval non-warship work.

Commercialization was very costly in terms of capital to refurbish the yard and modify the three dry docks to take modern merchant ships; and the risks in trying to attract a viable level of commercial work in the extremely depressed state of world shipping were alarmingly high. They advised adopting a hybrid plan, using naval management in a transitional period leading to full commercialization when conditions were more favourable. A three to five year period was envisaged, during which the navy would send its fleet auxiliaries for refitting while commercial operations were developed under a civilian contractor who would gradually take over the management. The modernization programme would be paid for under the catch-all Treasury heading of sustain and support.

Salvador and Isola were to accept this tentative hybrid plan in due course as a sensible way ahead if it could be negotiated with Whitehall. Joe Bossano also understood its logic, but he could not, as the TGWU leader of the public sector workers, let the Ministry of Defence close the dockyard unopposed. He decided to use trade union muscle in an attempt to force a rethink. He was in close touch with the TGWU in London and would make common cause with the Chatham and Portsmouth trade unions, who were bent on the same futile Luddite effort to turn back the effects of technological progress on the Royal Navy. Moreover, he thought that he held a special ace peculiar to Gibraltar. If Britain closed the yard and put his members out of work, he would ensure that Gibraltar naval base would be 'blacked' and become inoperable.

On 27th June, two days after the first meeting of the Consultative Committee, Bossano tried to hold a supposedly mass protest meeting in Casemates Square. Only about 200 turned up and they deserted him when it started to rain. He tried again more successfully three days later when 600 gathered. His speech contained the threat of blacking the naval base thus effectively shutting it if Britain closed the yard without finding an alternative livelihood for his members. His subsequent march to the Convent dispersed peacefully when the Governor explained to the GSLP leaders that he and they were on the same side in seeking to save the yard.

While Bossano mustered support from the Labour Party and the UK trade unions to halt the closure altogether, official negotiations with Whitehall became ever more tortuous and lengthy. No department wished to foot the bill caused by the Ministry of Defence's egocentric decision to close the yard before

the frontier was reopened by Spain. Salvador presented that bill
in the form of three requests: compensatory increases in support
and sustain to offset Spain's failure to implement Lisbon;
acknowledgement of Gibraltar's right to its land thus making it
possible for Gibraltar to take over surplus defence assets free of
charge; and financial assistance and provision of stopgap work
during the commercialization of the dockyard.

So fraught did negotiations with Whitehall become that
Salvador began to lose confidence again. At the end of
September, in a fit of uncharacteristic despair, he drafted a letter
of resignation, which he intended to send to the Secretary of State
if no satisfactory economic package could be agreed. He could
not carry on as Chief Minister with a closed dockyard and a closed
frontier without generous assistance from Britain. With mass
unemployment Gibraltar would become ungovernable, and
reversion to direct rule would become inevitable as local ministers
would no longer be willing to shoulder their responsibilities in
such an adverse situation, which was not of their own making.

The letter was never sent, because Ewen Ferguson, now an
Assistant Under-Secretary in the FCO, came out to Gibraltar
towards the end of November on a very useful fence-mending trip
which restored Salvador's and his ministers' confidence. The
Governor and Salvador were then invited to the FCO to meet Lord
Carrington on 14th December. The timing proved unfortunate
because the Polish situation was holding the British ministers'
attention and reduced the time available for discussion on
Gibraltar. Unfortunately, Salvador had over-prepared himself and
talked too long. Carrington, the great gentleman that he is, let
him speak for as long as time would allow, and then replied,
showing great sympathy for Gibraltar's plight, setting the tone for
his officials to follow. He gave the impression that most of
Salvador's requirements would be met as soon as the dockyard
consultant's reports had been completed and studied within the
Whitehall ministries concerned.

While Salvador had been grappling with the dockyard snake,
Parsons in Madrid and the Southern European Department in the

FCO, now under the sterling Dr David Wilson, who was to become Governor of Hong Kong during the Anglo-Chinese Treaty negotiations for ending British rule in the colony, were climbing one of the few ladders on the Lisbon board. Spain had applied officially to join NATO and negotiations were about to begin. This provided an ideal opportunity for Margaret Thatcher to get tough with the Spanish Prime Minister, Calvo Sotelo: lift restrictions now or you will not join NATO. They met in London at her invitation on 6th January 1982. He came, he saw and he surrendered: the frontier would be opened on 20th April when the two foreign ministers and their delegations would sit down at Sintra, near Lisbon, for the first ministerial meeting as required by the Lisbon agreement.

It was about this time that Salvador's health began to cause concern. Adolfo Canepa was appointed Deputy Chief Minister and thereafter attended all important official meetings with Salvador to ensure continuity of policy if anything were to happen to him. Moreover, it helped to give Canepa a wider perspective and experience in government. With hindsight, the decision was as unfortunate as it was inevitable: there was no one else of the necessary calibre, and Canepa had been second to Salvador amongst the AACR elected members at all the elections since 1972. While he was undoubtedly an able man and a good chief of staff, subsequent events were to show that either wrong timing, or his relative lack of charisma *vis-à-vis* Bossano, precluded him from becoming chief minister.

February and March sped by with final preparations for the opening of the frontier being rushed forward. Even the sceptical Salvador accepted that the gates were likely to open on 20th April: both prime ministers had been involved in the decision, and so it seemed most unlikely that another snake could intervene to stop it happening. Both sides prepared their briefs for Lisbon; travel arrangements were completed; and rooms allocated in the Sintra hotels. By coincidence, 20 British warships entered Gibraltar's harbour on 23rd March under the command of Rear-Admiral Sandy Woodward, Flag Officer 1st Flotilla, to take part in the annual *Spring Train* Exercises. That evening, Admiral Sir John Fieldhouse, C-in-C Fleet, arrived in Gibraltar to watch the ships at work. The two men, who were about to have great responsibilities thrust upon them, were in the Convent when, on 1st April, news came in that the Argentines had invaded the Falklands. Sir John Fieldhouse flew home to take command of the Falklands Task Force from Northwood, and Sandy Woodward sailed south with the leading ships from Gibraltar.

A totally unexpected international snake had appeared on Gibraltar's snakes and ladder board to save the game for Spain. Lord Carrington took the honourable course of resigning as Foreign Secretary over the failure of the FCO's Falklands policies. This gave Perez-Llorca an excuse for requesting a postponement of Lisbon. Britain's new Foreign Secretary, Francis Pym, would need time to read himself in before starting the complex Gibraltar negotiations. Moreover, the Spanish right-wing parties were banging anti-British and pro-Argentine drums. It was hardly the best time to open the gates and start negotiating on the delicate subject of Gibraltar when the Spanish people were in a very excitable and emotional state. The two foreign secretaries agreed to a new date of 25th June, and announced it as a 'joint' decision, although it was nothing of the sort.

Salvador and Peter Isola were furious when the Governor told them of Perez-Llorca's final evasion. They and the Governor had every right to show anger towards the media: Madrid had broken its word yet again; they had taken cover behind a dubiously 'joint' announcement when it was they who had actually ratted; and, most annoying of all, Spain would now be able to jump the British trip-wire across her path into NATO without opening the frontier because her accession date was 30th May. The Gibraltarians took the whole thing quite phlegmatically: 'typical of Spain' was the general comment.

Gibraltar played its full part in the Falklands campaign. The Rock became the first stop on the 'motorway' – the air supply and reinforcement route between England and Ascension Island – where RAF Hercules aircraft landed, refuelled and took off again in a steady stream, day and night. In some cases, the rear doors would open to land reinforcements and advanced weapons for Gibraltar's garrison. The dockyard did some memorable work such as the conversion of the British India schools cruise ship Uganda, into a fully equipped hospital ship over one weekend. She arrived in the dockyard on a Friday with a black hull and white superstructure and left on Monday brilliant white all over with large red crosses on her funnel. A helicopter landing pad had been built on her stern, and her medical staff and equipment, flown out from England, had been embarked.

The Rock itself was under threat, not from the Spanish government, who made it quite clear to Richard Parsons that Spain would remain neutral during the conflict, but from the possibility that one of the provincial generals might attempt to take the Rock by surprise attack and thus be able to make himself the new Franco of Spain. At times the garrison was down to two hours notice to deploy. The RAF was reinforced, and the naval guard ships were brought closer to the Rock. In all this military activity, Salvador and his ministers co-operated in every possible way with unimpeachable loyalty.

A week before the new date – 25th June – for Lisbon to be implemented, Port Stanley, the capital of the Falklands fell to the British task force. This was too much for Spanish pride. They reneged yet again on Lisbon, which was postponed *sine die*. Salvador's first reaction when the Governor told him the news was:

> Britain cannot close the dockyard now; if she does we [Salvador and Isola] cannot have a hand in government. (Jackson Diary, 21.6.82)

Two months later, Calvo Sotelo's government collapsed on 27th August and the Lisbon agreement appeared to have died with it. Opinion polls pointed to a socialist government winning the forthcoming general election. Salvador would be faced with what it was hoped would be a more humanitarian Spanish approach to the Gibraltar issue. He would also have to educate a new Governor. Admiral Sir David Williams replaced General Sir

William Jackson in October 1982, whose tenure had been extended twice to four and a half years. With Lisbon near dead and a new Spanish government in place, it was time for Salvador to have a new and fresher brain in the Convent.

CHAPTER 13

THE BRUSSELS AGREEMENT
AND RETIREMENT
1982-1987

Salvador's Last House of Assembly: elected January 1984

Government:

Sir Joshua Hassan	Chief Minister
A J Canepa	Deputy Chief Minister, Economic Development and Trade
M K Featherstone	Public Works
H J Zammitt	Tourism
F J Dellipiani	Housing, Labour and Social Security
R G Valarino	Municipal Services
B J Perez	Education and Health
G Mascarenhas	Sport and Postal Services

Opposition:

J Bossano	Leader of the Opposition
J E Pilcher	
M A Feetham	
Miss M I Montegriffo	
J C Perez	
J L Baldachino	
R Mor	

The autumn of 1982 was the beginning of Salvador's last five years in office. They were to be the most difficult of his whole career. He was 67 and had already been Gibraltar's Chairman of the City

Council, Mayor, Chief Member and Chief Minister for 37 years. Sir Geoffrey Howe referred to him as:

> One of the longest serving democratically elected leaders in post-war Europe, and a fellow Bencher of the Middle Temple. (Hassan 25.11.93, enclosing Howe 8.9.89)

It was not too surprising that there was a growing feeling that it was time to change the helmsman. His AACR had been in power, with only one short break of two years, since 1945, and in recent months Gibraltar's affairs seemed to many of the electorate to have taken a turn for the worse. After Spain's failure to implement the Lisbon agreement, and the announcement of the intended closure of the naval dockyard, there was a marked drop in Gibraltarian confidence. Many traders had stocked up, hoping for a bonanza when the frontier was opened. Left with unsaleable surplus stocks, several went into receivership. The Gibraltar government also suffered considerable financial loss in building parking for cars and buses, and improving traffic circuits. Unemployment had started to rise alarmingly because commercial firms were retrenching. The position would be made infinitely worse if the dockyard were to close without alternative employment being found for its workforce – a well nigh impossible task.

Inevitably, people started looking around for scapegoats. The old theories of perfidious Albion, in the usual guise of the Foreign and Commonwealth Office, plotting to slip Gibraltar unobtrusively into Spain, resurfaced. The recent sequence of events seemed too ominous for comfort: 1975, integration with Britain refused in the Hattersley memorandum; 1980, the Lisbon agreement did not, for the first time since the 18th century, specifically exclude discussion of sovereignty; 1981, the decision to close the dockyard before the 15th siege was lifted; and, 1982, the failure of the FCO to enforce more rigorously the implementation of the Lisbon agreement instead of lamely accepting Madrid's contention that the time was not right. Much of the criticism rubbed off on Salvador, whose close co-operation with the FCO had lost something of its local mystique as Britain, despite her great power status and reputed diplomatic skills, had continually failed to persuade or coerce the Spaniards, who were held in low esteem by the Gibraltarians, into lifting the frontier restrictions.

All this was grist to Joe Bossano's mill. Ever since he had achieved local trade union 'sainthood' by winning the wages parity battle in the mid-1970s, his driving ambition had been to become chief minister one day. It made him forage wider for issues through which he could challenge and embarrass Salvador. Coming second to him in the recent general election gave him additional confidence to dispute the hegemony of the AACR despite having no GSLP members to support him in the House of Assembly. Quite suddenly, however, not one but two major political issues had arisen on which he might mount a successful challenge to Salvador with a measure of popular backing. The first was opposing the commercialization of the dockyard; and the second was mounting a vicious and unrelenting offensive against Lisbon-style agreements. Both issues were to dominate all else during Salvador's last years in office.

With the Spanish general elections due in October 1982, there was little point in rushing the frontier issue until something was known about the complexion of the new Spanish government. The dockyard issue, on the other hand, was soon brought into the limelight by the completion of the consultant's reports on commercialization, which were avidly read in Whitehall and Gibraltar. They did recommend the hybrid solution, but they also shook Whitehall officials by their estimates of the large capital costs and high risk of failure. If the Gibraltarian workforce failed to meet the commercial productivity criteria and did not achieve a sharp enough competitive edge to secure a reasonable share of the depressed ship repair market, most of the capital, which had to be sunk into widening the docks to take fat merchant ship hulls instead of slim warships, would be lost.

Some Whitehall officials believed that the whole idea of entering the ship repair market, which was heavily over capacity already, was lunacy. It would be more sensible to make Gibraltar 'grant maintained' until an alternative source of employment and economic base could be developed. Salvador, after all he had done to give Gibraltar its own internal self-government, could not even contemplate such a solution, which would entail Whitehall officials taking over many of the key administrative and financial posts in the Gibraltar government. Fortunately the idea ran so counter to British colonial policy that it died on the vine.

Salvador and the Council of Ministers were carefully briefed on the implications of the consultants proposals by Reg Wallace, the Financial and Development Secretary, and Ernest Montado, the Economics Adviser, and after much hesitation agreed to back commercialization, provided – and this was the key issue – the British government was generous in putting together the financial package with the three distinct elements which Salvador had already sketched out: increased sustain and support funds to offset the Spanish failure to implement Lisbon; a settlement of the vexed issue of Crown lands in Gibraltar's favour; and adequate funds for the conversion of the dockyard for civilian shipping. So crucial were these demands that Salvador was invited back to London to meet the new Secretary of State, Francis Pym, for discussion of both the frontier and dockyard problems. Peter Isola was to join him to discuss the frontier situation since this was a bipartisan foreign policy matter. Adolfo Canepa, who accompanied Salvador to all London conferences to gain experience, provide continuity and advise on financial problems, would replace Isola for the dockyard session which was deemed to be part of Gibraltar's domestic and not foreign affairs.

Salvador put an enormous amount of work into the preparations for the meetings since he knew that Gibraltar's economic future depended largely on the outcome. Sadly, there was little rapport between him and Francis Pym, when they met in the Foreign Secretary's office on 24th September. The first meeting, dealing with the frontier, went reasonably well with Peter Isola making a sensible contribution. Canepa then replaced Isola for the dockyard session, which turned into a near disaster. Salvador started off on the wrong foot by criticizing the FCO for failing to come to Gibraltar's support with further financial assistance when Spain reneged on opening the frontier, and for allowing the Ministry of Defence to propose the closure of the Gibraltar dockyard before the Spanish restrictions were lifted. Francis Pym bridled, departed from his brief, and told Salvador a few home truths about Gibraltarian ingratitude, the world recession and Britain's own economic difficulties. Fortunately, Lord Belstead, the junior FCO minister responsible for Gibraltar, came to the rescue, calming the troubled waters and putting the more important points, which the Foreign Secretary had missed when he abandoned his brief. Recriminations were put aside and Salvador was invited to send a small team to put Gibraltar's requirements in detail to a Cabinet Office committee.

A very friendly post-conference lunch at Admiralty House was hosted by Lord Belstead, who assured Salvador that the FCO would not be ungenerous when an aid package had been properly worked out with the Treasury. All they needed was the Secretary of State's nod to go ahead. Despite appearances, they had got it thanks to Lord Belstead's intervention. The hard work of negotiating the aid package and selecting a contractor could begin. It was to take many months and involved Margaret Thatcher on two occasions.

There was a chance bonus for Salvador, which flowed from his altercation with Francis Pym. Canepa had listened wide-eyed while Salvador had loosed his verbal assaults, and confessed when he got back home that Salvador was certainly no lackey of British ministers when Gibraltar's vital interests were at stake. Once away from the Rock and treading the awe-inspiring corridors of the FCO, he had expected Salvador to adopt a much softer approach. The very opposite happened: Salvador's adrenalin flowed! Canepa made certain that all Salvador's critics knew the truth about their Chief Minister.

In the meantime Bossano had been seeking support from the Labour Party conference, from the London TGWU and from the trade unions at Chatham and Portsmouth, who were also fighting closure. His efforts in England were largely in vain because the

Chatham and Portsmouth men were quite naturally disinclined to help the Gibraltar dockyard survive at the expense of their own yards. However, he had no difficulty in persuading the majority of the dockyard workers in Gibraltar to oppose commercialization. Many non-dockyard people also sided with him because they believed that commercialization could not succeed. The only solution seemed to be to fight for the retention of naval dockyard management, whose costs were minute in defence budgetary terms but substantial in the scale of Gibraltar's economy. Surely there must be some way of helping Gibraltar without crippling the defence vote?

The hard fact had also to be faced that the workers had begun to trust Bossano more than Salvador to safeguard their jobs. If Joe was against commercialization, so were they: the unchallengeable technological, financial and naval strategic reasons for closure meant little to them. Bossano and his GSLP were building their power base on the class grievances in exactly the same way as Salvador and the AACR had done in 1943.

Calvo Sotelo's Spanish government had collapsed on 27th August. Felipe Gonzalez's socialist PSOE won its sweeping victory at the polls on 28th October, and bravely took a small step towards recognizing the inhumanity of the closed frontier at La Linea, which had split families living on both sides of it for so long. His new cabinet agreed to the restricted opening of the pedestrian gates ten days before Christmas as a goodwill gesture. Only Gibraltarian residents and Spaniards would be permitted to cross, but the Spaniards were not allowed to take anything back to Spain with them whereas the Gibraltarians could buy as much as they liked in the Campo and beyond. Other nationals and tourists were excluded.

This was a bold decision for Gonzalez to take. His government was very much on approval, and the PSOE were the most likely party to suffer a right-wing coup: 'going soft' on Gibraltar would be an obvious reason for the army to step in once more. Gonzalez hoped that a genuine consensus for a full opening of the frontier would be achievable in Madrid by the spring to honour Spain's signature on the Lisbon agreement. He had, by chance, made a brilliant and almost certainly unpremeditatedly successful move as we will see shortly.

Salvador quite naturally had to welcome Gonzalez's gesture as a step in the right direction, but he was disappointed by it. Not allowing tourists to cross the frontier would not help the stunted Gibraltar economy, and the outflow of cash through Gibraltarians shopping in Spain without any compensatory flow the other way could be financially damaging if it went on for very long. However, as Fernando Moran, Gonzalez's Foreign Minister, assured Francis Pym that Spain should be able to open the frontier fully in the spring, there was no point in turning the gesture down. The Gibraltarians should and did enjoy a united family Christmas with their families across the border for the first time since 1968.

To Salvador and the new Governor, Admiral Sir David Williams, the chances of the PSOE government being able to find an acceptable moment in the spring for lifting all restrictions seemed questionable. Their non-socialist predecessors had never succeeded in doing so. Calvo Sotelo had come nearest after Margaret Thatcher had threatened to obstruct Spain's entry into NATO, but he had been saved from the humiliation of defeat by the Falklands War. The hard fact was that no political party of the right, centre or left, could be seen to be failing to pursue one of Spain's stated national objectives, the recovery of Gibraltar. Only robust British obstruction to Spain's entry into the EC was likely to force the issue. However, the time was not yet ripe for another Thatcher intervention. Gonzalez had to be given time to follow up his preliminary gesture of opening the pedestrian gates with the complete dismantling of frontier restrictions.

For the time being, the frontier problem was best left to the diplomats in London and Madrid, who for the next two years circled round each other trying to find a way of revitalizing the Lisbon agreement. Spring and summer passed without Gonzalez being willing to risk a full opening. The British and Spanish foreign ministers met frequently in the 'margins' of international conferences, but the Spaniards never heard anything that they could put to their cabinet as an adequate reason for implementing Lisbon after hesitating so long. Indeed, they were to find the British, under Margaret Thatcher's leadership, tougher than ever as Spain's prospective date for EC entry approached. They were clearly warned at the highest level that a British veto hung poised over their negotiations. There was, however, little that Salvador could do to encourage them to 'bite on the bullet'. In any case, he had his hands full, fighting for an adequate dockyard package.

Throughout 1983 Salvador had two dockyard battles on his hands: with Whitehall and with Bossano. He spent more time than ever before in his career travelling to Whitehall, accompanied by Sir David Williams, to argue for and to clinch parts of the deal. His most important meetings were with Margaret Thatcher. The first was on 29th April at which she agreed to a £28 million grant for the conversion of the dockyard and £14 million of naval work to keep the yard going. These sums were in addition to £13 million of aid announced in March to cover Spain's failure to honour Lisbon. However, she was not prepared to offer more than a six-month extension to the dockyard's life which Salvador believed was inadequate. Rather than break the dialogue with her, he left a note with her of the points he needed to be satisfied about before a deal could be struck. They both agreed to restudy their positions and to meet again later.

The Under-Secretary for Procurement, Ian Stewart (now Lord Stewart) was sent out to negotiate an agreement with the Gibraltar government, which, although complex, was a success. Subsuming a lot of minor Crown land deals were two significant items: the extension of the dockyard closure for a year rather than six months; and the handover of Queensway, which was to cost the Ministry of Defence £8-10 million in re-provision costs, and Rosia Bay.

The second meeting with the Prime Minister was on 26th July when she gave her agreement to the deal, which was formally signed by the Foreign Secretary that evening at a dinner at Carlton Gardens. By no stretch of the imagination could the final package be called ungenerous. *The Times*, in its leader on 13th December, calculated that it amounted to £50 million, excluding redundancy payments. This was largely due to Salvador's determination and persuasive powers, and his co-operation with Sir David Williams, who, as a sailor, was fortuitously well placed to help fight the dockyard case. The generosity of the package was such that Salvador could claim convincingly that his long-standing policy of trusting the British government was once again fully vindicated and would be put to the test when the general election, which was expected in the new year of 1984, took place.

Salvador's concurrent battle with Bossano may have had far more to do with personal political rivalries than was good for Gibraltar. As soon as Mrs Thatcher announced in the Commons on 27th July that the ship repair firm of A & P Appledore had been selected as the contractors for the commercial yard, Bossano signalled out and out trade union opposition and blacking of all work connected with commercialization. The naval base was also embarrassed by the unions refusing to supply water to visiting warships. By 13th December, the Flag Officer Gibraltar was forced to grasp the nettle of union intransigence. Timing his move carefully with the government, he warned the unions that men who refused to work on measures to close the naval yard and reorganize the naval base would not be paid. All the usual union cries of 'management provocation' and 'lock out' were heard, but it was too near Christmas to risk serious loss of paypackets. Work went on with as much obstruction to Appledore as 'work to rule' and 'going slow' would allow. The real Salvador/Bossano battle, however, was to be fought at the polls after Christmas.

The election was held on 26th January. Each of the three main parties put up eight candidates: Salvador's GLP/AACR, Peter Isola's DPBG, Bossano's GSLP and there were also three independents. There was only one issue which polarized the electorate: the dockyard. Salvador called for a mandate to implement the Thatcher commercialization package, depending largely on his success in negotiating what was generally seen as an excellent deal. Bossano naturally fought for the electorate's support of his policy of opposing closure, and in this he was helped by rumours that almost 800 workers would lose their jobs as a result of commercialization. Isola, who wanted to renegotiate the Thatcher package, was squeezed out: the electorate knew that an answer 'yes' or 'no' to commercialization was what was needed and not some rather unconvincing halfway house. If the election had been about 'time for change', Isola might have had a chance, but confidence in the AACR had been restored by Salvador's spectacular negotiating success and a need for a change of party and leadership was no longer an electoral issue. So the contest became almost a straight fight between Salvador, the acknowledged statesman, and the militant left-wing Bossano.

The result, like the battle of Waterloo, was a close run thing. During the count, Bossano appeared on occasions to be winning, but in the end Salvador held the battlefield with a decisive victory. All his AACR candidates were elected with more votes than the GSLP, who lost their eighth man. None of Isola's DPBG survived. Salvador once again headed the poll with 6,644 votes; Adolfo Canepa surprisingly came second with 6,098; and Bossano third with 5,899. Paradoxically, unlike Waterloo, the vanquished Bossano emerged from defeat with his GSLP immensely strengthened. He had been the sole GSLP member in the last House of Assembly: now the GSLP were to occupy all seven opposition seats. Gibraltar politics were decisively polarized between the established right of centre and the new left, which was drawing its support from the AACR's original constituency. With age telling against Salvador and the risks involved in the dockyard commercialization being so high, Bossano had become a very dangerous political adversary for the AACR.

To be fair to Bossano, he accepted that Salvador had received a clear mandate from the electors for the commercialization of the dockyard. At a mass meeting on 14th February, the TGWU dockyard workers endorsed his revised policy of negotiations for better terms and larger numbers of workers with Gibraltar Ship Repair Ltd and its operating company, A & P Appledore, instead of continuing with their obstructive tactics. Both Bossano and Appledore were hard bargainers, the former seeking working conditions more in keeping with the comfortable naval traditions of the past than with a profit-making commercial yard; and the latter emphasizing the need to give the yard a telling competitive edge. For the moment, it was in Bossano's interests to negotiate a fair commercial deal to prove that his GSLP was a responsible and viable alternative government ready to replace Salvador's AACR. The commercial company, Gibraltar Ship Repair started work on 1st January 1985.

The total defeat of the DPBG destroyed the relatively harmonious bipartisan policy towards Spain, which Salvador and Isola had operated so successfully for so long. There was no common ground between Salvador and Bossano on relations with Madrid or Whitehall. Bossano believed fervently that Spain had no place in Gibraltar's affairs, and that Britain had no right to discuss Gibraltar with Spain. Unreal though this policy may have seemed it reflected a growing sense of Gibraltarian nationalism which was attractive to the younger generation whose votes he was bent on winning. Moreover, he had no soft spot for Britain whom he believed could not be trusted. Such sentiments could only lead to ruthlessly abrasive opposition in the House of Assembly to the statesmanlike Salvador, whose experience gave him good reasons for placing his trust in the British government.

Salvador's election victory was not his only cause for satisfaction at the turn of 1983/84. He was elected an Honorary Bencher of the Middle Temple and took his seat in March 1984.

Throughout the summer of 1984 there had been increasing diplomatic efforts between London and Madrid to find an agreed revised version of the Lisbon text. London, in theory, did not need to make any haste because Spain was bound to lift her restrictions if she wished to join the EC in January 1986 – only eighteen months ahead. Madrid knew from no lesser person than Margaret Thatcher that there was no way of bypassing the British veto on her EC entry unless Lisbon was honoured, and yet the Spanish cabinet needed some 'concession' that would save their faces in opening the frontier fully. They wanted two things: the word 'sovereignty' specifically spelt out in the list of items for discussion, and agreement to allow Spaniards EC status in Gibraltar as soon as the frontier was open instead of waiting for her actual entry to the EC.

Sovereignty had not been mentioned in the Lisbon text because it was covered in the catch-all paragraph, which read:

> 2. Both Governments have therefore agreed to start negotiations aimed at overcoming all the differences between them on Gibraltar.

As Gibraltar's interests were protected by the reiteration of the British guarantee inscribed in the preamble to the 1969 Constitution, Sir Geoffrey Howe, the Foreign Secretary, deemed it unnecessarily pedantic to refuse Madrid's first request. He and Salvador, however, had a very good, but confidential, reason for agreeing to the latter: Gibraltar was going broke as a consequence of the one-sided opening of the frontier. No amount of government cajoling would make the Rock's people heed warnings about the dire economic effects of overspending in Spain without any compensating income in pesetas. If the frontier was not opened quickly, Gibraltar would have to be grant-aided – and the accompanying constraints were anathema to Salvador and most Gibraltarians. In Margaret Thatcher's and Howe's judgement, giving the Spanish workers a few months' advance EC status was a small price to pay for stopping the financial haemorrhage.

Salvador, knowing the Spanish mentality far better than British ministers, protested vigorously over the inclusion of 'sovereignty', which would regenerate suspicions of British motives and cause him immense political difficulties in Gibraltar. Geoffrey Howe swept his protests aside, saying that if the word was take away from the agreement 'then the whole operation would come unstitched'. Salvador was also in difficulties over advance EC status. This could only be provided by House of Assembly legislation. Knowing the Gibraltarians' fears of losing their jobs to Spaniards, he could not guarantee that his government majority of one would hold.

Faced with Mrs Thatcher's endorsement of what became known

as the Brussels agreement, Salvador, with the Rock's bankruptcy staring him the face, had no option but to agree. The agreement was signed on 27th November 1984 [Text is in Appendix 6]. It was immediately condemned in Gibraltar by Bossano, the GSLP and many people, who could not understand – and still do not to this day – the reason for not waiting until Spain ran into the buffers of the British EC veto. Salvador, writing to the author recently, said of his decision to accept Brussels:

> The economy was at its lowest; the prospects were very bad; it was a decision I had to take myself. I approved it as an act of faith believing that Britain would not let us down as indeed she has not. My colleagues in the House of Assembly subsequently approved my action without dissent and later I brought a motion to the House of Assembly which approved it by a Government majority. The full opening of the frontier was a sheer necessity to survive. (Hassan letter of 5.10.94)

The January debates in the House of Assembly were unpleasantly acrimonious, but the AACR stood loyally behind Salvador. His motion commending Brussels, which he presented with great vigour as the best option available, and the legislation giving Spanish workers advance EC status, were passed by the government majority in the face of strident opposition from Bossano, the GSLP and much of the press and media. Bossano, for his part, set about generating opposition to Brussels. He organized and led a 1,300 strong march on the Convent on 31st January to hand in a protest with almost 10,000 signatures on it condemning Brussels.

Four days later the frontier gates were opened around midnight 4/5th February 1985. 'Around' is an apt description of the timing, which caused the Spanish officials some embarrassment. The Governor of Seville put his key in the lock, but it would not turn. A second official tried his hand without success. Then the local Spanish Commissioner of Police appeared with his key and the gates swung open!

The 15th siege of the Rock was over; and Salvador was the principal victor. Through his astute political leadership, he had maintained Gibraltarian morale through thick and thin. He was now faced with restoring the Rock's prosperity, and reaching a new *modus vivendi* with Spain, with a new generation of Gibraltarians baying at his heels.

This might have been the right moment to retire from office at the age 70, but how could he? He was the only Gibraltarian political leader who had the experience of negotiating with the Spaniards at the highest level. Sir Geoffrey Howe would have been aghast to have lost his wise counsel just as the post-Brussels talks were about to begin. Besides, to whom could he have handed over, if he had decided to retire – which he had, in fact, no thought of doing? He had already told Canepa that he was likely to be his political heir, but that he still needed time to mature and gain greater international experience before he could be expected to become a successful chief minister. Regrettably there was no one else in the AACR of the necessary calibre. Peter Isola had the experience and gravitas, but he was out of the House. And it was against Bossano's principles to have anything to do with Brussels. There was no way out: the new post-siege Gibraltar would have to be reshaped initially by the older generation – not that Salvador thought of doing anything else. It was to prove his most difficult task for which the younger generation were to give him scant thanks.

It is easy to make judgements a decade after a particular event has taken place because all the surrounding circumstances are forgotten and critics resort to special pleading and biased selection of quotes to support their particular theories and arguments. The Brussels agreement has been maligned to such an extent that it is barely recognizable. Its purpose has been deliberately distorted into an instrument for gradually transferring sovereignty to Spain in the longer term. From the British perspective it was nothing of the sort. It was an agreement, which could have been lived with so long as Britain stood by her word, and there was no suggestion – except in suspicious minds – that she would not do so. The reiteration of the preamble of the Constitution protected the issue of sovereignty, and the agreement itself opened the frontier just in time to save the Rock's economy. Such was the increase in economic activity with the frontier fully open that Salvador was able to reduce the very high level of taxes.

The first post-Brussels Anglo-Spanish meeting took place at Geneva on 5th February. Salvador attended as part of the British delegation. It is not true that each meeting was divided into two parts: the first between the two foreign secretaries, and the second with Salvador and the Campo mayors present. The two foreign secretaries did, indeed, meet first but only for a few minutes to settle how they would handle the agenda. In actual session, Sir Geoffrey Howe gave Salvador complete freedom of action, and Salvador felt himself in full partnership with Sir Geoffrey in fighting Gibraltar's case. In his principal contribution, he stressed the right of the Gibraltarians to determine their own future and the unfairness of Spain in trying to coerce them. He was not asked in advance what he was going to say by the British delegation, nor was he interrupted by either side as he spoke. He was treated as if he headed a separate Gibraltarian delegation.

As usual, Spain's Foreign Minister, Fernando Moran, put over his vision of how he saw the Rock's future within the Spanish realm, which he had convinced himself that the Gibraltarians would not be able to resist accepting. He was heard in silence, and then Sir Geoffrey replied:

> . . . well these proposals are not acceptable to the people of Gibraltar as you have heard from their Chief Minister nor are they acceptable to the British Government in these circumstances. Whenever the people of Gibraltar want to discuss their future relations with Spain on the basis on which they are made they can be looked at again. (Hassan letter 5.10.94)

No reply came from the Spanish side: they had played their routine opening gambit on sovereignty with the usual lack of success and were happy to go on to discussion of the practicalities of handling the open frontier.

There were three more post-Brussels meetings, which Salvador attended personally: Madrid, December 1985; London, January

1987; and Madrid, November 1987. They were all equally abortive as far as the primary issue was concerned because the Spaniards would only talk about transfer of sovereignty, and the British would only discuss improving relations between Gibraltar and Spain. Sir Geoffrey Howe, who was Foreign Secretary for all three meetings, always snubbed the routine Spanish peroration on sovereignty with the reply that such ideas could be looked at if and when the Gibraltarians wanted to discuss their future relations with Spain, which they had no wish to do at present. At the first Madrid meeting, however, there was agreement to study two of the secondary issues: the payment of pensions to former Spanish workers, who had been stopped entering Gibraltar by Franco; and the joint use of the airport.

Admiral Sir David Williams's tenure as Governor came to an end in October 1985. His successor was Air Chief Marshal Sir Peter Terry, who arrived soon after Spain had entered the EC on New Year's Day 1986. Salvador had the honour of greeting him just after his own appointment as KCMG in the New Year's Honours List. Like Sir David before him, Sir Peter soon established a rapport with Salvador. Sir Peter, however, was not given a very promising start by the FCO, who were trying to show that Spain's entry into the EC opened a new era in Anglo-Spanish relations. They suggested removing both British and Spanish ceremonial guards from the frontier as a symbolic gesture of close alliance. Salvador advised that the British guard should only be removed if the Spanish guard went too. In spite of the Spaniards refusing to follow suit unless the frontier fence was removed, the FCO persisted in setting a good example by withdrawing the British guard in July, much to the annoyance and despair of the Gibraltarians, who already saw that Spain would use her EC membership to harass Gibraltar instead of treating her as a new and friendly European ally. What was seen by the Whitehall mandarins as a minor gesture to Spain had an ominous whiff of British withdrawal to the naturally hypersensitive Gibraltarians.

Indeed, the Spaniards were already using the EC against the Rock. The first crisis was brought about by Spain being able to claim pensions under EC regulations for their former Gibraltar workers. The popular view was that as Franco had stopped his nationals working on the Rock, they had become a Spanish government commitment. The British government, however, was not prepared to breach EC regulations and expected the Gibraltar government to pay up the £21 million for the first three years from 1st January 1986 when Spain joined the EC. Salvador went back to London and offered to pay the £4.5 million which was held in the Spanish pensions fund and no more. After long and tedious negotiations with officials and ministers, the British government offered £6 million as a contribution, which Salvador rejected.

Early one morning, while he was still in London, Salvador and his team were summoned to breakfast with Sir Geoffrey Howe to take a new look at the problem. Salvador stuck firmly to his demand that the Treasury should pay the balance of £16.5 million. With Gibraltar's finances at their lowest ebb, there seemed no tenable alternative. He would never have been able to persuade the House of Assembly to pay the Spaniards any more than the £4.5 million which was rightfully theirs. Sir Geoffrey lost his temper and stormed out of his own breakfast party. Later that morning Salvador was summoned to the FCO where he saw Sir Geoffrey alone, and was told that it was imperative that the EC commitment be met on time. As a sign of generosity the British contribution would be raised to £9 million. If Sir Geoffrey believed that Salvador could be overawed, he was badly mistaken. Salvador said that £9 million would not solve the problem. Nothing short of £16.5 million would do so since Gibraltar was not prepared to pay more than the Spanish workers had paid into the pensions fund. Sir Geoffrey dashed off to accompany Margaret Thatcher and so the matter was left undecided for the time being.

On 23rd December 1985, a week before the first payment was due, the British government announced that it would be paying the £16.5 million contribution demanded by Salvador. Because the Gibraltar government had already made the necessary arrangements, the pensions were paid on time. With his long experience of Whitehall bargaining, Salvador knew when to co-operate and when to stick in his heels. The pensions battle is an excellent example of the latter.

Anglo-Spanish aviation experts started working on a plan for the joint use of the airport in March 1985, and the air space restrictions were eased for civil but not military aircraft in April. By June the following year, the work had stalled through excessive political demands by Spain aimed at undermining British sovereignty over the southern half of the isthmus, which was not ceded under Utrecht but was British under right of prescription (ie long usage). A version of these requirements was leaked to the Spanish press, which gave them as:

1. Access for Spaniards to the airport without passing through British customs and immigration.
2. Construction of a Spanish terminal in the Spanish neutral zone.
3. Spanish participation in the control of Gibraltar airspace.
4. Possible presence of Spanish air traffic controllers in Gibraltar control tower.
5. The use of installations at the Airport by Iberia and Spanish civil aviation.
6. Spain's eventual association with the management of the airport.

(Hassan quoting *El Pais* in the *Gibraltar Chronicle*, 1.11.93)

This and other leaks lead the House of Assembly on 18th December 1986 to pass a GSLP motion that the airport must remain under British and Gibraltarian control, and flights to and from Gibraltar should governed by the rules for international flights. There should be no special privileges for Spanish operators.

Britain was at this time leading negotiations for an EC Air Liberalization agreement, which Madrid decided to use to force through her requirements for the joint use of the Gibraltar Airport. Unless she got what she wanted, she was prepared to veto liberalization on the grounds that to include Gibraltar in it was tantamount to the EC recognising British sovereignty over the southern half of the isthmus. Sir Geoffrey Howe made strenuous efforts in Brussels to find a compromise but without success. So strong did the feeling become in Gibraltar that Salvador and Bossano joined hands in leading a mass march by 12,000 people on the Convent on 10th November with banners demanding 'NO CONCESSIONS', and handing in a petition with 16,000 signatures.

Sir Peter Terry relayed an account of the demonstration to Whitehall, and much to most people's surprise Sir Geoffrey appeared on Gibraltar television to announce that, in spite of the protest march, Britain would accept practical arrangements for joint use of the airport provided British sovereignty and control over the airport were not infringed. Next day, the House of Assembly attempted to tie the hands of the British negotiators by passing a unanimous motion calling on Britain never to agree to measures that might lead at any time in the future to joint control of the airport.

On 2nd December, Sir Geoffrey met Francisco Fernández Ordoñez in London under the auspices of Brussels, but without Salvador being present. The controversial airport agreement was signed that evening. Spanish passengers would have their own terminal to which there was no real political objection. Co-ordination would be through a joint committee of equal numbers appointed by both governments, and all measures taken were without prejudice to the dispute over sovereignty. The agreement was subject to Gibraltarian agreement. The full text is given in Appendix 7.

The reason for the inordinate haste in negotiating the agreement was the opening of the European Union Copenhagen Summit on 7th December at which it was to be presented as a part of the Air Liberalization agreement. It was an excellent example of 'more haste, less speed'. Salvador was particularly cautious, describing the text when he received it 'as the best available in the circumstances'. He agreed the text with Sir Geoffrey since it only gave away the first two Spanish requirements in the *El Pais* list – Spanish access through their own terminal – which were already seen as politically innocuous. There was no suggestion of Spanish control; and only an obviously necessary co-ordinating committee was to be established. Salvador had no valid reason for jeopardizing the EC Air Liberalization agreement by refusing consent, but wisely made it clear that he would not force the necessary legislation through the House of Assembly by using his government majority. He warned Sir Geoffrey that he needed a wider majority and more time for consultations.

The agreement was soon seen in Gibraltar as a Spanish Trojan Horse pushed into the British neutral zone to help Spain regain sovereignty over the isthmus. In Salvador's view this need not have been so if Madrid and the Spanish media had not started claiming a resounding victory in the battle for sovereignty over the isthmus. This killed all chances of the agreement ever being acceptable to the people of Gibraltar.

In private, Salvador told Sir Geoffrey that he would not be standing at the 1988 election. He had already taken his decision in August 1987, well before the crucial meetings on the airport Agreement, and so it is utterly wrong to claim, as many people have done, that unpopularity of the agreement was the main cause of his retirement. He delayed his announcement until the December talks were over to avoid embarrassing the Secretary of State.

In the meantime, Bossano had been hitting the headlines with an industrial relations dispute which he, as a union leader, had picked with Appledore. Relations between the workforce and the management had been steadily deteriorating for some time, resulting in a series of damaging strikes. In August 1987 a strike over pay resulted in the unions being warned that the yard would close if further disruption and failure to meet agreed productivity targets continued. The main political effect of this industrial aggro, however, was to boost Bossano's image as the protector of 'exploited' dockyard workers. For the first time the opinion polls in August 1987 started to show the GSLP ahead of the AACR, and they continued to do so until the 1988 election with an increasing margin favouring the GSLP.

Similarly, during the airport negotiations, Bossano had been exciting his supporters about Salvador's supposed submission to Spanish and British blackmail, and the iniquities of his making any deal at all with Spain. He spoke as if Salvador had given in to all the Spanish demands on the *El Pais* list, which was just not so. In the House of Assembly on 4th December, Salvador defended the airport agreement as the best deal on offer to give Gibraltar a proper international airport to boost the Rock's economy, and to enable the EC Air Liberalization agreement to go through. Next day, Bossano levelled a merciless attack on Salvador in the House, which seemed to many observers to have been the delivery of a *coup de grâce*. Salvador had misjudged the popular mood which Bossano had led. Certainly, Salvador's acute political antennae probably told him that confidence in his political leadership was draining away. He resigned as Chief Minister on 9th December and went to the back benches. Canepa took over four months before the 1988 election, timed for March, when Salvador had intended to retire anyway. But there was more to his resignation than this.

There were other factors which influenced his decision, such as the electorate's general feeling of a need for change; the GSLP lead in the opinion polls; his age and his family's wish to see him freed of the burden that he had carried for so long. These pale, however, into insignificance compared with the disloyal sapping and mining undertaken by his deputy, Adolfo Canepa, who was. growing more and more impatient to come into what he believed was his rightful political inheritance.

Trouble within the AACR had started as early as September 1986 when the executive were discussing potential candidates for the next election in 1987/88. Salvador felt two of his existing team of ministers were unlikely to be elected only to find that they were working with Canepa as if he was already chief minister. Canepa wanted the election held as early as possible in 1987. Salvador felt this was too soon, but agreed to review the matter in March 1987. By March 1987, Canepa was getting very impatient. He spoke at an AACR meeting of the suffering and anxiety of not knowing what was going to happen to him. As many influential people, including the Governor, were pressing him to stand once more, Salvador remained non-committal. Abraham Serfaty, one of Salvador's ardent supporters, naively asked Canepa whether he would stand again if Salvador did so too. Taken aback, Canepa replied that he could probably be persuaded to do so but not as deputy. Salvador still remained non-committal.

Some of the older members of the Party tried to point out that they would find it difficult to win the next election without Salvador at the helm. Canepa replied that if, as number two, he had won nearly 1,000 more votes than Bossano, then his block vote would enable him to muster the necessary forces to win. No amount of argument by friends would convince him that he would be in a new and adverse political environment. The GSLP was very much stronger now in electoral support due to Bossano's effective opposition to Brussels, the closure of the naval dockyard, the airport agreement, and the fight with Appledore, all of which had gained him supporters from the workers and the younger generation – the mass of the voters. Canepa was not to be convinced. He was certain that he would have no problem in being re-elected with seven other AACR candidates.

This situation continued into the autumn and Salvador's many friends tried to persuade him to stand again as the only man who could beat Bossano. Salvador, however, realized that it was, indeed, the right moment for change and that Bossano's time had come. He also wished to keep his unbroken record of election successes. It had been hard enough to decide not to stand again. He had told the Foreign Secretary, the Governor and, most important of all, Marcelle and his two daughters. There could be no turning back in spite the immense pressure from his friends to do so.

Salvador eventually told Canepa in confidence that he was not going to stand again, but he could not announce his decision until the Brussels talks were over early in December. Canepa then pressed Salvador to go early enough to enable him to be Chief Minister for at least one session of the House of Assembly. He got his wish but not in the way he or the electorate had expected.

Salvador's resignation after the airport debate instead of at the dissolution was in order to be fair to Canepa, who for his part felt he should have been given much more time to consolidate his position.

As many had predicted, Canepa fought and lost the March 1988 election. All eight GSLP candidates headed the poll. Canepa came ninth, at the top of the AACR candidates but with only 4,422 votes compared with Bossano's 8,128!

The long Salvador era in Gibraltar's history was over. He had retired at the age of 72 undefeated at the polls for 42 years.

Her Majesty the Queen honoured him with the Knight Grand Cross of the British Empire, and on 25th April 1988, the three services gave him a rousing farewell with a fly-past of RAF aircraft, a steam-past by five warships, and a marching display by the Band and Corps of Drums of the Royal Anglian Regiment, followed by a reception and luncheon in the assault ship HMS *Intrepid*.

In his retirement, he left politics altogether and devoted his life to his family and to his legal practice.

CHAPTER 14

EPILOGUE
A Legend in his Lifetime

It is far too early to assess the true magnitude of Salvador's great contribution to Gibraltar's emancipation from colonialism; to the United Nations debates on Gibraltar; to the international recognition of the Gibraltarians as a people; to the defeat of the Spanish 15th siege; and to the series of Anglo-Spanish negotiating processes – Strasbourg, Lisbon and Brussels – which might have led to a happier, fuller life for the people of the Rock without any loss of sovereignty if Brussels had not been repudiated by his successor. Less than a decade has passed since Salvador left office: too soon even to compare his policies with those of his immediate successor; and far too short a time to provide the depth of historical perspective. And so this Epilogue can only be an early assessment of his remarkable political life, spanning 44 years, only the first two of which were not as Gibraltar's principal political leader.

Salvador's long career can be divided into the three distinct and overlapping periods described in the Preface and forming the three parts of this book, but they now have greater significance with the unfolding of the story. The first can be called his 'constitutional reform' period, which lasted some 26 years and was crowned with the successful enactment of the 1969 Constitution, giving the Rock almost complete internal self-government – the political feat, which he, with absolute justification, sees as his life's greatest achievement. The second was his 'United Nations' period, from 1963 to 1969, which overlapped his first period. During this time, he became a world statesman and did more than anyone else to rebut the Franco/Castiella case, which divided the territory of the Rock from its people. And the third was the battle with Spain during the 16 years of the 15th siege, which, thanks to his steadfast leadership, was very reluctantly raised by Spain in 1985. But there was also a fourth short two-year tail-piece, which might be called 'an agreement too far' when he failed to carry the majority of the electorate with him over the airport agreement after he had already decided to retire from politics but had not announced the date.

Throughout these four periods he developed and pursued his distinctive policy of trusting Britain and co-operating with the many governors under whom he served. It was a partnership in which many disputes and arguments occurred, but in which confrontations were rarely carried to extremes. After his initial struggle in establishing himself as a radical political leader through AACR rallies, protest marches and other methods of confrontation, he found that reasoned argument was by far the best way forward in pressing the Convent for constitutional change. He was greatly encouraged by Mason-Mac, but had to turn briefly to generating popular political pressure when faced by reactionary governors like Sir Ralph Eastwood. Most governors were reasonable men who were as keen as he was to press ahead with constitutional reform, which was very much in fashion in the 1950s and 1960s as Britain deliberately sought to convert Empire into Commonwealth. The door to the advancement of civil rights was always ajar provided – and this was the key that Salvador recognized in dealing with the Convent and Whitehall – proposals were sensible, evolutionary and generally supported by the electorate.

This did not mean that Salvador did not have to fight for progress. No colonial administration, however paternalistic, welcomes changes that it is not itself initiating. Every step in

Salvador's long list of constitutional successes had to be lobbied and argued for; and, on occasions, stubbornly fought for as in the case of the elective majority for the City Council. Faced with Whitehall's refusal to allow the extra elective seat, Salvador and his elected colleagues refused to take their seats until the majority was agreed: Whitehall gave way and allowed the extra elective seat!

As long as Salvador was dealing with essentially internal affairs during his 'constitutional reform' period, there was little valid criticism of his close working relations with the Convent. Everything that the people of Gibraltar aspired to was within the British gift. There was no need to seek help elsewhere. Matters took on a different aspect when Spain entered Gibraltar's affairs in a big way from 1954 onwards, making British support even more essential. Paradoxically, Salvador's close relations with the Convent became something of an embarrassment as many of the electorate began to suspect a deliberate British plot to slide the Rock into Spain. This suspicion was never entirely expunged and, as the years went by, Salvador was tarred with being an FCO collaborator.

This widely held belief was entirely unjustified and unfair, and stemmed from Salvador's willingness to look at all Spanish proposals submitted to him. Provided they did not entail any change or dilution of British sovereignty, he was willing to discuss the ideas put forward. In his view, Spain was more likely to be co-operative if she thought there was some hope of a change of the Gibraltarian attitudes in two or three generations' time. This was the basis of the Lisbon and Brussels agreements, but such was the suspicion generated in the electorate of a British sellout that their promise has not been fulfilled – as yet!

There are two other important interlocking facets of Salvador's character, which have an impact on all four periods. The first is his unimpeachable loyalty to the Crown, which is shaded by the second: his ultimate loyalty to the Gibraltarian people whose identity he has done so much to establish. Opponents frequently forget or ignore these fundamental beliefs when they accuse him of colluding with Britain in plotting the Rock's return to Spain.

The retention of British sovereignty is of paramount importance to him until Gibraltar is freed of the shackles of the Treaty of Utrecht and can choose its future status, which he believes should be independence in free association with Britain in a way that Spain could come to accept. This belief set him against the integrationists, who risked the erosion and absorption of the Gibraltarian identity into British culture. Whatever happened, Gibraltar, in his view, must be Gibraltarian and true to itself alone. How long it will need close association with Britain will depend upon the length of time it takes for Spain to have the good grace to abandon her claim once and for all. The tragedy is that although Salvador is one of the greatest Gibraltarian nationalists, he is rarely seen as such because of his willingness to talk to Spain.

Salvador packed more into the 26 years of his 'constitutional reform' period, fighting for the advancement of civil rights, than most politicians manage to handle in a lifetime. Not only that, he did so as the Gibraltar's political leader, bearing responsibility for all the AACR's successes and failures, although he did not become its president until 1947. It took great personal dedication for a young lawyer in his early thirties to inspire the newly created AACR to challenge the traditionalists of the old representative bodies and to seize the leadership from them with so relatively little trouble. Where did his strength lie?

The short answer is that he knew more Gibraltarians personally and more of them knew and trusted him than any of the accepted politicians of the 1940s. This had come about through his work with the evacuees in 1940, and in a much greater way from 1943 onwards when he was fighting for the acceleration of their return to the Rock. The people had great confidence in him, and with his legal training and middle class background he was able to supply the working class membership of the AACR with the type of leadership it required. He was, indeed, the right man in the right place at the right time. It is never easy for men of such different backgrounds as those who came together to form the AACR, to unite, but Salvador was seen as a true man of the people and was strikingly able to hold them together and form them into an effective political machine. A measure of his achievement is that no other successful political party emerged in Gibraltar until Bob Peliza and Maurice Xiberras formed the IWBP in 1967. Parties such as Sergio Triay's Commonwealth Party never became established political forces.

Salvador's task was greatly eased by the loyalty of a number of his earliest and closest colleagues such as Aurelio Montegriffo, Abraham Serfaty, Emilio Salvado, Emilio Alvarez, Leopoldo Mannia, Anthony Morillo and many others. He was however indebted most to Albert Risso, who started the AACR with him. From Risso, Salvador derived inspiration and guidance on the attitudes of the working men and trade unionists, and Risso depended on Salvador's nimble mind and rhetoric. Both men complemented each other, and Salvador maintained that their close association was one of the cornerstones of his success.

Although Salvador was the prime-mover in all of the constitutional advances from the establishment of the post-war City Council in 1945 to internal self-government in 1969, he never acted alone. Proposals put to the governor were invariably the product of specially constituted committees, usually chaired by himself and working to one of his drafts, but taking full account of the opinions of his colleagues and opponents. He was essentially a consensus politician, who always sought to ensure that his policies were supported by a wide swathe of opinion. At the same time, he could be ruthless with dissenting minorities as Sol Seruya found to his cost.

There was little opposition in the formation of the post-war City Council and to Salvador's election as its first Chairman. The efficiency with which he ran it soon debunked the expatriate officials' contention that Gibraltarians were not competent to run the Rock's internal affairs. By one of his flashes of understanding of the British official mentality, he did not press for an elective majority on the first Legislative Council, believing that it was wiser to prove Gibraltarian administrative competence at city level first. In this he was proved right: the service commanders were adamantly opposed to Gibraltarians having a legislative veto, and ministers in Whitehall, including the Prime Minister, Clement Attlee, believed three tiers of government – City Council, Legislative Council and Executive Council were excessive for such a small territory. To have fought on for an elective majority could have been fatal to the embryo Legislative Council.

As it was, Salvador had to face up to Mr Attlee's personal criticism of the proposed three tiers of government when the Legislative Council proposals came before a Cabinet committee, which he was chairing. Salvador's forensic skills proved up to the task of convincing Attlee's envoy, Lord Listowel, who, like Baalam, was sent out to Gibraltar to curse, that the case was sound and should be allowed to go ahead. Working on the principle that constitutional change should be evolutionary and not revolutionary, and should be based upon experience gained so far, Salvador desisted from pressing for further change for five years. He and his colleagues, however, kept up a dialogue among themselves about the future evolution of the constitution, which would be presented at an appropriate moment when enough experience had been gained of the working of the current system.

It was towards the end of this sabbatical period that Salvador produced his brainchild: his substantive AACR paper on constitutional reform, which reached the Governor in 1955. It was so well thought through and logically argued that it was not surprising that over the next decade and a half most of its proposals became realities. The theme of the plan is worth repeating here. With the experience gained by the elected members of the City and Legislative Councils and their successes in local administration, it was now time to increase local government responsibilities. The elective seats on both Councils should be increased, and both should have an elective majority. It would be inappropriate for the Governor to chair an elected legislature so a speaker should be appointed. Each elected member of the Legislative Council should be associated with a government department to gain further experience of administration in anticipation of a full ministerial system being introduced with a chief minister and a council of ministers responsible for internal self-government. He further envisaged the eventual amalgamation of the City and Legislative Councils into a House of Assembly.

Logical though Salvador's plan may have been, Whitehall had to be softened up before agreement could be reached on each step forward. Salvador had stressed in his paper that advances should be made in an evolutionary way and be based on experience gained so far. Even he cannot have anticipated that it would take the tenures of seven governors, spanning fourteen years, to complete his programme in its entirety. The expansion of both councils and the appointment of a speaker were quite quickly and painlessly achieved, but it took the two constitutional conferences under Lord Lansdowne in 1964 and Lord Shepherd in 1968 to arrive at the goal of internal self-government with a House of Assembly and a full ministerial system. In the later stages, Salvador's freedom to negotiate was complicated by Bob Peliza's and Maurice Xiberras's IWBP drive for an indissoluble link with the United Kingdom. The happy outcome was the famous preamble to the 1969 Constitution, which has acted as Gibraltar's safety net ever since. Although there are many claims to authorship of the preamble, Salvador, as leader of the Gibraltar delegation, must be credited with the lion's share of responsibility for its drafting.

Salvador's second period, which was taking place simultaneously with these constitutional reforms, required very different talents. Called to New York at short notice in 1963 to present the Gibraltarian case before the United Nations Committee of 24, he and Peter Isola were thrust, with no experience of international debate and little help from the British delegation, into the lions' den of anti-colonial prejudice, and Hispanic and Afro-Asian hostility. They spoke with great authority as recently elected leaders of the people of Gibraltar, declaring that they were not Spaniards and had no wish to become part of the Spanish realm. Thereafter, speaking year after year at each autumn sessions of the United Nations General Assembly, they gave brilliant performances, but never managed to change the

Committee's acceptance of the Spanish interpretation of 'decolonization'. They did, however, bring to the world's attention the existence of the Gibraltarians as a small but legitimate nation with its own distinct culture and way of life.

The reception that Salvador and Peter Isola were given on their return home from New York in 1963 and 1964 might have turned the heads of any less responsible politicians. Never before or since has Gibraltar given its elected leaders such a heartfelt welcome; virtually the whole population turned out to cheer them back. Salvador resisted any triumphalism and wisely warned the over-excited crowd from the City Hall balcony that it was no time to celebrate. Gibraltar's problems were only just starting. Many difficult years lay ahead. Sadly he was to be proved right, but he also proved his growing statesmanship.

Salvador entered the third period of his career in 1969 as Franco slammed the frontier gates closed. He was no longer a minor local political leader of a small British colony. He was a recognized international statesman, able to talk on equal terms to other important personalities such as David Owen when he became Foreign Secretary and was hoping to make his name resolving the Gibraltar issue through a compromise with Spain over sovereignty. Owen was soon made aware that Salvador was heart and soul a Gibraltarian, and would not tolerate any dilution of British sovereignty to help to improve Anglo-Spanish relations. Indeed, it was perhaps the first time that any British foreign secretary had been so smartly rebuffed by the local leader of so small a dependent territory.

Owen never gave up hope that he could induce Oreja, his Spanish counterpart, to raise the siege as a democratic and humanitarian gesture, knowing that ideas such as condominions were anathema to Salvador. He initiated the Strasbourg process in the hopes of persuading Oreja to ease restrictions, but he was well aware that Salvador's and Xiberras's presence at the talks inhibited any British concessions on sovereignty. The Strasbourg process inevitably ran into the sand when the Labour government collapsed and Lord Carrington became the Conservative Foreign

Secretary.

The Lisbon process in Carrington's time was based upon the very different idea of seeking co-operation within the limits of the Spanish claim and the British pledge. It was largely initiated by the Convent and FCO officials with Salvador and Peter Isola consulted at each stage. Salvador never thought that the carefully crafted formula would work and so was caught off balance when Oreja signed the agreement. His instincts, regrettably, were in fact not far wrong: Oreja had exceeded his brief and Lisbon was never implemented by Spain.

Salvador's last five years in office was a time of triumph which displayed his strength of character, firmness of political judgement and negotiating skills at their best. Regrettably, they were also a time of tragedy when the generation gap had grown too great and he misjudged the general mood of the electorate.

Two crises hit him as Lisbon receded through the Spanish government's failure to summon up the courage to raise the siege. Both were of the FCO's making: the closure of the dockyard and the payment of Spanish pensions when Spain entered the EC. Salvador would take neither lying down and attacked Whitehall with the vigour only possible for a leader of great experience, who had built up the respect of British ministers over four decades. His successful struggle for the very generous compensation package for the dockyard was no mean feat, involving as it did personal negotiations up to Margaret Thatcher's level. It enabled him to win the 1984 election despite the growing strength of Bossano's GSLP. And he was just as relentless over Spanish pensions. He outfaced Sir Geoffrey Howe on no less than three occasions and won in the end.

These were not the actions of a weak and aging chief minister, nor was his willingness to take part in the Anglo-Spanish talks that led to and followed the much criticized Brussels agreement. In his judgement, allowing Spanish workers advanced EC status, and accepting discussion of 'sovereignty', safeguarded by the British pledge, was a price that had to be paid to prevent Gibraltar's bankruptcy. It was a difficult decision to take, but there was no viable alternative. Neither Sir Geoffrey Howe nor Margaret Thatcher were in any mood to accept Gibraltarian semantics over 'sovereignty', which they saw as more than adequately protected by the reiteration of the British constitutional pledge. Salvador was left to sell Brussels to the House of Assembly, which he succeeded in doing, but not to the electorate at large who, led on by Bossano, were emotionally against any agreement whatsoever with Spain.

A younger man might have fought Brussels through the anti-Spanish prejudice and used its full potential, but who can blame Salvador for deciding in August 1987 not to stand for re-election? As it was he even had opposition to his policy from members of his own party.

The all-important question, which only time can answer, is whether his fundamental philosophy of working with Britain while showing understanding and flexibility towards Spain was the soundest course, or whether the refusal to consider any concessions to Spain will eventually bring security and prosperity to the people of Gibraltar. Salvador never alienated British support, nor did he show a frigid face towards Spain. He left office with the frontier fully open and the sinews of trade regrowing in a satisfactory way. Bossano, by contrast, has done more for housing and infrastructure building, but his policy of no involvement with the Brussels Agreement (which has wide support from the electorate) has succeeded in alienating Britain as well as Spain. There are problems at the frontier and Gibraltar faces grave economic difficulties.

Every successful politician has his critics and quite rightly so. Four major criticisms are made about Salvador's actions, which should be answered. First of all, that his ambition led him to foster the cult of personality and set the pattern of Gibraltar looking for a *caudillo* as a saviour. This is nonsense. A better case can be made that the reverse is true. He was often accused with more justification of following public opinion rather than leading it. He was essentially a consensus politician, who had acute political antennae that warned him of dangers ahead. Consensus was so important to him that he worked out most of his major policies with colleagues, and often with opponents as well, in House of Assembly committees. His powers of persuasion were such that he usually had his way, but he was no dictator. On the other hand, he had to maintain the firm leadership needed by any successful prime or chief minister in a democracy if he or she is to remain in power, as Margaret Thatcher found out. But this did not amount to a cult of personality.

The second criticism was that he always took a short or medium term view and ignored the longer term. This may be so, but he was not a free enough agent to think very far ahead. The Foreign Office's responsibility for the Rock's external affairs and the unpredictability of Spain's coercive actions made any long term planning at the level of Gibraltar's chief minister a waste of time. Like the FCO, Salvador had to act pragmatically.

Almost the same defence can be made against the third criticism. He was said to have kept the Gibraltarians in ignorance of the true facts of life, particularly over his part in secret negotiations with Spain. Again, he was not a free agent. He was briefed by the governor on British policy and diplomatic activity on a confidential basis so that he could put the Gibraltarian point of view to Whitehall. To have released in public any of the information he was given without authority from the Convent would have resulted in his being excluded from confidential briefings, as happened to Bob Peliza. Gibraltar would have lost influence in the development of Whitehall policy. Salvador deserves credit for the way he walked the tightrope between Whitehall and the Gibraltar electorate.

The fourth criticism is rather different and has some validity. It has been suggested that by insisting on a ministerial system of government, Salvador foisted an unwieldy ministerial system of government on a small society like Gibraltar. But it was the service commanders in 1948 who caused the initial abandonment of a municipal style of government and forced Salvador to fight for the Legislative Council which was to develop into a ministerial government in 1969. Salvador's aim was simply to establish an elected Gibraltarian voice in the central government of the colony.

This could have been achieved by expanding the City Council into the municipal government of the colony. The all powerful service commanders – Gibraltar's strategic importance was on the increase at the time because of the Cold War – refused to release to City Council control those municipal services considered vital for the security of the fortress. In consequence the City Council could not be turned into the municipal government that would have suited Gibraltar very well, and as the Governor's Executive Council was an inappropriate forum for debates by elected Gibraltarian representatives, Salvador was compelled to fight for a Legislative Council through which their voice could be heard in government. Once the Atlee government had reluctantly accepted the establishment of the Legislative Council, all future constitutional development was inevitably along Westminster and not municipal lines.

Whatever the future holds, Salvador has undoubtedly carved his niche in history as the greatest Gibraltarian leader, who held the principal public office for 42 years, emancipating his people from British military rule, and successfully resisting the Spanish claim to 'sovereignty'. He is the worthy recipient of the style and titles of: The Honourable Sir Joshua Hassan, Knight Grand Cross of the British Empire, Knight of Saint Michael and Saint George, Knight Bachelor, Lieutenant of the Victorian Order, Queen's Counsel and Justice of the Peace.

A shorter and more appropriate title might be:

FATHER OF THE GIBRALTARIANS.

APPENDIX 1

Sir Joshua Hassan's paper on constitutional reform

AACR
Memorandum on Constitutional Reform

GENERAL

In 1945 the reconstitution of the City Council was effected with a majority of members elected by popular vote and the question of the constitution of a Legislative Council, which was then under consideration, was deferred for further discussion.

The Legislative Council was created in November 1950, following discussions with the representative bodies who, though not satisfied with many details of the constitutional set-up thus established, accepted it as a step towards constitutional advancement.

Since 1945 the City Council has been invested with increased responsibilities and the field of its activities has been considerably broadened with marked success which clearly evidences the capability of the people to manage public affairs.

The Legislative Council has now been in existence for nearly five years and the time is now ripe to take stock and see what further progress can be made in the way of constitutional development that will lead to the people being given full powers and responsibilities in civil matters.

It is appreciated that progress towards this justifiable aim should be gradual and methodical and it is considered that an advance thereto could now be achieved in two ways. Firstly, by altering the constitution of both the Legislative and City Council so that the composition of both Councils will be more in keeping with the proved capacity of the people to manage their own affairs and, secondly, by transferring to the City Council (subject to adequate financial arrangements) the control of such matters as Medical Services, Welfare, Education, Public Works, Housing and Town Planning.

From an administrative point of view, it is preferable that services which are essentially municipal in character should be managed by the City Council. When full control of all civil affairs is vested in the people through their elected representatives, it will be immaterial whether certain services are administered by the Government or by the City

Council and the question of merging the City Council into the Colonial Government could then be considered.

REFORM OF THE CITY COUNCIL

The composition of the City Council should be on a more democratic basis than the present one which gives only seven-thirteenths representation to the people who pay more than two-thirds of the Rates.

It is considered that the number of elected members should be double that of the nominated members and it is suggested that the numbers should be six and three respectively.

REFORM OF LEGISLATIVE COUNCIL

The composition of the Legislature of any particular territory must necessarily be governed by the nature of the territory and the circumstances prevailing therein. The extent of the elected representation must, however, be determined by the ability of people to manage their own affairs.

It is considered that as a step towards the ultimate goal of complete self-government in internal affairs, the two seats which are now held by nominated members should be relinquished to elected members so as to give the latter a majority in the Legislative Council. It is submitted that, in the circumstances which prevail in Gibraltar, it is unnecessary to have any nominated members in the Legislature. Should this proposition be unfavourably entertained, the desired objective could be attained by increasing the number of elected members to seven or ten. The Council would thus be composed of twelve or fifteen members, as the case may be, the larger number being advocated inasmuch as it would widen the scope for giving departmental responsibility to elected members.

It is furthermore considered that the disqualification for election to the Legislative Council which is contained in paragraph (j) of Section 11 of the Gibraltar Legislative Council Order-in-Council, 1950, should be limited to persons holding office under the Colonial Government. The present wide application of the said paragraph unduly restricts the field of prospective candidates for election, which is important in a relatively small community, and, inasmuch as the Legislative Council is not concerned with Imperial matters or matters of defence there appears to be no reason why persons in the employment of the Imperial Government should be debarred from standing for election.

REFORM OF EXECUTIVE COUNCIL

The Executive Council should be replaced by a Council of Ministers which should consist of the Governor as President, the three ex-officio members and four Ministers appointed from among the elected members of the Legislative Council of whom one should be styled 'Chief Minister'. The Chief Minister should be appointed by the Governor and the others should likewise be appointed by the Governor but after consultation with the Chief Minister.

The Ministers should be charged with responsibility for departments or subjects.

The Council of Ministers should be the principal instrument for the framing of policy and perform such functions and duties and exercise such powers as world from time to time be prescribed.

The Ministers should be collectively responsible to the Legislative Council.

The appointment of Ministers to exercise supervision over departments of Government has successfully implemented in many parts of the Commonwealth some of which have less capabilities for self government than Gibraltar.

RESERVED POWER OF GOVERNOR

The exercise of the reserved power by the Governor on the 27th July, 1955, has caused considerable, and justified resentment particularly because of the circumstances and manner in which it was used. This experience and the constitutional crisis which it occasioned should suffice to make clear the imperative necessity of re-drafting this part of the constitution in such a manner as will avoid a repetition of such a difficult situation.

It is accepted that things being as they are, the Governor should have some reserved power but it is considered that he should not be able to exercise such power without the approval of the Council of Ministers or of the Executive Council. This is, at this stage, more necessary in Gibraltar than elsewhere, inasmuch as the Governor is also the President of the Legislative Council, and the question of the exercise of such extraordinary powers should be considered not after a heated debate leading to the defeat of a measure but after due and calm deliberation taking all circumstances into account.

It is furthermore considered that the Legislative Council should be presided by an independent Speaker and not by the Governor.

CONCLUSION

The above cover the main proposals for constitutional reform. Other matters connected therewith such as the method of election both to the Legislative Council and the City Council will be raised in the course of the discussions that will necessarily take place in considering the said proposals.

Gibraltar.
October, 1955

APPENDIX 2

INTERVENTION OF THE PETITIONER FROM THE TOWN OF GIBRALTAR, SIR J HASSAN, BEFORE THE "COMMITTEE OF TWENTY-FOUR"

September 19th 1963

Mr HASSAN: In the first place, my colleague and I would like to express our thanks to you and to all the members of the Committee over which you so ably preside for acceding to our petition and giving us this opportunity of stating the case of the people of Gibraltar in the course of your deliberations on this matter which to us is of the utmost importance.

It is a clear sign of the enlightened times in which we live that small communities are not the less important because of their size and that their wishes must play a deciding factor in determining their future. I want to make it clear that we have come here to New York on our own initiative in order to make our views known to this Committee and to the world. This is an exclusively Gibraltarian delegation and we are expressing the views of the whole of the people of Gibraltar.

I think it would be useful if, before I deal with the matter of substance, I should say who we are and what we represent. I am the Chief Member of Gibraltar's Executive and Legislative Council, of which I will have more to say in detail later. I was elected to the Legislative Council by universal adult suffrage at the head of colleagues of my party, the Association for the Advancement of Civil Rights, the biggest political party in Gibraltar, a party which has the affiliation of the Gibraltar Confederation of Labour, the largest Trade Union of my city, which is itself completely free and is in turn an affiliated member of the British Trade Unions Congress and the International Confederation of Free Trade Unions.

By separate elections, also on universal adult suffrage, I am a City Councillor, in which capacity I have been re-elected at every general election held since its reconstitution after the war and I have had the privilege of having been unanimously elected by all the Councillors irrespective of party as its Mayor at sixteen annual elections, the last one having been held in January of this year. I continue as leader of the party to which I have referred and of which I was one of its founders during the war years with the aim of achieving self-government for the people of Gibraltar. I am sorry if I have appeared immodest in describing the above. This was not my intention, but I must establish my credentials to speak on behalf of the people of Gibraltar.

My colleague is Mr. Peter Isola, a member of the Gibraltar Bar, like myself, but much younger and indeed a product of the post-war men in public life in our city. He is an elected member of the Gibraltar Legislative Council, a member of the Executive Council and the member associated with education. For all intent and purposes, he is actually the Minister for Education, though not yet so-called. Mr. Isola does not belong to my party, he is an Independent. In fact in local politics in Gibraltar he is my most bitter and able opponent. His views and those of my party on certain aspects of internal Government are opposed but on the question of Gibraltar's future we are not only not opposed but we are entirely of the same mind and so is every other elected representative and indeed the whole population of Gibraltar. I shall have more to say on this matter later on. Mr. Isola was unanimously chosen by all our colleagues to come with me in order to make a delegation as widely representative as the circumstances and the time available permitted. Both Mr. Isola's family and my own have been established in Gibraltar for well over 200 years.

Spain has asked on many occasions that Gibraltar should be returned to it. Now the Spanish representative seeks to achieve this object under the guise of a passionate abhorrence of colonialism. We do not question Spain's dislike of colonialism, but we do most emphatically maintain that its application to Gibraltar is completely irrelevant.

What is meant by colonialism? The word has a number of unsavoury connotations. It implies surely, the subjugation of a people by an external and foreign power; the exploitation of the resources of the colony and of the labour of the people for the benefit of the colonial Power; the oppression of the people, economically, by not allowing them the opportunities of a high standard of living; socially, by refusing them opportunities for education and by distinctions of class, if not of race; morally, by not recognizing and respecting their worth as human beings; legally, by not granting them redress before the law and the fullest possible opportunities for seeking and attaining justice; and, perhaps most important of all, politically, by not allowing them the expression of their wishes as to the way in which they should be governed and preventing them from putting their wishes into effect.

To what extent are these qualifications for colonialism met in the case of Gibraltar? Gibraltar is a very small place and, understandably, the conditions of life there may not be very well known by the busy world outside, but it is not difficult to demonstrate – and to substantiate by every possible proof – that not one of the qualifications for colonialism is to be found in Gibraltar and that the case presented by the Spanish representative, in so far as it rests on this argument – and it does so to a very substantial extent – falls to the ground accordingly, based as it is on false premises, not on a desire to liberate or emancipate an oppressed people but on a centuries-old obsession to alter a historical fact.

Nothing could be further from the truth than to suggest that the people of Gibraltar are subjugated or exploited by a foreign Power. *The people of Gibraltar are descended from persons who came to Gibraltar after it had been conquered.* They came to Gibraltar and they settled there in the full knowledge that Gibraltar was a fortress and that the conditions of their lives would be subject to the overriding demands of the fulfilment of Gibraltar's role as a base of war. It is no secret that under modern conditions the value of Gibraltar as a fortress has declined from what it used to be. It may have been an accident of history that when this decline began, something else – the liberalization of colonial rule in the world at large – was gathering momentum. Be that as it may, the last forty years, and particularly the last twenty years, have seen changes in the whole way of life of Gibraltar which are entirely consonant with the gradual growth of Gibraltar as a political entity in proportion to its declining value or use as a fortress. In the light of the modern, enlightened concept of human rights, it may be argued that it was wrong that the democratic liberties of Gibraltarians should in the past been subordinated to the purely functional uses of war, defence or commercial strategy. The fact remains that our concern today is not with the past but with the present, not with Gibraltar as a military colony in the nineteenth and early twentieth centuries, but with Gibraltar as an enlightened, emancipated community in the 1960's, with a mind of its own and surely, within the spirit of the Charter of the United Nations, the right to determine its own future.

Let us take the next qualification for colonialism: the exploitation of the resources of the colony and of the labour of the people for the benefit of the colonial Power. Great Britain does not derive any revenue from Gibraltar nor from the labour of the Gibraltarian. On the contrary, the people of Gibraltar derive benefit from the presence of the armed forces of Great Britain, from the commercial turnover which this represents, from the opportunities for employment which are made available, from the grants made under the Colonial Development and Welfare Acts, and from the whole background of administrative expertise, judicial independence and responsible legislature which characterize a system of government at its best.

What shall we say about the economic oppression of the people? Prosperity is enjoyed by all sections of the community, which will not be satisfied except with the highest standards of food, housing and material prosperity generally.

In the educational sphere, the number of young men and women from Gibraltar who proceed from school to university, teacher-training colleges and technological studies is very great *pro rata*. How does this compare with other colonial territories where oppression and exploitation are being, or have been maintained and where over-all progress has been retarded by depriving the peoples of those territories of even the most elementary opportunities for educational advancement, with all that this implies in the economic, social and, political fields?

There are no distinctions of class, race or religion in Gibraltar. In such a tightly-knit community, with over 12,500 persons to the square mile, such distinctions would be as absurd in practice as they are detestable in principle.

The "Englishman" does not lord it over the Gibraltarian. We live in mutual respect; so too does Catholic with Jew, Jew with Protestant, Protestant with Catholic, Catholic with Hindu, Hindu with non-conformist or agnostic.

The moral aspect of Gibraltar's social conditions is, of course, intimately connected with the whole question of class, racial or religious distinction. It is in this sphere that, with all the modesty of which I am capable, I can claim – and challenge anyone to disprove it – that Gibraltar has achieved one of the very first objects of the Charter of the United Nations: its faith in fundamental human rights, in the dignity and worth of the human person and in the equal rights of men and women. This, to my mind, and to the minds of all those who have any knowledge of Gibraltar, is so self-evident a proposition that I am sure I do not need to labour the point.

The legal and judicial system of Gibraltar is based entirely on that of Great Britain. Justice is meted out to everybody, irrespective of class, creed or race and without fear or favour. There is a wholesome respect in Gibraltar for the impartiality of our courts. In my twenty-five years as a practising lawyer I have not had experience of a miscarriage of justice.

Lastly, we come to the political aspect, which, in the context of this discussion, is perhaps the most important question of all if only because politics cover practically every field of human activity. You will, I am sure, bear with me if, in order to drive home to the utmost the actual facts of the situation as it exists at present, *I remind you of sub-paragraph (b) of Article 73, Chapter XI of the Charter entitled "declaration Regarding Non-Self-Governing Territories". The relevant part of Article 73 reads as follows:*

"Members of the United Nations . . . accept as a sacred trust the obligation to promote to the utmost . . . the well-being of the inhabitants of these territories, and, to this end:

. . . . .

"b. to develop self-government, to take due account of the political aspirations of the peoples, and to assist them in the progressive development of their free political institutions, according to the particular circumstances of each territory and its peoples and their varying stages of advancement."

Gibraltar has not yet achieved full self-government. This, however, is the aim of Gibraltarian politicians and is an aim which has been accepted by the British Government. I will describe briefly the present formal constitutional position in Gibraltar; but before I do so I wish to make it quite clear to all of you that in practice the power of the Gibraltar politician extends well beyond the limits formally prescribed by the present constitutional instruments. This – with due modesty – is undoubtedly due to the proved integrity and ability of the people in public life in Gibraltar. Gibraltar's politics are municipal and governmental. In the municipal sphere, the Gibraltar City Council, of which I have already stated I have the honour to serve as Mayor, has a popularly elected majority and its decisions are not subject to the approval of Her Majesty's Government. In fact it is subject to less interference from the Central Government than any ordinary municipality in the United Kingdom. In the governmental sphere, there is a Legislative Council, an Executive Council and a Council of Members. The Legislative Council has a popularly elected majority. Its decisions are subject to the reserved powers of the Governor, who may refuse to assent to the enactment of legislation passed by the Council. In fact, and to illustrate my point about the extent of power wielded by the elected members beyond those set forth in the constitutional instruments, the Governor's reserved powers have been exercised on only one occasion since the establishment of the Legislature thirteen years ago. The use of these powers was followed immediately by the resignation of all the elected members, an emergency visit to Gibraltar by the Secretary of State for the Colonies himself, and the evolution of a compromise solution which took into account the wishes of the elected members, who then stood for election once again and were returned to power unopposed.

In 1956, a scheme was instituted for the association of members of the Legislature with government departments. This scheme has worked so satisfactorily that there can be no doubt that the appointment of members as fully responsible ministers will not be long delayed. My party put in a claim to this effect on 20 August this year and I am confident that the constitution will be changed in this respect in time for the general elections due in 1964. The scheme ensures that heads of government departments – who are, of course, responsible to Her Majesty's Government's representative in Gibraltar – do not take any policy decisions without consulting the member associated with the department. General matters of policy, not directly related to any particular department, are made the subject of consultation with the Chief Member.

The Executive Council sits under the chairmanship of the Governor and consists of equal numbers of official and elected members. By the constitutional instruments the Governor is entitled to disregard the advice tendered to him by the Council. In my recollection this has happened only once – and I refer to the occasion which I have already mentioned when the elected members resigned and thereby gained their objective. In practice the Governor acts on the advice of the elected representatives of the people.

Some eighteen months ago, as a further step in constitutional development, approval was given to the formation of a Council of Members. This body consists of the elected members in the Executive Council under the chairmanship of the Chief Member and its functions are to consider in detail items put before the Executive Council, the implications of which are wholly or mainly domestic – that is, not concerned with such matters as defence and external affairs – and should be considered in a forum consisting exclusively of locally elected representatives who are in a position, moreover, to call upon any member of the administration to appear before them. Again, this innovation has been extremely successful and there are now at least three meetings of the Council of Members to every meeting of the Executive Council. The conclusions arrived at by the Council of Members are subject to the endorsement of the Executive Council but no case has yet arisen of the recommendations of the former being negatived by the latter. Moreover, it has already been agreed that an additional elected member shall be appointed to Executive Council after the next general elections, thereby also broadening the representation in the Council of Members. Further, in the claim for further constitutional development which I have already mentioned, there is a demand for the creation of a Council of Ministers which will give formal sanction to the practice actually being followed now.

It must, I think, be evident to all you gentlemen that although Gibraltar is still, formally, a "Crown Colony", in spite of the fact that the word "colony" and its cognate expressions have been expunged from all local institutions, nothing could be further away from the generally accepted interpretation of "colonialism" than the situation in present-day Gibraltar.

We have such control of our own affairs that no one other than persons who belong to Gibraltar, by having been born there and by having parents belonging to the place, can live there as of right and without licence. Even United Kingdom nationals require such licence there, and in the case of those who have official functions to perform the nature of the exemptions are contained in legislation over which we have full control.

I have gone into this matter in some detail, because, with the greatest respect to the Spanish representative, it is my view that an attempt has been made to mislead the Committee by the application to Gibraltar of the word "colonialism", a word that in many instances in the past and, regrettably, in some instances in the present, bears a well-deserved stigma, but a word which cannot conceivably be applied to Gibraltar except in so far as Gibraltar, by an archaic relic of terminology, is still designated a Crown Colony.

Do not let us delude ourselves. We all of us know the true reasons why Spain has raised this matter in this Committee. And I, my colleagues, and the people of Gibraltar, knowing the Spanish character as we do and the Spaniard's regard, above all else, for his honour, not only understand his attitude towards Gibraltar but respect him for it. But, gentlemen, the people of Gibraltar also have a high regard for their honour. The land in which they live is their birthplace and was the birthplace of their forebears – for no less than 250 years.

There is no place for such notions of honour in a utilitarian, entirely materialistic world. But neither the Spaniard, nor the Gibraltarian, nor any other person who has a sense of nationalism consonant with international obligations and duties will regard his birthplace in so cynical a fashion. A man has an indefinable pull towards the land in which he was born. He wants to continue living in this land and he wants to decide for himself how he shall live there. The people of Gibraltar want to continue living in Gibraltar; they have decided how they want to live there; their objective has now been all but fulfilled, as is shown by the fact that my colleague and I are here to speak on this subject for ourselves. Our position before this Committee and before the world is a simple one and one which all members of the United Nations are in conscience bound to uphold. We ask for nothing except to be allowed to live our lives the way we want to live them without interference from outside, in friendliness with all peoples and in co-operation with our immediate neighbours for what, I assure you, can only be our mutual good, socially, culturally, economically, and in every other way. We are a community of only 25,000 persons, but we believe that the humanitarian ideals of this modern world, as enshrined in the United Nations Charter, have as much regard to the wishes and aspirations of small communities as they have to those containing millions,

I have every confidence that in acknowledging the justice of our position and endorsing our attitude this Committee will also support our view that the imposition by Spain of restrictions against Gibraltar, designed to destroy its well-being and undermine its prosperity, are as directly contrary to the spirit of the United Nations Charter is would be an act of open aggression.

Other arguments, besides the latest one of colonialism, have been adduced in the past by the Spaniards in support of their claim to Gibraltar. There are answers to those arguments and we are not afraid of taking issue on them. We submit, however, that the prime concern of this Committee is to ascertain whether colonialism is in fact being practised in Gibraltar and, if not, then to agree that, in the spirit and the letter of the United Nations Charter, the people of Gibraltar are entitled without any unwanted external influence to decide how they wish to shape their own future.

Even if, as the representative of Syria has said, Gibraltar should be dealt with as a colonial area within the terms of reference of this Committee, we say that the main concern of the Committee must be the right of self-determination of the people in accordance with paragraph 5 of resolution 1514 (XV), on which we should like to lay great stress and to which the representative of Denmark has referred in his short but pertinent intervention. In any case, I am very happy to see that the representative of Syria, in placing the order in which the interests of the interests of the three parties concerned should be taken, has put first those of the people of Gibraltar, and I am indeed grateful to him for doing so.

What, then, are the wishes of the people of Gibraltar? The United Nations, working through this Committee of Twenty-four is anxious to ensure that all Non-Self-Governing Territories reach a full measure of self-government. As you are all aware, Principle VI of the Annex to resolution 1514 (XV) defines three forms of what can constitute a "full measure of self-government". Principle 6 says:

"A non-self-governing territory can be said to have reached a full measure of self-government by:

(a) Emergence as a sovereign independent State;
(b) Free association with an independent State; or
(c) Integration with an Independent State."

If we were not sincere, we could argue here that we want complete independence followed by a treaty with Britain about defence and foreign affairs. However, Gibraltar is not and never can be a fully independent, self-supporting nation, relying on its own resources for its economy, its defence and conduct of its relations with other States. It can therefore never emerge as a sovereign independent State. This is, from the point of view of the people of Gibraltar, unfortunate, but there is nothing we can do to make Gibraltar bigger.

There are also practical reasons which make the third possibility of full self-government envisaged by the United Nations – that is, integration with an independent State – extremely difficult to implement. The conditions of life in Gibraltar are different, in a number of ways, from those in Britain, economically, culturally, and climatically. Geographical reasons, too, would make it very difficult.

But, apart from the practical reasons, there are also political reasons. How could the wishes of the people of Gibraltar, who, as I say, are in a number of ways different from the people of Britain, be implemented in Gibraltar if Gibraltar were integrated with Britain or with any other State? At most, Gibraltar would be represented in the British Parliament by one member – one among over 600 members. Gibraltar would not be integrated; it would be swallowed up, It would not have achieved self-government; it would have developed from a state of colonialism to a state where it would lose its individuality, its very self. Gibraltar cannot emerge as an independent State; it cannot and will not be integrated with another independent State.

The third possibility envisaged by the United Nations is "free association with an independent State". It is this that the people of Gibraltar aspire to, and it can surely be the people of Gibraltar alone who can decide with which independent State they wish to be freely associated. Any other way of association would not be a free association. It would be a continuation of the system of colonialism, or, even worse, an annexation of territory against the wishes of its inhabitants.

With whom, then, does Gibraltar wish to be freely associated?

For the reasons which I have already outlined in the earlier parts of my statement, Gibraltar wishes to be associated with Britain. This is the free choice of the people of Gibraltar, and I, their spokesman before this Committee, am entitled and empowered to say so with the full backing of the whole of the people of Gibraltar. It would be foolish to pretend that every country in this world, that every member of this Committee, agrees with the British way of life or with British institutions. The point is that the people of Gibraltar, of their own free will, have chosen this association and no other. We are not asking you to agree with the British way of life, or even with the Gibraltar version of this way of life. We are asking only that our right to choose our own way of life should not be impaired in any way.

And believe me when I tell you that, small though Gibraltar is, there is a distinct Gibraltarian way of life. No community can exist for over 250 years without creating its own individuality, its character, its personality. Gibraltar has achieved its own culture in the widest sense of that word. It has drawn for this culture from many sources, but naturally the two main sources have been Britain, for political, and Spain, for geographical reasons, and Italy where the bulk of the civilian population originated. We are not afraid to say that we have drawn something from Spain. It is precisely because our culture is eclectic that it has become individual, and it is precisely because it is individual that we do not desire to allow Gibraltar to be swallowed up by Spain, Britain, or anybody else.

Let me make it quite clear that we do not want to be under Britain; we want to be with Britain. The people of Gibraltar, as citizens of what until recently was primarily a fortress, have suffered as a result of that status. I referred before to the accident of history that combined the changing role of Gibraltar with the new breath of liberalism and liberty for the people of colonies throughout the world. But if these had not coincided in time, then the movement of liberalism, by itself, would have been enough – although the struggle might have been harder. I can tell you, as the leader of my political party – whose title is the Association for the Advancement of Civil Rights – that there has been a struggle. There has been a struggle for twenty years, and although it still continues, it is nearly over.

At this very moment the people of Gibraltar, all 25,000 of them, are waiting with anxiety to see what conclusions this Assembly will reach and how its members will react to our pleas. I have no doubt that the utter sincerity, the wholehearted unanimity and the severe anxiety of the people of Gibraltar at this crisis, this climax, of their political development, will find an echo and a response in the hearts as well as in the minds of the delegations of this Committee, whatever international political allegiances, affiliations or sympathies they may have.

We have nothing but a desire to be true friends of our neighbours, as we have been for well over two centuries, and to live in peace and amity with them. *We fully appreciate their strong feelings in this matter in attempting to recover peacefully what by conquest they gained and by conquest they lost.*

We, the people of Gibraltar, who had nothing to do with these war conflicts of the past, should not be made to give up what we hold most dear in order to reverse an accident of history.

Spain is a big country with a wonderful history of achievements and with a sense of honour and dignity which we and all the world admire. We feel sure that this grandeur will not in any way suffer if we, the people of Gibraltar, continue in our own way of life, which we cherish and which we fervently desire to preserve.

I stated in my original telegram to the Secretary-General that we wished for the continuation and development of the closest links with Britain, not only because of our centuries-old association with the mother country and of our traditional adherence to the British way of life, but also as a safeguard for the large measure of democratic control of our domestic affairs which, as I have already described, we have achieved and which, we are confident, will be increased.

The Committee of Twenty-four, representing as it does the big and the small nations, will strengthen their prestige as upholders of the rights of colonial peoples by reaffirming the principle of self-determination, thereby allowing us to continue the way of life which we have freely chosen for ourselves.

Many thanks, Mr. Chairman, for your patience and forbearance and for the patience and forbearance with which all the members of the Committee have listened to me.

Ref.: United Nations, Doc. A/AC.109/PV.214.

APPENDIX 3

The paper published by the Legislative Assembly in '64

THE FUTURE OF GIBRALTAR

Part 1: Gibraltar's Colonial Status

In September, 1963, the Committee of 24, in pursuance of its mandate to put a speedy and unconditional end to colonialism in all its forms and manifestations, turned its attention to Gibraltar. Gibraltar is indisputably a Crown Colony of Great Britain but it is a colony in which the evils of colonialism no longer exist and one which is on the verge of achieving internal self-government. This was demonstrated by the two petitioners from Gibraltar who appeared before the Committee in September, 1963. Their statements were not refuted by anyone: they are irrefutable. And yet, because Gibraltar has not yet in fact achieved full self-government, it is the duty of the Committee of 24, a duty which it owes both to the General Assembly of the United Nations and to the people of Gibraltar, to satisfy itself that self-government will be achieved with no unnecessary delay.

With its experience of the large number of colonial territories with which it has already dealt, the Committee of 24 is aware that circumstances between one territory and another differ widely and that the future of each territory must therefore be considered in relation to those circumstances and subject to the overriding right of the people of each territory to express their own wishes freely and, without any pressure, military, economic or political, from any other country.

The wishes of the people of Gibraltar are to achieve full internal self-government in a free association with Britain, This is a comparatively new concept and the terms and conditions under which it will be implemented require a considerable amount of study and negotiation. By having already achieved a very large measure of self-government the people of Gibraltar are confident as well as determined that they shall achieve full self-government in the very near future. But they are not prepared to embark on full self-government until they are satisfied that the arrangements under which it is obtained are such as to guarantee their economic prosperity and their international security in the future. They are sufficiently mature politically to run their own affairs and do so already to a very great extent, but the future constitutional relationship between the colony and the former administering power is, in the case of Gibraltar, as important to the future welfare of its people as the achievement of full self-government. Other former colonies may have desired only to rid themselves of the status of colony, able and willing as they were to stand on their own, economically, politically and militarily, as viable self-sustaining entities. Because of its size, Gibraltar is unable to do this without entering into an association with another country on whom the responsibility for guaranteeing the future security and independence of Gibraltar can be reliably laid.

In discussing the termination of Gibraltar's colonial status, there are three aspects to be considered, the political aspect, the economic aspect and the question of defence and foreign affairs.

(1) The Political Aspect.

In September, 1963, the petitioners from Gibraltar made it clear to the Committee of 24 that the people of Gibraltar already enjoyed a very large measure of self-government under the existing constitution. They also stated that further constitutional changes had been sought and that it was expected that these would be introduced before the next elections to the Legislature in the autumn of 1964.

In April, 1964. the Minister of State for Commonwealth Relations and Colonial Affairs visited Gibraltar for a constitutional conference.

The results of the conference, which are to be implemented in time for the elections in the autumn, represent a very significant advance in Gibraltar's progress towards full internal self-government, both by consolidating in legal form certain powers already enjoyed in practice by the elected members and by introducing a number of important measures to accelerate the complete devolution of internal powers.

Nominated members have been abolished; the Chief Secretary, who is the Colonial Office representative in Gibraltar, will no longer be a member of the Legislative Council, and the number of elected members has been increased from 7 to 11. Accordingly, after the elections to be held this year, the Legislature will consist of 11 elected members and two official members, the Attorney-General and the Financial Secretary, who will be virtually in the position of officers of the House and who will be expected to vote with the majority of elected members who will form the Government.

Members forming the Government will be known as Ministers and will enjoy full ministerial responsibility within their Departments. The Council of Members will be known as the Council of Ministers and its composition will be decided at the discretion of the Chief Minister. The Chief Minister will be the Leader of the Legislative Council and will be vested with the direction of Government business.

The Executive Council is being replaced by the Gibraltar Council and the number of Ministers in the Council will be increased from 4 to 5, thus providing an elected majority in this Council also.

The constitutional changes which have been made are fully in accordance with the wishes of the elected members. They represent the last step before the formal achievement of full internal self-government which now awaits only the conclusion of an agreement between Britain and Gibraltar as to the terms and conditions of the association between them. These terms and conditions are now being studied and will be discussed with the British Government when agreement has been reached among the elected members. It is fully expected therefore that the final, formal achievement of self-government will take place during the life of the next Legislature

Because of the large extent to which the people of Gibraltar already govern themselves, the political aspect of Gibraltar's colonial status is that which troubles them least of all. To the people of Gibraltar this presents no problem. There is no question of their requiring emancipation from colonialist oppression.

In the stage of political development which has been reached in Gibraltar and in the face of the attitude of the United Nations towards colonial territories, the British Government would not today lightly override the wishes of the people of Gibraltar in any matter affecting the government of their city.

It is true that technically some remnants of the forms of a

Crown Colony remain, with the legal trappings of the Governor's constitutional prerogatives. It cannot be too strongly emphasised, however, that the real effective voice in the Government of Gibraltar today is that of the elected members. For many years now Governors have acted on the advice of the people's elected representatives and it is inconceivable that the Governor would thwart their wishes or attempt to act without their agreement.

(2) The Economic Aspect.

Under the impetus of imminent self-government, urgent measures are being taken to change the basis of the economy of Gibraltar in such a way as to lessen its dependence on external factors and enable Gibraltar to become economically viable. The remarkable growth of tourism in recent years is one important element in this transformation. Record figures are achieved each year and the further expansion of the tourist industry continues to be energetically pursued. Other plans include the setting up of light industries, an even fuller development of the Port of Gibraltar, the attraction of important business firms, encouraged by low taxation, to establish their offices in Gibraltar and the provision of housing and other facilities to induce "permanent tourists" to come and settle in Gibraltar.

If from a political point of view Gibraltar's present formal status of Crown Colony is of no practical consequence in the lives of its people, from the economic point of view that status represents, perhaps paradoxically, their safeguard for the future and one which they will not give up until the guarantees which they seek are negotiated, agreed and formally embodied in articles of association with Britain.

In the case of large colonies, rich in raw materials and other resources, some administering powers have at times been reluctant to grant independence because of the economic losses which such transfer of power has entailed. In such circumstances the Committee of 24 has rightly demanded the immediate grant of independence. To apply this principle to Gibraltar, however, from which Britain derives no revenue but to whose economy she contributes, would be to relieve Britain from the obligations and responsibilities which she owes to a former colony. Far from releasing the people of Gibraltar from bondage the Committee of

24 would unwittingly be rendering them a disservice.

(3) Defence and Foreign Affairs.

The people of Gibraltar are British, but this does not mean that they are English: they live very near to Spain, but this does not mean that they are Spanish. They are a unique community which has a character of its own and which seeks to continue to live as such. While the political aspirations of this community are virtually satisfied, and while its economic development is rapidly being completed, the people of Gibraltar cannot ever hope to be able to defend themselves against an aggressor. Nor can they hope to establish and maintain foreign relations with other countries. These are the two requirements in which Gibraltar has to place its reliance elsewhere. It was for this kind of situation that the principle of free association was intended by the United Nations. The people of Gibraltar do not want to rush into full self-government until the details of the manner in which the British Government will meet these responsibilities on behalf of its former colony have been settled.

The people of Gibraltar are making steady and intelligent progress towards full *de jure* as well as *de facto* self-government. Should the British Government at any stage refuse to agree to the wishes of the people of Gibraltar in any matter concerning their future, petitioners from Gibraltar would seek to appear before the United Nations for protection as promptly and as fiercely as they appeared before the Committee of 24 in September, 1963, when it became evident that the truth about Gibraltar was being distorted by those who sought not the emancipation of the people of Gibraltar from a colonial regime, but the fulfilment of their own territorial ambitions.

What Gibraltarians seek from the Committee of 24, therefore, is an affirmation of their right to self-government in a free association with Britain, the terms of such an association to be agreed freely between Gibraltar and Britain and fully implemented at a time to be chosen by the people of Gibraltar themselves.

Part 2: Sovereignty over Gibraltar.

While the terms of the mandate which governs the activities of the

Committee of 24 do not specifically include any reference to the question of the sovereignty of colonial territories, and while it would seem, on the face of it, that questions of sovereignty are outside the scope of the Committee's sphere of action, we are aware that some members of the Committee believe that the question of sovereignty should not be kept entirely outside the auspices of the Committee. For this reason, we feel it desirable to record our views on this important aspect of the future of Gibraltar.

It is a matter of fact that sovereignty over Gibraltar is at present exercised by Britain. The Spanish claim to sovereignty has been brought before the Committee of 24. It has been stated that the British have a colony on Spanish soil and an attempt has been made to suggest that the people of Gibraltar are Spanish in their outlook and traditions and desire unification with Spain.

The soil of Gibraltar should belong to no-one but the people of Gibraltar and the people of Gibraltar do not desire to be united with Spain. Part I of this publication dealt with the right of a colonial people to end their colonial status by the exercise of self-determination. But emergence from a colonial status is not of itself enough if it does not also ensure that the right to self-determination is exercised at the same time and enjoyed securely thereafter.

Sovereignty over Gibraltar is not a matter for discussion between Britain and Spain. That is why Gibraltar objected to the suggestion made last September that talks to decide Gibraltar's future should be held between those two countries. The question of sovereignty over Gibraltar must be decided solely according to the wishes of the people of Gibraltar. If the people of Gibraltar wished to be associated with Spain, then Britain would have to surrender Gibraltar to Spain if the principle of self-determination were not to be abused. Similarly, if the people of Gibraltar wish to be associated with Britain – as they do – then Spain's territorial claim to Gibraltar must fail, if the grant of self-government under the auspices of the Committee of 24 is not to be vitiated, nullified and made into a mockery.

It must be made clear that the people of Gibraltar want nothing but the friendliest possible relations with their neighbours, including Spain. Because of the geographical position of Gibraltar they inevitably have many links with Spain. But they also have many links with Britain and the link which, in this matter of sovereignty and the future of Gibraltar, is the most important, overriding the claims and demands of all others, is the political link.

The work of the Committee of 24 is essentially political in its nature and it is on political considerations, above all else, that it, and its parent body, make their decisions. The people of Gibraltar wish to be politically associated with Britain and not with Spain. At this moment in their history when, as part of the work of the Committee of 24, they are given the right to choose freely what their future shall be, they decide that they want to follow the British tradition of Parliamentary democracy.

The Spanish system of government is no concern of the people of Gibraltar. They believe that it is up to each country to govern itself as it chooses to do so. But in so far as the people of Gibraltar are concerned, they want a parliamentary democracy on the lines of the British form of government and nothing else.

It is essential therefore that the political aspect of Gibraltar's future should be a matter solely for Britain and Gibraltar. In all other matters, such as economic problems, Gibraltar is always prepared to co-operate with Spain and to resolve difficulties by discussion and negotiation between Spain and Britain acting on behalf of Gibraltar in international affairs. If Spain requires assurances that Gibraltar will never pose a threat to her internal political or economic stability these will be freely given by Britain on behalf of Gibraltar. But from the internal political and constitutional affairs of Gibraltar, which are two of the constituents of the concept of sovereignty, Spain must be excluded.

If, therefore, the Committee of 24 considers that it cannot altogether exclude from its consideration of Gibraltar's future the dispute which exists over Gibraltar's sovereignty, then the people of Gibraltar also seek from the Committee of 24 an affirmation that, while it may not be the function of the Committee to settle disputes about sovereignty, the Committee's mandate cannot be effectively carried out in the case of Gibraltar unless, when the question of sovereignty is discussed, the wishes of the people of Gibraltar as to where that sovereignty should lie are taken fully into account.

Appendix 4

STATEMENT OF THE PETITIONER OF THE TOWN OF GIBRALTAR SIR JOSHUA HASSAN, BEFORE THE 4TH COMMITTEE OF THE UNITED NATIONS GENERAL ASSEMBLY

17 December 1966

Mr. Chairman: At the outset my colleague and I would like to express our gratitude to you and all the members of the "Committee", for acceding at such short notice to our petition, and for allowing us to be heard on matters of vital interest to ourselves and to all the people of Gibraltar whom we represent. We are both aware of the pressure under which you are working to dispose of the rest of the problems before you, and we shall endeavour to be as brief as possible in what we have to say. We had the honour in 1963 and 1964 of being heard as petitioners before the "Committee of 24", and distinguished Delegates who want to know the whole background of the struggle of the people of Gibraltar and their process towards full internal self government, I would respectfully refer them to the speeches we then delivered on the matter. But, very briefly, I must state that we enjoy a very full measure of self-government in our internal affairs; we have a Legislative Council elected by universal adult suffrage, one man one vote, and a Government and opposition in the best traditions of democratic government. Since July of last year, however, because of the situation brought about in Gibraltar as a result of the severe restrictions imposed on us by Spain, there is now a coalition Government. In Gibraltar political parties of all shades of opinion operate freely, our trade unions are completely free. *Habeas corpus* is in existence, which means that no arrest without trial is possible. The process of decolonisation started in 1950 by the setting up of the first Legislative Council. Since then, we have achieved the great measure of self-government that we enjoy. My colleague, Mr. Isola, will tell you of steps that are being taken internally to reconcile differing views about the nature of our future association with Britain which will lead to the complete decolonisation of Gibraltar in accordance with the Charter of the United Nations and *Resolution 1514 (XV)*, which is not, I repeat, contrary to the Treaty of Utrecht.

It is this form of complete decolonisation that the people of Gibraltar passionately want. Once talks were started between Britain and Spain on the question of Gibraltar following on the United Nations General Assembly Resolution, we hoped that these would succeed and that, in the friendly atmosphere of these talks, Spain would have thought fit to remove all the pressures that she has been exercising against Gibraltar and against the people of Gibraltar – who are not in any party to the dispute – no doubt in an endeavour to weaken our determination to maintain the way of life that we have developed over the years. However, the opposite has been the case: since the talks started, the restrictions have been more severe with the consequence that the people's determination to withstand them has been strengthened. The people of Gibraltar have suffered not only restrictions at the hand of Spain but a major hostile propaganda against us through their information services, radio and television, which has certainly not helped to endear us more to the Spaniards and much less to take seriously their offers of guarantees for our future, contained in their vague proposals made on May 18th, 1966, for a special status for the Gibraltarians under Spanish sovereignty. We were incidentally guaranteed in these proposals freedom of religion, a freedom which we have enjoyed for the last two centuries. Despite all this, the people of Gibraltar want to live in peace and in good relations with their neighbours. However, what is more important, the people of Gibraltar want to be allowed to continue exercising the rights and freedom we enjoy and which we have fought for over the years. It seems that both Britain and Spain are willing to carry on the talks to solve the dispute and, in this respect, we appeal to this "Committee" to do nothing at this stage that might seem to take Spain's side on the question of the negotiation and which would no doubt bring further restrictions against our people. This would only have the result, without in any way solving the problem, of making the situation more difficult for the people of Gibraltar.

I would like to state at this stage that the people of Gibraltar, through their freely elected representatives, have been kept fully informed by the British Government of the progress of the talks and there has been full consultation with us on all matters affecting our people. They are, however, confident that they can rely on the U.N. to help them in preserving their rights and in achieving greater rights and they would naturally feel betrayed by the U.N. if this world organ departed from the entire impartiality shown by the "Committee of 24" in their Resolution of November 17th, 1966, which seems to us the people of Gibraltar, to be fair and constructive. Article 73 of the U.N. Charter entrusts the U.N. to look after the inhabitants of territories who have not achieved a full measure of self-government, recognising "the principle that the interests of the inhabitants of these territories are paramount". The fact that the people of my territory are only 25,000 inhabitants does not make the responsibility of the U.N. any the less.

I have already referred to some of the many rights that we enjoy and that we naturally wish to preserve. I consider it necessary, however, for the record that I should briefly set out the most important ones:

1. Constitutional.
(a)   The right to a Legislative body with power to enact and amend Laws for Gibraltar.

2.   The right to free elections as provided under the Elections Ordinance.

3.   The right to exercise all powers and rights vested in existing legislations to amend or extend such legislation and to introduce new legislation.

4.   The right to modify the internal constitution without external interference in accordance with the freely expressed wishes of the people and with due constitutional processes which include, in particular, consultation with and the agreement of Her Majesty's Government in the United Kingdom.

5.   Political.
(a)   The right to free assembly for all lawful purposes.

(b)   The right to form political parties of any kind of political belief.

(c)   The right to the peaceful and lawful expression of any kind of political belief.

(d)   The right to the peaceful and lawful advocacy of any kind of political belief.

(e) The right to free and unrestricted choice of reading matter of a political nature of any kind.

(f) The right to leave Gibraltar and return to it and all the other rights which Gibraltarians enjoy in virtue of their status as such.

(g) The right to the continuous possession of British nationality, its acquisition by birth in Gibraltar and its transmission by descent in accordance with the provisions of the British Nationality Acts.

6. Administrative.
(a) The right to maintain full and exclusive control over the internal administration of Gibraltar.

(b) Freedom of the press.
1. The right to complete freedom of the press and all other information services.

7. Trade unions and industrial relations.
(a) The right to form trade unions.

(b) The right to maintain and, if considered necessary, extend the existing powers and functions of trade unions.

(c) The right to strike.

8. Social.
(a) The right to a reasonable standard of living.

(b) The right of employment.

(c) The right to social security.

In the final analysis, it is the individual rights that count, the rights of men, women and children, whatever the number that must be safeguarded. These are the people we represent.

I ask this "Committee", therefore, which is entrusted under the Charter to safeguard the rights of people, to do nothing that may in any way affect adversely the people of Gibraltar.

(Ref.: *United Nations*. Doc. A/C.4/SR.1,679.)

APPENDIX 5

The Castiella Proposals

18 May, 1966

(Translation)

Today, on the 18th of May 1966, complying with the invitation contained in the Resolution of the General Assembly of the United Nations of December láth 1965, which ratifies the "Consensus" of the "Committee of Twenty-four" on October 16th 1964, the United Kingdom and Spain are ready to start negotiations on the Status and situation of the Territory of Gibraltar.

The mandate of the United Nations.

The international mandate we are here to comply with, deals with the problem of applying to Gibraltar the principles contained in the Declaration on the granting of independence to colonial countries and peoples. This problem had been raised by Great Britain as one to be solved on the basis of self-determination for the present inhabitants of what she considers to be the Colony of Gibraltar. However, the United Nations did not admit that Gibraltar can be unilaterally decolonized by Great Britain in that manner. Instead, the United Nations have invited the Governments of Spain and Great Britain and Northern Ireland to "undertake without delay conversations in order to find, in accordance with the principles of the Charter of the United Nations, a negotiated solution, in keeping with the provisions of *Resolution 1514 (XV)*, taking duly into account the opinions expressed by the members of the "Committee" and bearing in mind the interests of the population of the territory".

Thus, the United Nations have not admitted a unilateral solution and have fundamentally recognized the existence of a serious problem between the two countries, the solution of which they entrust to a dialogue between them. In these circumstances, Spain considers that today is a date of extreme and even historical importance for our two peoples, because it enables us to attempt to solve permanently a problem that has seriously disturbed relations between Spain and England for 262 years.

A summary of this statement.

We must now define and analyse objectively the problem of Gibraltar.

In this analysis I wish to lay aside all pathos and emotion. In spite of the enormous importance of this question for Spain and of the very deep feelings it arouses, I wish to speak objectively and calmly, and to try and focus a clear light of understanding on this complex and often-debated subject.

I intend, firstly, to attempt to define the structure of the problem in its three main aspects – military, demographic and economic – and to describe the currents of forces affecting British interests to which they have given rise. Then, I will explain the significance for Spain of Gibraltar and its evolution through history, and the repercussion on our country of its political, military, human and socio-economic aspects. Next, I will refer to the grave "frontier question" raised by Gibraltar, and finally, I shall present the formula of the solution offered by Spain and some conclusions which may perhaps contain some surprises for many of you.

Although it is entirely obvious, I would like to emphasize that my colleagues and I are here to explain the Spanish points of view, clearly and honestly, and that all we ask for is to be heard with the same attention and patience with which we are ready to listen to your points of view. We hope that our statements will contain nothing offensive, because it has been our firm intention to frame them in a spirit of equanimity and friendship.

A legal title and its limitations.

For us the Rock is above all a British military Base installed in Spain. The legal title conferring this Base is Article 10 of the Treaty of Utrecht of 1713, fully ratified in various subsequent Conventions and especially by the Treaty of Versailles of 1783.

It is necessary to point out that Great Britain lacks any other title to justify her presence in Gibraltar.

The right of conquest cannot be alleged for the Rock, as this was occupied during the War of the Spanish Succession on behalf of a possible King of Spain – the Pretender to the Spanish Crown, Archduke Charles of Austria – by an allied force, carried by the British ships of Admiral Rooke, which was composed of German, Dutch, Irish, British and even Spanish troops under the command of the German-Austrian Landgrave of Hesse-Darmstadt; who, on occupying the Rock, acted as the representative and plenipotentiary of the Austrian Pretender, appointed Spanish authorities and later received the Archduke in triumph as King of Spain. So true is it that Gibraltar was originally involved exclusively in a conflict between Pretenders to the Spanish throne, that Queen Anne of England made a statement, published on May 1st 1705 by Lord Peterborough, in which she indicated that she was sending her forces to the Peninsula to uphold the just claim of the House of Austria to the Throne of Spain, and not to take possession of any place in the name of Her Britannic Majesty. (General Collection of Treaties, Vol. IV, p. 336.)

It is evident that the only rights possessed by Great Britain in this matter are those which derive from a correct interpretation of Article 10 of the Treaty of Utrecht.

And Article 10 – I apologize for briefly repeating facts which are already well known – contains not only a statement of the rights conceded to Great Britain in respect to the Rock but also, concurrently, some limitations which may be summarized as follows:

1) Territorial limitations
Gibraltar is ceded only in respect of the Town, Castle, port, fortifications and fortress as they were in 1704 – the date of British occupation – and there is absolutely no inclusion of other territories.

2) Legal limitations
The cession is made "without any territorial jurisdiction".

3) Economic limitations
All communication by land and all commerce between the Town and the surrounding territory were forbidden.

4) Limitations based on military reasons
For security reasons, the residence in Gibraltar of certain classes of persons was prohibited.

5) Limitation as to its future disposal
It was stipulated that Great Britain could neither grant, sell, or otherwise alienate Gibraltar without first offering Spain the right to recover it.

All these limitations, to be found in the full text, which is still in force, of Article 10 of the Treaty of Utrecht have not only been ignored but specifically violated, and this has impaired the legal basis of the British presence on the Rock.

The anatomy of the problem:
a) The Fortress and its expansion.
With reference to Gibraltar considered as a Military Base the violations have consisted: firstly, in the invasion of adjacent territories which had not been ceded by the Treaty of Utrecht and which still belong to the absolute sovereignty of Spain. Secondly, in the British expansion over territorial waters in the Bay of Algeciras which are equally under Spanish sovereignty. And, finally, in an aspect which touches on the very essence of the Base, as this was ceded strictly to Great Britain, in the context of a bilateral Anglo-Spanish relationship – in which some Spanish interests were or might be involved – but not in order to serve the ends of an International Organization to which Spain does not belong. And it is generally known that, *de facto* if not *de jure*, the Base of Gibraltar is now serving the purposes of NATO – an Organization in which Spanish interests are not directly involved.

b) An artificially constituted human group.
Gibraltar is also a human aggregate, and this is another aspect of the problem. Great Britain's pretension is today that the inhabitants of the Rock should decide upon its future, thus linking by the method of self-determination the territory with its inhabitants; this basically alters the original terms of the situation, which was that of a bilateral relationship between England and Spain, but from which, however, Spain has been ousted for the benefit of a third party. But this third party is not valid because, firstly, Gibraltar is merely a military Base and a Base can only belong, either to the country that occupies it or to the country in whose territory it stands. Anything else would be as absurd as, for instance, to maintain that the American Base at Guantánamo, in Cuba, should stop being American, without reverting to Cuba either, but should have its fate decided by an alleged population residing there. Hong Kong presents a similar, though not formally identical situation. The Observer expressed the opinion, on July 10th 1949, that there could be no question of preparing the island for independence, as Hong Kong should either continue being British, or else revert to China.

Secondly, there is no real or profound link between the inhabitants of Gibraltar and the territory, because, apart from the fact that the authentic population of the Rock was obliged to abandon it by reason of the military occupation, the later inhabitants are a product of a British political operation aimed at successively fabricating and refabricating the so-called population with ethnical groups uprooted from their original countries; they are inhabitants without any real political identity of their own or any real autonomy as such, and they constitute a demographic group which is entirely subsidiary to a Base enclosed in a territory of two square miles, almost all of it a military zone and Crown property. How can this group be considered a true population capable of political self-determination and with a right to dispose of a territory which belongs to it neither historically nor legally?

The London *Times* of January 4th 1946 frankly pointed out these characteristics when it said the following about the inhabitants of the Rock:

> "A people which gains its livelihood largely by importing a commodity and selling it to someone who is on the spot or who comes to fetch it, be it tons of coal or a packet of cigarettes and a bottle of beer to a soldier, or sailor, has not hitherto developed racial or national characteristics as do tillers of the soil or fishers of the sea."

c) An economy based on smuggling.

Thirdly, the problem of Gibraltar consists of an economy which sprang up under the shadow of a British military force planted on Spanish soil, and which in itself is inevitably bound to raise problems, for there can be no normal economy in a military Base with a small area and which has no resources of its own, no agriculture or industry and whose trade is principally contraband. W. C. Atkinson (*Fortnightly Review*, February 1951, page 90) wrote with sincerity:

> "As for smuggling, there has never been any attempt on the English side to conceal that for long this *was the chief industry of the Rock's inhabitants*, including the garrison."

The objective description we have given is the true anatomy of the problem of Gibraltar, a military Base with an essentially unsound legal foundation, an artificial population without any genuine autonomy, and an economy partly sustained by unnatural and illegal means; all of which reveals the importance of the question of Gibraltar and the urgent need for a solution.

Dynamics of the problem.
These three aspects of the question – the Base, the inhabitants and the economy – have produced a set of vital problems and an interplay of British and Spanish interests that lie at the very root of the question which brings us here today, at the request of the United Nations.

a) A fortress transformed into a Base.
Firstly, Gibraltar has experienced a profound evolution through history. In 1713 Spain ceded a fortress from which some guns with a limited range merely defended a British Base of great strategic importance which was destined one day to become a key point in the communications of the British Empire; but the great political and technical changes of our times – which have seen Empires disappear, brought forth new alliances and World Wars and created new nations, and above all transformed every aspect of the old military art and the principles of strategy – have also radically changed the nature of Gibraltar as a Base.

With this background of strategic change, the Rock was bound to play its part in vast alliances and it became a pivot for collective military operations on a world scale. Its purely relative value then became even more evident, that is to say, the indissoluble relationship between Gibraltar and its natural geographical environment, namely, Spain.

Military efficiency dependent on Spain.
The Second World War laid bare the essential problem of Gibraltar, without any possible euphemism or insincerity. It could he seen sharply and clearly. The statesmen and soldiers of Great Britain and her allies realized that a hostile attitude on the part of Spain could nullify this Rock, which was indispensable to the whole allied military machine, and that the results might be catastrophic. Indeed, during those sombre days of 1940 when the greater part of Continental Europe was in enemy hands, Gibraltar became, in the words of Field-Marshal Lord Alanbrooke, Chief of the Imperial General Staff, ". . . the sole remaining foothold in Europe". (Sir Arthur Bryan, *The Turn of the Tide.* Doubleday and Co. Inc. New York, 1957, page 405.) Thanks to Spanish neutrality and Spain's diplomatic resistance to the Axis powers, this foothold of Gibraltar was fully efficient as a key piece of the Allied war strategy; and, as General Eisenhower wrote in his *Memoirs*, "made possible the invasion of northwest Africa", a decisive Allied military operation of which he said: ". . . if the Spaniards should take hostile action against us immediately

315

upon the beginning of landing operations, it would be practically impossible to secure any land-based fighter craft for use in northern Africa (. . .) and would prevent our use of the Strait of Gibraltar." (Dwight D. Eisenhower, *Crusade in Europe*. Doubleday and Co. Inc. New York, 1948, pages 91, 92 and 95.) This operation was carried out, as Sir Arthur Bryant reminds us, "with nothing to protect its flank and rear but the Rock of Gibraltar and its minute airstrip", (Id. page 403.) This was the most severe and crippling blow inflicted on the enemies of Great Britain as Sir Ivone Kirkpatrick – who was Permanent Under-Secretary of the Foreign Office and in the confidence of Mr. Ernest Bevin – states in his Memoirs, *"The Inner Circle"* (MacMillan & Co., Ltd., London, 1959), when he tells of his interview with Goering in the Nuremberg prison and gives us the German marshal's opinion on Hitler's terrible handicap in not having at his disposal Spain and Gibraltar to prevent the later Allied penetration of Africa. The fact is that Gibraltar had had a free hand thanks to Spanish neutrality, which enabled it to develop its full potential as a military Base. Sir Anthony Eden referred to such a problem many years later when he said in the House of Commons on July 29th 1954 that in the modern world nations "do not want foreign troops on their territory" and that what is needed is "a Base that works, and not a beleaguered garrison".

a) *Authoritative opinions.*

The many testimonies to the fact that Gibraltar was able to function thanks to Spain and Spanish neutrality, which we find in the words or works of men like Winston Churchill and Franklin Roosevelt, are an irrefutable proof that the problem of Gibraltar as a viable Base exists and cannot be solved without Spain. This fact must have been gloomily impressed on the mind of the Governor of the Rock. When General Marshall visited Gibraltar with Mr. Churchill during the Second World War, there occurred an incident that the veteran British statesman described later in his *Memoirs* with his usual eloquence. I apologise for the length of this quotation which I think is worth while:

> "We did not leave Gibraltar for Algiers until the following afternoon. There was therefore an opportunity to show General Marshall the Rock, and we all made a few hours' pilgrimage, and inspected the new distillery which assures the fortress a permanent supply of fresh water, and various important guns, some hospitals, and a large number of troops. I finally went below

to see the Governor's special pet, the new Rock gallery, cut deep into the rock, with its battery of eight quick-firing guns commanding the isthmus and the neutral ground between Britain and Spain. An immense amount of work had been put into this, and it certainly seemed, as we walked along it, that whatever perils Gibraltar might have to fear, attack from the mainland was no longer one of them. The Governor's pride in his achievement was shared by his British visitors. It was not until we said good-bye upon the flying-boat that General Marshall somewhat hesitatingly observed, "I admired your gallery, but we had one like it at Corregidor. The Japanese fired their artillery at the rock several hundred feet above it, and in two or three days blocked it off with an immense bank of rubble." (Winston Churchill's *Memoirs*, The Hinge of Fate, Chap. XL.)

The War, in fact, provided supreme evidence that the Rock was in the very centre of a total revolution in the conception of military Bases in foreign lands; because today we can no longer imagine a Base isolated from the geopolitical environment around it, or indifferent to the neighbouring territory. Only by the friendship and cooperation of the adjoining country, and by understanding that its daily efficiency depends on that country's goodwill, can a Base in foreign lands be of any use. The old idea of a military Base installed by a unilateral decision, and isolated like a "ghetto", has given way to the idea of zones of bilateral and multilateral cooperation, and of great strategic spaces shared by common consent and agreement in the service of common objectives.

Behind this doctrine there is a specific reality which lies at the end of Gibraltar's long historical evolution: that Gibraltar can only be used with full efficiency if it can rely on Spanish cooperation. The fact that Gibraltar has in practice been attached to NATO objectives in recent days, gives a greater emphasis to this truth.

b) Contradictory interests.

In so far as the second aspect is concerned, the inhabitants of Gibraltar have also become a problematic factor. At present, this human group is creating some urgent problems for Great Britain, and is demanding the solution of difficulties that arise inevitably from its having been artificially planted on the Rock and from the equally artificial character of its way of livelihood, economy, etc. It is evident that these inhabitants, whose necessary environment lies beyond the Rock, so that many of them have fixed their residence and commercial activities on Spanish soil, and whose economic life is bound up intimately with the economy of the neighbouring region, cannot be reconciled to any restrictions that may be applied by Spain, even if these consist merely in the strict application of her current Laws. It must be remembered that the way of life a of a great number of the inhabitants has been based up to the present on the benevolent interpretation by Spain of the articles of the Treaty of Utrecht. The Spanish Government understands that all this constitutes a problem for Great Britain because, without any doubt, it will be very difficult and expensive to protect their interests. But we cannot admit that this protection should be effected at the expense of Spain interests.

c) The crisis of Gibraltar's economy.
Finally, there is the economy of Gibraltar, the port of Gibraltar, and a Gibraltarian commerce that have also historically evolved. They would have evolved legitimately if the limitations to which Gibraltar was subjected by the Treaty of Utrecht and by Spanish laws had been modified by an agreement between England and Spain. This did not take place and an illegal commerce was resorted to. At present this Gibraltarian economy is in danger of paralysis, and consequently requires Great Britain to undertake a complete revision of its structure.

d) The "proud Fortress" a thorn in Spanish flesh.
The currents of forces we have described lead up to a fact which should not be ignored merely because it touches on a question of sentiment. Gibraltar is not only a Base with its attendant difficulties, but also a symbol for Great Britain: "The Proud Fortress", symbolic of British power and of her glorious naval and military traditions. We realize this and we understand that in raising this question we are touching a sensitive and painful area. For this reason we believe that we ought to arrive at an agreement by which neither of the two nations should feel humiliated or resentful. For it is necessary to understand that, for Spain, Gibraltar has also been a symbol: of a series of inquiries and affronts; there is the memory of the way in which it was taken from us, the humiliations we have suffered, the intolerable political, military and economic servitudes that were imposed on us in times of national prostration. Such memories are lasting. It is the only foreign colony in a European nation. One can speak about Gibraltar in the words used recently by the eminent British historian Arnold Toynbee:

"Gibraltar? It is a thorn in Spain's flesh. Would the British people like to see a Russian or Chinese fortress at Land's End or in the Channel Islands?"

Up till now we have described a series of problems created by the historical evolution of the Rock of Gibraltar and the play of forces which has taken place around it, problems which affect the interests of Great Britain, and which condition radically the viability of Gibraltar as a military Base, as a human aggregate and as an economy.

But for Spain also the passing of the years has made Gibraltar into a focus of very serious wrongs, a centre of pernicious influence on the neighbouring regions and a place of friction and discord; in short, a disturbing and negative element in Anglo-Spanish relations. It is permissible to ask if the English people fully understand this reality, which will probably surprise many who are not acquainted with its various aspects.

Consequences for Spain:
a) Violation of territorial integrity.
For Spaniards, Gibraltar remains fundamentally a foreign Base on national territory, a foreign body in our own organism, serving alien interests that often clash with those of Spain. It represents the amputation of our territory, a break in the continuity of our coasts, a sort of military wedge and obstacle in the communications between two seas and the relations between two continents. Gibraltar is situated in one of the vital parts of Spanish geography, and it has always deeply troubled the people of Spain who over the centuries have sought to retain it, or recover it if it was in alien hands. So true is this, that in one of the most important clauses in the political testament of Queen Isabella, at a historical moment when both the idea and the national unity of Spain had crystallized, she commanded her descendants to retain Gibraltar inflexibly and forbade them ever to give away or dispose of it.

b) Spain interfered with.
For Spain Gibraltar is not only a territorial amputation. It has produced a constant interference in Spanish affairs, both in her home politics and foreign policies. It has interfered, firstly in Spain's own defensive system, sometimes demanding the dismantlement of neighbouring military installations, as when in 1810 – with the excuse that they should be prevented from falling into French hands – the Governor of Gibraltar,

General Campbell, levelled the Spanish forts of San Felipe and Santa Bárbara that protected the neighbouring town of La Línea from the Fortress of Gibraltar. The war with France ended but Great Britain continued to oppose the rebuilding of the Forts. Nearly a century later – in 1898, when Spain was fighting an ill-matched war with the United States and passing through a serious and difficult time in her history; when she had lost her overseas provinces, at perhaps her weakest moment, Great Britain once again insisted on Spanish disarmament, objecting to the installation of artillery in the neighbouring Spanish zone of the Bay of Algeciras. (Diplomatic Notes from August 9th to December 9th of 1898.) Spain was alone at that critical moment of her history, as alone as England in 1940.

Behind this specific British action we may perceive Britain's permanent desire to establish round Gibraltar a military neutralized zone, subject to the influence of the Rock and even to a possible occupation. The British Press towards the end of the 19th century and commencement of the 20th often admitted this objective (*The Times*, 4-XII-1899, *Daily Telegraph*, 29-III-1901, *The Sun*, 13-II-1901) and in the House of Commons a Member, Mr. Gibson Bowles, on June 13th 1901 quoted the opinion of the Military experts in the same sense. This British preoccupation was so vivid that in 1905 the then Foreign Secretary Lord Landsdowne suggested to the Spanish Minister in London, Marqués de Villaurrutia, that both countries should reach an agreement by which Spain should guarantee Great Britain the possession of Gibraltar in exchange for a guarantee given by Great Britain of Spain's possession of the Balearic Islands, a concept which from the point of view of the dignity and unity of the Spanish Nation was tantamount to guaranteeing us the possession of the Province of Madrid (Marqués de Villaurrutia, *"Palique Diplomático"*, page 137). The Ex-Governor of Gibraltar General Sir Charles Harrington on February 13th, 1939, explained to the Royal Empire Society, with perhaps excessive sincerity, this constant British pretension:

"It is the area round Gibraltar which is of more importance in view of the range of modern guns. I would like to see the neutral ground between us and Spain, now some 300 yards, extended to an arc of some 25 miles from Tarifa via Castellar to the Mediterranean to make both Gibraltar and the *Royal Calpe Hunt* safe." (United Empire, volume XXX, No. 3, March 1939.)

And even in the Teheran conference in November 1943 where the Allies discussed the gravest military and political problems of the Second World War, the question of Gibraltar was touched upon, and the possibility of broadening the Gibraltar territory was discussed, as André Fontaine reports in his "*Histoire de la Guerre Froide*" (Fayard, Paris, 1966, p. 222).

This interference carried out from the Rock in such a fundamental question of Spain's own defences was even to affect our foreign policy. The British Government, for instance in the middle of last century, intervened in our North African policy, attempting to condition and limit the Spanish Government's decision for the defence of its interests in that region, with the argument that those decisions would endanger the security of the Fortress of Gibraltar.

c) Gratuitous risk for Spain and the diplomatic reaction.

Lastly, as a military base, Gibraltar implies a constant danger to Spain. The Rock has undergone many historical changes, from its days as one more British fortress in the 18th century, down to the present day when it has become a place of international military cooperation in which we do not share; and these changes have turned it into a hazard for the whole national territory of Spain, which Spain endures gratuitously. It the Gibraltar Base caused Spain to suffer loss of lives and property on the occasion of the Second World War – a war of conventional weapons – and if even in times of peace Spain has received damage during manoeuvres and military concentrations on the adjoining Rock, it is easy to imagine what Spaniards may have to fear from the Base in a nuclear war. And while Spain is prepared to accept risks of that kind on account of alliances in which Spanish interests are served, she is not prepared to do the same for the benefit of interests or alliances that are foreign to her, least of all when the prospects of a modern war may turn Gibraltar into a sure objective for nuclear weapons.

Gibraltar and NATO.

The practical attachment of Gibraltar to the service of NATO has increased the dangers, and further still, the accusing finger of an entire military *bloc* which rivals that of NATO has heightened that danger, by suggesting at the United Nations that, in not purely and simply demanding the elimination of the Gibraltar Base, Spain was voluntarily assuming the risks which the Base implies.

The Spanish Government, aware of this new and sombre menace hanging over all of Spain, has found itself obliged to declare in unmistakable terms that as far as we are concerned Gibraltar is not a base in the service of NATO. As a result, on January 20th 1966 all the members of the Atlantic Alliance, except Great Britain, were sent a Note in which, after declaring that the status of Gibraltar – which is at the present moment under discussion – had been bilaterally laid down by Spain and Great Britain, our country could not regard Gibraltar as a Base in the service of the Atlantic Alliance, and was accordingly not prepared to grant the facilities depending on this country for its use by the members of that Alliance. Spain moreover indicated that she viewed with the greatest reserve any military, naval or air exercises and operations, that might be carried out with support at Gibraltar and in which a part was played by countries other than Great Britain.

We are aware that this Spanish reaction, imposed by the real circumstances of the Gibraltar problem, was fully discussed at the NATO Council. The individual replies that Spain has been receiving have been on the whole positive towards my country's thesis.

The Soviet affirmation that Gibraltar is being used in a massive degree by NATO, that is, by Great Britain's allies, was no fantasy, and the decision which led Spain to send the Atlantic Alliance countries the Note of January 20th was thus fully justified.

In the first place, the British Government not only makes use of Gibraltar waters that do not belong to her, but also uses for military purposes the airport built in a zone of Spanish territory which was never ceded, which is occupied by Great Britain without any title whatsoever, and which, in view of its neutral character, should never have been made to serve military purposes. And that use of it, in addition to violating our sovereignty, frequently violates an air space which is also Spanish.

The massive use of Spanish air space.

In order to use that airport, England applies to Spain for overflight authorizations in respect of military aircraft proceeding from the British Isles, with a frequency which is reflected in the following facts: From November 23rd 1965 down to May 5th 1966, that is, in less than half a year, the British Embassy in Madrid has requested the Spanish Government, in 61 Notas Verbales, to authorize 274 overflights by machines of the Royal Air Force in our air space, and all these authorizations were granted.

But it is not only the British Armed Forces that have made use of the Gibraltar military facilities. From January 1st 1966 down to the sending of the Note mentioned, the Gibraltar airport was used by about twenty military aircraft of the United States, and from January 20th to the beginning of May by only twelve. The rate of arrival of American aircraft at Gibraltar has fallen roughly from one a day to one a week. Fourteen aircraft of the Royal Canadian Air Force operated from the Rock through February 22nd to 26th, on February 28th and March 27th; that is to say after the Ottawa Government had received the Spanish Note of January 20th 1966 which explained our position in respect of a Gibraltar placed at the service of an Organization to which Spain does not belong. One French military aircraft, of January 21st 1966, and two Dutch aircraft on January 28th last, also wished to use it, with previous Spanish authorization, but these applications had to be replied to negatively, in terms of the arguments set forth in the Note of January 20th already mentioned.

Navies of countries other than Great Britain also use Gibraltar, which has been called at, in the course of the present year, by warships of the United States, Germany, Norway, Italy and other NATO countries which, like Holland, make the Rock a port of call for their fleets when operating or holding exercises in the Mediterranean,

The Governments of all these countries are now perfectly well aware of Spain's view regarding this mass use of the Gibraltar Base. Hence it should have caused no surprise when the Spanish Government, on January 24th this year, refused to grant facilities for operating in Spanish waters to the Italian ship *Maria Paolina G*, in the service of NATO at the Base of La Spezia: or when Spain did not facilitate, on February 22nd, the telegraph and telephone link-ups to connect Gibraltar with the bases of Brest and Montijo (Lisbon) during the naval exercises of the Atlantic Alliance that were held in Portuguese waters during last March.

No matter in what way it may be sought to disguise Gibraltar's connexion with the Atlantic Organization, the fact remains that it exists, as is proved by the presence on the Rock of the Headquarters of the Admiral Commanding the Gibraltar-Mediterranean zone, dependent on the Malta Command, and a permanent liaison officer of the United States of America.

This connexion, moreover, was carefully explained by the Minister of Her Britannic Majesty's Embassy in Madrid to the Spanish Ministry of Foreign Affairs, as is recorded on pages 69 to 73 of the Spanish *Red Book*

(English edition), when he sought to show that if England remained at Gibraltar it was on account of her obligations for collective defence in view of the Soviet menace.

The Soviet Union is right in saying that the Rock is linked to the Atlantic Alliance. It is wrong when insinuating that this connexion takes place with Spain's tacit or explicit consent. So opposed is Spain to the use of the Rock for purposes other than those which justified its cession in other times, that she also formally objects to the provisioning which is periodically carried out at Gibraltar by the Russian whaling fleet, some of whose ships, in view of the instruments they are equipped with, can scarcely be regarded as ordinary vessels engaged in a peaceful commercial pursuit.

Spanish deference towards Britain. A frank notification.
These circumstances which have been briefly set forth made it advisable for the Spanish Government to apply, with gradually increasing intensity, the measures that were becoming necessary in order to reduce to the greatest possible extent the dangers involved in the present military situation of the Rock. If that step has yet been taken, the sole reason for withholding it is a desire to assist the Anglo-Spanish conversations which are now opening and which Spain has tried to envelop in an atmosphere of good will and harmony, even at the risk of postponing any possible defence against the hazards described. Spain hopes that this token of good will may be appreciated at its true value by the British Government, which the Spanish Ambassador in London informed, on April 20th, of the reasons why, in the interest of Anglo-Spanish understanding. Great Britain had not been sent a Note similar to those sent to the other members of the NATO.

On receiving for the first time Her Britannic Majesty's present Ambassador in Madrid on the same day of April 20th, I also had occasion to inform him that since receiving on February 14th the British acceptance of the holding of the conversations that we commence today, Spain had abstained from adopting any fresh measure that could be interpreted, directly or indirectly, as aimed against Gibraltar. The revision of our European military policy, largely forced on us by the new Gibraltar situation, involved among other things, refusal of authorization for British overflights of our air space, a measure which, if adopted, would mainly affect British military aircraft bound for Gibraltar.

As we sit down now at the table, I think it my duty as an honourable negotiator to make it perfectly clear that as Spain does not accept the militarization carried out by Great Britain in the southern part of the former neutral ground, she not only is under no obligation to grant permits for overflights bound for the Rock, but unless she wishes her silence to be taken as tacit consent, she must also oppose the use of that airport by military aircraft.

If that reason were not enough, the dangers which the present military significance of Gibraltar involves for my country would make it advisable for the Spanish Government to refuse authorizations for overflights by British Gibraltar-bound planes, as it has refused them to aircraft of other NATO countries.

Only an Anglo-Spanish agreement on Gibraltar can justify Spain's not putting these measures into effect in the shortest possible space of time, as the Spanish Government has in view. If I have succeeded in making you understand clearly the spirit in which we are describing the problem of Gibraltar as we are so doing, I think you will also easily understand that the measures I have mentioned in all honesty are aimed only at protecting legitimate Spanish interests and re-establishing the rightful and legal situation.

The consequences for a region of Spain:
a) Military "glacis" and economic void.
But besides all these detriments caused by the Military Base and its activity, Gibraltar has made a great void around itself. This began with the actual demographic void on the Rock, which owing to the forced exodus of its original Spanish population, declined from the 6,000 inhabitants it had before the occupation, to only 900 in 1721, seventeen years later, and to 2,890 in 1791, almost a century later – a period in which it had not even succeeded in reaching half the population it possessed in the Spanish period. This brought about the mutilation of a Spanish population complex which formerly had its centre in Gibraltar and was thus profoundly altered.

Side by side with the void on the Rock, inhabited almost solely by the garrison, a void came into being in the neighbouring zone of Spain, not perhaps strictly demographic, but certainly in respect of economic life and development. The warfare at the foot of the Rock, the sieges and blockades, the British disarmament exactions, in short the military reality, which created an area of distrust, anxiety, alarms and external interferences, prevented a normal development of the district and maintained it in the situation of a real devitalized military "glacis".

From these two voids, an authentic colonial situation was to arise; but not in the sense that might normally be given to that expression; in other words, not a colonial situation which was confined to the Rock and to which it is now necessary to put an end, but a real colonialism exercised outside the Rock and upon a zone of Spain and its inhabitants. The process that led to this was as follows:

b) Demography and smuggling.
First of all, Great Britain needed to fill her own demographic void on the Rock. It was indispensable to procure a civilian support for the almost solitary garrison, and this – as was outlined when the problem of Gibraltar was briefly sketched – was achieved through a constant intake of ethnical groups which generally came from countries not yet constituted into national States. These groups, suddenly cut off from their traditional human background, and coming from the most widely varying places, were marked by instability and lack of roots. The 19th-century epidemics almost wiped out this group of people several times, and Great Britain, several times also, hastened to reconstruct it through mass operations of importing and recruiting people from those parts of the Mediterranean where the chance of doing good business on the Rock – or else, for instance, of escaping the military levies in the times of the Napoleonic wars – formed enticing incentives to go to Gibraltar.

The statistics for population and professions at Gibraltar in 1834 already show the curious nature of this group so artificially formed, for the prevailing occupations among these improvised inhabitants are those of commercial agents, exchange agents, sellers of tobacco and wine, tavern-keepers and the like. And in the 1860 census, out of the 12,679 inhabitants of Gibraltar, 132 are given as Government officials, 1,978 as traders, 5,565 miscellaneous employments, and 4,994 as unemployed; in other words, more than 10,000 inhabitants had no clearly justified occupation.

The Report which the Governor of Gibraltar himself, Sir Robert Gardiner, drew up for Lord Palmerston on the inhabitants of the Rock and their growth, contains a sincere analysis of this demographic phenomenon which was to have so many consequences for the future of Gibraltar:

> "The excess of population has its rise in the increase of smuggling; aliens having flocked to the Fortress in vast numbers

to pursue that trade, since it was made a Colony." (Page 48.)

Later, he adds:

"If such promised to be the result, it is still a question for the Imperial Government to decide, whether the general interests of England, and of the fair British trader, should be sacrificed to promote those of the persons who, for the most part, have but a footing here, to pass contraband goods into Spain." (Page 114.)

This aggregate of people, assembled throughout the years in a way so opposed to the normal biological increase of natural populations, has been brought in and taken out again by Great Britain whenever necessary, and the last time it occurred was the great exodus of the Second World War when there were some 18,000 Gibraltarians resident on the Rock – to which Lord Merrivale referred in his recent speech on March 9th 1966, when he stated:

"In 1940, 16,700 men over 45, women and children were evacuated to this country from Gibraltar, and by 1951 repatriation was complete for all those Gibraltarians who had homes to go back to."

c) A non-viable political organization.
Naturally enough, this collective group had never possessed a political being of its own, nor had Great Britain attached any political importance or standing to its components. This could not have been otherwise, in view of the character, essentially subsidiary to the military base, which it has possessed. Its basic nature has been clearly recognised by W. A. Ebsworth in a study on Gibraltar and its problems published in *The Quarterly Review* for April 1951 (Vol. 289, No. 588), in which he states:

"The relationships between the Services and civilians is of unusual importance in so small a community, and everything possible must always be done to improve it. Each party depends on the other. Although the Services say emphatically that there are too many civilians in Gibraltar, few would go so far as to contend that there should be none at all; while for the civilians their very existence depends on the Services. If there were no garrison Gibraltar would not remain a British Colony for long, and if once the frontier with Spain were to disappear, its trade would dwindle to nothing."

The characteristics of a necessary political dependence and real lack of autonomy as also brought out in the article as follows:

> "Politically Gibraltar has developed slowly, and it is natural that this should be the case. From time to time the local Press will protest that government in the Fortress is not democratic. Of course it is not democratic in the accepted way in which a modern State is democratic! A fortress must be ruled with authority, and to talk about 'a democratic fortress' is a contradiction in terms. If we refer to the history of Gibraltar we remind ourselves that it is not, like other colonies, a civilian settlement in which military authority rightly keeps in the background, but it is a military fortress into which a civilian community has made its way because catering for the needs of the garrison and trading under its protection are lucrative propositions."

d) *Gibraltar has no labour force of its own.*

A human group which has not even been able to constitute a solid, rooted population with permanent interests, or an essentially autonomous political entity, was also incapable of creating its own labour force. This incapacity is bound up with the situation and has become typical, even nowadays, for the inhabitants of the Rock, of whom a British daily, the *Manchester Guardian* of May 11th 1950, said: "The Gibraltarian has an innate objection to manual work, preferring the 'white collar' or the 'white apron'."

At that time also a labour population had to be imported. After an effort to provide one by the use of convicts had failed, it had to be looked for in Spain, because Spain is Gibraltar's natural space. The Rock became an absorption point for labour, not only from the immediate vicinity but also from the provinces of southern Spain. English recruiting agents operated at great distances from the Rock, and even in our own days, in 1945, a British Consul at Cádiz caused an incident when he had advertisements offering work in Gibraltar published. Throughout long periods of time, this absorption went on attracting into the zone of the Campo groups of persons uprooted from the regions of their birth, who approached the Rock in the hope of getting jobs there. This created a real colonial situation, since the Campo de Gibraltar was becoming peopled with workers who depended on employers across the frontier, and it was these employers who dictated the conditions of work. In turn, as almost the sole activity of the Rock's inhabitants was illicit trade over this zone, it did much to deprive the region of sound economic business, by keeping it in a condition as closely as possible resembling that of a mere labour pool at Gibraltar's disposal.

The development of works and installations on the Rock gradually increased the number of Spanish workers, and at the end of the 19th century the figure rose rapidly from about 2,500 or 3,000 to 6,500 or 7,000 when the great harbour works of the town and the installation of the modern Base were carried out, and above all, when the tunnels that perforate the Rock were under construction. These were also the years of economic depression in Spain – even those when Spanish defence works in the zone were paralysed by British imposition – and labour resorted rapidly and in mass to Gibraltar, which thus had at its disposal an entire region which served it as a veritable colony. The other great increase of the Spanish labour force occurred with the Second World War, when the workers that went in from Spain every day reached 13,000. As we have seen, the vast majority – 16,700 – of the 18,000 resident Gibraltarians were evacuated, and thus the Spaniards, during those years, were the real population of the Rock, where they kept up its entire working activity under the difficulties and risks inherent in a war, and made a decisive contribution to British interests at that time.

c) Colonial exploitation of the workers.

This labour force, the real muscle of Gibraltar's life, has worked under a régime for which colonial is the only fitting word. Wages have been fixed at caprice, the working hours have reached 90 and more a week, holiday periods did not exist, social insurance and family care have been ignored and when the first trade unions were set up in Gibraltar, the Spanish workers were forbidden to belong to them on equal terms, so that even union protection was denied. There were periods when part of their wages was paid in kind, and when that was no longer possible, a system was used by which a portion of the workers' wages consisted purely and simply of goods for smuggling into Spain. And when the Spanish Government, for elementary reasons of economic protection and dignity, imposed restrictions on this illicit traffic, protests arose in the British Press (letter from Lt.-Gen. Martin to the *Daily Telegraph*, August 26th 1954) and even in the British Parliament a debate was staged on February 13th 1956, in which the Hon. Member Kenneth Robinson criticized a series of measures taken by Spain, one of which, to his apparent surprise and displeasure, was that "the Spanish workers can no longer take goods out of Gibraltar as they used to do before", and that they were "moreover forced to change part of their wages, I think the greater part, on the frontier at the official rate," which the speaker considered "much less favourable to them than the rate they can get at any tobacconist's in Gibraltar, for I understand that all tobacco shops in Gibraltar are also unofficial money-changing offices."

But the Spanish workers, the real active population of Gibraltar, have never been able to reside in Gibraltar because the British laws forbid it. Every day they have had to go back across the border from the territory where they left the results of their daily effort. They are the exiles of Gibraltar, the historical pariahs of the town, who have had no voice in the affairs of Gibraltar; they are truly the "other" Gibraltar population, whom nobody mentions, of whom nothing is said when the future of the Rock is discussed, but who are there just the same; and the daily life of Gibraltar, at least nowadays, depends upon them. Behind them, in the adjacent Spanish zone, are their families, forming a demographic group of as many as forty or fifty thousand, upon whom, I repeat, a real colonialism has operated.

These facts make it quite clear that in face of the vacuum created by the military presence of Great Britain on the Rock, a demographic reality has arisen – inhabitants of the Town, Spanish workers and families of the Campo – upon which a colonial situation has operated and which calls for consideration at the moment of examining the problem of Gibraltar and its future.

f) Prosperity at Spain's expense.

Lastly, Gibraltar is a permanent source of economic harm to Spain. Since its activities rest upon the abnormal demographic situation which has just been analysed, the Gibraltar economy was necessarily bound to operate through illegal channels. Thus Gibraltar has been a veritable cancer applied to a part of Spain's flesh, operating as it does fundamentally through contraband.

This assertion is proved by a mass of Spanish and British documents, to which reference is made in the recent Spanish Red Book. An ample British bibliography, too, has accumulated in the course of the years with books such as Captain F. Sayer's *History of Gibraltar* (Chapman and Hall, London, 1865); G. T. Garratt's *Gibraltar and the Mediterranean* (Jonathan Cape, London, 1939); H. Howe's *The Gibraltarian*, the origin and development of the population of Gibraltar from 1704, published in

1951; and others. A passage from the last-named work is exceptionally telling:

> "There has been and probably always will be smuggling from Gibraltar. Anyone, local or English, who could say he or she had never broken a revenue regulation deserves a halo!" (Page 201,)

g) Smuggling as a weapon in commercial policy.
Already the Report sent to Lord Palmerston by Sir Robert Gardiner, Governor of Gibraltar, and published in 1856, examined the problem of smuggling and touched on a vital point for Spain in this illicit trade. Gardiner wrote:

> "We believe that Spain could beneficially lower her tariff to a scale that would render smuggling unprofitable. But Spain cannot do that yet." (Page 51.)

And he concluded thus:

> "If we desire to see Spain lower her tariff, we cannot take surer steps to induce her to do so, than by suppressing smuggling at Gibraltar, and leaving to Spain the time for her own commercial regeneration." (Page 52.)

It follows clearly enough from this consideration of the problem that smuggling was in fact a commercial weapon against Spain. This appears to have been the view of the British Government when on June 3rd 1882, in a Note signed by the Minister Plenipotentiary of Great Britain and sent to the Spanish Minister of State, no less a proposal was made than that the two Governments should negotiate a commercial treaty in which Spain would offer Great Britain most-favoured-nation treatment, and Great Britain would undertake to suppress smuggling at Gibraltar in return.

Smuggling has in effect had that character throughout the 19th century and in the 20th to the present day. The Spanish *Red Book* gives figures for recent years in which smuggling based on the Rock amounted, as we said, to a real economic cancer for Spain. By sea alone this illicit traffic in 1959 reached the figure of 1,794 million pesetas, and it was carried on from the Rock, in that year, by 299 sorties of smuggling launches. Though Spanish repression gradually reduced these figures in the following years, in 1961 seaborne contraband still totalled 840 million, with 140 sorties, that is, an average of roughly eleven sorties a month. The Spanish Minister of Information and Tourism has stated publicly that the sum total of the losses caused by Gibraltar smuggling to the Spanish State in the years from 1961 to 1965 attained the figure of twelve million pounds sterling. We shall get a clear idea of the volume of clandestine traffic carried out from Gibraltar if we recall that the annual imports of American tobacco by Gibraltar – with its population of 25,000 – is 5,048,767 dollars, whereas the whole of Spain, with 32 million inhabitants, imports no more than 4,779,227 dollars' worth, and Germany, with 55 million inhabitants, imports only 2,520,183 dollars' worth.

Quite clearly this exaggerated importation of tobacco is made for the sole purpose of smuggling it into Spain. As a further testimony to its existence, our Ministry of Foreign Affairs is in possession of samples of sixteen brands of tobacco with labels printed in Spanish – brands which were in circulation at a time when those really manufactured in Spain were far fewer.

The fact is that smuggling has been a logical outcome of the unnatural character of the human assemblage that resides at Gibraltar. Since it has not been capable of creating its own labour force, and the civilian and military posts of the Base were filled, this floating collectivity, with no economic basis of its own and no definite range of professions, has drifted into illicit trade with Spain in order to enrich itself.

h) Interdependence and inequality.

But at the same time the inhabitants of Gibraltar have inevitably had to fit into their natural economic background, namely the neighbouring economy of Spain. The voids created by Gibraltar as a Base have had to be filled up somehow or other, and in addition to illegal trade, an economic interdependence has arisen between Gibraltar and its Campo or hinterland.

As a result of this, many inhabitants of Gibraltar established their residences in the Campo or other neighbouring parts of Spain – thus evading taxation by both countries – acquired urban properties – there are 500 houses registered in their names in the Campo Zone – in addition to numerous rural estates which they entered in the names of third parties so as to escape fiscal obligations; and they also set up, in Spanish territory, prosperous businesses of hotelkeeping, transport, etc., thus creating an important current of outlet for Gibraltar into Spain, for economic reasons which redounded to their own profit. Meanwhile, no similar Spanish current into Gibraltar could ever be created, because the British laws – the 1873 *Order in Council* the *Immigrants and Aliens Order* of 1885 of the *Gibraltarian Status Ordinance* of 1962 – at all times prohibited residence on the Rock by Spaniards, who were only authorized, during all those years, to enter Gibraltar every day, for the mere purpose of working in the service of the British fortress.

Again, Gibraltar's daily supplies, whether foodstuffs or building materials, have been dependent on the products of Spain, and in this respect the Spanish statistics show very considerable figures, they prove that the Rock is part of a social and economic continuum which is naturally much larger than the perimeter of the Base and is the latter's real living space. A single fact is enough to prove this argument, clear as it is: in the town of Gibraltar, in 1964, there were 6,869 vehicles licensed to be driven on the roads (Gibraltar, 1964, *Report of the Year*). Clearly these vehicles are not used merely to carry Gibraltarians around the two square miles of the Rock and along its 12½ miles of roads and streets.

All that we have said about the economic complex of Gibraltar proves that its sole lawful and natural basis is Spain. This has also been recognized by the *Manchester Guardian* of May 11th 1950, when it stated, in referring to the economy of Gibraltar, that "the sole practical solution is to regard the surrounding area and Gibraltar as one economic unit". This undeniable fact makes it necessary to renovate completely such an economy, which has hitherto been nothing but a dead weight on Anglo-Spanish relations.

National sentiments.
We said earlier that Gibraltar was not only a set of problems of Great Britain but also the "proud fortress" symbolizing a past which still stirs the British soul. But it must also be said that Gibraltar is equally the symbol of a "proud nation", namely Spain, who has never really accepted the present situation and who likewise has her own Gibraltarian tradition – the history of an outcry that has never ceased, against what she regards as an historical wrong.

Spain is unanimous. A contrast.
Concerning this sentiment, Spanish opinion has been totally unanimous. Spaniards of every political ideology and every social class have always coincided in a reclamation which, in the course of 262 years, has taken the form of three military sieges, thousands of combatants killed,

innumerable diplomatic approaches, numerous conversations between statesmen, six attempts at exchange and a vast, unanimous bibliography, which is the most important moral force behind the Spanish Government at the moment these conversations. Perhaps British readers may find special significance and effectiveness in some words written by Salvador de Madariaga, who was then the representative of Spain at the League of Nations, in a Report to the Spanish Minister of State. The document is on the files of our Ministry of Foreign Affairs. When referring to a conversation he had with Mr. Anthony Eden (as he then was), Señor Madariaga states that he dealt "once more with the matter of the occupation of a territory so obviously national as Gibraltar, reminding him that this was not an island of more or less debatable nationality such as Malta, but a piece of unquestionably Spanish national territory, a unique case in European geography". This Spanish unanimity, which emphasizes that the problem is permanently alive, contrasts with the fact that, like a sort of counterpoint, there have always been, on the British side, free and open minds which have been capable of comprehending the Spaniards' feelings and thereby bringing out the injustice of the situation. More than a century ago, a man so incapable of disloyalty and so well acquainted with the facts as the British Governor of Gibraltar, Sir Robert Gardiner, used these words:

"What must be the feelings of every Spaniard, with this noble Rock for ever in view, occupied by strangers? Our own feelings, as we reach the deep shade of its high summit, in returning from our daily course into Spain, teaches us what those of a Spaniard must be." (Page 167.)

A few years later an eminent British statesman, John Bright, actually proposed in a speech that Gibraltar should be ceded to Spain, and declared that the Rock had been captured by Great Britain when she was not at war with Spain and "retained against every law of morality and honour" (*The war and the supply of cotton*, Birmingham, December 18th 1862, *Speeches on questions of public policy* MacMillan and Co., London, 1883).

In our own day the eminent British historian, Sir Charles Petrie, who has written pages showing a great understanding of the Gibraltar problem, has recognized that "British occupation of Gibraltar has been a running sore for Spaniards ever since its original seizure". (Introduction to the book *Gibraltar* by José Pla; Hollis and Carter, London, 1955.) The same has been recognized by a historian of the prestige of Arnold Toynbee, whom we have already quoted, and even by a British Member of Parliament, Mr. Wyatt, who stated in the House of Commons on December 20th 1961, with remarkable frankness: "I think General Franco has a perfect right to claim Gibraltar, but I hope that we are strong enough to resist him."

And even the compilers of the *Encyclopaedia Britannica*, in its 1879 edition, when speaking of the occupation of Gibraltar by British troops, had written:

"It is hardly to the honour of England that it was unprincipled enough to sanction and ratify the occupation."

We have examined the accumulation of military, demographic and economic processes which have originated and developed from Gibraltar and the effects of all kinds that they have had on Spain. They are the inevitable result of the alien enclave of the Rock, and they all imperiously demand a radical solution without loss of time. That is why we are here: to negotiate about them; and any objective examination of the problem must necessarily take into account this unanimity of Spanish feeling on the claim to Gibraltar.

The second Gibraltar:
a) The British occupation of the isthmus.
But there is one very grave problem that is not in itself a logical outcome of the Gibraltar enclave, and concerning which the only thing to be done is to restore the situation immediately to its original terms. I refer to the British advance on the Isthmus of Gibraltar, to the north of the fortifications that enclosed the Town in 1704, and hence outside the limits conceded to England in the Treaty of Utrecht. This has been a pure and simple British invasion of Spanish territory which, although militarily neutralized by the free decision of Spain, was and still is, entirely Spanish sovereign territory, and in which Great Britain has built the present airfield of Gibraltar. The Treaty of Utrecht can give legal grounds for a British presence which has proved, in essence, a usurpation and has moreover evolved through so many violations of its original legal intentions that it makes these conversations indispensable today; but what the Treaty can most certainly not justify is the occupation and utilization, by the abusive employment of force, of Spanish territory outside that which was ceded at Utrecht. Upon this point there cannot

be any shadow of doubt; neither is it possible to plead any right of prescription to consolidate a permanently illegal situation, and I will say why. In addition to prescription being a debatable and vague institution, both in judicial decisions and in doctrine – which I will not go into here, though I admit I am tempted to do so in my capacity as a Professor of International Law – in addition to that, I say the following is evident, even to those who accept prescription: in order that prescription may produce legal effects it is necessary to take into account the behaviour of both the interested parties; in other words, the indifference or tacit abandonment on the part of one side, and the occupation as owner on the part of the other. And that is something that has certainly not occurred here. The Spanish Government has continually declared that its act of tolerance did not imply any extension of the concessions made in the Treaty of Utrecht, and the Government of Great Britain has repeatedly assured it that in their actions there was no intention of altering the *status quo ante*. Consequently, it is not possible to speak of any legitimization of the British presence in part of the neutral ground, by reason of the long series of Spanish protests and refusals which have been made uninterruptedly from 1713 down to the present day. These are presented, with documents, in the Spanish Red Book, and they incontrovertibly prove Spain's unchanging attitude of not ceding her rights in a zone belonging to her exclusive sovereign competence.

In short, to apply to our case the words of a former legal adviser to the Foreign Office, Sir Gerald Fitzmaurice, in his lectures at The Hague Academy of International Law (*Recueil des cours*, 92-1957, II, 146) "such acts, far from conferring title, are merely violations of another State's sovereignty and are simply attempts at an illegal usurpation of title". The same holds good for the British expansion over some waters in Algeciras Bay which are waters coming under unquestionable Spanish competence, and in which there is no alternative to a strict respect for that competence.

The Spanish *Red Book* of 1965 describes the pretexts which were employed by Great Britain in order to advance 850 metres in a straight line northwards, occupying roughly a square kilometre of Spanish sovereign territory in the isthmus. Great Britain used every means, from the deceit by which she blew up the Spanish forts facing the Rock, to the humanitarian motives put forward on the occasion of epidemics in the Town, to continue advancing her positions and encampments, interspersed with absurd discussions about the position of sentry-boxes, and crowning her illegal encroachment by erecting the so-called fence which was set up in 1909 and which, like another "wall of shame", separates Spain from a piece of her own territory.

b) An emergency airfield.
The construction, already mentioned, of the Gibraltar aerodrome within that territory, has military implications which aggravate an invasion that was of itself inadmissible. In 1939, a year after the airfield was constructed, during Spain's difficult moments of the civil war, the British Government, replying to the Spanish protests, said that it was merely a question of "an emergency landing ground" (Memorandum of the Foreign Office, attached to the dispatch of the Spanish Ambassador in London of May 17th 1939). But this "emergency landing ground" was consolidated, and became a key piece in British strategy, a point of support for the Allied military machine in the Second World War, and finally – if not juridically, at least in fact – a very important element, like the Base as a whole, in the structure of NATO, a fact which has obliged Spain to take the measures about overflights to which we have already referred. Captain Alan Hillgarth, who was the British Naval Attaché at Madrid during the war and who was specially praised by Winston Churchill in his Memoirs (*Their Finest Hour*) for his "profound knowledge of Spanish Affairs", in a letter on the subject of this airfield to the *Daily Telegraph* of April 28th 1955, wrote among other things:

> "The airstrip is on the so-called neutral ground, which strict observance of the spirit of the treaties should logically have left inviolable. The extension into Algeciras Bay is so directed that it infringes on water which is not even neutral but definitely Spanish."

In the same letter, realizing, the precarious character of Gibraltar because of modern conditions and through its own development and enlargements, Captain Hillgarth emphasized its vulnerability, saying: "Gibraltar itself is only feasible as a modern base with Spanish consent. The port and airstrip are completely vulnerable."

c) The seriousness of a frontier problem.
The advance up the isthmus is a genuine "frontier question" with all the gravity that such questions imply. It is one on which Spain cannot give way, and which in itself alone would justify international action.

Frontiers are either zones of collaboration and friendship under a legal order, or else zones of violence; and in Gibraltar, Spain cannot accept anything that is not either a free agreement between the parties or a removal of the present British line back to its original position.

It is also necessary to repeat here that any measure which Spain may take in this respect, or in any other of the matters that constitute the problem of Gibraltar, cannot in any way be described as a policy of aggression or a measure of retort. Any such measure will be merely a return to normality, that is to say, to the existing norm, to the legal position from which Gibraltar has been steadily departing throughout the years. It will be the redress of a situation damaged by the British violations of the Treaty of Utrecht and by the unnatural – not to say pathological – evolution of Gibraltar. For if the Treaty of Utrecht is a legal instrument that needs renovation, its 10th Article is fully in force, and in addition to certain rights, it lays down certain obligations which must also be complied with. It would be senseless that Article 10 should have a one-way validity only, that is to say, to justify the British presence at Gibraltar, but should be invalid in the other sense, namely that of the limitation it imposes, and the Spanish rights and interests it expressly protects. This would be a legal monstrosity which Spain cannot accept.

Here, then, in broad lines, expressed bluntly but sincerely is the problem of Gibraltar as seen through Spanish eyes. It is not a fictitious problem but a real one; it is not the reclamation of a political régime, but the demand of an entire people. Neither Great Britain nor Spain could ignore or evade it any longer, and that is why we are here today.

Firmness and friendship.
As I said in my speech of December 20th 1965 to the Spanish Cortes, Spain approaches this problem in a firm and friendly spirit. We know we have behind us a unanimous people and we are also encouraged by world public opinion, eloquently expressed by the United Nations. But we who are here today represent two great European peoples, experienced and mature, who may sometimes have been rivals because of that very greatness; but who are bound also by many old friendships, and who belong to the same historic community. We would be betraying our present mission if we were not capable of putting aside any psychological obstacle or ideological prejudice standing in the way of a friendly and peaceful understanding. Let us not delay, let us not invent artificial pretexts such as supposedly incompatible political systems; for

such distinctions are usually as unprofitable as in the case of the Spanish politician Sagasta, who on the advent of the I Republic naively attempted to get the British to give Gibraltar back to Spain saying that there no longer existed the obstacle of the Spanish Monarchy, and that the country was now *Bourbonless Spain.*

Let us not waste our time when the question is so clear. The opportunity beckons because of many factors: not only an elementary sense of political usefulness, but also the possibility of strengthening Gibraltar's position with the full weight of Spanish friendship and with an area of cooperation that would be of fundamental importance for Europe; we can also think of our ever-growing commercial relations as a symbol of what our general relationship might be if we removed all the existing obstacles.

Some eloquent trade-figures.
I wish to remark at this point that while Great Britain has been our principal client over many years, although Germany has now gone ahead, Spain is also an important market for Great Britain. According to figures given in the Official British publication *Overseas Trade Accounts of the United Kingdom* (December 1965), British exports to Spain were £96,314,000 in 1965, an increase of 300 per cent since 1952, the increase having been constant, from £24,341,254 in 1952 to £40,511,000 in 1961, with a further increase as mentioned up to 1965. On the other hand, Spanish exports to Great Britain reached £74,021,000 which gives a favourable balance to British exports of £22,293,000.

Spain is hopeful that Great Britain, whose political talent and genius has enabled her to liquidate so many colonial situation, facing problems even more complicated than this one – even through the trials of war – may also avoid what Salisbury called: "the commonest error is politics: sticking to the carcases of dead policies". We hold that the British Government, with its clarity of vision, will be guided by the words of the Prime Minister Mr. Harold Wilson, in his book *Purpose in Politics* (Weidenfeld and Nicholson, 1964, page 7):

> ". . . I believe we are on the eve of a new greatness for Britain, a greatness based not on military oppression or the ability to mount a colonial expedition, not on economic imperialism or colonialism, but on a contribution we have it in our unique power to make to the peace and happiness of mankind. A contribution

based not on separatism, or nationalism, or on outdated concepts of sovereignty, but on leadership in an inter-dependent world."

When we think of this problem of Gibraltar which is in essence so easy to solve, we expect a gesture of understanding on the part of Great Britain. We for our own part are ready to meet her half-way, in a spirit of generosity which we are prepared to carry through to its maximum limit.

Spanish offers.

In view of these hopes and intentions, the Spanish Government realises that there is only one definite solution to the Gibraltar problem. The one recommended by the resolution of the United Nations, and made necessary by the true present situation of Gibraltar which we have described.

The Consensus of the "Committee of Twenty-four" noted the existence of a dispute between Spain and the United Kingdom over the status and situation of the territory of Gibraltar, and clearly defined, as we have seen, the two key factors of the colonial problem of Gibraltar. On the one hand, the administering power, Great Britain, and on the other, the nation colonized on a part of its territory: Spain. The Committee entrusted to these two countries the authentic decolonization of the Rock, and they were to bear in mind the interests of the inhabitants of the territory; for though the Committee did not recognize them as a people legally endowed with the right to self-determination, neither did it want to make them the exclusive victims of this final colonial phase. Spain shares these wishes; she wants to avoid the consequences for them of a persistent colonialism which would oblige our country to take self-protective measures.

The United Nations decided in favour of a negotiation between the colonized nation and the colonizing power, and at the same time pointed out the way for a rightful solution of the problem: To apply to it the Declaration on the granting of independence to colonial nations and peoples, contained in *Resolution 1514* approved by the XV General Assembly.

The United Nations have denied self-determination to the inhabitants of the Rock; Spain does not admit the possibility that these inhabitants should have at their disposal a piece of Spanish territory; the British Government is aware that the Gibraltarians lack a sufficient political entity to enable them to take part in these negotiations, as admitted in the House of Commons by the Colonial Secretary of May 5th. Therefore, the only principle applicable to the Colonial situation of Gibraltar is paragraph 6 of the aforementioned *Resolution 1514* (XV) which says literally:

"Any attempt aimed at the partial or total disruption of the national unity and the territorial integrity of a country is incompatible with the purposes and principles of the Charter of the United Nations."

Certain countries in the "Committee of Twenty-four" laid stress on the need to apply this paragraph; they were Uruguay, Venezuela, Syria, Tunisia, Mali and Iraq, and only the representative of Australia, a Commonwealth country, expressed some doubts; his stand in the United Nations was that the Gibraltarians were the exclusive masters of their future, a position far in advance of what the Gibraltarians themselves want or Great Britain is prepared to grant them.

The United Nations therefore recommend the restoration of the national unity and territorial integrity of Spain as a means to ensure the end of the Colonial problem on our soil. This also is what Spain asks for: The cancellation through cordial and sincere negotiations with Great Britain of Article 10 of the Treaty of Utrecht of July 17th 1713 by which our national unity was disrupted and our territory amputated.

a) A present-day Base.
Spain upholds this solution not merely as a territorial claim which would objectively, in its own right, be worthy of taking into account. Present-day Gibraltar, as we have seen, must necessarily violate the Spanish military and economic space in a thousand different ways: because otherwise it would suffocate. Even with the best will in the world, Great Britain, though she alone is responsible for what happens on the Rock, cannot avoid the consequences – however foreseeable – of having an active military and economic stronghold set in the midst of the Spanish national community. But Spain is the exclusive victim of these consequences; so she cannot take into consideration any guarantee that Gibraltar will not develop in a manner harmful to Spain, because she knows by experience that the British Government has never been able to make such a guarantee effective to the full satisfaction of my country.

Any other formula for Gibraltar that ignores these facts could only be successful with a completely passive Government resigned to have on Spanish soil a foreign sovereign power with a say in Spain's destiny which could subvert Spanish sovereignty not only on the Rock but in the country as a whole. In 262 years there has been no Spanish Government willing to accept this situation, and I dare to prophesy that there will never be. Either through weakness or through the stress of circumstances, there have been silent Governments or Governments disposed only to put a momentary brake on the national aspirations. But these have never been renounced to; not by any régime, nor aspirations. But these have never been renounced to; not by any régimen, nor by any sector whatsoever of Spanish politics.

Nor could a shared sovereignty be considered a fair and rightful solution, because it would leave in the hands of the Gibraltarians a control of Anglo-Spanish relations. Stern economic needs would oblige the future inhabitants of the Rock, uncertain as to where their allegiance lay, to try and keep Spain and the United Kingdom in a state of permanent rivalry, a situation which would not be improved by the probable efforts of other Powers who might think it in their interest to prevent the development of a sincere and lasting friendship between London and Madrid.

I must repeat that the British sovereignty over a piece of our territory is based on the status of Gibraltar, established bilaterally by Spain and Great Britain in Article 10 of the Treaty of Utrecht of 1713, as was admitted by the British Delegation of the "Committee of Twenty-four" and in the IV Committee of the XX General Assembly, when they made status and sovereignty synonymous in their addresses of September 11th 1963, September 23rd and October 16th 1964 and November 16th, December 1st and 7th 1965.

The United Nations have invited Spain and the United Kingdom to put an end to the dispute about the *status* of Gibraltar which is by now anachronistic, as the Prime Minister, Mr. Wilson, quite rightly pointed out in the House of Commons on April 29th 1966. My country therefore considers that the moment has come to cancel Article 10 of the Treaty of Utrecht through friendly and sincere negotiations, as this article is the basis of an old-fashioned idea of sovereignty which has given rise to the colonial situation of Gibraltar. Our territorial integrity and National unity will thus be restored and the old and bitter quarrel which divides us will be at last surmounted.

I think that this opportunity now presented to us of being, so to speak, taken by the hand by the United Nations should not be cast aside. We hope that Great Britain will not give an example, which is all too easy to follow, of disregarding or misapplying the Recommendation of the United Nations.

We understand perfectly that in considering this solution there arises also a vital interest for the United Kingdom: the need to meet military undertakings that in modern times – it is only proper for us to admit it – are rather the results of your country's cooperation in a common defensive effort, than of a selfish imperialism that would now be irrelevant. Although during the debates of the "Committee of Twenty-four" various members of the United Nations have cast doubts on the legitimacy of Great Britain's military interests in Gibraltar, the Spanish Government considers that they ought to be taken into account, and is prepared to give them formal recognition. Such a recognition would not contradict the Charter of the United Nations, that admits the possibility of Agreements in benefit of a common security when their aim is to maintain peace in specific areas of the world.

In the consideration given by the United Nations to the decolonisation of Gibraltar, both the "Consensus" of the "Committee of Twenty-four" and the General Assembly Resolution that ratifies it, provide freedom of action for Spain and the United Kingdom to agree on the best manner of protecting and coordinating these military interests.

The Declaration of the British Government of 1966 on the Military Budgets says briefly that "the garrison, the Arsenal and other establishments" will be maintained in Gibraltar.

It would not be difficult for Spain to agree to the continuation in Gibraltar of the defensive military establishment. However, if this British military effort in Spain were to remain disconnected from the common defensive background, this would be in contradiction of the ideas in the *White Book on Defense*: for you would then have a very expensive and inefficient Base, a sort of old-fashioned bastion at the service of purposes to which the British Government says it has renounced for ever.

It would seem advisable to think of this matter courageously and decisively in up-to-date terms and to consider a wider form of cooperation between our two countries, for which we find a good example in the Spanish-American Bases jointly utilized, which resulted from the Agreement signed between Spain and the United States in 1953 and which over the years have shown their soundness and efficiency.

It is not for nothing that the Iberian Peninsula has such an essential role in the security of the Strait of Gibraltar. These few names: Gibraltar and Rota in Spain, Alverca and Beja in Portugal, are the real coordinates of a strategy extensively covering the entry to the Mediterranean, which is needful of Spanish air space, which is perhaps the most useful training ground for the air forces of the Western world in Europe, but which cannot be used without the cooperation of Spain, a cooperation which it will be logically difficult to provide while the present arbitrary situation of Gibraltar continues.

These realities of the situation, which transcend the specific problem of Gibraltar and to a certain extent leave it on a secondary plane in the light of the present international scene, are not ignored by the Spanish Government. But the Spanish Government is not prepared to accept risks without the corresponding benefits, merely to satisfy the selfishness of others and to the detriment of Spanish security. These are matters which deserve to be deeply considered at a later and proper moment.

b) International guarantees for the inhabitants.
In considering the fair solution to the problem which the United Nations exclusively recommends and which meets the facts of the case, and which, as we have seen, naturally implies the need to cancel Article 10 of the Treaty of Utrecht, a second element arises which the United Nations has also advised us to protect and respect: the interests of the present inhabitants of the territory.

From an economic point of view it is obvious that they are closely bound to Spain. All the efforts carried out since last year to create in Gibraltar an "island economy" independent of the Spanish economy, have so far failed, and they can only succeed through massive financial grants to the Rock, deriving entirely from the British Budget. If my country does not contribute to achieving a high standard of living for the Rock – and this she cannot do if we do not reach an Anglo-Spanish understanding – the high standard of living will either be paid for in good measure by the British tax payer, or will have to he considerably reduced. Lord Merrivale on March 9th 1966, quoted some figures in the House of Lords to explain the losses suffered by the economy of Gibraltar through some Spanish measures which consisted merely in cancelling certain facilities which had been a profitable boon for smugglers. The figures he quoted were sufficiently explicit to realize that an economic régime independent of Spain offers very scarce possibilities to the inhabitants of the Rock.

From a demographic point of view, only Spain can offer the

Gibraltarians a normal area of expansion, which they lack on the Rock, unless they prefer to set themselves a population limit.

Individually the inhabitants are linked to the British Crown by their British nationality and its legal consequences.

It is very difficult for Spain to define *a priori* what are the interests of the inhabitants of the Rock which we must take into account in this negotiation. To judge by the statements of their representatives of the "Committee of Twenty-four", and by many other statements made during 1965 and the present year, one obtains the impression that they wish to maintain close association with the United Kingdom, in whom it appears that they see the only guarantee for some interests which they have never really defined publicly with the necessary clarity or precision. But at the same time, from their petition to the British Government; from their statements in the United Nations to which we have referred; and from others in the international Press, it can be clearly deduced that the inhabitants of the Rock also wish to maintain close links with Spain, although they have accused her recently of creating economic and other difficulties, and of destroying the interdependence between the Rock and adjoining territory; an interdependence which, we should add has so far developed only to the detriment of the Spanish economy and sovereignty.

It is very difficult, we repeat, to try and define at this stage of the negotiations the true interests of the present inhabitants of the Rock. No one better than the inhabitants themselves could explain their needs to Spain through the British Government that represents them, once they are convinced that the possible solution to the problem of Gibraltar is at the same time the only one which offers them a guarantee for the future.

In so far as my country is concerned, it is enough to say that, except for the right to have at her disposal a piece of her own territory, Spain is prepared to consider the most generous formulae for establishing the most adequate legal régime for the defence of the interests of the inhabitants as indicated by the United Nations, this legal régime would be fully guaranteed by an Anglo-Spanish Convention registered in the United Nations according to Article 102 of the Charter, the enactment of which would therefore be protected by the United Nations.

This Convention would establish a Personal Statute, in which, in addition to other basic rights – such as freedom of religion – the British nationality of the present inhabitants of Gibraltar would be respected, and their right of residence be guaranteed, as also the free exercise of their lawful activities, and their permanence in their place of work. Also, Spain is prepared to grant a special Charter to Gibraltar that will integrate the interests of the present inhabitants with those of the rest of the Campo, by means of an administrative organization and an economic and financial system based on a Free Port régime, which would give rise to a considerable development of the whole region through its co-operation with the neighbouring territory.

c) A healthy and developing economy.

We are making our proposal, not only because we wish to meet the requirements of the United Nations and to do this as generously as possible, but also because the Spanish Government has the firm intention of associating Gibraltar to the great enterprise, which has already begun, of developing economically the whole zone of the Campo; of restoring its unity and making it in a short time a rich and flourishing region, which will have as its centre a great city in the Bay of Algeciras, that is to link up the dispersed urban centres of Gibraltar, La Línea, San Roque, Los Barrios and Algeciras.

No matter whether Gibraltar becomes integrated with this vast urban complex or whether the Rock becomes definitely isolated, Spain has in any case engaged herself on this project on her honour, and she will carry it out.

For if on the one hand Great Britain has obligations towards the present inhabitants of the Rock, Spain also has very serious obligations towards the inhabitants of the Campo de Gibraltar and especially of La Línea and San Roque. We have to fill in the deplorable economic vacuum that surrounded the Rock in former times, the "glacis" of Gibraltar, the depressed area which was nothing but a passive labour market for the Base.

We must replace all this with a prosperous region in one of the crucial zones of the Mediterranean. San Roque, where live the descendants of the old Spanish population of the Rock, who have been gazing for two and a half centuries at their lost homes; La Línea, the humble camp of a community of daily exiles, of pariahs at the service of an old-fashioned capitalist régime: these townships, like the rest of the Campo, deserve a historic compensation. Many things have changed in the region of Gibraltar, and one of them is the Spanish resolve to find a permanent remedy for a colonial situation, and to give a region – whose situation should have made it one of the most flourishing in modern Spain – the position and wealth that it never attained because it was a victim of one of those imperialist situations which Mr. Wilson mentioned in the quotation we have referred to.

We have described with full clarity from the beginning the factors that must be taken into consideration for the only possible solution that can be given to the problem of Gibraltar, and have avoided for this negotiation the classical gambits of diplomatic bargaining and compromise. Precisely because we are dealing with such serious matters as the integrity of Spain, the military security of the free world and the interests of human beings who should not be made to pay for situations that they have no power to remedy, it seems to us that any bargaining over the principles of the solution should in all honesty be excluded.

d) Formal proposal.

In view of all these considerations, Spain proposes to the Government of Great Britain that a Convention should be signed, the *First Article* of which should contain the cancellation of Article 10 of the Treaty of Utrecht of 1713 and the restoration of the national unity and territorial integrity of Spain through the reversion of Gibraltar, thus complying with the mandate of the United Nations.

In the *Second Article* my Country would accept the presence at Gibraltar of a British Military Base whose structure, legal situation, and co-ordination with the defense organization of Spain or the Free World would be the subject of a negotiation for an especial Agreement to be attached to the Convention we are proposing.

Spain proposes a *Third Article* stipulating that a legal régime to protect the interests of the present citizens of Gibraltar should be the subject of an additional Anglo-Spanish agreement registered in the United Nations, as has been stated. In this agreement, in addition to the appropriate economic and administrative formulae, a Personal Statute would be established, by which, among other fundamental rights – such as freedom of religion – the British nationality of the present inhabitants of Gibraltar would be respected, and their right of residence would be guaranteed, as also the free exercise of their lawful activities, and a guarantee of permanence in their place of work.

Finally in a *Fourth Article*, it would be specified that this Convention will be effective after the two additional agreements to which reference has been made in the Second and Third Articles, shall have been signed and registered in the United Nations.

Thus, the peace of the world will be reinforced, with the commencement of a new era in Anglo-Spanish relations.

APPENDIX 6

The Brussels Agreement

27 November 1984

The Foreign and Commonwealth Secretary, the Rt Hon Sir Geoffrey Howe, and the Spanish Foreign Minister, His Excellency Sr Don Fernando Moran Lopez, held a meeting in Brussels on 27 November 1984 during which they agreed on the way in which the Spanish and British Governments will apply by not later than 15 February 1985 the Lisbon Declaration of 10 April 1980 in all its parts. This will involve simultaneously:

a) The provision of equality and reciprocity of rights for Spaniards in Gibraltar and Gibraltarians in Spain. This will be implemented through the mutual concession of the rights which citizens of EC countries enjoy taking into account the transitional periods and derogations agreed between Spain and the EC. The necessary legislative proposals to achieve this will be introduced in Spain and Gibraltar. As concerns paid employment, and recalling the general principle of community preference, this carries the implication that during the transitional period each side will be favourably disposed to each other's citizens when granting work permits.

(b) The establishment of the free movement of persons, vehicles and goods between Gibraltar and the neighbouring territory.

(c) The establishment of a negotiating process aimed at overcoming all the differences between them over Gibraltar and at promoting cooperation on a mutually beneficial basis on economic, cultural, touristic, aviation, military and environmental matters. Both sides accept that the issues of sovereignty will be discussed in that process. The British Government will fully maintain its commitment to honour the wishes of the people of Gibraltar as set out in the preamble of the 1969 Constitution.

Insofar as the airspace in the region of Gibraltar is concerned, the Spanish Government undertakes to take the early actions necessary to allow safe and effective air communications.

There will be meetings of working groups, which will be reviewed periodically in meetings for this purpose between the Spanish and British Foreign Ministers.

APPENDIX 7

The Airport Agreement

2 December 1987

The Minister of Foreign Affairs of the Kingdom of Spain, His Excellency Sr Don Francisco Fernandez Ordoñez, and the Foreign and Commonwealth Secretary of the United Kingdom, the Right Honourable Sir Geoffrey Howe, meeting in London on 2 December 1987,

taking into account the joint communiqué agreed at Brussels on 27 November 1984 which established a negotiating process between both countries aimed at overcoming all the differences between them over Gibraltar and at promoting cooperation on a mutually beneficial basis on a number of matters including aviation;

taking into account also the discussions within the Council of the European Community about the European Commission's proposals for liberalising air transport;

understanding, as a result of the conversations which have taken place between the two Ministers, that both Governments consider that greater cooperation over the use of Gibraltar Airport be beneficial for both countries and for the population of Gibraltar and the Campo de Gibraltar;

and in view of the fact that the application of the European Community air transport policy to Gibraltar airport will mean an increase in its civil use,

have agreed the following arrangements:

1. The aeronautical authorities of the two sides will hold regular consultations about all questions relating to the development of the civil use of the airport, including those relating to the establishment of new services to third countries.
Permission for Spanish airlines to operate services between airports of

the Kingdom of Spain and Gibraltar, under paragraph 1 of Article 6 of the draft EC Decision on capacity and market access, will be given by the Spanish authorities.

2. The Spanish authorities will build a new terminal at La Linea de la Concepción adjacent to the northern side of the existing frontier-fence. Passengers using this terminal will have direct access to the airport through a gate in the south side of the terminal.

3.1. The Spanish terminal will be used by the following categories of passengers:
– Passengers from any country, flying in aircraft of any company, and of any nationality, whose destination on disembarking is any point on the territory situated to the north of the frontier-fence.
– Passengers proceeding from any point of the territory situated to the north of the frontier-fence who embark in aircraft of any company and of any nationality, for any destination.

3.2. The British terminal will be used by all other passengers.

3.3. When appropriate, passengers will be subject to customs and immigration controls in the respective terminals.

4.1. A committee will be established to coordinate the civil air transport activities of the British and Spanish terminals and their relation with the airport's other services. The committee will consist of an equal number of members appointed by each Government.

4.2. The arrangements in paragraph 4.1 will be kept under review by the Working Group on Civil Aviation Questions established in 1985 under the auspices of the Anglo/Spanish Coordinators. This working group will report regularly to the Coordinators. The reports will contain any recommendations for further cooperation in the use of Gibraltar airport.

5. The British and Spanish Governments will ensure that effective measures are taken within the existing and new terminals respectively, to screen passengers and their carry-on items, and to carry out appropriate checks on crew, cargo and aircraft stores prior to and during boarding. There will be close cooperation between the authorities responsible for

security, within the two terminals and between them and the existing authorities responsible for security elsewhere at the airport, so as to ensure that the highest standards of security are maintained.

6. There will be continued discussions between the two sides about further strengthening of air safety and traffic control arrangements in the area.

7. The present arrangements and any activity or measure undertaken in applying them or as a consequence of them are understood to be without prejudice to the respective legal positions of Spain and the United Kingdom with regard to the dispute over sovereignty over the territory in which the airport is situated.

8. The above arrangements will come into operation when the British authorities have signified to the Spanish authorities that the legislation necessary to give effect to paragraph 3.3 above is in force, or on completion of the construction of the Spanish terminal, whichever is the later, but in any event not more than one year after the notification referred to above.

BIBLIOGRAPHY

MANUSCRIPT SOURCES

Admiral of the Fleet Sir Varyl Begg, Gibraltar papers

General Sir William Jackson, Gibraltar diary

Sir Joshua Hassan, notes

CO.91 files at the Public Records Office

PRINTED SOURCES

Benady, Samuel M, *Memoirs of a Gibraltarian*
           (Gibraltar Books 1993)

Command Paper 2632, *Gibraltar. Recent Differences with Spain*
           (HMSO 1965)

Command Paper 3131, *Gibraltar: Talks with Spain May-October 1966*
           (HMSO 1966)

Command Paper 3325, *Further Documents on Gibraltar: October*
           1966 - June 1967 (HMSO 1967)

Command paper 3735, *Further Documents on Gibraltar: June 1967 -*
           June 1968 (HMSO 1968)

Finlayson, T J, *The Fortress Came First* (Gibraltar Books 1991)

Garcia, J J, *Gibraltar: the Making of a People* (Medsun 1994)

Morris, D S, Haig, R H, *Britain Spain and Gibraltar 1945-90:*
           The Eternal Triangle (Routledge 1992)

The Spanish Red Book on Gibraltar (Madrid 1965)

A New Spanish Red Book: Negotiations on Gibraltar (Madrid 1968)

INDEX

Index